# Lecture Notes in Computer Science    8324

*Commenced Publication in 1973*
Founding and Former Series Editors:
Gerhard Goos, Juris Hartmanis, and Jan van Leeuwen

Matthew Flatt   Hai-Feng Guo (Eds.)

# Practical Aspects of Declarative Languages

16th International Symposium, PADL 2014
San Diego, CA, USA, January 20-21, 2014
Proceedings

 Springer

Volume Editors

Matthew Flatt
University of Utah
School of Computing
50 Central Campus Drive, Salt Lake City, UT 84112-9205, USA
E-mail: mflatt@cs.utah.edu

Hai-Feng Guo
University of Nebraska
Department of Computer Science
6001 Dodge Street, Omaha, NE 68182, USA
E-mail: haifengguo@unomaha.edu

ISSN 0302-9743                                    e-ISSN 1611-3349
ISBN 978-3-319-04131-5                            e-ISBN 978-3-319-04132-2
DOI 10.1007/978-3-319-04132-2
Springer Cham Heidelberg New York Dordrecht London

Library of Congress Control Number: 2013956505

CR Subject Classification (1998): D.3, D.1, F.3, D.2

LNCS Sublibrary: SL 2 – Programming and Software Engineering

*Typesetting:* Camera-ready by author, data conversion by Scientific Publishing Services, Chennai, India

Printed on acid-free paper

Springer is part of Springer Science+Business Media (www.springer.com)

# Preface

This volume contains the proceedings of the 16th International Symposium on Practical Aspects of Declarative Languages (PADL 2014), held during January 20–21, 2014, in San Diego, California. PADL is an annual forum where researchers and practitioners present original work emphasizing new ideas and approaches pertaining to applications and implementation techniques of declarative languages.

PADL solicits both full technical papers and shorter application papers. This year, the Program Committee received 27 submissions (26 technical papers and one application paper) and accepted 15 papers (including one application paper). Each submission was reviewed by at least three Program Committee members.

The accepted papers span a range of topics related to logic and functional programming, including language support for parallelism and GPUs, constructs and techniques for modularity and extensibility, and applications of declarative programming to document processing and DNA simulation. The conference program includes invited talks by Molham Aref of LogicBlox and David Walker of Princeton.

The symposium was sponsored by the Association of Logic Programming and the ACM. We also thank the University of Nebraska at Omaha, the University of Utah, and the University of Texas at Dallas for supporting the organization of the symposium. The support of many individuals was crucial to the success of the symposium. We thank all Program Committee members and additional reviewers for giving constructive feedback on each paper. We thank Gopal Gupta for coordinating the organization of the symposium. We thank David Van Horn for the general organization and coordination with POPL. We thank Roni Myers and Zac Fowler, from the University of Nebraska at Omaha, for maintaining the symposium website. Last but not least, we thank the Springer staff responsible for producing the LNCS series and the developers of EasyChair, which is a wonderful conference management system for assisting the paper reviewing process and preparation of symposium proceedings.

November 2013

Matthew Flatt
Hai-Feng Guo

# Organization

## Program Committee

| | |
|---|---|
| Matthew Flatt | University of Utah, USA |
| Ronald Garcia | University of British Columbia, USA |
| Hai-Feng Guo | University of Nebraska at Omaha, USA |
| Manuel Hermenegildo | IMDEA Software Institute and T.U. Madrid (UPM), Spain |
| Joohyung Lee | Arizona State University, USA |
| Yuliya Lierler | University of Nebraska at Omaha, USA |
| Sam Lindley | University of Edinburgh, UK |
| Leaf Petersen | Intel |
| Rinus Plasmeijer | Radboud University Nijmegen, The Netherlands |
| C.R. Ramakrishnan | Stony Brook University, USA |
| Sukyoung Ryu | KAIST, South Korea |
| Manuel Serrano | Inria Sophia-Antipolis, France |
| Yi-Dong Shen | Institute of Software, the Chinese Academy of Sciences, China |
| Tran Cao Son | New Mexico State University, USA |
| Peter Stuckey | University of Melbourne, Australia |
| Peter Thiemann | University of Freiburg, Germany |
| Hans Tompits | Vienna University of Technology, Austria |
| Aaron Turon | Max Planck Institute for Software Systems (MPI-SWS), Germany |
| David Van Horn | Northeastern University |
| German Vidal | MiST, DSIC, Universitat Politecnica de Valencia, Spain |

## Additional Reviewers

| | |
|---|---|
| Atkey, Robert | Johnson, J. Ian |
| Banks, Chris | Koopman, Pieter |
| Correas Fernandez, Jesus | Lipovetzky, Nir |
| De Cat, Broes | Mariño, Julio |
| Deng, Jun | Morales, Jose F. |
| Domoszlai, László | Oetsch, Johannes |
| Du, Jianfeng | Pontelli, Enrico |
| Gutiérrez, Raúl | Pührer, Jörg |
| Harrison, Amelia | Redl, Christoph |
| Inclezan, Daniela | Segura, Clara |

Stivala, Alex
Stutterheim, Jurrien
Tack, Guido

Toups, Zachary
Yallop, Jeremy
Yang, Fangkai

# Abstracts of Invited Talks

# The Frenetic Project: Declarative Languages for Programming Networks

David Walker

Princeton University
dpw@cs.princeton.edu

For decades, traditional network devices such as switches, firewalls, load balancers and routers have been closed, proprietary platforms controlled by the major hardware vendors. Each device contains a combination of (1) hardware to forward packets efficiently along chosen network paths, and (2) software to run the distributed protocols that decide which network paths to choose. To configure or specialize these devices, network operators have had to learn a myriad of complex, vendor-specific interfaces and protocols. Moreover, there was no easy way to change the basic distributed routing algorithms these network devices implement.

Over the last few years, however, *software-defined networking* (SDN) has taken both the academic and industrial networking communities by storm. In a software-defined network, each switch exports a simple, standard and relatively direct interface to its underlying hardware. These switches are organized and managed by a separate, logically centralized *controller* machine or cluster of machines. A controller runs a general-purpose computation that reacts to network events such as changes in topology or traffic volume and decides how to route packets across the network. Based on these decisions, it sends commands to configure the switches it controls. By standardizing the hardware interface and separating out the decision-making software, this new architecture makes it possible to control and optimize networks in ways that were previously impossible. Google is already taking advantage of this technology to control the global backbone network that connects its data centers together [1]. Many other networking companies, both large and small, have also begun to innovate in this new space. However, despite the genesis of SDN in the networking community, many of the key problems are actually programming problems. Hence, researchers who understand the design of declarative programming languages have much to offer in this important new domain.

In this talk, we will discuss the Frenetic project [2], whose goal over the last several years has been to develop new, high-level, declarative, domain-specific languages for programming software-defined networks. In particular, we will discuss several of the core abstractions and programming language features we have developed, what key problems they solve, their formal semantics, and how to compile them to the underlying switch hardware. We will also touch on the next generation of software-defined networks and future opportunities for declarative language design.

The Frenetic Project is a large collaborative project centered between Cornell and Princeton universities. Since it began in 2009, the project has been led by Nate Foster, Jennifer Rexford and David Walker. We thank the wonderful contributions to the project made by Carolyn Jane Anderson, Shrutarshi Basu, Rebecca Coombes, Michael Freedman, Arjun Guha, Steven Gutz, Rob Harrison, Jean-Baptiste Jeannin, Nanxi Kang, Naga Praveen Katta, Dexter Kozen, Zhenming Liu, Matthew Meola, Matthew Milano, Christopher Monsanto, Nayden Nedev, Josh Reich, Mark Reitblatt, Cole Schlesinger, Emin Gün Sirer, Robert Soulé, Alec Story, Laure Thompson, and Todd Warszawski.

*Acknowledgement.* This work is supported in part by the NSF under grants CNS-1111520, SHF-1016937 and a Google Research Award. Any opinions, findings, and recommendations are those of the author and do not necessarily reflect the views of the NSF or Google.

# References

1. Sushant Jain, Alok Kumar, Subhasree Mandal, Joon Ong, Leon Poutievski, Arjun Singh, Subbaiah Venkata, Jim Wanderer, Junlan Zhou, Min Zhu, Jonathan Zolla, Urs Hölzle, Stephen Stuart, and Amin Vahdat. B4: Experience with a globally-deployed software defined WAN. In *ACM SIGCOMM*, 2013.
2. The Frenetic Project, 2013. See `http://frenetic-lang.org`.

# Declarative Programming for the Cloud

Molham Aref

LogicBlox
molham.aref@logicblox.com

**Abstract.** I will present the LogicBlox database and describe business applications that use it. The LogicBlox database marries declarative programming (logic-based specifications) with cloud deployment over large datasets. The database is programmed with a variant of the Datalog programming language. The flexibility of declarative programming allows us to integrate both traditional business application development and "probabilistic" applications: machine-learning or search-based solutions, as required by the domain. Our approach aims to eliminate the distance between prototyping and deployed, high-performance implementations. I will discuss real customer applications and actual deployment instances that elastically adapt to several thousands of machines.

# Table of Contents

R$^{\text{CML}}$: A Prescription for Safely Relaxing Synchrony .................. 1
*K.C. Sivaramakrishnan, Lukasz Ziarek, and Suresh Jagannathan*

Partial Type Signatures for Haskell................................. 17
*Thomas Winant, Dominique Devriese, Frank Piessens, and
Tom Schrijvers*

The F# Computation Expression Zoo ............................. 33
*Tomas Petricek and Don Syme*

Abstract Modular Inference Systems and Solvers ..................... 49
*Yuliya Lierler and Miroslaw Truszczynski*

Sunroof: A Monadic DSL for Generating JavaScript .................. 65
*Jan Bracker and Andy Gill*

Compiling DNA Strand Displacement Reactions Using a Functional
Programming Language.......................................... 81
*Matthew R. Lakin and Andrew Phillips*

Two Applications of the ASP-Prolog System: Decomposable Programs
and Multi-context Systems ....................................... 87
*Tran Cao Son, Enrico Pontelli, and Tiep Le*

Towards Modeling Morality Computationally with Logic
Programming..................................................... 104
*Ari Saptawijaya and Luís Moniz Pereira*

A Declarative Specification of Giant Number Arithmetic .............. 120
*Paul Tarau*

Embedding Foreign Code ......................................... 136
*Robert Clifton-Everest, Trevor L. McDonell,
Manuel M.T. Chakravarty, and Gabriele Keller*

Exploring the Use of GPUs in Constraint Solving ................... 152
*Federico Campeotto, Alessandro Dal Palù, Agostino Dovier,
Ferdinando Fioretto, and Enrico Pontelli*

On the Correctness and Efficiency of Lock-Free Expandable Tries for
Tabled Logic Programs .......................................... 168
*Miguel Areias and Ricardo Rocha*

Typelets — A Rule-Based Evaluation Model for Dynamic, Statically
Typed User Interfaces .......................................... 184
    *Martin Elsman and Anders Schack-Nielsen*

Expand: Towards an Extensible Pandoc System..................... 200
    *Jacco Krijnen, Doaitse Swierstra, and Marcos O. Viera*

Generic Generic Programming ..................................... 216
    *José Pedro Magalhães and Andres Löh*

**Author Index** ................................................ 233

# $\mathbb{R}^{\text{CML}}$: A Prescription for Safely Relaxing Synchrony

K.C. Sivaramakrishnan[1], Lukasz Ziarek[2], and Suresh Jagannathan[1]

[1] Purdue University
{chandras,suresh}@cs.purdue.edu
[2] SUNY Buffalo
lziarek@buffalo.edu

**Abstract.** A functional programming discipline, combined with abstractions like Concurrent ML (CML)'s first-class synchronous events, offers an attractive programming model for concurrency. In high-latency distributed environments, like the cloud, however, the high communication latencies incurred by synchronous communication can compromise performance. While switching to an explicitly asynchronous communication model may reclaim some of these costs, program structure and understanding also becomes more complex. To ease the challenge of migrating concurrent applications to distributed cloud environments, we have built an extension of the MultiMLton compiler and runtime that *implements* CML communication asynchronously, but guarantees that the resulting execution is *faithful* to the synchronous semantics of CML. We formalize the conditions under which this equivalence holds, and present an implementation that builds a decentralized dependence graph whose structure can be used to check the integrity of an execution with respect to this equivalence. We integrate a notion of speculation to allow ill-formed executions to be rolled-back and re-executed, replacing offending asynchronous actions with safe synchronous ones. Several realistic case studies deployed on the Amazon EC2 cloud infrastructure demonstrate the utility of our approach.

**Keywords:** Message-passing, Speculative Execution, Axiomatic Semantics, Cloud Computing.

## 1 Introduction

Concurrent ML [18] (CML) provides an expressive concurrency mechanism through its use of first-class composable synchronous events. When synchronized, events allow threads to communicate data via message-passing over first-class channels. Synchronous communication simplifies program reasoning because every communication action is also a synchronization point; thus, the continuation of a message-send is guaranteed that the data being sent has been successfully transmitted to a receiver. The cost of synchrony comes at a high price in performance, however; recent proposals therefore suggest the use of asynchronous variants of CML's synchronous events [28] to overcome this cost. While asynchronous extensions can be used to gain performance, they sacrifice the simplicity provided by synchronous communication in favor of a more complex and sophisticated set of primitives.

One way to enhance performance without requiring new additions to CML's core set of event combinators is to give the underlying runtime the freedom to allow a sender

M. Flatt and H.-F. Guo (Eds.): PADL 2014, LNCS 8324, pp. 1–16, 2014.
© Springer International Publishing Switzerland 2014

to communicate data asynchronously. In this way, the cost of synchronous communication can be masked by allowing the sender's continuation to begin execution even if a matching receiver is not yet available. Because asynchrony is introduced only by the runtime, applications do not have to be restructured to explicitly account for new behaviors introduced by this additional concurrency. Thus, we wish to have the runtime enforce the equivalence: $[\![\, \mathtt{send}\, (c, v)]\!]k \equiv [\![\, \mathtt{asend}\, (c, v)]\!]k$ where $k$ is a continuation, $\mathtt{send}$ is CML's synchronous send operation that communicates value $v$ on channel $c$, and $\mathtt{asend}$ is an asynchronous variant that buffers $v$ on $c$ and does not synchronize with matching receiver.

**Motivation.** To motivate the utility of safe relaxation of synchronous behavior, consider the problem of building a distributed chat application. The application consists of a number of participants, each of whom can broadcast a message to every other member in the group. The invariant that must be observed is that any two messages sent by a participant must appear in the same order to all members. Moreover, any message Y broadcast in response to a previously received message X must always appear after message X to every member. Here, message Y is said to be *causally dependent* on message X.

```
datatype 'a bchan = BCHAN of ('a chan list (*val*) * unit chan list (*ack*))

(* Create a new broadcast channel *)
fun newBChan (n: int) (* n = number of participants *) =
  BCHAN(tabulate(n,fn _ => channel()), tabulate(n,fn _ => channel()))

(* Broadcast send operation *)
fun bsend (BCHAN (vcList, acList), v: 'a, id: int) : unit =
let
   val _ = map (fn vc => if (vc = nth (vcList, id)) then () else send (vc, v))
             vcList (* phase 1 -- Value distribution *)
   val _ = map (fn ac => if (ac = nth (acList, id)) then () else recv ac)
             acList (* phase 2 -- Acknowledgments *)
in ()
end

(* Broadcast receive operation *)
fun brecv (BCHAN (vcList, acList), id: int) : 'a=
let val v = recv (nth (vcList, id))
         val _ = send (nth (acList, id), ())
in v
end
```

**Fig. 1.** Synchronous broadcast channel

Building such an application using a centralized server is straightforward, but hinders scalability. In the absence of central mediation, a causal broadcast protocol [2] is required. One possible encoding of causal broadcast using CML primitives is shown in Figure 1. A broadcast operation involves two phases. In the first phase, values (i.e., messages) are synchronously communicated to all receivers (except to the sender). In the second phase, the sender simulates a barrier by synchronously receiving acknowledgments from all recipients.

The synchronous nature of the broadcast protocol along with the fact that the acknowledgment phase occurs only after message distribution ensure that no member can proceed immediately after receiving a message until all other members have also received the message. This achieves the desired causal ordering between broadcast messages since every member would have received a message before the subsequent causally ordered message is generated. We can build a distributed group chat server using the broadcast channel as shown below.

```
(* bc is broadcast chan, daemon is spawn as a separate thread *)
fun daemon id = display (brecv (bc, id)); daemon id
fun newMessage (m, id) = display m; bsend (bc, m, id)
```

Assume that there are $n$ participants in the group, each with a unique identifier $id$ between 0 and $n - 1$. Each participant runs a local *daemon* thread that waits for incoming messages on the broadcast channel bc. On a reception of a message, the daemon displays the message and continues waiting. The clients broadcast a message using newMessage after displaying the message locally. Observe that remote messages are only displayed after all other participants have also received the message. In a geo-distributed environment, where the communication latency is very high, this protocol results in a poor user experience that degrades as the number of participants increases.

Without making wholesale (ideally, zero!) changes to this relatively simple protocol implementation, we would like to improve responsiveness, while preserving correctness. One obvious way of reducing latency overheads is to convert the synchronous sends in bsend to an asynchronous variant that buffers the message, but does not synchronize with a matching receiver. There are two opportunities where asynchrony could be introduced, either during value distribution or during acknowledgment reception. Unfortunately, injecting asynchrony at either point is not guaranteed to preserve causal ordering on the semantics of the program.

Consider the case where the value is distributed asynchronously. Assume that there are three participants: $p_1$, $p_2$, and $p_3$. Participant $p_1$ first types message x, which is seen by $p_2$, who in turn types the message y after sending an acknowledgment. Since there is a causal order between the message x and y, $p_3$ must see x followed by y. The key observation is that, due to asynchrony, message x sent by the $p_1$ to $p_3$ might be *in-flight*, while the causally dependent message y sent by $p_2$ reaches $p_3$ out-of-order. This leads to a violation of the protocol's invariants. Similarly, it is easy to see that sending acknowledgments message asynchronously is also incorrect. This would allow a participant that receives a message to asynchronously send an acknowledgment, and proceed before all other participants have received the same message. As a result, causal dependence between messages is lost.

To quantify these issues in a realistic setting, we implemented a group chat simulator application using a distributed extension of the MultiMLton Standard ML compiler. We launched three Amazon EC2 instances, each simulating a participant in the group chat application, with the same communication pattern described in the discussion above. In order to capture the geo-distributed nature of the application, participants were placed in three different availability zones – EU West (Ireland), US West (Oregon), and Asia Pacific (Tokyo), resp.

During each run, $p_1$ broadcasts a message x, followed by $p_2$ broadcasting y. We consider the run to be successful if the participant $p_3$ sees the messages x, y, in that order. The experiment was repeated for 1K iterations. We record the time between protocol initiation and the time at which each participant gets the message Y. We consider the largest of the times across the participants to be the running time. The results are presented below.

The *Unsafe Async* row describes the variant where both value and acknowledgment
distribution is performed asynchronously; it
is three times as fast as the synchronous variant. However, over the total set of 1K runs, it

| Execution | Avg. time (ms) | Errors |
|---|---|---|
| Sync | 1540 | 0 |
| Unsafe Async | 520 | 7 |
| Safe Async ($R^{CML}$) | 533 | 0 |

produced seven erroneous executions. The *Safe Async* row illustrates our implementation, $R^{CML}$, that detects erroneous executions on-the-fly and remediates them. The results indicate that the cost of ensuring safe asynchronous executions is quite low for this application, incurring only roughly 2.5% overhead above the unsafe version. Thus, in this application, we can gain the performance benefits and responsiveness of the asynchronous version, while retaining the simplicity of reasoning about program behavior synchronously.

**Contributions.** The formalization of *well-formed executions*, those that are the result of asynchronous evaluation of CML send operations, but which nonetheless are observably equivalent to a synchronous execution, and the means by which erroneous executions can be detected and repaired, form the focus of this paper. Specifically, we make the following contributions:

- We present the rationale for a *relaxed execution model* for CML that specifies the conditions under which a synchronous operation can be safely executed asynchronously. Our model allows applications to program with the simplicity and composability of CML synchronous events, but reap the performance benefits of implementing communication asynchronously.
- We develop an axiomatic formulation of the relaxed execution model which is used to reason about correctness in terms of causal dependencies captured by a *happens-before* relation (§ 2).
- A distributed implementation, $R^{CML}$, that treats asynchronous communication as a form of *speculation* is described. A mis-speculation, namely the execution that could not have been realized using only synchronous communication, is detected using a runtime instantiation of our axiomatic formulation. An un-coordinated, distributed checkpointing mechanism is utilized to rollback and re-execute the offending execution synchronously, which is known to be safe (§ 3).
- Several case studies on a realistic cloud deployment demonstrate the utility of the model in improving the performance of CML programs in distributed environments without requiring *any* restructuring of application logic to deal with asynchrony (§ 4).

## 2   Axiomatic Semantics

We introduce an axiomatic formalization for reasoning about the relaxed behaviors of a concurrent message-passing programs with dynamic thread creation. Not surprisingly, our formulation is similar in structure to axiomatic formalizations used to describe, for example, relaxed memory models [7, 19, 21].

An *axiomatic execution* is captured by a set of *actions* performed by each thread and the relationship between them. These actions abstract the relevant behaviors possible in a CML execution, relaxed or otherwise. Relation between the actions as a result of sequential execution, communication, thread creation and thread joins define the dependencies that any sensible execution must respect. A relaxed execution, as a result of speculation, admits more behaviors than observable under synchronous CML execution. Therefore, to understand the validity of executions, we define a *well-formedness* condition that imposes additional constraints on executions to ensure their observable effects correspond to correct CML behavior.

We assume a set of $\mathbb{T}$ threads, $\mathbb{C}$ channels, and $\mathbb{V}$ values. The set of actions is provided below. Superscripts $m$ and $n$ denote a unique identifier for the action.

| Actions $\mathbb{A} :=$ | $b_t$ | (t starts) | | $e_t$ | (t ends) |
|---|---|---|---|---|---|
| | $\mid j_t^m t'$ | (t detects t' has terminated) | | $f_t^m t'$ | (t forks a new t') |
| | $\mid s_t^m c, v$ | (t sends value v on c) | | $r_t^m c$ | (t receives a value v on c) |
| | $\mid p_t^m v$ | (t outputs an observable value v) | | | |

$$c \in \mathbb{C} \text{ (Channels)} \quad t, t' \in \mathbb{T} \text{ (Threads)} \quad v \in \mathbb{V} \text{ (Values)} \quad m, n \in \mathbb{N} \text{ (Numbers)}$$

Action $b_t$ signals the initiation of a new thread with identifier $t$; action $e_t$ indicates that thread $t$ has terminated. A join action, $j_t^m t'$, defines an action that recognizes the point where thread $t$ detects that another thread $t'$ has completed. A thread creation action, where thread $t$ spawns a thread $t'$, is given by $f_t^m t'$. Action $s_t^m c, v$ denotes the communication of data $v$ on channel $c$ by thread $t$, and $r_t^m c$ denotes the receipt of data from channel $c$. An external action (e.g., printing) that emits value $v$ is denoted as $p_t^m v$. We can generalize these individuals actions into a family of related actions:

$$\mathbb{A}_r = \{r_t^m c \mid t \in \mathbb{T}\} \text{ (Receives)} \qquad \mathbb{A}_s = \{s_t^m c, v \mid t \in \mathbb{T}, v \in \mathbb{V}\} \text{ (Sends)}$$
$$\mathbb{A}_c = \mathbb{A}_s \cup \mathbb{A}_r \qquad \text{(Communication)} \quad \mathbb{A}_o = \{p_t^m v \mid t \in \mathbb{T}, v \in \mathbb{V}\} \quad \text{(Observables)}$$

**Notation.** We write $T(\alpha)$ to indicate the thread in which action $\alpha$ occurs, and write $V(s_t^m c, v)$ to extract the value $v$ communicated by a send action. Given a set of actions $A \in 2^{\mathbb{A}}$, $A_x = A \cap \mathbb{A}_x$, where $\mathbb{A}_x$ represents one of the action classes defined above.

**Definition 1 (Axiomatic Execution).** *An axiomatic execution is defined by the tuple* $\mathsf{E} := \langle \mathsf{P}, \mathsf{A}, \rightarrow_{po}, \rightarrow_{co} \rangle$ *where:*

- $\mathsf{P}$ *is a program.*
- $\mathsf{A}$ *is a set of actions.*
- $\rightarrow_{po} \subseteq \mathsf{A} \times \mathsf{A}$ *is the program order, a disjoint union of the sequential actions of each thread (which is a total order).*
- $\rightarrow_{co} \subseteq (\mathsf{A}_s \times \mathsf{A}_r) \cup (\mathsf{A}_r \times \mathsf{A}_s)$ *is the communication order which is a symmetric relation established between matching communication actions (i.e., $\alpha \rightarrow_{co} \beta \implies \beta \rightarrow_{co} \alpha$). Moreover, a send and its matching receive must operate over the same channel (i.e., $s_t^m c, v \rightarrow_{co} r_{t'}^n c' \implies c = c'$).*

Additionally, there is an obvious ordering on thread creation and execution, as well as the visibility of thread termination by other threads:

**Definition 2 (Thread Dependence).** *If* $\alpha = f_t^m t'$ *and* $\beta = b_{t'}$ *or* $\alpha = e_t$ *and* $\beta = j_{t'}^m t$ *then* $\alpha \rightarrow_{td} \beta$ *holds.*

**Definition 3 (Happens-before relation).** *The happens-before order of an execution is the transitive closure of the union of program order, thread dependence order, and actions related by communication and program order:*

$$\rightarrow_{hb} = (\rightarrow_{po} \cup \rightarrow_{td} \cup$$
$$\{(\alpha, \beta) \mid \alpha \rightarrow_{co} \alpha' \wedge \alpha' \rightarrow_{po} \beta\} \cup$$
$$\{(\beta, \alpha) \mid \beta \rightarrow_{po} \alpha' \wedge \alpha' \rightarrow_{co} \alpha\})^+$$

For any two actions $\alpha, \beta \in A$, if $\alpha \leftrightarrow_{hb} \beta$, then $\alpha$ and $\beta$ are said to be *concurrent* actions. Importantly, our happens-before relation defines a preorder. A preorder is a reflexive transitive binary relation. Unlike partial orders, preorders are not necessarily anti-symmetric, i.e. they may contain cycles.

**Definition 4 (Happens-before Cycle).** *A cycle exists in a happens-before relation if for any two actions* $\alpha, \beta$ *and* $\alpha \rightarrow_{hb} \beta \rightarrow_{hb} \alpha$.

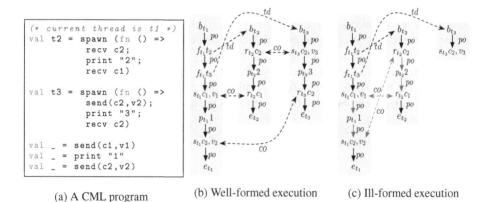

(a) A CML program    (b) Well-formed execution    (c) Ill-formed execution

**Fig. 2.** A CML program and its potential axiomatic executions

We provide an example to illustrate these definitions and to gain an insight into erroneous executions that manifest as a result of speculative communication. Consider the example presented in Figure 2 which shows a simple CML program and two possible executions. The execution in Figure 2b imposes no causal dependence between the observable actions (i.e., print statements) in $t_2$ or $t_3$; thus, an interleaving derived from this execution may permute the order in which these statements execute. All interleavings derivable from this execution correspond to valid CML behavior.

In contrast, the execution depicted in Figure 2c, exhibits a happens-before cycle between $t_1$ and $t_2$, through a combination of program and communication order edges.

*Such cyclic dependences never manifest in any correct CML execution.* Cyclic dependences may however manifest when synchronous sends are speculatively discharged asynchronously. We must therefore strengthen our notion of correct executions to discard those that contain such cycles.

To do so, we first note that the semantics as currently presented is concerned only with actions that introduce some form of causal dependence either within a thread (via program order) or across threads (via thread dependence or communication order). However, a real program also does computation, and reasoning about an execution's correctness will require us to specify these actions as well. To facilitate this reasoning, we abstract the intra-thread semantics, and parameterize our definition of an axiomatic execution accordingly.

**Intra-thread semantics.** The intra-thread semantics is abstracted in our formulation via a labeled transition system. Let State$_{intra}$ denote the intra-thread state of a thread; its specific structure is not interesting for the purposes of the axiomatic definition[1]. A labeled transition between intra-thread states is captured by the relation, $\twoheadrightarrow \subseteq$ State$_{intra} \times$ Label$_{intra} \times$ State$_{intra}$, given to each thread $t \in \mathbb{T}$. The transition labels are in the set Label$_{intra} = (\mathbb{A} \setminus \mathbb{A}_r) \cup (\mathbb{A}_r \times \mathbb{V}) \cup \{\tau\}$. Thus, a thread can either take a global action step (e.g., creating another thread, performing a send action, ending a thread, etc.), execute a *silent* thread-local computation (denoted by label $\tau$), or execute a receive action that receives the value associated with the label. The requirements on the intra-thread semantics are:

- $\twoheadrightarrow$ can only relate states belonging to the same thread.
- there is an initial state READY: no transition leads to it, and a thread $t$ steps from it if and only if it emits a begin action $b_t$.
- there is a final state DONE: a thread leads to it if and only if it emits an end action $e_t$ and no transition leads from it.

**Definition 5 (Intra-trace).** *Let $tr = \overline{\alpha}$ be a sequence of actions in set A, and $\rightarrow_{co}$ be a communication order on A. Given a thread $t \in \mathbb{T}$ in a program P, tr is a valid intra-trace for t if there exists a set of states $\{\delta_0, \delta_1, \ldots\}$, and a set of labels $\overline{l} = \{l_0, l_1, \ldots\}$ such that:*

- *for all $\alpha_i \in \overline{\alpha}, T(a) = t$*
- *$\delta_0$ is the initial state READY*
- *for all $0 \leq i, \delta_i \xrightarrow{l_i} \delta_{i+1}$*
- *the projection $\overline{\beta}$ of $\overline{l}$ to non-silent labels is such that $\beta_i = (\alpha_i, V(\gamma_i))$ if $\alpha_i \in$ A$_r$ and $\alpha_i \rightarrow_{co} \gamma_i$, or $\beta_i = \alpha_i$ otherwise.*

We write In Tr$^P$[t] set of such pairs $(tr, \rightarrow_{co})$ for P.

**Definition 6 (Well-formed Execution).** *An execution $E := \langle P, A, \rightarrow_{po}, \rightarrow_{co} \rangle$ is well-formed if the following conditions hold:*

---

[1] The concrete instantiation of the intra-thread state, and an operational semantics for the language are given in a technical report, available from:
http://multimlton.cs.purdue.edu/mML/rx-cml.html

1. *Intra-thread consistency: for all threads* $t \in \mathbb{T}$, $([\rightarrow_{po}]_t, \rightarrow_{co}) \in \mathsf{InTr}^P[t]$
2. *Happens-before correctness: The happens-before relation* $\rightarrow_{hb}$ *constructed from E has no cycles.*
3. *Observable correctness: Given* $\alpha \in \mathsf{A}_o$ *and* $\beta \in \mathsf{A}_c$ *if* $\beta \rightarrow_{hb} \alpha$ *then there exists* $\beta' \in \mathsf{A}_c$ *s.t.* $\beta \rightarrow_{co} \beta'$.

For an axiomatic execution $\mathsf{E} := \langle \mathsf{P}, \mathsf{A}, \rightarrow_{po}, \rightarrow_{co} \rangle$ to be well-formed, the actions, program order and communication order relations must have been obtained from a valid execution of the program $\mathsf{P}$ as given by the intra-thread semantics defined above (1). As we noted in our discussion of Figure 2, no valid execution of a CML program may involve a cyclic dependence between actions; such dependencies can only occur because of *speculatively* performing what is presumed to be a synchronous send operation (2).

Finally, although the relaxed execution might speculate, i.e., have a send operation transparently execute asynchronously, the observable behavior of such an execution should mirror some valid non-speculative execution, i.e., an execution in which the send action was, in fact, performed synchronously. We limit the scope of speculative actions by requiring that they complete (i.e., have a matching recipient) before an observable action is performed (3). Conversely, this allows communication actions not preceding an observable action to be speculated upon. Concretely, a send not preceding an externally visible action can be discharged asynchronously. The match and validity of the send needs to be checked only before discharging the next such action. This is the key idea behind our speculative execution framework.

**Safety.** An axiomatic execution represents a set of interleavings, each interleaving defining a specific total order that is consistent with the partial order defined by the execution[2]. The well-formedness conditions of an axiomatic execution implies that any observable behavior of an interleaving induced from it must correspond to a synchronous CML execution. The following two definitions formalize this intuition.

**Definition 7 (Observable dependencies).** *In a well-formed axiomatic execution* $\mathsf{E} := \langle \mathsf{P}, \mathsf{A}, \rightarrow_{po}, \rightarrow_{co} \rangle$, *the observable dependencies* $\mathsf{A}_{od}$ *is the set of actions that precedes (under* $\rightarrow_{hb}$) *some observable action, i.e.,* $\mathsf{A}_{od} = \{\alpha \mid \alpha \in \mathsf{A}, \beta \in \mathsf{A}_o, \alpha \rightarrow_{hb} \beta\}$.

**Definition 8 (CML Execution).** *Given a well-formed axiomatic execution* $\mathsf{E} := \langle \mathsf{P}, \mathsf{A}, \rightarrow_{po}, \rightarrow_{co} \rangle$, *the pair* $(\mathsf{E}, \rightarrow_{to})$ *is said to be in* CML(P) *if* $\rightarrow_{to}$ *is a total order on* $\mathsf{A}_{od}$ *and* $\rightarrow_{to}$ *is consistent with* $\rightarrow_{hb}$.

In the above definition, an interleaving represented by $\rightarrow_{to}$ is only possible since the axiomatic execution is well-formed, and thereby does not contain a happens-before cycle.

**Lemma 1.** *If a total order* $\rightarrow_{to}$ *is consistent with* $\rightarrow_{hb}$, *then* $\rightarrow_{hb}$ *does not contain a cycle involving actions in* $\mathsf{A}_{od}$.

Next, we show that a well-formed axiomatic execution respects the safety property of non-speculative execution of a CML program. When a CML program evaluates non-speculatively, a thread performing a communication action is blocked until a matching

---

[2] Two ordering relations $P$ and $Q$ are said to be *consistent* if $\forall x, y, \neg(xPy \wedge yQx)$.

communication action is available. Hence, if $(\langle \mathsf{P}, \mathsf{A}, \rightarrow_{po}, \rightarrow_{co} \rangle, \rightarrow_{to}) \in \text{CML}(\mathsf{P})$, and a communication action $\alpha$ on a thread $t$ is followed by an action $\beta$ on the same thread, then it must be the case that there is a matching action $\alpha \rightarrow_{co} \alpha'$ that happened before $\beta$ in $\rightarrow_{to}$. This is captured in the following theorem.

**Theorem 1.** *Given a CML execution* $(\mathsf{E}, \rightarrow_{to}) \in \text{CML}(\mathsf{P})$, $\forall \alpha, \beta$ *such that* $\alpha \in \mathbb{A}_c$, $T(\alpha) = T(\beta), \alpha \rightarrow_{to} \beta$, *there exists an action* $\alpha \rightarrow_{co} \alpha'$ *such that* $\alpha' \rightarrow_{to} \beta$.

*Proof.* Let $\mathsf{E} := \langle \mathsf{P}, \mathsf{A}, \rightarrow_{po}, \rightarrow_{co} \rangle$. First, we show that $\alpha' \in \mathsf{A}$. Since $\alpha \rightarrow_{to} \beta, \alpha \in \mathsf{A}_{od}$, by Definition 8. By Definition 7, there exists some $\gamma \in \mathsf{A}_o$ such that $\alpha \rightarrow_{hb} \gamma$. Since $\mathsf{E}$ is well-formed and $\alpha \rightarrow_{hb} \gamma$, by Definition 6, there exists an $\alpha' \in \mathsf{A}$ such that $\alpha \rightarrow_{co} \alpha'$.

Next, we show that $\alpha' \in \mathsf{A}_{od}$. By Definition 3, $\alpha' \rightarrow_{co} \alpha \rightarrow_{hb} \gamma$ implies $\alpha' \rightarrow_{hb} \gamma$. Hence, $\alpha' \in \mathsf{A}_{od}$, and is related by $\rightarrow_{to}$. Finally, since $T(\alpha) = T(\beta)$ and $\alpha \rightarrow_{to} \beta$, $\alpha \rightarrow_{po} \beta$. And, $\alpha' \rightarrow_{co} \alpha \rightarrow_{po} \beta$ implies $\alpha' \rightarrow_{hb} \beta$. By Lemma 1 and Definition 8, $\alpha' \rightarrow_{to} \beta$. ∎

## 3  Implementation

The axiomatic semantics provides a declarative way of reasoning about correct CML executions. In particular, a well-formed execution does not have a happens-before cycle. However, in practice, a speculative execution framework that discharges synchronous sends asynchronously (speculatively), needs to track the relations necessary to perform the integrity check *on-the-fly*, detect and remediate any execution that has a happens-before cycle.

To do so, we construct a *dependence graph* that captures the dependencies described by an axiomatic execution, and ensure the graph has no cycles. If a cycle is detected, we rollback the effects induced by the offending speculative action, and re-execute it as a normal synchronous operation. By definition, this synchronous re-execution is bound to be correct. The context of our investigation is a distributed implementation of CML called R$^{\text{CML}}$(RELAXED CML)[3] built on top of the MultiMLton SML compiler and runtime [15]. We have extended MultiMLton with the infrastructure necessary for distributed execution.

### 3.1  System Architecture

An R$^{\text{CML}}$ application consists of multiple *instances*, each of which runs the *same* MultiMLton executable. These instances might run on the same node, on different nodes within the same datacenter, or on nodes found in different data centers. Each instance has a scheduler which preemptively multiplexes execution of user-level CML threads over multiple cores. We use the ZeroMQ messaging library [26] as the transport layer over which the R$^{\text{CML}}$ channel communication is implemented. In addition to providing reliable and efficient point-to-point communication, ZeroMQ also provides the ability to construct higher-level multicast patterns. In particular, we leverage ZeroMQ's publish/subscribe support to implement CML's first-class channel based communication.

---

[3] `http://multimlton.cs.purdue.edu/mML/rx-cml.html`

The fact that every instance in an $R^{CML}$ application runs the same program, in addition to the property that CML channels are strongly-typed, allows us to provide typesafe serialization of immutable values as well as function closures. Serializing mutable references is disallowed, and an exception is raised if the value being serialized refers to a mutable object. To safely refer to the same channel object across multiple instances, channel creation is parameterized with an identity string. Channels created with the same identity string refer to the same channel object across all instances in the $R^{CML}$ application. Channels are first-class citizens and can be sent as messages over other channels to construct complex communication protocols.

## 3.2 Communication Manager

Each $R^{CML}$ instance runs a single communication manager thread, which maintains globally consistent replica of the CML channels utilized by its constituent CML threads. The protocol for a single CML communication is illustrated in Figure 3. Since CML channel might potentially be shared among multiple threads across different instances, communication matches are determined dynamically. In general, it is not possible to determine the matching thread and its instance while initiating the communication action. Hence, whenever a thread intends to send or receive a value on the channel, its intention (along with a value in the case of a send operation), is broadcast to every other $R^{CML}$ instance. Importantly, the application thread performing the send does not block and *speculatively* continues execution.

Subsequently, an application thread that performs a receive on this channel consumes the send action, sends a *join message* to the sender thread's instance, and proceeds immediately. In particular, receiver thread does not block to determine if the send action was concurrently consumed by a thread in another instance. This corresponds to speculating on the communication match, which will succeed in the absence of concurrent receives for the same send action. On receiving the join message, a *match message* is broadcast to every instance, sealing the match. Those instances that speculatively matched with the send, except the one indicated in the match message, treat their re-

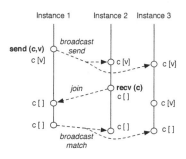

**Fig. 3.** Communication manager behavior during a send and its matching receive

ceive action as a mis-speculation. Other instances that have not matched with this particular send remove the send action from the corresponding local channel replica.

## 3.3 Speculative Execution

Aborting a mis-speculation requires restoring the computation to a previously known consistent state. Achieving this entails rolling back all threads that communicated with the offending action, transitively. In this regard, *stabilizers* [27] provide a suitable abstraction for restoring consistent checkpoints in message-passing programs. A stabilizer builds a dependence graph that takes into account intra-thread program order and inter-thread communication dependence. However, the implementation reported in [27] assumes a centralized structure, and a global barrier that stops all execution while a checkpoint is restored; neither condition is reasonable in a high-latency, distributed environment.

**Replicated Dependence Graph.** Instead, R$^{CML}$ exploits the broadcast nature of the match message (Section 3.2) to incrementally construct a globally-consistent replica of the dependence graph at every instance. The nodes in the dependence graph correspond to the actions in the axiomatic definition. Thread spawn and join actions are broadcast to allow other instances to add necessary nodes and edges. Maintaining a replica of the dependence graph at each replica allows ill-formed executions to be detected locally and remediated.

**Well-Formedness Check.** To ensure observable behavior of an R$^{CML}$ program to its synchronous equivalent, the compiler automatically inserts a *well-formedness check* before observable actions in the program. R$^{CML}$ treats system calls, access to mutable references, and foreign function calls as observable actions. On reaching a well-formedness check, a *cycle-detector* is invoked which checks for cycles in the dependence graph leading up to this point. If the execution is well-formed (no cycles in the dependence graph), then the observable action is performed. Since there is no need to check for well-formedness of this fragment again, the verified dependence graph fragment is garbage collected on all instances.

**Checkpoint.** After a well-formedness check, the state of the current thread is consistent. Hence, right before the next (speculative) communication action, we checkpoint the current thread by saving its current continuation. This ensures that the observable actions performed after the well-formedness check are not re-executed if the thread happens to rollback. In addition, this checkpointing scheme allows multiple observable actions to be performed between a well-formedness check and the subsequent checkpoint. Unlike Stabilizers [27], every thread in an R$^{CML}$ application has exactly one saved checkpoint continuation during the execution. Moreover, R$^{CML}$ checkpointing is un-coordinated [10], and does not require that all the threads that transitively interacted capture their checkpoint together, which would be unreasonable in geo-distributed application.

**Remediation.** If the well-formedness check does report a cycle, then all threads that have *transitively* observed the mis-speculation are rolled back. The protocol roughly follows the same structure described in [27], but is asynchronous and does not involve a global barrier. The recovery process is a combination of checkpoint (saved continuation) and log-based (dependence graph) rollback and recovery [10]. Every mis-speculated thread is eventually restored to a consistent state by replacing its current continuation with its saved continuation, which was captured in a consistent state.

Recall that R$^{CML}$ automatically captures a checkpoint, and only stores a single checkpoint per thread. As a result, rolling back to a checkpoint might entail re-executing, in addition to mis-speculated communication actions, correct speculative communications as well (i.e., communication actions that are not reachable from a cycle in the dependence graph). Thus, after the saved continuation is restored, correct speculative actions are *replayed* from the dependence graph, while mis-speculations are discharged non-speculatively (i.e., synchronously). This strategy ensures progress. Finally, we leverage ZeroMQ's guarantee on FIFO ordered delivery of messages to ensure that messages in-flight during the remediation process are properly accounted for.

### 3.4   Handling Full CML

Our discussion so far has been limited to primitive send and recv operations. $\mathbb{R}^{CML}$ also supports base events, wrap, guard, and choice combinators. The wrap and guard combinators construct a complex event from a simpler event by suffixing and prefixing computations, resp. Evaluation of such a complex event is effectively the same as performing a *sequence* of actions encapsulated by the event. From the perspective of reasoning about well-formed executions, wrap and guard are purely syntactic additions.

Choices are more intriguing. The choose combinator operates over a list of events, which when discharged, non-deterministically picks one of the enabled events. If none of the choices are already enabled, one could imagine speculatively discharging every event in a choice, picking one of the enabled events, terminating other events and rolling back the appropriate threads. However, in practice, such a solution would lead to large number of mis-speculations. Hence, $\mathbb{R}^{CML}$ discharges choices non-speculatively. In order to avoid spurious invocations, negative acknowledgment events (withNack) are enabled only after the selection to which they belong is part of a successful well-formedness check.

### 3.5   Extensions

Our presentation so far has been restricted to speculating only on synchronous sends. Speculation on receives is, in general, not possible since the continuation might depend on the value received. However, if the receive is on a unit channel, speculation has a sensible interpretation. The well-formedness check only needs to ensure that the receive action has been paired up, along with the usual well-formedness checks. Speculating on these kinds of receive actions, which essentially serve as synchronization barriers, is useful, especially during a broadcast operation of the kind described in Figure 1 for receiving acknowledgments.

## 4   Case Studies

### 4.1   Online Transaction Processing

Our first case study considers a CML implementation of an online transaction processing (OLTP) system. Resources are modeled as actors that communicate to clients via message-passing, each protected by a lock server. A transaction can span multiple resources, and is implemented pessimistically. Hence, a transaction must hold all relevant locks before starting its computation. We can use our relaxed execution semantics to allow transactions to effectively execute optimistically, identifying and remediating conflicting transactions *post facto*; the key idea is to model conflicting transactions as an ill-formed execution. We implement each lock server as a single CML thread, whose kernel is:

```
fun lockServer (lockChan: unit chan) (unlockChan: unit chan) =
  (recv lockChan; recv unlockChan; lockServer lockChan unlockChan)
```

which protects a single *resource* by ensuring atomic access. It is up to the application to ensure that the lock servers are correctly used, and when obtaining multiple locks, locks are sorted to avoid deadlocks.

In the absence of contention, the involvement of the lock server adds unnecessary overhead. By communicating with lockChan asynchronously, we can allow the client (the thread performing the transaction), to concurrently proceed with obtaining other locks or executing the transaction. However, the transactional guarantees are lost in this case. Under R$^{CML}$ such serializability violation shows up as a cycle in the happens-before dependence graph. R$^{CML}$ rejects such executions, causing the transaction to abort, and re-execute non-speculatively.

For our evaluation, we implemented a distributed version of this program ( vacation ) taken from the STAMP benchmark suite [4]. To adapt the benchmark for a distributed environment, we partitioned resources into 16 *shards*, each protected by a lock server. The workload was setup for moderate contention, and each transaction involves 10 operations. The shards were spread across 16 EC2 M1 large instances within the same EC2 availability zone. The clients were instantiated from all of the different regions on M1 small instances to simulate the latencies involved in a real web-application. A benchmark run involved 10K transactions, spread equally across all of the available clients. Each benchmark run was repeated 5 times.

The performance results are presented in the Figure 4. The number of clients concurrently issuing transaction requests was increased from 1 to 48. R$^{CML}$ is the speculative version, while Sync is the synchronous, non-speculative variant. The 1-client Sync version took 1220 seconds to complete. For comparison, we extended the original C version with a similar shared distribution structure. This run was 1.3× faster than the CML baseline. The benchmark execution under R$^{CML}$ scales much better than the Sync version due to optimistic transactions. With 48 clients, R$^{CML}$ version was 5.8× faster

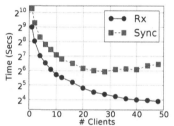

**Fig. 4.** Performance comparison on distributed vacation (OLTP) benchmark. Lower is better.

than then Sync version. Under R$^{CML}$, the number of transaction conflicts does increase with the number of clients. With 48 clients, 9% of the transactions executed under R$^{CML}$ were tagged as conflicting and re-executed non-speculatively. This does not, however, adversely affect scalability.

## 4.2 Collaborative Editing

Our next case study is a real-time, decentralized collaborative editing tool. Typically, commercial offerings such as Google Docs, EtherPad, etc., utilize a centralized server to coordinate between the authors. Not only does the server eventually become a bottleneck, but service providers also need to store a copy of the document, along with other personal information, which is undesirable. We consider a fully decentralized solution, in which authors work on a local copy of the shared document for responsiveness, with remote updates merged incrementally. Although replicas are allowed to diverge, they are expected to converge eventually. This convergence is achieved through *operational transformation* [22]. Dealing with operational transformation in the absence of a centralized server is tricky [16], and commercial collaborative editing services like Google Wave impose additional restrictions with respect to the frequency of remote updates [24] in order to build a tractable implementation.

We simplify the design by performing *causal atomic broadcast* when sending updates to the replicas. Causal atomic broadcast ensures that the updates are applied on all replicas in the same global order, providing a semblance of a single centralized server. Implemented naïvely, i.e., performing the broadcast synchronously, however, is an expensive operation, requiring coordination among all replicas for every broadcast operation compromising responsiveness. Our relaxed execution model overcomes this inefficiency. The key advantage of our system is that the causal atomic broadcast is performed speculatively, allowing client threads to remain responsive.

We use a collaborative editing benchmark generator described in [14] to generate a random trace of operations, based on parameters such as trace length, percentage of insertions, deletions, number of replicas, local operation delay, etc. Our benchmarking trace contains 30K operations, 85%(15%) of which are insertions(deletions), and 20% of which are concurrent operations. We insert a 25 ms delay between two consecutive local operations to simulate user-interaction. Updates from each replica is causal atomically broadcasted every 250 ms. Each replica is represented by a $\mathcal{R}^{CML}$ instance placed in widely distributed Amazon EC2 availability zones chosen to capture the geo-distributed nature of collaborative editing. The average inter-instance latency was 173 ms, with a standard deviation of 71.5. Results are reported as the average of five runs.

We consider the time taken by a collaborative editing session to be the time between the first operation generation and the completion of the last broadcast operation, at which point the documents at every replica would have converged. Figure 5 shows results with respect to total running time. Sync represents an ordinary CML execution, while $\mathcal{R}^{CML}$ represents our new implementation. With 2-authors, $\mathcal{R}^{CML}$ version took 485 seconds to complete, and was 37% faster than the synchronous version. As we increase the number of concurrent authors, the number of communication actions per broadcast operation increases. Hence, we expect the benchmark run to

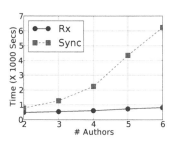

**Fig. 5.** Performance comparison on collaborative editing benchmark. Lower is better.

take longer to complete. The non-speculative version scales poorly due to the increasing number of synchronizations involved in the broadcast operations. Indeed, Sync is 7.6× slower than $\mathcal{R}^{CML}$ when there are six concurrent authors. Not surprisingly, $\mathcal{R}^{CML}$ also takes longer to complete a run as we increase the number of concurrent authors. This is because of increasing communication actions per broadcast as well as increase in mis-speculations. However, with six authors, it only takes 1.67× longer to complete the session when compared to having just two authors, and illustrates the utility of speculative communication.

## 5   Related Work

Causal-ordering of messages is considered an important building block [2] for distributed applications. Similar to our formulation, Charron-Bost *et al.* [5] develop an axiomatic formulation for causal-ordered communication primitives, although their focus is on characterizing communication behavior and verifying communication protocols, rather than latency hiding. Speculative execution has been shown to be beneficial in other circumstances under high latency environments such as distributed file systems [17], asynchronous virtual machine replication [6], state machine replication [25], deadlock detection [13] etc., although we are unaware of other attempts to use it for transparently converting synchronous operations to asynchronous ones.

Besides Erlang [1], there are also several distributed implementations of functional languages that have been proposed [23, 20]. More recently, Cloud Haskell [11] has been proposed for developing distributed Haskell programs. While all these systems deal with issues such as type-safe serialization and fault tolerance central to any distributed language, R$^{CML}$'s focus is on enforcing equivalence between synchronous and asynchronous evaluation. The formalization used to establish this equivalence is inspired by work in language and hardware memory models [21, 7, 3]. These efforts, however, are primarily concerned with visibility of shared-memory updates, rather than correctness of relaxed message-passing behavior. Thus, while language memory models [3, 7] are useful in reasoning about compiler optimizations, our relaxed communication model reasons about safe asynchronous manifestations of synchronous protocols.

Transactional events(TE) [8, 9] combine first-class synchronous events with an all-or-nothing semantics. They are strictly more expressive than CML, although such expressivity comes at the price of an expensive runtime search procedure to find a satisfiable schedule. Communicating memory transactions (CMT) [12] also uses speculation to allow asynchronous message-passing communication between shared-memory transactions, although CMT does not enforce any equivalence with a synchronous execution. Instead, mis-speculations only arise because of a serializability violation on memory.

## 6    Conclusions and Future Work

CML provides a simple, expressive, and composable set of synchronous event combinators that facilitate concurrent programming, albeit at the price of performance, especially in high-latency environments. This paper shows how to regain this performance by transparently implementing synchronous operations asynchronously, effectively treating them as speculative actions. We formalize the conditions under which such a transformation is sound, and describe a distributed implementation of CML called R$^{CML}$ that incorporates these ideas. Our reported case studies illustrate the benefits of our approach, and provide evidence that R$^{CML}$ is a basis upon which we can build clean, robust, and efficient distributed CML programs. An important area of future work is the integration of fault tolerance into the system. Note that the state of a failed instance can be recovered from the dependence graph (which includes all saved continuations), enabling the use of checkpoint restoration and replay as a feasible response mechanism to node failures.

## References

[1] Armstrong, J., Virding, R., Wikström, C., Williams, M.: Concurrent Programming in Erlang, 2nd edn. (1996)
[2] Birman, K.P., Joseph, T.A.: Reliable Communication in the Presence of Failures. ACM Trans. Comput. Syst. 5(1), 47–76 (1987)
[3] Boehm, H.J., Adve, S.V.: Foundations of the C++ Concurrency Memory Model. In: PLDI, pp. 68–78 (2008)

[4] Cao Minh, C., Chung, J., Kozyrakis, C., Olukotun, K.: STAMP: Stanford transactional applications for multi-processing. In: IISWC (2008)

[5] Charron-Bost, B., Mattern, F., Tel, G.: Synchronous, Asynchronous, and Causally Ordered Communication. Distrib. Comput. 9(4), 173–191 (1996)

[6] Cully, B., Lefebvre, G., Meyer, D., Feeley, M., Hutchinson, N., Warfield, A.: Remus: High Availability via Asynchronous Virtual Machine Replication. In: NSDI, pp. 161–174 (2008)

[7] Demange, D., Laporte, V., Zhao, L., Jagannathan, S., Pichardie, D., Vitek, J.: Plan B: A Buffered Memory Model for Java. In: POPL, pp. 329–342 (2013)

[8] Donnelly, K., Fluet, M.: Transactional Events. In: ICFP, pp. 124–135 (2006)

[9] Effinger-Dean, L., Kehrt, M., Grossman, D.: Transactional Events for ML. In: ICFP, pp. 103–114 (2008)

[10] Elnozahy, E.N.M., Alvisi, L., Wang, Y.M., Johnson, D.B.: A survey of rollback-recovery protocols in message-passing systems. ACM Comput. Surv. 34(3), 375–408 (2002)

[11] Epstein, J., Black, A.P., Peyton-Jones, S.: Towards Haskell in the Cloud. In: Haskell Symposium, pp. 118–129 (2011)

[12] Lesani, M., Palsberg, J.: Communicating Memory Transactions. In: PPoPP, pp. 157–168 (2011)

[13] Li, T., Ellis, C.S., Lebeck, A.R., Sorin, D.J.: Pulse: A Dynamic Deadlock Detection Mechanism Using Speculative Execution. In: USENIX ATC, pp. 31–44 (2005)

[14] Martin, S., Ahmed-Nacer, M., Urso, P.: Controlled Conflict Resolution for Replicated Documents. In: CollaborateCom, pp. 471–480 (2012)

[15] MultiMLton: MLton for Scalable Multicore Architectures (2013), http://multimlton.cs.purdue.edu

[16] Nichols, D.A., Curtis, P., Dixon, M., Lamping, J.: High-latency, Low-bandwidth Windowing in the Jupiter Collaboration System. In: UIST, pp. 111–120 (1995)

[17] Nightingale, E.B., Chen, P.M., Flinn, J.: Speculative Execution in a Distributed File System. In: SOSP, pp. 191–205 (2005)

[18] Reppy, J.: Concurrent Programming in ML. Cambridge University Press (2007)

[19] Sarkar, S., Sewell, P., Nardelli, F.Z., Owens, S., Ridge, T., Braibant, T., Myreen, M.O., Alglave, J.: The Semantics of x86-CC Multiprocessor Machine Code. In: POPL, pp. 379–391 (2009)

[20] Sewell, P., Leifer, J.J., Wansbrough, K., Nardelli, F.Z., Allen-Williams, M., Habouzit, P., Vafeiadis, V.: Acute: High-level Programming Language Design for Distributed Computation. J. Funct. Program. 17(4-5), 547–612 (2007)

[21] Sewell, P., Sarkar, S., Owens, S., Nardelli, F.Z., Myreen, M.O.: x86-TSO: A Rigorous and Usable Programmer's Model for x86 Multiprocessors. Commun. ACM 53(7), 89–97 (2010)

[22] Suleiman, M., Cart, M., Ferrié, J.: Serialization of Concurrent Operations in a Distributed Collaborative Environment. In: GROUP, pp. 435–445 (1997)

[23] Wakita, K., Asano, T., Sassa, M.: D'Caml: Native Support for Distributed ML Programming in Heterogeneous Environment. In: Amestoy, P.R., Berger, P., Daydé, M., Duff, I.S., Frayssé, V., Giraud, L., Ruiz, D. (eds.) Euro-Par 1999. LNCS, vol. 1685, pp. 914–924. Springer, Heidelberg (1999)

[24] Wang, D., Mah, A., Lassen, S.: Operational Transformation (2010), http://www.waveprotocol.org/whitepapers/operational-transform

[25] Wester, B., Cowling, J.A., Nightingale, E.B., Chen, P.M., Flinn, J., Liskov, B.: Tolerating Latency in Replicated State Machines Through Client Speculation. In: NSDI, pp. 245–260 (2009)

[26] ZeroMQ: The Intelligent Transport Layer (2013), http://www.zeromq.org

[27] Ziarek, L., Jagannathan, S.: Lightweight Checkpointing for Concurrent ML. Journal of Functional Programming 20(2), 137–173 (2010)

[28] Ziarek, L., Sivaramakrishnan, K., Jagannathan, S.: Composable Asynchronous Events. In: PLDI, pp. 628–639 (2011)

# Partial Type Signatures for Haskell

Thomas Winant[1], Dominique Devriese[1], Frank Piessens[1], and Tom Schrijvers[2]

[1] KU Leuven, Celestijnenlaan 200A, 3001 Leuven, Belgium
firstname.lastname@cs.kuleuven.be
[2] Ghent University, Krijgslaan 281 S9 WE02, 9000 Gent, Belgium
tom.schrijvers@ugent.be

**Abstract.** Strong type systems can be used to increase the reliability and performance of programs. In combination with type inference the overhead for the programmer can be kept small. Nevertheless, explicit type signatures often remain needed or useful. In languages with standard Hindley-Milner-based type systems, programmers have a binary choice between omitting the type signature (and rely on type inference) or explicitly providing the type entirely; there are no intermediate options. Proposals for partial type signatures exist, but none support features like local constraints and GHC's non-generalisation of local bindings. Therefore we propose and motivate a practical form of partial type signatures for present-day Haskell. We formally describe our proposal as an extension of the OUTSIDEIN(X) system and prove some of its properties. We have developed a (not yet complete) implementation for the GHC Haskell compiler. Our design fits naturally in both the OUTSIDEIN(X) formalism and the compiler.

**Keywords:** Haskell, Hindley-Milner type inference, (partial) type signatures, wildcards.

## 1 Introduction

Static type checking can help catch errors at compile-time and provide useful information for compiler optimisations. Through the use of type inference, programmers are not required to provide explicit type signatures for all values in a program. Nevertheless, explicit signatures can still be needed or useful: type signatures provide a form of machine-checked documentation, they can be used to make general inferred types more specific, and help to verify whether the program corresponds to the programmer's intentions.

Haskell's overloaded math operators exemplify the need for type signatures:

**let** *harmonic* $x$ $y$ = $\frac{2}{\frac{1}{x} + \frac{1}{y}}$ **in** *print* (*harmonic* 3 2)

Under Haskell's defaulting rule[1], $x$ and $y$ are interpreted as floating point numbers leading to the inexact output 2.400000000000004. The exact output $\frac{12}{5}$

---

[1] Haskell lets programmers manually specify to which type the ambiguous type variables satisfying the *Num* class should resolve.

M. Flatt and H.-F. Guo (Eds.): PADL 2014, LNCS 8324, pp. 17–32, 2014.

is produced with the signature $harmonic :: Rational \to Rational \to Rational$. Without defaulting, an ambiguous type variable would make a type signature mandatory.

Additionally, type inference is fundamentally limited. It is impossible to infer types for all programs that are typeable in more complex type systems. Consider the following Haskell program:

$foo\ x = (x\ [\mathit{True}, \mathit{False}], x\ [\text{'a'}, \text{'b'}])$

$test = foo\ reverse$

This program is rejected by Haskell's type checker, because of the Damas-Milner rule that *a lambda-bound argument (like x) must have a monomorphic type*. $x$ could be assigned the type $[\mathit{Bool}] \to [\mathit{Bool}]$, or $[\mathit{Char}] \to [\mathit{Char}]$, but not $\forall a.[a] \to [a]$, see e.g. [9]. With a correct signature, the program is accepted:

$foo :: (\forall a.[a] \to [a]) \to ([\mathit{Bool}], [\mathit{Char}])$
$foo\ x = (x\ [\mathit{True}, \mathit{False}], x\ [\text{'a'}, \text{'b'}])$

Haskell, like many other programming languages provides a binary, all-or-nothing choice when it comes to type signatures: either the programmer writes the whole signature or none at all. Nevertheless, in many of the situations where type signatures are needed or useful, it suffices to pin down certain parts of the type. Providing the full type is unneeded and sometimes tedious or distracting. For example, when types are intended to document the code or to make its inferred type more specific, this is often only needed for one argument of a function or for the monad in which a computation runs, but not its result type. For example, only the type of *foo*'s argument cannot be inferred, but its result type can. In cases where we want or need to specify only a part of a type, it can be beneficial to *not* specify the rest. That remainder can be boilerplate, tedious or obscure the intention of the type signature. Not providing this information can save the programmer some thought and work, especially if the uninteresting bits of the type are unknown or prone to frequent change during development.

For such cases, *partial type signatures* can specify a type only partially and leave the rest for the type inferencer to decide. For *foo*, we could use:

$foo :: (\forall a.[a] \to [a]) \to \_$
$foo\ x = (x\ [\mathit{True}, \mathit{False}], x\ [\text{'a'}, \text{'b'}])$

This partial signature specifies that *foo* is a function and defines the polymorphic type of *foo*'s first argument. The result type is unspecified, as indicated by a type wildcard (written _). Similarly, for the *harmonic* example, it would suffice to write the shorter signature $harmonic :: Rational \to \_$ .

At this point, we should mention some partial workarounds for the lack of partial signatures in Haskell. *foo* could for example use a pattern type signature:

$foo\ (x :: \forall a.[a] \to [a]) = ...$

Expression type signatures similarly provide a partial solution. Another way to simulate partial type signatures uses a helper function, *isTypeFor*, which forces its second argument to have the same type as the first. Combined with an explicitly typed dummy value, we could write for example *foo* as follows:

$$isTypeFor :: a \rightarrow a \rightarrow a$$
$$\_\,\text{'}isTypeFor\text{'}\ x = x$$
$$foo = (\bot :: (\forall a.[a] \rightarrow [a]) \rightarrow b)\ \text{'}isTypeFor\text{'}$$
$$(\lambda x \rightarrow (x\,[\,True, False\,], x\,[\,\text{'a'}, \text{'b'}\,]))$$

The type variable $b$ acts as a type wildcard and will be instantiated to the result type. A downside is that $foo$'s implementation is obscured with computationally insignificant code. A combinator library supports this technique [2]. Kiselyov also proposes a trick using *fake clauses* to partially annotate constraints [5]:

$$addOrd :: Ord\ x \Rightarrow x \rightarrow a$$
$$addOrd = \bot$$
$$foo_2\ x\ |\ False = addOrd\ x$$
$$foo_2\ x = x$$

The first clause of $foo_2$ is never executed but it does make the type inferencer produce an additional constraint $Ord\ x$, leading to the type $Ord\ a \Rightarrow a \rightarrow a$ instead of $a \rightarrow a$. Not every partial signature can be emulated though: we do not see a way to forbid the inference of additional constraints and there may be other limitations w.r.t. our work as well.

These workarounds are generally poorly legible, cumbersome to use (e.g. requiring lambda functions instead of left-hand-side patterns) and limited (e.g. only a lower bound on type constraints). Their existence does prove the need for actual partial type signatures.

We propose and study a form of partial type signatures in the context of a language with HM-based type inference. Our partial type signatures extend normal signatures with type wildcards (_). During type inference, such wildcards can be instantiated to arbitrary types, e.g. the type $\_ \rightarrow \_$ can be instantiated to $Int \rightarrow (Bool \rightarrow Int)$ or $(Int \rightarrow Bool) \rightarrow String$. They map nicely to the unification variables used internally by most type inferencers.

In the context of HM-based type inference, we take care to properly interact with the type generalisation that is performed to achieve let-polymorphism. If (part of) the type instantiating a wildcard is not restricted by type inference, a HM-style type inferencer will quantify over it. Consider the following program:

$$bar :: \_ \rightarrow \_$$
$$bar\ \_ = True$$

From the return value $True$, the type checker learns that the second wildcard in the partial signature of $bar$ must be instantiated to $Bool$. However, the first wildcard remains open. In this case, type generalisation will infer $bar$'s principal type $\forall a.a \rightarrow Bool$, as when the type signature is omitted entirely.

A second, related challenge is dealing with constraints, for example type class constraints (e.g. $\forall a.Num\ a \Rightarrow a$) and equality constraints (e.g. $(Fun1\ a \sim (b \rightarrow b)) \Rightarrow a \rightarrow b$) supported by GHC. Our partial signatures allow the inference of additional constraints if and only if the type contains an *extra-constraints wildcard*, written as an underscore just before the double arrow: $\_ \Rightarrow a \rightarrow b$. For example, the signature $\_ \rightarrow b$ (without an extra-constraints wildcard) forbids types with additional constraints like $Num\ b \Rightarrow Int \rightarrow b$. That type can be allowed explicitly with the signature $\_ \Rightarrow \_ \rightarrow b$. Only one extra-constraints wildcard can be present and allows any number of constraints to be added.

In a GHC ticket discussion, Peyton Jones has argued the usefulness of an extra-constraints wildcard based on the following example [12]. By placing a wildcard, the programmer tells the type checker to infer the context for him.

$f :: \_ \Rightarrow [a] \rightarrow String$    -- Inferred constraints: $(Num\ a, Show\ a)$
$f\ xs = show\ (sum\ xs)$

We also allow multiple references to a wildcard within a signature using *named wildcards* (written as $\_a$). They can be used to shorten tedious type signatures:

$isMeltdown :: NukeMonad\ param_1\ param_2\ Bool$
$unlessMeltdown :: \_nm\ () \rightarrow \_nm\ ()$
$unlessMeltdown\ c = \textbf{do}\ m \leftarrow isMeltdown$
                    $\textbf{if}\ m\ \textbf{then}\ return\ ()\ \textbf{else}\ c$

To make our proposal precise, we give a formal account based on Vytiniotis et al.'s OUTSIDEIN(X) formalism [13]. We define natural and algorithmic typing rules and prove their correspondence. Additionally, we prove that our new rules generalise the old ones for signatures without wildcards and that a partial signature $f :: \_ \Rightarrow \_$ has the same effect as no signature at all. Such correspondences are important for consistency and to align with users' expectations.

We have an implementation of our proposal in the Glasgow Haskell Compiler, but it is not yet complete at the time of writing. Our current version correctly unifies wildcards and named wildcards with concrete types, but unifying with open types, generalisation, and the extra-constraints wildcard are not yet working as we intend. We hope to finish our modifications in the coming months.

*Contributions* The idea of partial type signatures is not novel. Several languages support them in some form or other [7,6,10] and they have been proposed for Haskell several times before [14,15]. Dijkstra [4] and Sulzmann and Wazny [11,16] have detailed proposals for Haskell-like languages. Still, we believe that ours is the first rigorous formalisation of partial type signatures for a HM-style inference that supports all the features of present-day Haskell. Specifically, we support local constraints (that arise e.g. from pattern matching on GADTs) and align with GHC's non-generalisation of local bindings. More specifically, our contributions are the following:

- A formalised proposal for partial type signatures, including generalisation, in a Hindley-Milner-style type inference system. Our work plugs into the constraint-based type inference approach OUTSIDEIN(X) [13], currently employed by the de facto standard Haskell compiler GHC.
- We align our partial type signatures with the OUTSIDEIN(X) policy that *let should not be generalised.*
- We formally show that the new typing rules generalise the existing rules for signatures without wildcards and for omitted signatures.
- A (not yet complete) implementation in the GHC Haskell compiler.

| Term variables | | $\in x, y, z, f, g, h$ |
|---|---|---|
| Type variables | | $\in a, b, c$ |
| Named wildcards | | $\in \_a, \_b, \_c$ |
| Data constructors | | $\in K$ |
| | $\nu$ | $::= K \mid x$ |
| Programs | $prog$ | $::= \epsilon \mid f = e, prog \mid$ |
| | | $f :: \underline{\sigma} = e, prog$ |
| Expressions | $e$ | $::= \nu \mid \lambda x . e \mid e_1\, e_2 \mid$ |
| | | $\textbf{case } e \textbf{ of } \{\overline{K\,\overline{x} \to e}\}$ |
| Type schemes | $\sigma$ | $::= \forall \overline{a} . Q \Rightarrow \tau$ |
| Type schemes with wildcards | $\underline{\sigma}$ | $::= \forall \overline{a} . \underline{Q} \Rightarrow \underline{\tau}$ |
| Constraints | $Q$ | $::= \epsilon \mid Q_1 \wedge Q_2 \mid \tau_1 \sim \tau_2 \mid \mathsf{D}\,\overline{\tau} \mid \ldots$ |
| Constraints with wildcards | $\underline{Q}^w$ | $::= Q \mid \underline{Q}_1^w \wedge \underline{Q}_2^w \mid \underline{\tau}_1 \sim \underline{\tau}_2 \mid \mathsf{D}\,\overline{\underline{\tau}} \mid \ldots$ |
| Constraints with extra constraints wildcard | $\underline{Q}$ | $::= \underline{Q}^w \mid \underline{Q}^w \wedge \_$ |
| Monotypes | $\tau, \upsilon$ | $::= tv \mid \texttt{Int} \mid \texttt{Bool} \mid [\tau] \mid \mathsf{T}\,\overline{\tau} \mid \ldots$ |
| Monotypes with wildcards | $\underline{\tau}, \underline{\upsilon}$ | $::= \tau \mid \_ \mid \_a \mid [\underline{\tau}] \mid \mathsf{T}\,\overline{\underline{\tau}}$ |
| Type environments | $\Gamma$ | $::= \epsilon \mid (\nu{:}\sigma), \Gamma$ |
| Free type variables | $ftv(\cdot)$ | |
| Top-level axiom schemes | $\mathcal{Q}$ | $::= \epsilon \mid \mathcal{Q} \wedge \mathcal{Q} \mid \forall \overline{a} . Q \Rightarrow Q$ |
| Unification variables | | $\in \alpha, \beta, \gamma, \omega, \ldots$ |
| Unifiers | $\theta, \varphi$ | $::= [\overline{\alpha \mapsto \tau}]$ |
| Unification or rigid (skolem) variables | $tv$ | $::= \alpha \mid a$ |
| Algorithm-generated constraints $C$ | | $::= Q \mid C_1 \wedge C_2 \mid \exists \overline{\alpha} . (Q \supset C)$ |
| Free unification variables | $fuv(\cdot)$ | |
| Named wildcards | $nwc(\cdot)$ | |

**Fig. 1.** Wildcard syntax extension of [13, Fig. 1, page 12] and [13, Fig. 5, page 17]

*Outline* In Sect. 2, we describe our additional syntax, both informally and formally. Formal rules for handling wildcard syntax are listed in Sect. 3. We extend OUTSIDEIN(X) typing rules to support wildcards in Sect. 4. Local bindings with partial type signatures are described in Sect. 5. We prove the correspondence of our rules to the standard ones for the uninformative signature $\_ \Rightarrow \_$ and for signatures without wildcards in Sect. 6. We discuss our implementation in Sect. 7, related work in Sect. 8 and conclude in Sect. 9. Proofs of our results can be found in an extended version of this paper [17].

## 2 Wildcard Syntax

In the introduction we already gave an informal account of the wildcard syntax we support. We quickly reiterate and formalise the syntax of wildcards as an extension of the syntax in OUTSIDEIN(X) [13]. Figure 1 contains the formal definitions with additions and changes highlighted in grey.

First of all, *type wildcards* can take the place of monotypes, e.g. $f :: \_ \to \_$. For type inference, they are translated to unification variables (see Sect. 3.2). By convention, we write unification variables that arise from wildcards as $\omega_1, \omega_2, \cdots$.

A wildcard *in* a constraint is called a *constraint wildcard*, e.g. $Eq \_ \Rightarrow a$. A wildcard occurring *as* a constraint is an *extra-constraints wildcard*, e.g. $\_ \Rightarrow a$. When it is present, any number of constraints may be added to the type during inference. Because one extra-constraints wildcard can be instantiated to any number of constraints, more than one such wildcard would be pointless. For clarity, we allow only one and require that it comes last in the list of constraints.

Additionally, we support *named wildcards*, e.g. $\_a \to \_a$. All instances of a named wildcard within a partial type signature must unify with the same type. Named wildcards are particularly useful to express constraints on wildcard types, e.g. $Eq \_a \Rightarrow \_a$ or $(\_a \sim b) \Rightarrow \_a \to [b]$. Although syntactically similar, named wildcards should not be confused with type variables: they can unify with concrete types. Only when not unified with concrete types, they are generalised over and behave like type variables.

In Fig. 1 we provide variants of type schemes $(\sigma)$, constraints $(Q)$, and monotypes $(\tau)$ that *can* contain wildcards, respectively $\underline{\sigma}$, $\underline{Q}$, and $\underline{\tau}$. A distinction between *constraints with wildcards* $(\underline{Q}^w)$ and *constraints with [an] extra-constraints wildcard* $(\underline{Q})$ is made to enforce that the extra-constraints wildcard can occur at most once and must come last.

# 3 Wildcard Instantiation and Desugaring

Before we introduce the adapted typing rules, we formalise the relation between wildcards and types. To this end, we define two judgments: the *wildcard instantiation judgment* and the *wildcard desugaring judgment*. They are employed in Sect. 4 by the natural and algorithmic typing rules respectively and the latter should be understood as algorithmic variants of the former.

## 3.1 Wildcard Instantiation

The wildcard instantiation judgment $\underline{Q} ; \underline{\tau} \Rrightarrow Q ; \tau$ can be read as "The wildcards in constraints $\underline{Q}$ and monotype $\underline{\tau}$ can be instantiated to obtain constraints $Q$ and monotype $\tau$". Each wildcard in $\underline{Q}$ and $\underline{\tau}$ corresponds to a concrete type or a type variable in $Q$ and $\tau$. Remember that $\underline{Q}$ and $\underline{\tau}$ can contain wildcards, whereas $Q$ and $\tau$ cannot. This judgment will be used by the adapted typing rules to instantiate a partial type signature to a type signature without wildcards.

The rules of the judgment are shown in Fig. 2. The rule NAMEDWC requires monotypes $\overline{\upsilon}$ that are substituted by the named wildcards in $\underline{Q}$ and $\underline{\tau}$. We then delegate to two subjudgments that instantiate the unnamed wildcards in respectively $\underline{Q}^w$ and $\underline{\tau}$. The rule EXTRAWC states that an extra-constraints wildcard can be instantiated to an arbitrary conjunction of constraints $Q_{res}$, which can consist of zero or more constraints. Remember that $\underline{Q}$ can contain an extra-constraints wildcard and $\underline{Q}^w$ cannot.

$$\boxed{Q ; \underline{\tau} \Rrightarrow Q ; \tau}$$

$$\frac{\underline{a} = nwc(\underline{\tau}) \cup nwc(\underline{Q^w}) \qquad [\underline{a} \mapsto \overline{v}]\underline{Q^w} \Rrightarrow^c Q \qquad [\underline{a} \mapsto \overline{v}]\underline{\tau} \Rrightarrow^t \tau}{\underline{Q^w} ; \underline{\tau} \Rrightarrow Q ; \tau} \; \textsc{NamedWc}$$

$$\frac{\underline{Q^w} ; \underline{\tau} \Rrightarrow Q ; \tau}{\underline{Q^w} \wedge \_ ; \underline{\tau} \Rrightarrow Q \wedge Q_{res} ; \tau} \; \textsc{ExtraWc}$$

$$\boxed{\underline{\tau} \Rrightarrow^t \tau}$$

$$\frac{}{\_ \Rrightarrow^t \tau} \; \textsc{TyWc} \qquad \frac{}{\tau \Rrightarrow^t \tau} \; \textsc{TyNoWc} \qquad \frac{\forall i . \underline{\tau_i} \Rrightarrow^t \tau_i}{T \, \underline{\overline{\tau_i}} \Rrightarrow^t T \, \overline{\tau_i}} \; \textsc{TyApp}$$

$$\boxed{\underline{Q^w} \Rrightarrow^c Q}$$

$$\frac{}{Q \Rrightarrow^c Q} \; \textsc{ConNoWc} \qquad \frac{\underline{Q_1^w} \Rrightarrow^c Q_1 \qquad \underline{Q_2^w} \Rrightarrow^c Q_2}{\underline{Q_1^w} \wedge \underline{Q_2^w} \Rrightarrow^c Q_1 \wedge Q_2} \; \textsc{ConConj}$$

$$\frac{\forall i . \underline{\tau_i} \Rrightarrow^t \tau_i}{D \, \underline{\overline{\tau_i}} \Rrightarrow^c D \, \overline{\tau_i}} \; \textsc{ConTc} \qquad \frac{\underline{\tau_1} \Rrightarrow^t \tau_1 \qquad \underline{\tau_2} \Rrightarrow^t \tau_2}{\underline{\tau_1} \sim \underline{\tau_2} \Rrightarrow^c \tau_1 \sim \tau_2} \; \textsc{ConEq}$$

**Fig. 2.** Natural wildcard instantiation judgment rules

The first subjudgment $\underline{\tau} \Rrightarrow^t \tau$ instantiates wildcards in a monotype to concrete types or type variables. The rule TyWc states that a type wildcard can be instantiated to any monotype $\tau$. A monotype without wildcards is instantiated to itself (TyNoWc) and there is a congruence rule for type constructor applications (TyApp). Note that function types: ($\rightarrow$), tuples: (,), lists: [], ... are all treated as type constructor applications.

The second subjudgment $\underline{Q^w} \Rrightarrow^c Q$ instantiates wildcards in constraints to concrete types or type variables. Constraints without wildcards need no further wildcard instantiation (ConNoWc). A conjunction of constraints is handled recursively in ConConj. A type-class constraint can also contain wildcards (ConTc), which will be instantiated using the previously described subjudgment. Type wildcards in equality constraints are handled in ConEq.

### 3.2  Wildcard Desugaring

We also define an algorithmic variant of the wildcard instantiation judgment, the *wildcard desugaring judgment*. Instead of instantiating wildcards to concrete types or type variables as the wildcard instantiation judgment does, the wildcard desugaring judgment replaces them by fresh unification variables in order to participate in OutsideIn(X)'s type inference.

The wildcard desugaring judgment $Q ; \underline{\tau} \Rrightarrow_a Q ; \tau ; extra$ can be read as: replacing all the wildcards in $Q$ and $\underline{\tau}$ with fresh unification variables, gives us $Q$, $\tau$, and $extra$. This last boolean output parameter indicates whether the constraints contained an extra-constraints wildcard or not, e.g. the underscore in $\_ \Rightarrow a$. If and only if $extra = $ true, extra constraints can be generated.

$$\boxed{Q\,;\underline{\tau} \Rrightarrow_a Q\,;\tau\,;extra}$$

$$\dfrac{\overline{a} = nwc(\underline{\tau}) \cup nwc(\underline{Q}^w) \qquad \overline{\omega}\,\text{fresh}}{\dfrac{[\overline{a \mapsto \omega}]\underline{Q}^w \Rrightarrow_a^c Q \qquad [\overline{a \mapsto \omega}]\underline{\tau} \Rrightarrow_a^t \tau}{\underline{Q}^w\,;\underline{\tau} \Rrightarrow_a Q\,;\tau\,;\text{false}}}\ \text{ANamedWc} \qquad \dfrac{\underline{Q}^w\,;\underline{\tau} \Rrightarrow_a Q\,;\tau\,;\text{false}}{\underline{Q}^w \wedge {}_-\,;\underline{\tau} \Rrightarrow_a Q\,;\tau\,;\text{true}}\ \text{AExtraWc}$$

$$\boxed{\underline{\tau} \Rrightarrow_a^t \tau}$$

$$\dfrac{\omega\,\text{fresh}}{{}_- \Rrightarrow_a^t \omega}\ \text{ATyWc} \qquad \dfrac{}{\tau \Rrightarrow_a^t \tau}\ \text{ATyNoWc} \qquad \dfrac{\forall i\,.\,\underline{\tau}_i \Rrightarrow_a^t \tau_i}{T\,\underline{\tau}_i \Rrightarrow_a^t T\,\overline{\tau}_i}\ \text{ATyApp}$$

$$\boxed{\underline{Q}^w \Rrightarrow_a^c Q}$$

$$\dfrac{}{Q \Rrightarrow_a^c Q}\ \text{AConNoWc} \qquad \dfrac{\underline{Q}_1^w \Rrightarrow_a^c Q_1 \qquad \underline{Q}_2^w \Rrightarrow_a^c Q_2}{\underline{Q}_1^w \wedge \underline{Q}_2^w \Rrightarrow_a^c Q_1 \wedge Q_2}\ \text{AConConj}$$

$$\dfrac{\forall i\,.\,\underline{\tau}_i \Rrightarrow_a^t \tau_i}{D\,\underline{\tau}_i \Rrightarrow_a^c D\,\overline{\tau}_i}\ \text{AConTc} \qquad \dfrac{\underline{\tau}_1 \Rrightarrow_a^t \tau_1 \qquad \underline{\tau}_2 \Rrightarrow_a^t \tau_2}{\underline{\tau}_1 \sim \underline{\tau}_2 \Rrightarrow_a^c \tau_1 \sim \tau_2}\ \text{AConTc}$$

**Fig. 3.** Algorithmic wildcard desugaring judgment rules

The rules of this judgment are shown in Fig. 3. As they strongly resemble the corresponding natural rules, we shall only highlight the differences. If $\underline{Q}$ contains an extra-constraints wildcard, *extra* will be true (AExtraWc). Subsequently, or if it did not, the named wildcards in $\underline{Q}^w$ and $\underline{\tau}$ are replaced with fresh unification variables $\omega_1, \omega_2, \ldots$ (ANamedWc). Note that multiple occurrences of a named wildcard are replaced with the same unification variable. Unnamed wildcards in $\underline{\tau}$ and $\underline{Q}^w$ are desugared separately by two subjudgments $\underline{\tau} \Rrightarrow_a^t \tau$ and $\underline{Q}^w \Rrightarrow_a^c Q$ respectively. The only difference with the corresponding wildcard instantiation subjudgments is that in the rule ATyWc, a wildcard is replaced with a fresh unification variable instead of a monotype $\tau$.

## 4   Typing Rules

When checking a partial type signature, the wildcards are unified with concrete types if necessary, otherwise they are replaced with fresh universally quantified type variables, i.e. the type is generalised. If an extra-constraints wildcard is present, additional constraints may be generated and added to the annotated constraints. We formalise this by adapting the OUTSIDEIN(X) typing rules [13].

### 4.1   Natural Typing Rules

Figure 4 shows the three top-level natural typing rules in [13]: EMPTY, the base case, BIND, for definitions without a type signature, and BINDA, for definitions with a signature. It also shows the new rule BINDPA which replaces BINDA. Changes in BINDPA w.r.t. BINDA are greyed. The rules refer to the *constraint entailment* judgment $\mathcal{Q} \Vdash Q$, which should be read as: "the axioms $\mathcal{Q}$ imply $Q$".

$$\boxed{\mathcal{Q};\Gamma \vdash prog} \qquad \frac{ftv(\Gamma) = fuv(\mathcal{Q}) = \emptyset}{\mathcal{Q};\Gamma \vdash \epsilon}\ \textsc{Empty}$$

$$\frac{\begin{array}{c} Q_1;\Gamma \vdash e:\tau \qquad \overline{a} = ftv(Q) \cup fuv(\tau) \qquad \mathcal{Q} \wedge Q \Vdash Q_1 \\ \mathcal{Q};\Gamma,(f:\forall\overline{a}\,.\,Q \Rightarrow \tau) \vdash prog \end{array}}{\mathcal{Q};\Gamma \vdash f = e, prog}\ \textsc{Bind}$$

$$\frac{\begin{array}{c} Q_1;\Gamma \vdash e:\tau \qquad \overline{a} = ftv(Q) \cup fuv(\tau) \qquad \mathcal{Q} \wedge Q \Vdash Q_1 \\ \mathcal{Q};\Gamma,(f:\forall\overline{a}\,.\,Q \Rightarrow \tau) \vdash prog \end{array}}{\mathcal{Q};\Gamma \vdash f :: \forall\overline{a}\,.\,Q \Rightarrow \tau = e, prog}\ \textsc{BindA}$$

$$\frac{\begin{array}{c} \underline{Q};\underline{\tau} \Rrightarrow Q;\tau \qquad Q_1;\Gamma \vdash e:\tau \qquad \overline{a} \uplus \overline{b} = ftv(Q) \cup fuv(\tau) \\ \mathcal{Q} \wedge Q \Vdash Q_1 \qquad \mathcal{Q};\Gamma,(f:\forall\overline{a}\overline{b}\,.\,Q \Rightarrow \tau) \vdash prog \end{array}}{\mathcal{Q};\Gamma \vdash f :: \forall\overline{a}\,.\,\underline{Q} \Rightarrow \underline{\tau} = e, prog}\ \textsc{BindPA}$$

**Fig. 4.** Natural top-level typing rules, adapted from [13, Fig. 4, p. 15]

Compared to BindA, BindPA supports partial type signatures. It is extended with the premise $\underline{Q};\underline{\tau} \Rrightarrow Q;\tau$, i.e. $\underline{Q}$ and $\underline{\tau}$ are instantiated to $Q$ and $\tau$ (see Sect. 3.1). Additional type variables that were not present in the partial type signature but arose from the generalisation of the type, are captured in $\overline{b}$, and are also universally quantified over in the final type of the top-level definition.

### 4.2 Constraint Solver

Before discussing the new top-level algorithmic typing rules, which make use of OutsideIn(X)'s constraint solver, we shall briefly describe the constraint solver [13, Sect. 5.5]. The OutsideIn(X) type inference system is parameterised by a constraint domain X. For present-day Haskell, X would be instantiated to a constraint domain that contains type-class and equality constraints (and Vytiniotis et al. present a concrete solver for this X [13]), but the OutsideIn(X) typing rules and algorithms are designed to support alternative domains as well. In this text, we keep X abstract. We will only describe the form of the constraint solver, not the implementation, which is specific to X.

We have already seen the natural constraint entailment relation $\mathcal{Q} \Vdash Q$. On the algorithmic side, the constraint solver (Fig. 5) has the following signature.

$$\mathcal{Q};Q_{given};\overline{\alpha}_{tch} \overset{solv}{\mapsto} C_{wanted} \leadsto Q_{residual};\theta$$

The inputs in this signature are:

- $\mathcal{Q}$: the top-level axiom scheme. In a concrete setting, it will contain e.g. class instances or reduction rules of type functions, but we will leave it abstract.
- $Q_{given}$: the given constraints that arise from type annotations (or pattern matching),
- $\overline{\alpha}_{tch}$: the *touchable* unification variables that the solver is allowed to instantiate, and
- $C_{wanted}$: the constraints to be solved.

The outputs are:

- $Q_{residual}$: residual constraints that the solver has not been able to solve, and
- $\theta$: a substitution mapping unification variables to types, with $dom(\theta) \subseteq \overline{\alpha}_{tch}$.

Vytiniotis et al. keep the constraint solver abstract, but require certain properties of it. It is required to be *sound* and yield *guess-free solutions*, two formal properties (specified in terms of the natural constraint entailment relation $\Vdash$) that we do not go into further. We will however require the solver to support a somewhat larger form of inputs. In the next section, we explain this further.

### 4.3   Wildcards in Constraints

We have chosen to allow both named and unnamed wildcards in constraints. Nevertheless, it is important to point out a limitation of such wildcards in our system. The OUTSIDEIN(X) infrastructure will never apply unification to two constraints. Consider the following example:

$$h :: Eq \_ \Rightarrow a \to a \to Bool$$
$$h = (\equiv)$$

In this case, $h$'s implementation generates the wanted constraint $Eq\ a$, which one might expect to be unified with $Eq\ \_$, so that the wildcard is instantiated with type $a$, but this is not what happens. The OUTSIDEIN(X) constraint solver does not unify the given constraint $Eq\ \_$ with the wanted constraint $Eq\ a$. In general, it will never unify one constraint with another; the algorithm will only instantiate wildcards $\_a$ in constraints $C$ if

- $\_a$ is a named wildcard also mentioned in the non-constraint part of the signature and it is instantiated during unification with the inferred type.
- The instantiation follows semantically from the constraint, i.e. $C \supset \_a \sim ....$

In OUTSIDEIN(X), unifying the non-constraint part of a signature with the inferred type happens through the generation of equality constraints, so in this sense the first case is comprised in the second. As a result, for $h$ we get an error that the constraint $Eq\ a$ cannot be solved from given constraints $Eq\ \_$.

Nevertheless, this limitation does not mean that wildcards in constraints are useless. Consider the following example:

$$f :: Monad\ \_m \Rightarrow \_m\ Bool$$

For this signature, $\_m$ can either be unified with a concrete type constructor like *Maybe* for which there is a *Monad* instance or be generalised to a universally quantified monad $m$. Similarly, we can say something like:

$$g :: (\_a, \_) \sim F\ \_b \Rightarrow \_b \to \_a$$

This signature states that $g$ is a function whose domain type is mapped by type function F to a tuple whose first element is its range type.

Contrary to the behaviour of wildcards in the non-constraint part of a signature, some of the behaviour of wildcards in constraints we just discussed could be unexpected by programmers. Because of this, one might consider disallowing

$$\boxed{\mathcal{Q};\Gamma \Vdash prog}\qquad \dfrac{}{\mathcal{Q};\Gamma \Vdash \epsilon}\ \text{EMPTY}$$

$$\dfrac{\Gamma \Vdash e:\tau \rightsquigarrow C \quad \mathcal{Q};\epsilon;fuv(\tau)\cup fuv(C) \overset{solv}{\Vdash} C \rightsquigarrow \mathcal{Q};\theta \quad \bar{a}\ \text{fresh}}{\bar{\alpha}=fuv(\theta\tau)\cup fuv(\mathcal{Q}) \quad \mathcal{Q};\Gamma,(f:\forall \bar{a}.[\bar{\alpha}\mapsto \bar{a}](Q\Rightarrow \theta\tau)) \Vdash prog \\ \mathcal{Q};\Gamma \Vdash f=e,prog}\ \text{BIND}$$

$$\dfrac{\Gamma \Vdash e:\upsilon \rightsquigarrow C \quad \mathcal{Q};Q;fuv(\upsilon)\cup fuv(C) \overset{solv}{\Vdash} C\wedge \upsilon \sim \tau \rightsquigarrow \epsilon;\theta \\ \mathcal{Q};\Gamma,(f:\forall \bar{a}.Q\Rightarrow \tau)\Vdash prog}{\mathcal{Q};\Gamma \Vdash f::\forall \bar{a}.Q\Rightarrow \tau = e,prog}\ \text{BINDA}$$

$$\boxed{\mathcal{Q};Q_{given};\bar{\alpha}_{tch} \overset{solv}{\Vdash} C_{wanted} \rightsquigarrow Q_{residual};\theta}$$

**Fig. 5.** Top-level algorithmic rules, taken from [13, Fig. 12, page 39]

$$\dfrac{\Gamma \Vdash e:\upsilon \rightsquigarrow C \qquad\qquad \boxed{\mathcal{Q};\underline{\tau} \Rrightarrow_a \mathcal{Q};\tau\,;extra} \\ \mathcal{Q};Q;fuv(\upsilon)\cup fuv(C)\cup \boxed{fuv(\tau)\cup fuv(Q)} \overset{solv}{\Vdash} C\wedge \upsilon\sim\tau \rightsquigarrow \boxed{Q_{res}};\theta \\ extra \vee (Q_{res}=\epsilon) \qquad \bar{\beta}=fuv(\theta\tau)\cup fuv(\theta Q\wedge Q_{res}) \qquad \bar{b}\ \text{fresh} \\ \mathcal{Q};\Gamma,(f:\forall \bar{a}\bar{b}.\boxed{[\bar{\beta}\mapsto \bar{b}]}(\theta Q\wedge Q_{res}\Rightarrow \theta\tau)) \Vdash prog}{\mathcal{Q};\Gamma \Vdash f::\forall \bar{a}.\underline{Q}\Rightarrow \underline{\tau} = e,prog}\ \text{BINDPA}$$

**Fig. 6.** New top-level algorithmic rule, adapted from Fig. 5

both named and unnamed type wildcards in constraints. This is a viable and safe option, but we have currently chosen not to do so. Our impression is that the limitations of wildcards in constraints can be explained to the user, and our examples show that they can be useful despite the limitations.

Formally, the choice to allow wildcards in constraints implies that we have to drop an invariant of the constraint solver. For the constraint solver, Vytiniotis et al. mention two invariants that should hold: $\bar{\alpha}_{tch}\#fuv(Q_{given})$ and $dom(\theta)\#fuv(Q_{given})$, i.e. the free unification variables in $Q_{given}$ should not be unified. In order to support wildcards in constraints, it is required to remove this restriction. This also requires corresponding modifications in Definition 3.2 and subsequent proofs in Vytiniotis et al.'s paper [13, p. 20]. We suspect potential issues when the wildcards are under a GADT pattern match, but this remains to be further investigated in future work.

### 4.4 Algorithmic Typing Rules

In addition to the top-level natural typing rules, we also adapt the top-level algorithmic typing rules. The original top-level algorithmic typing rules are shown in Fig. 5. As wildcards can only occur in a type signature, only the rule BINDA that handles declarations with a type annotation has to be adapted. The adapted rule is presented in Fig. 6, with changes w.r.t. BINDA highlighted in grey.

The BINDPA rule works as follows. First, the type $\upsilon$ of $e$ is inferred using the constraint generation judgment from [13] while generating the constraints $C$. The wildcards in $Q$ and $\underline{\tau}$ are replaced with fresh unification variables with the wildcard desugaring judgment we defined earlier. The *extra* output parameter indicates whether we are allowed to infer extra constraints.

On the second line, the invocation of the constraint solver has been slightly modified. The free unification variables in $\tau$ and $Q$, introduced during the wildcard desugaring, are added to the set of touchable unification variables that the constraint solver is allowed to instantiate. We also capture the residual constraints, which were not allowed in the previous version of the rule, in $Q_{res}$. Now they are allowed, but only if *extra* is true.

In the next step, we collect the remaining free unification variables in $\theta\tau$ and $\theta Q \wedge Q_{res}$. These unification variables were not instantiated to concrete types while solving the constraints and so we generalise over them. They are replaced with fresh, universally quantified type variables, $\bar{b}$. The residual constraints, i.e. the extra constraints that have not been solved by the constraint solver, are added to the annotated constraints.

**Theorem 1 (Algorithm soundness).** *If $Q;\Gamma \Vdash prog$ then $Q;\Gamma \vdash prog$ in a closed top-level $\Gamma$.*

## 5   Typing of Local Definitions

Advanced type system features like GADTs have a profound impact on a type system. Crucially, the clean and simple principal typing property that the HM system satisfies is no longer valid [13]. This makes type inference a harder problem and Vytiniotis et al. present one possible way out. They advocate the policy that the types of local (unannotated) definitions should not be generalised, with the slogan "Let should not be generalised".

For partial type signatures of local definitions, we align with the policy to not generalise local definitions. Next, we present the adapted typing rules for local definitions, but we omit natural typing rules as the required changes are minimal. The existing algorithmic rules and our adapted rule are shown in Fig. 7.

The rule LETA applies to definitions with an annotated monomorphic type, GLETA for polymorphic type signatures and LET for definitions without a signature. The rule LET is remarkably simple, as it applies the NOGEN policy of not generalising the inferred type at all. Our adapted typing rule GLETPA extends this policy to partial type signatures.

The GLETPA rule applies to local bindings with a partial type signature, either polymorphic or monomorphic. It first desugars the partial type signature. The *extra* parameter must be false, i.e. we forbid an extra-constraints wildcard, since the NOGEN policy forbids additional constraints. We verify that the type signature was indeed partial by requiring free unification variables in the desugared type and constraints. Next, the set of unification variables allowed to unify, i.e. the *touchables*, is extended with those resulting from the wildcard desugaring. Solving the implication constraint should unify them, fixing the definition's actual type. The local binding, annotated with the desugared type, is added

$$\frac{\Gamma \Vdash e_1 : \tau_1 \rightsquigarrow C_1 \qquad \Gamma, (x : \tau_1) \Vdash e_2 : \tau_2 \rightsquigarrow C_2}{\Gamma \Vdash \mathbf{let}\ x = e_1\ \mathbf{in}\ e_2 : \tau_2 \rightsquigarrow C_1 \wedge C_2}\ \text{LET}$$

$$\frac{\Gamma \Vdash e_1 : \tau \rightsquigarrow C_1 \qquad \Gamma, (x : \tau_1) \Vdash e_2 : \tau_2 \rightsquigarrow C_2}{\Gamma \Vdash \mathbf{let}\ x :: \tau_1 = e_1\ \mathbf{in}\ e_2 : \tau_2 \rightsquigarrow C_1 \wedge C_2 \wedge \tau \sim \tau_1}\ \text{LETA}$$

$$\frac{\begin{array}{c} \sigma_1 = \forall \overline{a}.\, Q_1 \Rightarrow \tau_1 \qquad Q_1 \neq \epsilon\ \text{or}\ \overline{a} \neq \epsilon \qquad \Gamma \Vdash e_1 : \tau \rightsquigarrow C \\ \overline{\beta} = (fuv(\tau) \cup fuv(C)) - fuv(\Gamma) \qquad C_1 = \exists \overline{\beta}.\,(Q_1 \supset C \wedge \tau \sim \tau_1) \\ \Gamma, (x : \sigma_1) \Vdash e_2 : \tau_2 \rightsquigarrow C_2 \end{array}}{\Gamma \Vdash \mathbf{let}\ x :: \sigma_1 = e_1\ \mathbf{in}\ e_2 : \tau_2 \rightsquigarrow C_1 \wedge C_2}\ \text{GLETA}$$

$$\boxed{\Gamma \Vdash e : \tau \rightsquigarrow C}$$

$$\frac{\begin{array}{c} \underline{\sigma_1} = \forall \overline{a}.\, \underline{Q_1} \Rightarrow \underline{\tau_1} \qquad \Gamma \Vdash e_1 : \tau \rightsquigarrow C \qquad \underline{Q_1 ; \tau_1 \Rightarrow_a Q_1 ; \tau_1 ; \text{false}} \\ Q_1 \neq \epsilon\ \text{or}\ \overline{a} \neq \epsilon\ \underline{\text{or}\ fuv(\tau_1) \cup fuv(Q_1) \neq \emptyset} \\ \overline{\beta} = ((fuv(\tau) \cup fuv(C)) - fuv(\Gamma)) \underline{\cup fuv(\tau_1) \cup fuv(Q_1)} \\ C_1 = \exists \overline{\beta}.\,(Q_1 \supset C \wedge \tau \sim \tau_1) \qquad \Gamma, (x : \forall \overline{a}.\, Q_1 \Rightarrow \tau_1) \Vdash e_2 : \tau_2 \rightsquigarrow C_2 \end{array}}{\Gamma \Vdash \mathbf{let}\ x :: \underline{\sigma_1} = e_1\ \mathbf{in}\ e_2 : \tau_2 \rightsquigarrow C_1 \wedge C_2}\ \text{GLETPA}$$

**Fig. 7.** Constraint generation for local `let`-bound definitions, taken and adapted from [13, Fig. 13, page 40]

to the environment to type check the body $e_2$. Following the NoGen policy, no generalisation is performed. The example *foo* shows the effect of not generalising:

$$foo = \mathbf{let}\ g :: \_ \to \_$$
$$g\ x = x$$
$$h :: Eq\ \_a \Rightarrow \_a \to \_a \to Bool$$
$$h\ x\ y = x \equiv y$$
$$\mathbf{in}\ (g\ True, g\ \text{'v'}, h\ True\ True, h\ \text{'a'}\ \text{'b'})$$

Instead of being quantified over, the free unification variables in the type of $g$ unify with the *Bool* type at the first call of $g$. Thus, $g$'s type is *Bool* $\to$ *Bool*. As $g$ is also called with a *Char* argument, the program will be rejected. Similarly, the unification variable for the named wildcard $\_a$ in $h$'s type is not generalised. Instead, it unifies with the *Bool* type, producing the type $Eq\ Bool \Rightarrow Bool \to Bool \to Bool$ for $h$.

## 6   Alignment with Existing Rules

Partial type signatures are a generalisation of the binary choice between a full signature or none at all. Using wildcards, partial type signatures can mix annotated and inferred types. To demonstrate that partial type signatures truly are a generalisation of the existing inference, we prove two properties.

First, partial type signatures are a conservative extension: the adapted typing rules are equivalent to the original rules for signatures without wildcards.

Second, (top-level) definitions without a type signature are equivalent to definitions with the partial type signature $\_ \Rightarrow \_$. More formally: the BindPA rule

(Fig. 6) can be used to type check a definition $f = e$ without a type signature by treating it as if it had the partial type signature $f :: \_ \Rightarrow \_ = e$. The ALTBIND rule provides the definitions without type signature with the equivalent partial type signature.

$$\frac{\mathcal{Q}\,;\Gamma \Vdash f :: \_ \Rightarrow \_ = e,\, prog}{\mathcal{Q}\,;\Gamma \Vdash f = e,\, prog}\ \text{ALTBIND}$$

**Theorem 2.** *Given a program prog in which every definition f has either a type signature without wildcards, i.e. $f :: \forall \overline{a} \,.\, \mathcal{Q} \Rightarrow \tau = e$, or no type signature at all, i.e. $f = e$. If $\mathcal{Q}\,;\Gamma \Vdash prog$, using* BIND, BINDA, *and* EMPTY *(Fig. 5), then $\mathcal{Q}\,;\Gamma \Vdash prog$, using* ALTBIND, BINDPA *(Fig. 6), and* EMPTY *(Fig. 5).*

These properties show that our proposal aligns well with the existing behaviour of type inference. This is not just theoretically important, but also shows that our proposal is natural and unsurprising for existing users.

## 7   Implementation and Extensions

We have developed an implementation of our proposal in the de facto standard Haskell compiler GHC. GHC's inferencer is based on the OUTSIDEIN(X) type inference system. As a result, our proposal fits relatively nicely into the compiler's inference infrastructure. Nevertheless, GHC's actual inferencer is (unavoidably) more complex than Vytiniotis et al.'s elegant theory, notably when it comes to the inference and generalisation of mutually recursive blocks and higher-rank types. Hence, our prototype currently implements only part of our theoretical development. More specifically, it correctly unifies wildcards and named wildcards with closed types, but does not yet support unifying with open types, generalisation and extra-constraints wildcards. The prototype code is available for download at `http://github.com/mrBliss/ghc`. We still intend to check and ensure compatibility with the ScopedTypeVariables [8] and ConstraintKinds [1,18] extensions, but we expect no major problems there.

## 8   Related Work

Vytiniotis et al. provide a comprehensive overview of work on constraint-based type systems and type inference for advanced type system features that we do not repeat here [13], except to discuss aspects related to *partial* type signatures. Vytiniotis et al. claim that their presentation is the first one that deals with local assumptions introduced by type signatures and data constructors, and where those local assumptions may include type equalities.

The idea of partial type signatures is not new. The topic regularly comes up on the Haskell community mailing lists. In two 2006 tickets on the Haskell Prime wiki (where the Haskell community proposes and tracks future language changes), Malcolm Wallace proposes a form of partial type signatures [14,15].

His proposal seems similar to ours, but it does not contain a lot of detail. A GHC feature request has also been logged to request a form of constraint wildcards [12].

The *Agda* programming language [7] has a dependent type system, which allows terms in types and vice versa. The type system allows more powerful type-level computations, so that type inferencing becomes harder. On the other hand, the inferencer can sometimes infer terms as well. In Agda, any value or type can be replaced by an underscore, in which case Agda will try to infer it. Agda's inference does not perform generalisation: if the type checker cannot infer the value of such a meta-variable, it reports an error.

Our work was inspired by the partial signatures in Dijkstra and Swierstra's *Explicit Haskell* [4][3, Chapt. 10]. They also use wildcards and allow predicate wildcards very similar to our extra-constraints wildcards. However, where we follow Vytiniotis et al. in using a rather standard form of HM style type generalisation, Dijkstra and Swierstra use *quantifier location inference* rules that differ significantly, both for normal and partial type signatures. They argue that depending on the structure of the type in which a type variable appears, it should either be existentially or universally quantified to align with user expectations. For example, the type $a \to a$ is interpreted as $\forall a. a \to a$ but $(a \to a) \to Int$ is interpreted as $(\forall a. a \to a) \to Int$, unlike in Haskell. In a product type, the variables are quantified existentially instead of universally, e.g. $(a, a)$ is interpreted as $\exists a.(a, a)$ and $(a, a) \to Int$ as $(\exists a.(a, a)) \to Int$. Dijkstra and Swierstra formalise Explicit Haskell, but do not prove results like our Theorem 1 and Theorem 2.

For the *Chameleon* programming language, Sulzmann and Wazny describe a form of *existential type signatures*, supported in addition to standard *universal* signatures [11,16]. Type variables in a universal signature $f :: a \to a$ are interpreted in the same way as Haskell, i.e. as $f :: \forall a. a \to a$. However, in an existential type signature $f ::: a \to a$ (note: three colons) the variables are interpreted more or less like our named wildcards, so that it becomes equivalent to our $f :: \_a \to \_a$. A mixture of existential and universal annotations is not supported, but can be encoded by nesting existential in universal annotations.

Both $F_{ML}$ [10] and *HMF* [6] combine the expressiveness of System F with the convenience of Hindley-Milner type inference, while remaining a conservative extension of ML and HM respectively. Both solutions employ *partial type annotations* to avoid the *guessing* of polymorphic types during type inference. These partial type annotations are similar to the ones in the introduction, which use the ScopedTypeVariables extension. Furthermore, they support partial type annotations of the following form: $e :: \exists \overline{\alpha} . \sigma$, where the free variables $\overline{\alpha}$ in $\sigma$ are locally bound. This should be read as "for some types $\overline{\alpha}$, the expression $e$ has type $\sigma$" and the $\overline{\alpha}$ correspond to our named wildcards. The authors formalised these partial type annotations, including generalisation, for a HM-based type system, but without considering GADTs or local type assumptions.

# 9   Conclusion

Partial type signatures are a useful feature that has often been requested and proposed for Haskell. They bridge the gap between complete type annotations and none at all. Our proposal pins down the precise behaviour and we formally prove its well-behavedness. The result fits naturally in both the existing formal description of GHC's type inferencer (OUTSIDEIN(X)) and the implementation. The idea of partial type signatures is not novel, but we believe our proposal is the first that supports all the features necessary for present-day GHC Haskell, esp. local constraint assumptions.

**Acknowledgments.** This research is partially funded by the Research Foundation - Flanders (FWO), and by the Research Fund KU Leuven. Dominique Devriese holds a Ph.D. fellowship of the Research Foundation - Flanders (FWO).

# References

1. Bolingbroke, M.: Constraint kinds for GHC (2011),
   `http://blog.omega-prime.co.uk/?p=127`
2. Claessen, K., Axelsson, E.: The patch-combinators package. Hackage (2012),
   `http://hackage.haskell.org/package/patch-combinators`
3. Dijkstra, A.: Stepping Through Haskell. Ph.D. thesis, Universiteit Utrecht (2005)
4. Dijkstra, A., Swierstra, D.S.: Making implicit parameters explicit. Tech. Rep. UU-CS-2005-032, Universiteit Utrecht (2005)
5. Kiselyov, O.: Partial signatures (August 2004), `http://okmij.org/ftp/Haskell/types.html#partial-sigs` (visited on December 31, 2012)
6. Leijen, D.: HMF: simple type inference for first-class polymorphism. In: ICFP, pp. 283–294. ACM (2008)
7. Norell, U.: Towards a practical programming language based on dependent type theory. Ph.D. thesis, Chalmers University and Göteborg University (2007)
8. Peyton Jones, S., Shields, M.: Lexically-scoped type variables (2004)
9. Peyton Jones, S., Vytiniotis, D., Weirich, S., Shields, M.: Practical type inference for arbitrary-rank types. J. Funct. Program. 17(1), 1–82 (2007)
10. Rémy, D.: Simple, partial type-inference for System F based on type-containment. In: ICFP, pp. 130–143. ACM (2005)
11. Sulzmann, M., Wazny, J.: Lexically scoped type annotations (2005) (manuscript),
    `http://www.cs.mu.oz.au/~sulzmann/manuscript/lexical-annot.ps`
12. Various authors: Infer type context in a type signature. GHC Ticket (2011),
    `http://hackage.haskell.org/trac/ghc/ticket/5248`
13. Vytiniotis, D., Peyton Jones, S., Schrijvers, T., Sulzmann, M.: OutsideIn(X): Modular type inference with local assumptions. J. Funct. Program. 21(4-5), 333–412 (2011)
14. Wallace, M.: Partial type signatures/annotations. Haskell Prime Wiki (February 2006), `http://ghc.haskell.org/trac/haskell-prime/wiki/PartialTypeAnnotations`
15. Wallace, M., et al.: Partial type signatures. Haskell Prime Wiki (January 2006),
    `http://ghc.haskell.org/trac/haskell-prime/wiki/PartialTypeSigs`
16. Wazny, J.: Type inference and type error diagnosis for Hindley/Milner with extensions. Ph.D. thesis, University of Melbourne (2006)
17. Winant, T., Devriese, D., Piessens, F., Schrijvers, T.: Partial type signatures for Haskell: Extended version with proofs of the theorems. Tech. Rep. 649, Department of Computer Science, KU Leuven (November 2013),
    `http://www.cs.kuleuven.be/publicaties/rapporten/cw/CW649.abs.html`
18. Yorgey, B.A., Weirich, S., Cretin, J., Peyton Jones, S., Vytiniotis, D., Magalhães, J.P.: Giving haskell a promotion. In: TLDI, pp. 53–66 (2012)

# The F# Computation Expression Zoo

Tomas Petricek[1] and Don Syme[2]

[1] University of Cambridge, UK
[2] Microsoft Research Cambridge, UK
tp322@cam.ac.uk, dsyme@microsoft.com

**Abstract.** Program logic can often be structured using abstract computation types such as monoids, monad transformers or applicative functors. Functional programmers use those abstractions directly while main-stream languages often integrate concrete instances as language features – e.g. generators in Python or asynchronous computations in C# 5.0. The question is, is there a sweet spot between convenient, hard-wired language features, and an inconvenient but flexible libraries?

F# *computation expressions* answer this question in the affirmative. Unlike the "do" notation in Haskell, computation expressions are not tied to a single kind of abstraction. They support a wide range of abstractions, depending on what operations are available. F# also provides greater syntactic flexibility leading to a more intuitive syntax, without resorting to full macro-based meta-programming.

We present computation expressions in a principled way, developing a type system that captures the semantics of the calculus. We demonstrate how computation expressions structure well-known abstractions including monoidal list comprehensions, monadic parsers, applicative formlets and asynchronous sequences based on monad transformers.

## 1 Introduction

Computations with non-standard aspects like non-determinism, effects, asynchronicity or their combinations can be captured using a variety of abstract computation types. In Haskell, we write such computations using a mix of combinators and syntactic extensions like monad comprehensions [5] and "do" notation. Languages such as Python and C# emphasize the syntax and provide single-purpose support e.g. for asynchrony [1] and list generators.

Using such abstractions can be made simpler and more intuitive if we employ a general syntactic machinery. F# computation expressions provide *uniform* syntax that supports monoids, monads [22], monad transformers [10] and applicative functors [13]. They reuse familiar syntax including loops and exception handling – the laws of underlying abstractions guarantee that these constructs preserve intuition about code. At the same time, the mechanism is *adaptable* and enables appropriate syntax depending on the abstraction.

Most languages, including Haskell, Scala, C#, JavaScript and Python have multiple syntactic extensions that improve computational expressivity: queries, iterators, comprehensions, asynchronous computations are just a few. However,

M. Flatt and H.-F. Guo (Eds.): PADL 2014, LNCS 8324, pp. 33–48, 2014.

"syntactic budget" for such extensions is limited. Haskell already uses three notations for comprehensions, monads and arrows [15]. C# and Scala have multiple notations for queries, comprehensions, asynchronicity and iterators. The more we get with one mechanism, the better. As we show, computation expressions give a lot for relatively low cost – notably, without resorting to full-blown macros.

Some of the technical aspects of the feature have been described before[1] [20], but this paper is novel in that it uses more principled approach by developing a new type system and relating the mechanism to well-known abstractions.

**Practical Examples.** We demonstrate the breadth of computations that can be structured using F# computation expressions. The applications include asynchronous workflows and sequences (§2.1, §2.3), list comprehensions and monadic parsers (§2.2) and formlets for web programming (§2.4).

**Abstract Computations.** We show that the above examples fit well-known types of abstract computations, including additive monads and monad transformers, and we show that important syntactic equalities hold as a result (§4).

**Syntax and Typing.** We give typing rules that capture idiomatic uses of computation expressions (§3.2), extend the translation to support applicative functors (§2.4) and discuss the treatment of effects (§3.4) needed in impure languages.

We believe that software artifacts in programming language research matter [9], so all code can be run at: `http://tryjoinads.org/computations`. The syntax for applicative functors is a reserch extension; other examples require F# 2.0.

## 2   Computation Expressions by Example

Computation expressions are blocks of code that represent computations with a non-standard aspect such as laziness, asynchronicity, state or other. The code inside the block is re-interpreted using a *computation builder*, which is a record of operations that define the semantics, but also syntax available in the block.

Computation expressions mirror the standard F# syntax (let binding, loops, exception handling), but support additonal computational constructs. For example let! represents the computational (monadic) alternative of let binding.

We first introduce the syntax and mapping to the underlying operations informally, but both are made precise later (§3). Readers unfamiliar with F# may find additional explanation in previous publications [20]. To show the breadth of applications, we look at five examples arising from different abstractions.

### 2.1   Monadic Asynchronous Workflows

Asynchronous workflows [19] allow writing non-blocking I/O using a mechanism based on the *continuation monad* (with error handling etc.) The following example compares F# code with an equivalent in C# using a single-purpose feature:

---

[1] F# 3.0 extends the mechanism further to accomodate extensible query syntax. To keep this paper focused, we leave analysis of these extensions to future work.

```
let getLength url = async {              async Task⟨string⟩ GetLength(string url) {
  let! html = fetchAsync url                var html = await FetchAsync(url);
  do! Async.Sleep 1000                      await Task.Delay(1000);
  return html.Length                        return html.Length;
}                                        }
```

Both functions return a computation that expects a *continuation* and then downloads a given URL, waits one second and passes content length to the continuation. The C# version uses the built-in await keyword to represent non-blocking waiting. In F#, the computation is enclosed in the async {...} block, where async is an identifier that refers to a library-defined computation builder.

The computation builder async is an F# object with instance members such as *async.Bind*. The members determine which of the pre-defined keywords are allowed – e.g. *Bind* member enables let! which represents (monadic) binding. *Bind* also enables the do! *e* expression, which is a shortcut for let! () = *e*. Finally, the return keyword is mapped to the *Return* operation:

$$\text{async.Bind}(fetchAsync(url), \textbf{fun } html \rightarrow$$
$$\text{async.Bind}(\text{Async.Sleep } 1000, \textbf{fun } () \rightarrow$$
$$\text{async.Return}(html.\text{Length})))$$

The *Bind* and *Return* operations form a monad. As usual, *Return* has a type $\alpha \rightarrow A\alpha$ and the required type of *Bind* is $A\alpha \times (\alpha \rightarrow A\beta) \rightarrow A\beta$ (we write $\alpha, \beta$ for universally qualified type variables and $\tau$ as for concrete types)[2].

**Sequencing and Effects.** Effectful expressions in F# return a value () which is the only value of type unit. Assuming $e_1$ has a type unit, we can sequence expression using $e_1; e_2$. We can also write effectful if condition without the else clause (which implicitly returns the unit value () in the false case). Both have an equivalent computation expression syntax:

$$\text{async } \{ \textbf{ if } delay \textbf{ then do! } \text{Async.Sleep}(1000)$$
$$\text{printfn "Starting..."}$$
$$\textbf{return! } \text{asyncFetch}(url) \}$$

If *delay* is true, the workflow waits one second before downloading the page and returning it. The translation uses additional operations – *Zero* represents monadic unit value, *Combine* corresponds to the ";" operator and *Delay* embeds an effectful expression in a (delayed) computation. For monads, these can be defined in terms of *Bind* and *Return*, but this is not the case for all computations (e.g. monoidal computations discussed in §2.2 require different definitions).

We also use the return! keyword, which returns the result of a computation and requires an operation *ReturnFrom* of type $A\alpha \rightarrow A\alpha$. This is typically implemented as an identity function – its main purpose is to enable the return! keyword in the syntax, as this may not be alway desirable.

---

[2] For the purpose of this paper, we write type application using a light notation $T\tau$.

async.Combine
( ( **if** *delay* **then** async.Bind(Async.Sleep(1000), **fun** () → async.Zero())
    **else** async.Zero() ), async.Delay(**fun**() →
      printfn "Starting..."
      async.ReturnFrom(asyncFetch(*url*)))))

*Zero* has a type unit → $A$ unit and is inserted when a computation does not return a value, here in both branches of if. A computation returning unit can be composed with another using *Combine* which has a type $A$ unit × $A\alpha$ → $A\alpha$ and corresponds to ";". It runs the left-hand side before returning the result of the right-hand side. Finally, *Delay*, of type (unit → $A\tau$) → $A\tau$, is used to wrap any effectful computations (like printing) in the monad to avoid performing the effects before the first part of sequential computation is run.

## 2.2   Additive Parsers and List Comprehensions

Parsers or list comprehensions differ in that they may return multiple values. Such computations can be structured using additive monads (MonadPlus in Haskell). These abstractions can be used with F# computation expressions too. Interestingly, they require different typing of *Zero* and *Combine*.

**Monadic Parsers.** For parsers, we use the same notation as previously. The difference is that we can now use return and return! repeatedly. The following parsers recognize one or more and zero or more repetitions of a given predicate:

**let rec** zeroOrMore $p$ = parse {
  **return!** oneOrMore $p$
  **return** [] }

**and** oneOrMore $p$ = parse {
  **let!** $x = p$
  **let!** $xs$ = zeroOrMore $p$
  **return** $x :: xs$ }

The oneOrMore function uses just the monadic interface and so its translation uses *Bind* and *Return*. The zeroOrMore function is more interesting – it combines a parser that returns one or more occurrences with a parser that always succeeds and returns an empty list. This is achieved using the *Combine* operation:

**let rec** zeroOrMore $p$ = parse.Delay(**fun** () →
    parse.Combine( parse.ReturnFrom(oneOrMore $p$),
        parse.Delay(**fun**() → parse.Return( [] ) )))

Here, *Combine* represents the monoidal operation on parsers (either left-biassed or non-deterministic choice) and has the type $P\alpha \times P\alpha \to P\alpha$. Accordingly, the *Zero* operations is the unit of the monoid. It has a type unit → $P\alpha$, representing a parser that returns no $\alpha$ values (rather than returning a single unit value).

For effectful sequencing of monads, it only makes sense to use unit-returning computations in the left-hand side of *Combine* and as the result of *Zero*. However, if we have a monoidal computation, we can define *Combine* that combines multiple produced values. This shows that the computation expression mechanism needs certain flexibility – the translation is the same, but the typing differs.

**List Comprehensions.** Although list comprehensions implement the same abstract type as parsers, it is desirable to use different syntax if we want to make the syntactic sugar comparable to built-in features in other languages. The following shows an F# list comprehension and a Python generator side-by-side:

$$\begin{array}{ll} \text{seq } \{ \text{ for } n \text{ in } \mathit{list} \text{ do} & \text{for } n \text{ in } \mathit{list} : \\ \quad \text{yield } n & \quad \text{yield } n \\ \quad \text{yield } n * 10 \ \} & \quad \text{yield } n * 10 \end{array}$$

The computations iterate over a source list and produce two results for each input. Monad comprehensions [5] allow us to write [ $n * 10$ | $n \leftarrow \mathit{list}$ ] to multiply all elements by 10, but they are not expressive enough to capture the duplication. Doing that requires rewriting the code using combinators.

The F# syntax works similarly to what we have seen for monads. The for and yield constructs are translated to *For* and *Yield* operations which have the same types as emphBind and *Return*, but provide backing for a different syntax (each keyword is mapped to a specific named operation of the builder e.g. for uses *seq.For*, so the members defined by *seq* determine which keywords are enabled):

seq.For($\mathit{list}$, **fun** () →
    seq.Combine(seq.Yield($n$), seq.Delay(**fun** () → seq.Yield($n * 10$))) )

*Combine* concatenates multiple results and has the standard monoidal type $[\alpha] \times [\alpha] \rightarrow [\alpha]$. *For* has the type of monadic bind $[\alpha] \rightarrow (\alpha \rightarrow [\beta]) \rightarrow [\beta]$ and *Yield* has a type of monadic unit $\alpha \rightarrow [\alpha]$. We could have provided the *Bind* and *Return* operations in the seq builder instead, but this leads to a less intuitive syntax that requires users to write let! for iteration and return for yielding.

As the Python comparison shows, the flexibility of computation expressions means that they are often close to a built-in syntax. The author of a concrete computation (parse, seq, async, . . . ) chooses the appropriate syntax. For additive monads, the choice can be made based on the laws that hold §4.2.

## 2.3   Layered Asynchronous Sequences

It is often useful to combine non-standard aspects of multiple computations. This is captured by monad transformers [10]. Although F# does not support higher-kinded types, monad transformers still provide a useful conceptual framework.

For example, *asynchronous sequences* [16] combine non-blocking asynchronous execution with the ability to return multiple results – a file download can then produce data in 1kB buffers as they become available. Using Async $\tau$ as the base type, we can follow the list monad transformer [7] and define the type as:

$$\begin{array}{lll} \textbf{type AsyncSeqInner } \tau & = & \text{AsyncNil} \mid \text{AsyncCons of } \tau \times \text{Async } \tau \\ \textbf{type AsyncSeq } \tau & = & \text{Async (AsyncSeqInner } \tau) \end{array}$$

When given a continuation, an asynchronous sequence calls it with either the end of the sequence AsyncNil or with AsyncCons that carries a value together with the tail of the asynchronous sequence. The flexibility of computation expression makes it possible to provide an elegant syntax for writing such computations:

```
let rec urlPerSecond n = asyncSeq {        let pagePerSecond urls = asyncSeq {
  do! Async.Sleep 1000                       for url in urlPerSecond 0 do
  yield getUrl i                               let! html = asyncFetch url
  yield! iterate (i + 1) }                     yield url, html }
```

The urlPerSecond function creates an asynchronous sequence that produces one URL per second. It uses bind (do!) of the asynchronous workflow monad to wait one second and then composition of asynchronous sequences, together with yield to produce the next URL. The pagePerSecond function uses for to iterate over (bind on) an asynchronous sequence and then let! to wait for (bind on) an asynchronous workflow. The for loop is asynchronous and lazy – it's body is run each time the caller asks for the next result.

Asynchronous sequences form a monad and so we could use the standard notation for monads with just let! and return. We would then need explicit lifting function that turns an asynchronous workflow into an asynchronous sequence that returns a single value. However, F# computation expressions allow us to do better. We can define both For and Bind with the following types:

$$\text{asyncSeq.For} \;:\; \text{AsyncSeq}\,\alpha \to (\alpha \to \text{AsyncSeq}\,\beta) \to \text{AsyncSeq}\,\beta$$
$$\text{asyncSeq.Bind} \;:\; \text{Async}\,\alpha \quad\;\; \to (\alpha \to \text{AsyncSeq}\,\beta) \to \text{AsyncSeq}\,\beta$$

We omit the translation of the above example – it is a straightforward variation on what we have seen so far. A more important point is that we use the fact that operations of the computation builder are not restricted to a specific type (the above *Bind* is not an ordinary binding making let! behave differently).

As previously, the choice of the syntax is left to the author of the computation. Asynchronous sequences are an additive monad and so we use for/yield. Underlying asynchronous workflows are just monads, so it makes sense to add let! that automatically lifts a workflow to an asynchronous sequence.

An important aspect of the fact that asynchronous sequences can be described using a monad transformer is that certain laws hold. We discuss how these map to the computation expression syntax later (§4.3).

### 2.4  Applicative Formlets

*Applicative functors* [13,11] are weaker (and thus more common) abstraction than monads. The difference between applicative and monadic computations is that a monadic computation can perform different effects depending on values obtained earlier during the computation. Conversely, the effects of an applicative computation are fully determined by its structure.

In other words, it is not possible to choose which computation to run (using let! or do!) based on values obtained in previous let! bindings. The following example demonstrates this using a web form abstraction called formlets [2]:

```
formlet { let! name = Formlet.textBox
          and gender = Formlet.dropDown ["Male"; "Female"]
          return name + " " + gender }
```

The computation describes two aspects – the rendering and the processing of entered values. The rendering phase uses the fixed structure to produce HTML with text-box and drop-down elements. In the processing phase, the values of *name* and *gender* are available and are used to calculate the result of the form.

The structure of the form needs to be known without having access to specific values. The syntax uses parallel binding (let!... and...), which binds a fixed number of independent computations. The rest of the computation cannot contain other (applicative) bindings.

There are two equivalent definitions of applicative functors. We need two operations known from the less common definition. *Merge* of type $F\alpha \times F\beta \to F(\alpha \times \beta)$ represents composition of the structure (without considering specific values) and *Map* of type $F\alpha \times (\alpha \to \beta) \to F\beta$ transforms the (pure) value. The computation expression from the previous example is translated as follows:

formlet.Map
  ( formlet.Merge(Formlet.textBox, Formlet.dropDown ["Male"; "Female"]),
   **fun** $(name, gender) \to name + $ " " $+ gender$ )

The computations composed using parallel binding are combined using *Merge*. In formlets, this determines the structure used for HTML rendering. The rest of the computation is turned into a pure function passed to *Map*. Note that the translation allows uses beyond applicative functors. The let!... and... syntax can also be used with monads to write zip comprehensions [5].

Applicative functors were first introduced to support *applicative* programming style where monads are not needed. The *idiom brackets* notation [13] fits that purpose better. We find that computation expressions provide a useful alternative for more complex code and fit better with the impure nature of F#.

## 3   Semantics of Computation Expressions

The F# language specification [20] documents computation expressions as a purely syntactic mechanism. They are desugared before type-checking, which is then performed on the translated code using standard F# typing rules. Similarly to Haskell's rebindable syntax, but to a greater level, this provides flexibility that allows the users to invent previously unforseen abstractions.

The purely syntactic approach allows more experimentation, but does not disallow erroneous uses. In this section, we present new typing rules that capture such common uses and make the system more robust. Aside from guaranteeing idiomatic use of computation expressions, it also enables better error messages.

### 3.1   Syntax

The full syntax of computation expressions is given in the language specification, but the following lists all important constructs that we consider in this paper:

$$
\begin{aligned}
expr &= \ldots \mid expr \ \{ \ cexpr \ \} &&\text{(computation expression)} \\
binds &= v = expr &&\text{(single binding)} \\
&\mid v = expr \ \textbf{and} \ binds &&\text{(parallel binding)}
\end{aligned}
$$

$$
\begin{aligned}
cexpr = \ &\textbf{let}\ v = expr\ \textbf{in}\ cexpr && \text{(binding value)} \\
\mid\ &\textbf{let!}\ binds\ \textbf{in}\ cexpr && \text{(binding computation)} \\
\mid\ &\textbf{for}\ v\ \textbf{in}\ expr\ \textbf{do}\ cexpr && \text{(for loop computation)} \\
\mid\ &\textbf{return}\ expr && \text{(return value)} \\
\mid\ &\textbf{return!}\ expr && \text{(return computation)} \\
\mid\ &\textbf{yield}\ expr && \text{(yield value)} \\
\mid\ &\textbf{yield!}\ expr && \text{(yield computation)} \\
\mid\ &cexpr_1;\ cexpr_2 && \text{(compose computations)} \\
\mid\ &expr && \text{(effectful expression)}
\end{aligned}
$$

We omit do! which is easily expressed using let! To accommodate the applicative syntax, *binds* is used to express one or more parallel variable bindings.

For space reasons, we also omit imperative while and exception handling constructs, but both of these are an important part of computation expressions. They allow taking existing code and wrapping it in a computation block to augment it with non-standard computational aspect.

## 3.2 Typing

The Figure 1 uses three judgments. Standard F# expressions are typed using $\Gamma \vdash expr : \tau$. Computation expressions always return computation of type $M\tau$ and are typed using $\Gamma \Vdash_\sigma cexpr : M\tau$. A helper judgement $\Gamma \rhd_\sigma binds : M\Sigma$ checks bindings of multiple computations and produces a variable context with newly bound variables, wrapped in the type $M$ of the bound computations.

The latter two are parameterized by the type of the computation expression builder (such as seq or async). The operations supported by the builder determine which syntactic constructs are enabled. Typing rules that require a certain operation have a side-condition on the right, which specifies the requirement.

In most of the side-conditions, the functions are universally quantified over the type of values (written as $\alpha, \beta$). This captures the fact that computation should not restrict the values that users can work with. However, this is not the case in the rules (*seq*) and (*zero*). Here, we can only require that a specific instantiation is available – the reason is that these operations may be used in two different ways. As discussed earlier (§2.1), for monads the result of *Zero* and the first argument of *Combine* are restricted to $M$ unit. They can be universally quantified only if the computation is monoidal (§2.2).

Another notable aspect of the typing is that a single computation expression may use multiple computation types (written $M, N, L$ and $D$). In *Bind* and *For*, the type of bound argument is $M$, but the resulting computation is $N$ (we require that bind returns the same type of computation as the one produced by the function). This corresponds to the typing used by computations arising from monad transformers (§2.3). Although combining multiple computation types is not as frequent, computations often have a delayed version which we write as $D$. This is an important consideration for impure langauges (§3.4).

Finally, we omitted typing for yield and yield! because it is similar to the typing of return and return! (using *Yield* and *YieldFrom* operations, respectively).

$$\boxed{\Gamma \vdash expr : \tau} \quad \text{and} \quad \boxed{\Gamma \vartriangleright_\sigma binds : M\Sigma}$$

$$\text{(run)} \quad \frac{\Gamma \vdash expr : \sigma \quad \Gamma \Vdash_\sigma cexpr : M\tau}{\Gamma \vdash expr \; \{ \; cexpr \; \} : N\tau} \qquad (\forall \alpha : \sigma.Run \; : \; D\alpha \to N\alpha$$
$$\forall \alpha : \sigma.Delay : (\mathsf{unit} \to M\alpha) \to D\alpha)$$

$$\text{(bind-one)} \quad \frac{\Gamma \vdash expr : M\tau}{\Gamma \vartriangleright_\sigma v = expr : M(v{:}\tau)}$$

$$\text{(bind-par)} \quad \frac{\Gamma \vdash expr : \tau \quad \Gamma \vartriangleright_\sigma binds : M\Sigma}{\Gamma \vartriangleright_\sigma v = expr \; \textbf{and} \; binds : M(\Sigma, v{:}\tau)} \qquad (\forall \alpha, \beta : \sigma.Merge \; :$$
$$M\alpha \to M\beta \to M(\alpha \times \beta))$$

$$\boxed{\Gamma \Vdash_\sigma cexpr : M\tau}$$

$$\text{(let)} \quad \frac{\Gamma \vdash expr : \tau_1 \quad \Gamma, v{:}\tau_1 \Vdash_\sigma cexpr : M\tau_2}{\Gamma \Vdash_\sigma \textbf{let} \; v = expr \; \textbf{in} \; cexpr : M\tau_2}$$

$$\text{(bind)} \quad \frac{\Gamma \vartriangleright_\sigma binds : M\Sigma \quad \Gamma, \Sigma \Vdash_\sigma cexpr : N\tau}{\Gamma \Vdash_\sigma \textbf{let!} \; binds \; \textbf{in} \; cexpr : N\tau} \qquad (\forall \alpha, \beta : \sigma.Bind \; :$$
$$M\alpha \to (\alpha \to N\beta) \to N\beta)$$

$$\text{(map)} \quad \frac{\Gamma \vartriangleright_\sigma binds : M\Sigma \quad \Gamma, \Sigma \vdash expr : \tau}{\Gamma \Vdash_\sigma \textbf{let!} \; binds \; \textbf{in return} \; expr : N\tau} \qquad (\forall \alpha, \beta : \sigma.Map \; :$$
$$M\alpha \to (\alpha \to \beta) \to N\beta)$$

$$\text{(for)} \quad \frac{\Gamma \vdash expr : M\tau_1 \quad \Gamma, v{:}\tau_1 \Vdash_\sigma cexpr : N\tau_2}{\Gamma \Vdash_\sigma \textbf{for} \; v \; \textbf{in} \; expr \; \textbf{do} \; cexpr : N\tau_2} \qquad (\forall \alpha, \beta : \sigma.For \; :$$
$$M\alpha \to (\alpha \to N\beta) \to N\beta)$$

$$\text{(return-val)} \quad \frac{\Gamma \vdash expr : \tau}{\Gamma \Vdash_\sigma \textbf{return} \; expr : M\tau} \qquad (\forall \alpha : \sigma.Return \; : \; \alpha \to M\alpha)$$

$$\text{(return-comp)} \quad \frac{\Gamma \vdash expr : M\tau}{\Gamma \Vdash_\sigma \textbf{return!} \; expr : N\tau} \qquad (\forall \alpha : \sigma.ReturnFrom \; : \; M\alpha \to N\alpha)$$

$$\text{(seq)} \quad \frac{\Gamma \Vdash_\sigma cexpr_1 : M\tau_1 \quad \Gamma \Vdash_\sigma cexpr_2 : N\tau_2}{\Gamma \Vdash_\sigma cexpr_1; cexpr_2 : L\tau_1} \qquad (\forall \alpha : \sigma.Delay \; : \; (\mathsf{unit} \to N\alpha) \to D\alpha$$
$$\forall \alpha : \sigma.Combine : M\tau_1 \to D\alpha \to L\alpha)$$

$$\text{(zero)} \quad \frac{\Gamma \vdash expr : \mathsf{unit}}{\Gamma \Vdash_\sigma expr : M\tau} \qquad (\sigma.Zero \; : \; \mathsf{unit} \to M\tau)$$

**Fig. 1.** Typing rules for computation expressions

## 3.3   Translation

The translation is defined as a relation $\llbracket - \rrbracket_m$ that is parameterized by a variable $m$ which refers to the current instance of a computation builder. This parameter is used to invoke members of the builder, such as $m.Return(\dots)$. Multiple variable bindings are translated using $\langle\!\langle binds \rangle\!\rangle_m$ and we define a helper mapping $\langle binds \rangle$ that turns bindings into a pattern that can be used to decompose a tuple constructed by merging computations using the $Merge$ operation.

As can be easily checked, our typing guarantees that a well-typed computation expression is always translated to a well-typed F# expression. The side-conditions ensure that all operations are available and have an appropriate type.

Some readers have already noticed that our definition of $\llbracket - \rrbracket_m$ is ambiguous. The let! binding followed by return can be translated in two different ways. We intentionally do not specify the behaviour in this paper – the laws (§4.2) require

$$
\begin{aligned}
expr\ \{\ cexpr\ \} \ &= \ \textbf{let}\ m = expr\ \textbf{in}\ m.\mathsf{Run}(m.\mathsf{Delay}(\textbf{fun}\ ()\to [\![\,cexpr\,]\!]_m)) \\
[\![\,\textbf{let}\ v = expr\ \textbf{in}\ cexpr\,]\!]_m \ &= \ \textbf{let}\ v = expr\ \textbf{in}\ [\![\,cexpr\,]\!]_m \\
[\![\,\textbf{let!}\ binds\ \textbf{in}\ cexpr\,]\!]_m \ &= \ m.\mathsf{Bind}(\langle\!\langle binds\rangle\!\rangle_m, \textbf{fun}\ \langle binds\rangle \to [\![\,cexpr\,]\!]_m) \\
[\![\,\textbf{let!}\ binds\ \textbf{in return}\,expr\,]\!]_m \ &= \ m.\mathsf{Map}(\langle\!\langle binds\rangle\!\rangle_m, \textbf{fun}\ \langle binds\rangle \to expr) \\
[\![\,\textbf{for}\ v\ \textbf{in}\ expr\ \textbf{do}\ cexpr\,]\!]_m \ &= \ m.\mathsf{For}(expr, \textbf{fun}\ ()\to [\![\,cexpr\,]\!]_m) \\
[\![\,\textbf{return}\ expr\,]\!]_m \ &= \ m.\mathsf{Return}(expr) \\
[\![\,\textbf{return!}\ expr\,]\!]_m \ &= \ m.\mathsf{ReturnFrom}(expr) \\
[\![\,cexpr_1; cexpr_2\,]\!]_m \ &= \ m.\mathsf{Combine}([\![\,cexpr_1\,]\!]_m, m.\mathsf{Delay}(\textbf{fun}\ ()\to [\![\,cexpr_2\,]\!]_m)) \\
[\![\,expr\,]\!]_m \ &= \ expr;\ m.\mathsf{Zero}() \\[4pt]
\langle\!\langle v = expr\rangle\!\rangle_m \ &= \ expr \\
\langle\!\langle v = expr\ \textbf{and}\ binds\rangle\!\rangle_m \ &= \ m.\mathsf{Merge}(expr, [\![\,binds\,]\!]_m) \\[4pt]
\langle v = expr\rangle \ &= \ v \\
\langle v = expr\ \textbf{and}\ binds\rangle \ &= \ v, \langle binds\rangle
\end{aligned}
$$

**Fig. 2.** Translation rules for computation expressions

the two translations to be equivalent. For monads, this equivalence is easy to see by considering the definition of *Map* in terms of *Bind* and *Return*.

In earlier discussion, we omitted the *Run* and *Delay* members in the translation of *expr* { *cexpr* }. The next section discusses these two in more details.

### 3.4   Delayed Computations

We already mentioned that side-effects are an important consideration when adding sequencing to monadic comptuations (§2.1). In effectful languages, it becomes apparent that we need to distinguish betwccn two types of monads.

We use the term *monadic computation* for monads that represent a delayed computation such as asynchronous workflows or lazy lists; the term *monadic containers* will be used for monads that represent a wrapped non-delayed value (such as the option type, non-lazy list or the identity monad).

**Monadic Computations.** The defining feature of *monadic computations* is that they permit a *Delay* operation of type (unit $\to M\alpha$) $\to M\alpha$ that does not perform the effects associated with the function argument. For example, in asynchronous workflows, the operation builds a computation that waits for a continuation – and so the effects are only run when the continuation is provided.

Before going further, we revisit the translation of asynchronous workflows using the full set of rules to show how *Run* and *Delay* are used. Consider the the following simple computation with a corresponding translation:

```
let answer = async {            let answer = async.Run(async.Delay(fun () →
  printfn "Welcome..."            printfn "Welcome..."
  return 42 }                     async.Return(42) ))
```

For monadic computations such as asynchronous workflows, we do not expect that defining answer will print "Welcome". This is achieved by the wrapping the specified computation in the translation rule for the *expr* { *cexpr* } expression.

In this case, the result of *Delay* is a computation $A$ int that encapsulates the delayed effect. For monadic computations, *Run* is a simple identity (of type $M\alpha \rightarrow M\alpha$). Contrary to what the name suggests, it does not run the computation (that might be an interesting use beyond standard abstract computations). The need for *Run* becomes obvious when we look at monadic containers.

**Monadic Containers.** For monadic containers, it is impossible to define a *Delay* operation that does not perform the (untracked) side-effects and has a type (unit $\rightarrow M\alpha) \rightarrow M\alpha$, because the resulting type has no way of capturing unevaluated code. However, the (*seq*) typing rule in Figure 1 permits an alternative typing. Consider the following example using the Maybe (option) monad:

$$\text{maybe} \; \{ \; \textbf{if} \; b = 0 \; \textbf{then return!} \; \text{None}$$
$$\text{printfn "Calculating..."}$$
$$\textbf{return} \; a \, / \, b \; \}$$

Using the same translation rules, *Run*, *Delay* and *Delay* are inserted as follows:

```
maybe.Run(maybe.Delay(fun () → maybe.Combine
   ( (if b = 0 then maybe.ReturnFrom(None) else maybe.Zero()),
      maybe.Delay(fun () → printfn "Calculating..."
                  maybe.Return(a / b)) ) ))
```

The key idea is that we can use two different types – $M\alpha$ for varlues representing (evaluated) monadic containers and unit $\rightarrow M\alpha$ for delayed computations. The operations then have the following types:

$$
\begin{array}{lll}
Delay & : & (\text{unit} \rightarrow M\alpha) \rightarrow (\text{unit} \rightarrow M\alpha) \\
Run & : & (\text{unit} \rightarrow M\alpha) \rightarrow M\alpha \\
Combine & : & M \, \text{unit} \rightarrow (\text{unit} \rightarrow M\alpha) \rightarrow M\alpha
\end{array}
$$

Here, the *Delay* operation becomes just an identity that returns the function created by the translation. In the translation, the result of *Delay* can be passed either to *Run* or as the second argument of *Delay*, so these need to be changed accordingly. The *Run* function now becomes important as it turns the delayed function into a value of the expected type $M\alpha$ (by applying it).

**Unified Treatment of Effects.** In the typing rules (§3.2), we did not explicitly list the two options, because they can be generalized. We require that the result of *Delay* is some (possibly different) abstract type $D\alpha$ representing delayed computations. For monadic computations, the type is just $M\alpha$ and for monadic containers, it is unit $\rightarrow M\alpha$. Our typing is even more flexible, as it allows usage of multiple different computation types – but treatment of effects is one example where this additional flexibility is necessary.

Finally, it should be noted that we use a slight simplification. The actual F# implementation does not strictly require *Run* and *Delay* in the translation of *expr* { *cexpr* }. They are only used if they are present.

## 4   Computation Expression Laws

Although computation expressions are not tied to any specific abstract computation type, we showed that they are usually used with well-known abstractions.
This means three good things. First, we get better understanding of what computations can be encoded (and how). Second, we can add a more precise typing
§3.2. Third, we know that certain syntactic transformations (refactorings) preserve the meaning of computation. This section looks at the last point.

To keep the presentation in this section focused, we assume that there are no
untracked side-effects (such as I/O) and we ignore *Run* and *Delay*.

### 4.1   Monoid and Semigroup Laws

We start from the simplest structures. A semigroup $(S, \circ)$ consists of a set $S$ and
a binary operation $\circ$ such that $a \circ (b \circ c) = (a \circ b) \circ c$. A computation expression
corresponding to a semigroup defines only *Combine* (of type $M\alpha \times M\alpha \to M\alpha$).
To allow appropriate syntax, we also add *YieldFrom* which is just the identity
function (with a type $M\alpha \to M\alpha$). The associativity implies the following syntactic equivalence (we use $m$ as a placeholder for concrete computation builder):

$$\text{m } \{ \ cexpr_1; \ cexpr_2; \ cexpr_3 \ \} \ \equiv \ \text{m } \{ \ \textbf{yield! } \text{m } \{cexpr_1; \ cexpr_2 \ \}; \ cexpr_3 \ \}$$

A monoid $(S, \circ, \epsilon)$ is a semigroup $(S, \circ)$ with an identity element $\epsilon$ meaning that
for all values $a \in S$ it holds that $\epsilon \circ a = a = a \circ \epsilon$. The identity element can be
added to computation builder as the *Zero* member. This operation is used when
a computation uses conditional without else branch. Thus we get:

$$\text{m } \{ \ \textbf{if false then } cexpr_1 \atop cexpr_2 \ \} \ \equiv \ \text{m } \{ \ cexpr_2 \ \} \ \equiv \ {\text{m } \{ \ cexpr_2 \atop \textbf{if false then } cexpr_1 \ \}}$$

Although these are simple laws, they can be used to reason about list comprehensions. The associativity means that we can move a sub-expression of computation
expression (that uses yield! repeatedly) into a separate computation. To use the
identity law, consider a recursive function that generates numbers up to 100:

$$\begin{aligned} &\textbf{let rec } \text{range } n = \text{seq } \{ \\ &\quad \textbf{yield } n \\ &\quad \textbf{if } n < 100 \textbf{ then yield! } \text{range } (n+1) \ \} \end{aligned}$$

The law guarantees that for $n = 100$, the body equals seq { yield 100 }. This is
an expected property of the if construct – the law guarantees that it holds even
for if that is reinterpreted by some (monoidal) computation expression.

### 4.2   Monad and Additive Monad Laws

Monad laws are well-understood and the corresponding equivalent computation
expressions do not significantly differ from the laws about Haskell's do notation:

$$\begin{aligned} \text{m } \{ \ \textbf{let! } y = \text{m } \{ \ \textbf{return } x \ \} \textbf{ in } cexpr \ \} \ &\equiv \ \text{m } \{ \ \textbf{let } y = x \textbf{ in } cexpr \ \} \\ \text{m } \{ \ \textbf{let! } x = c \textbf{ in return } x \} \ &\equiv \ \text{m } \{ \ \textbf{return! } c \} \end{aligned}$$

$$m \; \{ \; \textbf{let!} \; x = m \; \{ \; \textbf{let!} \; y = c \; \textbf{in} \; cexpr_1 \; \} \; \textbf{in} \; cexpr_2 \; \} \; \equiv$$
$$\equiv m \; \{ \; \textbf{let!} \; y = c \; \textbf{in} \; \textbf{let!} \; x = m \; \{ \; cexpr_1 \; \} \; \textbf{in} \; cexpr_2 \; \}$$

**Resolving ambiguity.** When discussing the translation rules (§3.3), we noted that the rules are ambiguous when both *Map* and *Bind* operations are present. The following can be translated both monadically and using the *Map* operation:

$$m \; \{ \; \textbf{let!} \; x = c \; \textbf{in return} \; expr \; \}$$

The two translations are shown below. Assuming that our computation is a monad, this is a well-known definition of *Map* in terms of *Bind* and *Return*:

$$m.\mathsf{Map}(x, \textbf{fun} \; x \to expr) \; \equiv \; m.\mathsf{Bind}(x, \textbf{fun} \; x \to m.\mathsf{Return}(expr))$$

More generally, if a computation builder defines both *Map* and *Bind* (even if they are not based on a monad), we require this equation to guarantee that the two possible translations produce equivalent computations.

**Additive Monads.** Additive monads are computations that combine monad with the monoidal structure. As shown earlier (§2.2), these can be embedded using let!/return or using for/yield. The choice can be made based on the laws that hold.

The laws required for additive monads is not fully resolved [8]. A frequently advocated law is *left distributivity* – binding on the result of a monoidal operation is equivalent to binding on two computations and then combining the results:

$$m.\mathsf{For}(m.\mathsf{Combine}(a, b), f) \; \equiv \; m.\mathsf{Combine}(m.\mathsf{For}(a, f), m.\mathsf{For}(b, f))$$

We intentionally use the *For* operation (corresponding to the for keyword), because this leads to the following intuitive syntactic equality:

$$m \; \{ \; \textbf{for} \; x \; \textbf{in} \; m \; \{ \; cexpr_1; \; cexpr_2 \; \} \; \textbf{do} \; \equiv \; m \; \{ \; \textbf{for} \; x \; \textbf{in} \; m \; \{ \; cexpr_1 \; \} \; \textbf{do} \; cexpr$$
$$cexpr \; \} \qquad\qquad\qquad\qquad\qquad \textbf{for} \; x \; \textbf{in} \; m \; \{ \; cexpr_2 \; \} \; \textbf{do} \; cexpr \; \}$$

If we read the code as an imperative looping construct (without the computational reinterpretation), then this is, indeed, a valid law about for loops.

Another law that is sometimes required about additive monads is *left catch*. It states that combining a computation that immediately returns a value with any other computation results in a computation that just returns the value:

$$m.\mathsf{Combine}(m.\mathsf{Return}(v), a) \; \equiv \; m.\mathsf{Return}(v)$$

This time, we intentionally used the *Return* member instead of *Yield*, because the law corresponds to the following syntactic equivalence:

$$m \; \{ \; \textbf{return} \; v; \; cexpr \; \} \; \equiv \; m \; \{ \; \textbf{return} \; v \; \}$$

The fact that *left catch* corresponds to an intuitive syntactic equality about let!/return while *left distributivity* corresponds to an intuitive syntactic equality about for/yield determines the appropriate syntax. The former can be used for list comprehensions (and other collections), while the latter is suitable e.g. for the option monad or the software transactional memory monad [6].

## 4.3   Monad Transformers

There are multiple ways of composing or layering monads [10,12]. Monad transformers are perhaps the most widely known technique. A monad transformer is a type constructor $T\,m$ together with a *Lift* operation. For some monad $M$ the operation has a type $M\,\alpha \to T\,M\,\alpha$ and it turns a computation in the underlying monad into a computation in the transformed monad.

The result of monad transformer is also a monad. This means that we can use the usual syntactic sugar for monads, such as the do notation in Haskell. However, a more specific notation can use the additional *Lift* operation.

We looked at computation expression for a composed monad when discussing asynchronous sequences (§2.3). An asynchronous sequence AsyncSeq $\alpha$ is a computation obtained by applying the list monad transformer [7] to the monad Async $\alpha$. Asynchronous sequences are *additive monads* satisfying the left distributivity law, so we choose the for/yield syntax for working with the composed computation. We also provided additional *Bind* to support awaiting a single asynchronous workflow using let! This operation is defined in terms of *Lift* of the monad transformer and *For* (monadic bind) of the composed computation:

$$\mathsf{asyncSeq.Bind}(a, f) = \mathsf{asyncSeq.For}(\mathsf{asyncSeq.Lift}(a), f)$$

There are two laws that hold about monad transforers. To simplify the presentation, we use asynchronous workflows and sequences rather than showing the generalised version. The first law states that composing *Return* of asynchronous workflows with *Lift* should be equivalent to the *Yield* of asynchronous sequences. The other states that *Lift* distributes over monadic bind.

Our syntax always combines *Lift* with *For*, so the following syntactic equivalences also require right identity for monads and function extensionality:

$$\mathsf{asyncSeq}\;\{\;\mathbf{let!}\;x = \mathsf{async}\;\{\;\mathbf{return}\;v\;\}\;\mathbf{in\;return}\;x\;\}\;\equiv\;\mathsf{asyncSeq}\;\{\;\mathbf{return}\;v\;\}$$

$$\mathsf{asyncSeq}\;\{\;\mathbf{let!}\;x = \mathsf{async}\;\{\;\mathbf{let!}\;y = c\;\mathbf{in}\;cexpr_1\;\}\;\mathbf{in}\;cexpr_2\;\}\;\equiv$$
$$\equiv\;\mathsf{asyncSeq}\;\{\;\mathbf{let!}\;y = c\;\mathbf{in\;let!}\;x = \mathsf{async}\;\{\;cexpr_1\;\}\;\mathbf{in}\;cexpr_2\;\}$$

The first equation returns $v$ without any asynchronous waiting in both cases (although, in presence of side-effects, this is made more complicated by cancellation). The second equation is more subtle. The left-hand side awaits a single asynchronous workflow that first awaits $c$ and then does more work. The right-hand side awaits $c$ lifted to an asynchronous sequence and then awaits the rest.

## 4.4   Applicative Computations

The last type of computations that we discussed (§2.4) is *applicative functor*. We use the less common definition called Monoidal [13]. It consists of *Map* and *Merge*, together with a unit computation. The unit computation can be used to define *Zero*. This is used only in the translation of empty computations f { () }.

The identity law guarantees that merging with a unit and then projecting the non-unit value produces an equivalent computation:

$$\mathsf{f}\;\{\;\mathbf{let!}\;x = \mathsf{f}\;\{\;()\;\}\qquad\qquad\qquad \mathsf{f}\;\{\;\mathbf{let!}\;x = c$$
$$\mathbf{and}\;y = c\;\mathbf{in\;return}\;y\;\}\}\quad\equiv\;c\;\equiv\quad \mathbf{and}\;y = \mathsf{f}\;\{\;()\;\}\;\mathbf{in\;return}\;x\;\}\}$$

The naturality law specifies that *Merge* distributes over *Map*, which translates to the following code (assuming $x_1$ not free in $expr_2$ and $x_2$ not free in $expr_1$):

$$\begin{aligned}
&\textsf{f \{ let! } y_1 = \textsf{f \{ let! } x_1 = c_1 \textsf{ in return } expr_1 \textsf{ \}}\\
&\quad\textsf{and } y_2 = \textsf{f \{ let! } x_2 = c_2 \textsf{ in return } expr_2 \textsf{ \} in } expr \textsf{ \}}
\end{aligned} \equiv$$

$$\equiv\ \textsf{f \{ let! } x_1 = c_1 \textsf{ and } x_2 = c_2 \textsf{ in let } y_1, y_2 = expr_1, expr_2 \textsf{ in } expr \textsf{ \}}$$

As with the earlier syntactic rules, we can leave out the non-standard aspect of the computations, read them as ordinary functional code and get correct and expected laws. This means that the laws, again, guarantee that intuition about the syntax used by computation expressions will be correct.

Finally, the *Merge* operation is also required to be associative – this does not have any corresponding syntax, but it means that the user does not need to know implementation details of the compiler – it does not matter whether the parsing of *binds* in let!... and... is left-associative or right-associative.

## 5 Related Work

Haskell and its extensions support monad comprehensions [12] and "do" notation for monads, idiom brackets [13] for applicatives and arrows [15]. These are similar to computation expressions in that they are not tied to concrete computations. However, they differ syntactically – they add multiple new notations, while computation expressions add a uniform notation resembling standard language structures. Adding arrows to computation expressions is an open question.

Python and C# generators, LINQ [14] in C# and "for" comprehensions in Scala are just a few examples of syntax for concrete computations. Although they can all be used with other computations, this is not generally considered idiomatic use. Similarly to F#, the Scala async library [21] supports loops and exception handling. However, it is implemented through full macro system.

Other encodings of effectful computations include effect handlers [17] and continuations [3]. Providing syntactic support for these may be an interesting alternative to our encoding. Interestingly, our *Run* operation resembles *reset* of delimited continuations [18] and our *Delay* is similar to *reify* of Filinsky [4].

## 6 Conclusions

This paper is presents a principled treatment of F# *computation expressions*. We develop a type system that captures the static semantics and relate the feature to well-known abstract computation types. Computation expressions provide a unified way for writing a wide range of computations including monoids, monads, applicative formlets and monads composed using monad transformers.

Computation expressions follow a different approach than e.g. Haskell "do" notation. They integrate a wide range of abstractions and flexibly reuse existing syntax (including loops and exception handling). The library developer can choose the appropriate syntax and use laws of abstract computations to guarantee that the computation preserves intuition about the syntax.

Such reusable syntactic extensions are becoming increasingly important. We cannot keep adding new features to support comprehensions, asynchronicity, queries and more as the "syntactic budget" is rapidly running out.

**Acknowledgements.** We are grateful to Dominic Orchard, Alan Mycroft, Sam Lindley, anonymous reviewers and the audience of TFP 2012.

# References

1. Bierman, G., Russo, C., Mainland, G., Meijer, E., Torgersen, M.: Pause 'n' play: formalizing asynchronous C$^\sharp$. In: Noble, J. (ed.) ECOOP 2012. LNCS, vol. 7313, pp. 233–257. Springer, Heidelberg (2012)
2. Cooper, E., Lindley, S., Wadler, P., Yallop, J.: The essence of form abstraction. In: Ramalingam, G. (ed.) APLAS 2008. LNCS, vol. 5356, pp. 205–220. Springer, Heidelberg (2008)
3. Filinski, A.: Representing layered monads. In: POPL, pp. 175–188 (1999)
4. Filinski, A.: Monads in action. In: POPL, pp. 483–494 (2010)
5. Giorgidze, G., Grust, T., Schweinsberg, N., Weijers, J.: Bringing back monad comprehensions. In: Haskell Symposium, pp. 13–22 (2011)
6. Harris, T., Marlow, S., Peyton-Jones, S., Herlihy, M.: Composable memory transactions. In: PPoPP, pp. 48–60 (2005)
7. HaskellWiki. Listt done right (2012),
   `http://www.haskell.org/haskellwiki/ListT_done_right`
8. HaskellWiki. Monadplus (2012),
   `http://www.haskell.org/haskellwiki/MonadPlus`
9. Krishnamurthi, S.: Artifact evaluation for software conferences (2012),
   `http://cs.brown.edu/~sk/Memos/Conference-Artifact-Evaluation/`
10. Liang, S., Hudak, P., Jones, M.: Monad transformers and modular interpreters. In: POPL (1995)
11. Lindley, S., Wadler, P., Yallop, J.: Idioms are oblivious, arrows are meticulous, monads are promiscuous. Electron. Notes Theor. Comput. Sci. 229(5) (March 2011)
12. Lüth, C., Ghani, N.: Proceedings of the Seventh ACM SIGPLAN International Conference on Functional Programming, ICFP, pp. 133–144 (2002)
13. Mcbride, C., Paterson, R.: Applicative programming with effects. J. Funct. Program. 18(1), 1–13 (2008)
14. Meijer, E., Beckman, B., Bierman, G.: LINQ: reconciling object, relations and XML in the.NET framework. In: SIGMOD, p. 706 (2006)
15. Paterson, R.: A new notation for arrows. In: ICFP (2001)
16. Petricek, T.: Programming with F# asynchronous sequences (2011),
    `http://tomasp.net/blog/async-sequences.aspx`
17. Plotkin, G., Pretnar, M.: Handlers of algebraic effects. In: Castagna, G. (ed.) ESOP 2009. LNCS, vol. 5502, pp. 80–94. Springer, Heidelberg (2009)
18. Rompf, T., Maier, I., Odersky, M.: Implementing first-class polymorphic delimited continuations by a type-directed selective cps-transform. In: ICFP (2009)
19. Syme, D., Petricek, T., Lomov, D.: The F# asynchronous programming model. In: Rocha, R., Launchbury, J. (eds.) PADL 2011. LNCS, vol. 6539, pp. 175–189. Springer, Heidelberg (2011)
20. The F# Software Foundation. F# language specification (2013)
21. Typesafe Inc. An asynchronous programming facility for scala (2013)
22. Wadler, P.: Monads for functional programming. In: Jeuring, J., Meijer, E. (eds.) AFP 1995. LNCS, vol. 925, pp. 24–52. Springer, Heidelberg (1995)

# Abstract Modular Inference Systems and Solvers

Yuliya Lierler[1] and Miroslaw Truszczynski[2]

[1] University of Nebraska at Omaha
ylierler@unomaha.edu
[2] University of Kentucky
mirek@cs.uky.edu

**Abstract.** Integrating diverse formalisms into modular knowledge representation systems offers increased expressivity, modeling convenience and computational benefits. We introduce the concepts of *abstract inference modules* and *abstract modular inference systems* to study general principles behind the design and analysis of model-generating programs, or *solvers*, for integrated multi-logic systems. We show how modules and modular systems give rise to *transition graphs*, which are a natural and convenient representation of solvers, an idea pioneered by the SAT community. We illustrate our approach by showing how it applies to answer-set programming and propositional logic, and to multi-logic systems based on these two formalisms.

## 1 Introduction

Knowledge representation and reasoning (KR) is concerned with developing formal languages and logics to model knowledge, and with designing and implementing corresponding automated reasoning tools. The choice of specific logics and tools depends on the type of knowledge to be represented and reasoned about. Different logics are suitable for common-sense reasoning, reasoning under incomplete information and uncertainty, for temporal and spatial reasoning, and for modeling and solving boolean constraints, or constraints over larger, even continuous domains. In applications in areas such as distributed databases, semantic web, hybrid constraint modeling and solving, to name just a few, several of these aspects come to play. Accordingly, often diverse logics have to be accommodated together.

Modeling convenience is not the only reason why diverse logics are combined into modular hybrid KR systems. Another motivation is to exploit in reasoning the transparent structure that comes from modularity, computational strengths of individual logics, and synergies that arise when they are put together. Constraint logic programming [10] and satisfiability modulo theories (SMT) [20,2] are well-known examples of formalisms stemming directly from such considerations. More recent examples include constraint answer-set programming (CASP) [13] that integrates answer-set programming (ASP) [16,18] with constraint modeling languages [22], and "multi-logic" formalisms PC(ID) [17], SM(ASP) [14] and ASP-FO [4] that combine modules expressed as logic theories under the classical semantics with modules given as answer-set programs.

The key computational task arising in KR is that of *model generation*. Model-generating programs or *solvers*, developed in satisfiability (SAT) and ASP proved to be

M. Flatt and H.-F. Guo (Eds.): PADL 2014, LNCS 8324, pp. 49–64, 2014.

effective in a broad range of KR applications. Accordingly, model generation is of critical importance in modular multi-logic systems. Research on formalisms listed above resulted in fast solvers that demonstrate gains one can obtain from their heterogeneous nature. However, the diversity of logics considered and low-level technical details of their syntax and semantics obscure general principles that are important in the design and analysis of solvers for multi-logic systems.

In this paper we address this problem by proposing a language for talking about modular multi-logic systems that (i) abstracts away the syntactic details, (ii) is expressive enough to capture various concepts of inference, and (iii) is based only on the weakest assumptions concerning the semantics of underlying logics. The basic elements of this language are *abstract inference modules* (or just *modules*). Collections of abstract inference modules constitute *abstract modular inference systems* (or just *modular systems*). We define the semantics of abstract inference modules and show that they provide a uniform language capturing different logics, diverse inference mechanisms, and their modular combinations. Importantly, abstract inference modules and abstract modular inference systems give rise to *transition graphs* of the type introduced by Nieuwenhuis, Oliveras, and Tinelli [20] in their study of SAT and SMT solvers. As in that earlier work, our transition graphs provide a natural and convenient representation of solvers for modules and modular systems. In this way, abstract modular inference systems and the corresponding framework of transition graphs are useful conceptualizations clarifying computational principles behind solvers for multi-logic knowledge representation systems and facilitating systematic development of new ones.

We start the paper by introducing abstract inference modules. We then adapt transition graphs of Nieuwenhuis et al. [20] to the formalism of abstract inference modules and use them to describe algorithms for finding models of modules. In Section 4, we introduce abstract modular inference systems, extend the concept of a transition graph to modular systems, and show that transition graphs can be used to formalize search for models in this setting, too. We conclude by discussing related work, recapping our contributions, and commenting on future work. Throughout the paper, we illustrate our approach by showing how it applies to propositional logic and answer-set programming, and to multi-logic systems based on these two formalisms. A version of the paper containing proofs is available at `http://www.cs.uky.edu/ai/ams.pdf`.

## 2   Abstract Inference Modules

We start with some notation. Let $\sigma$ be a fixed infinite vocabulary (a set of propositional atoms). We write $Lit(\sigma)$ for the set of all literals over $\sigma$. For a set $M \subseteq Lit(\sigma)$, we define $M^+ = \sigma \cap M$ and $M^- = \{a \in \sigma : \neg a \in M\}$. A literal $l \in Lit(\sigma)$ is *unassigned* by a set of literals $M \subseteq Lit(\sigma)$ if $M$ contains neither $l$ nor its dual literal $\bar{l}$. A set $M$ of literals over $\sigma$ is *consistent* if for every literal $l \in Lit(\sigma)$, $l \notin M$ or $\bar{l} \notin M$. We denote the set of all consistent subsets of $Lit(\sigma)$ by $C(\sigma)$.

**Definition 1.** *An* abstract inference module *over a vocabulary $\sigma$ (or just a* module, *for short) is a finite set of pairs of the form $(M, l)$, where $M \in C(\sigma)$, $l \in Lit(\sigma)$ and $l \notin M$. These pairs are called* inferences *of the module. For a module $S$, $\sigma(S)$ denotes the set of all atoms that appear in inferences of $S$.*

Intuitively, an inference $(M, l)$ in a module indicates support for inferring $l$ whenever all literals in $M$ are given. We note that if $(M, l)$ is an inference and $\bar{l} \in M$, the inference is an explicit indication of a contradiction. Figure 1(a) shows all inferences over the vocabulary $\{a\}$. Figures 1(b) and 1(c) give examples of modules over the vocabulary $\{a\}$. Here and throughout the paper, we present inferences as directed edges and modules as bipartite graphs.

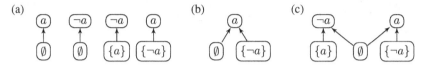

**Fig. 1.** All inferences and two inference modules over the vocabulary $\{a\}$

A set $M \subseteq Lit(\sigma)$ is *consistent with* a set $X \subseteq \sigma$ if $M^+ \subseteq X$ and $M^- \cap X = \emptyset$. A literal $l \in Lit(\sigma)$ is *consistent with* a set $X \subseteq \sigma$ if $\{l\}$ is consistent with $X$. Let $S$ be an abstract inference module. A set $X \subseteq \sigma$ of atoms is a *model* of $S$ if for every inference $(M, l) \in S$ such that $M$ is consistent with $X$, $l$ is consistent with $X$, too. For example, any set of atoms that contains $a$ is a model of the module in Figure 1(b), whereas no set of atoms that does not contain $a$ is such. The module in Figure 1(c) has no models due to inferences $(\emptyset, a)$ and $(\emptyset, \neg a)$. A module is *satisfiable* if it has models, and is *unsatisfiable* otherwise. The module in Figure 1(b) is satisfiable, the one in Figure 1(c) is unsatisfiable.

Two modules that have the same models are *equivalent*.

**Proposition 1.** *Abstract inference modules $S_1$ and $S_2$ are equivalent if and only if they have the same models contained in the set $\sigma(S_1) \cup \sigma(S_2)$.*

The semantics of modules is given by the set of their models. A module $S$ over a vocabulary $\sigma$ *entails* a literal $l \in Lit(\sigma)$, written $S \approx l$, if for every model $X$ of $S$, $l$ is consistent with $X$. Furthermore, $S$ *entails* $l$ with respect to a set $M \subseteq Lit(\sigma)$ of literals, written $S \approx_M l$, if whenever $M$ is consistent with a model $X$ of $S$, $l$ is consistent with $X$, too. Modules are *sound* with respect to their semantics:

**Proposition 2.** *Let $S$ be a module and $(M, l)$ an edge in $S$. Then $S \approx_M l$.*

In the paper we often consider unions of (finitely many) modules. We use the symbol $\cup$ to denote the union of modules.

**Proposition 3.** *Let $S_1$ and $S_2$ be abstract inference modules. A set $X$ of atoms is a model of $S_1 \cup S_2$ if and only if $X$ is a model of $S_1$ and $S_2$.*

Modules are not meant for modeling knowledge. Representations by means of logic theories are usually more concise. Furthermore, the logic languages align closely with natural language, which facilitates modeling and makes the correspondence between logic theories and knowledge they represent direct. Modules lack this connection. The power of modules comes from the fact that they provide a uniform, syntax-independent way to describe theories and inference methods from *different* logics. We illustrate this property of modules by showing that they can capture theories and inferences in classical propositional logic and in answer-set programming [8,16,18] (where theories are commonly called programs).

Let $T$ be a finite CNF propositional theory over $\sigma$ and let $\sigma_T$ be the set of atoms that actually appear in $T$. We first consider the inference method given by the classical entailment. By $Ent(T)$ we denote the module consisting of pairs $(M, l)$ that satisfy the following conditions: $M \in C(\sigma_T)$, $l \in Lit(\sigma_T) \setminus M$, and $T \cup M \models l$. Figure 1(b) shows the module $Ent(\{a\})$. Similarly, Figure 2 presents the module $Ent(T)$, where $T$ is the theory:

$$\{a \vee b, \neg a \vee \neg b\}. \tag{1}$$

We note that $Ent(T)$ has two models contained in $\{a, b\}$: $\{a\}$ and $\{b\}$.[1] More generally, every model $X$ of $Ent(T)$ contains exactly one of $a$ and $b$.

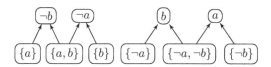

**Fig. 2.** Abstract module $Ent(T)$ for the theory $T$ given by (1)

Focusing on specific inference rules of propositional logic also gives rise to abstract modules. *Unit Propagate* is a standard inference rule commonly used when reasoning with CNF theories. This inference rule is essential to all satisfiability (SAT) solvers, programs that compute models of CNF theories or determine that no models exist. The *Unit Propagate* rule gives rise to the module $UP(T)$ that consists of all pairs $(M, l)$ that satisfy the following conditions: $M \in C(\sigma_T)$, $l \in Lit(\sigma_T) \setminus M$, and $T$ has a clause $C \vee l$ (modulo reordering of literals) such that for every literal $u$ of $C$, $\overline{u} \in M$.

Let $T$ be the theory (1). The module $Ent(T)$ in Figure 2 coincides with $UP(T)$. Thus, for the theory (1) the *Unit Propagate* rule captures entailment.

We say that a module $S$ is *equivalent* to a propositional theory $T$ if they have the same models. Clearly, the module in Figure 2 is equivalent to the propositional theory (1). This is an instance of a general property.

**Proposition 4.** *For every propositional theory $T$ (respectively, CNF formula $T$ containing no empty clause), $Ent(T)$ (respectively, $UP(T)$) is equivalent to $T$.*

*Unit Propagate* is the primary inference rule of most SAT solvers. In the case of answer-set programming, most solvers rely on several inference rules associated with reasoning under the answer-set semantics. For instance, the classical answer-set solver SMODELS [19] exploits four inference rules: the *Unit Propagate* rule, the *Unfounded* rule, the *All Rules Cancelled* rule, and the *Backchain True* rule. To state these rules we introduce some definitions and notations commonly used in logic programming.

---

[1] We identify a model, an interpretation, of a propositional theory with the set of atoms that are assigned $True$ in the model.

A *logic program*, or simply a *program*, over $\sigma$ is a finite set of *rules* of the form

$$a_0 \leftarrow a_1, \ldots, a_\ell, \textit{not } a_{\ell+1}, \ldots, \textit{not } a_m, \tag{2}$$

where each $a_i$, $0 \leq i \leq m$, is an atom from $\sigma$. The expression $a_0$ is the *head* of the rule. The expression on the right hand side of the arrow is the *body*. For a program $\Pi$ and an atom $a$, $Bodies(\Pi, a)$ denotes the set of the bodies of all rules in $\Pi$ with the head $a$. We write $\sigma_\Pi$ for the set of atoms that occur in a program $\Pi$.

For the body $B$ of a rule (2), we define $s(B) = \{a_1, \ldots, a_\ell, \neg a_{\ell+1}, \ldots, \neg a_m\}$. In some cases, we identify $B$ with the conjunction of the elements in $s(B)$, and we often interpret a rule (2) as the propositional clause

$$a_0 \vee \neg a_1 \vee \ldots \vee \neg a_\ell \vee a_{\ell+1} \vee \ldots \vee a_m. \tag{3}$$

For a program $\Pi$, we write $\Pi^{cl}$ for the set of clauses (3) corresponding to all rules in $\Pi$. We assume the reader is familiar with the definition of an *answer set* [8], as well as the concept of *unfounded sets* [25]. For a set $M$ of literals and a program $\Pi$, we write $U(M, \Pi)$ to denote a set that is unfounded on $M$ w.r.t. $\Pi$ (typically, such set will be identified by some algorithmic method, but a specific way in which we find it is immaterial for the purposes of this paper).

We are now ready to define the SMODELS inference rules. For a program $\Pi$, a set $M \in C(\sigma_\Pi)$ of literals, and a literal $l \in Lit(\sigma_\Pi) \setminus M$:

*Unit Propagate*: derive $l$ if $\Pi^{cl}$ contains clause $C \vee l$ such that for every $u \in C, \overline{u} \in M$;

*Unfounded*: derive $l$ if $l = \neg a$ and $a \in U(M, \Pi)$;

*All Rule Cancelled*: derive $l$ if $l = \neg a$ and for every $B \in Bodies(\Pi, a)$, there is $u \in s(B)$ such that $\overline{u} \in M$;

*Backchain True*: derive $l$, if for some rule $a \leftarrow B \in \Pi, a \in M, l \in s(B)$, and for every $B' \in Bodies(\Pi, a) \setminus \{B\}$, there is $u \in s(B')$ such that $\overline{u} \in M$;

Note that $UP(\Pi)$ and $UP(\Pi^{cl})$ are identical (and equivalent) even though they concern different logics.

The four rules above give rise to abstract inference modules $UP(\Pi)$, $UF(\Pi)$, $ARC(\Pi)$ and $BC(\Pi)$, respectively, each defined by taking the definition of the rule as the condition for $(M, l)$ to be an inference of the module. We note that the inference rule *All Rule Cancelled* is subsumed by the inference rule *Unfounded*. That is, $ARC(\Pi) \subseteq UF(\Pi)$. This is the only inclusion relation between distinct modules in that set that holds for every program.

We say that a module $S$ is *equivalent* to a program $\Pi$ if for every $X \subseteq \sigma_\Pi$, $X$ is a model of $S$ if and only if $X$ is an answer set of $\Pi$.[2] None of the four modules $UP(\Pi)$, $UF(\Pi)$, $ARC(\Pi)$ and $BC(\Pi)$ alone is equivalent to the underlying program $\Pi$. However, some combinations of these modules are. Let us define

$$UPUF(\Pi) = UP(\Pi) \cup UF(\Pi)$$

---

[2] This is not the standard concept of equivalence as it is restricted to models over the vocabulary of the program. It is sufficient, however, for our purpose of studying algorithms to compute answer sets.

and
$$smodels(\Pi) = UP(\Pi) \cup UF(\Pi) \cup ARC(\Pi) \cup BC(\Pi).$$

Since $ARC(\Pi) \subseteq UF(\Pi)$, it is not necessary to list the module $ARC(\Pi)$ explicitly in the union above. We do so, as the rule *All Rule Cancelled* is computationally cheaper than the rule *Unfounded* and in practical implementations the two are distinguished.

The following result restates well-known properties of the inference rules [12] in terms of equivalence of modules and programs.

**Proposition 5.** *Every logic program $\Pi$ is equivalent to the modules $UPUF(\Pi)$ and $smodels(\Pi)$.*

Let $\Pi$ be the program
$$\begin{aligned} a &\leftarrow not\ b \\ b &\leftarrow not\ a. \end{aligned} \tag{4}$$

This program has two answer sets $\{a\}$ and $\{b\}$. Since these are also the only two models over the vocabulary $\{a, b\}$ of the module in Figure 2, the program and the module are equivalent. The module represents the reasoning mechanism of entailment with respect to the answer sets of the program. Furthermore, that module also represents the program (4) and the reasoning mechanism captured by the module $smodels(\Pi)$.

Two other modules associated with program (4) are given in Figure 3. Figure 3(a) shows the module $UP(\Pi)$, which represents the program (4) and the reasoning mechanism based on *Unit Propagate*. This module is not equivalent to program (4). Indeed, $\{a, b\}$ is its model but not an answer set of (4). Figure 3(b) shows the module $ARC(\Pi)$ (which in this case happens to coincide with both $UF(\Pi)$ and $BC(\Pi)$). Also this module is not equivalent to program (4) as $\emptyset$ is its model but not an answer set of $\Pi$. The union of the two modules in Figure 3 captures all four inference rules and is indeed equal to the module in Figure 2.

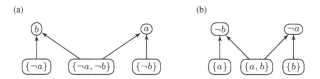

**Fig. 3.** Two abstract modules based on the program (4)

## 3   Abstract Modular Solver: AM$_S$

Finding models of logic theories and programs is a key computational task in declarative programming. Nieuwenhuis et al. [20] proposed to use *transition graphs* to describe search procedures involved in model-finding algorithms commonly called *solvers*, and developed that approach for the case of SAT. Their transition graph framework can express DPLL, the basic search procedure employed by SAT solvers, and its enhancements with techniques such as the conflict driven clause learning. Lierler and Truszczynski [12,14] proposed a similar framework to describe and analyze the answer-set programming solvers SMODELS, CMODELS [9] and CLASP [6], as well as a PC(ID) solver

MINISAT(ID) [17]. In the previous section, we argued that theories and programs can be represented by equivalent abstract inference modules (Propositions 4 and 5). We now show that the idea of a transition graph can be generalized to the setting of modules, leading to an abstract perspective on the problem of search for models of modules, and unifying the approaches to the model-finding task.

Let $\delta$ be a *finite* vocabulary. A *state over* $\delta$ is either a special state $\perp$ (the *fail* state) or a sequence $M$ of *distinct* literals over $\delta$, some possibly annotated by $\Delta$, which marks them as *decision* literals, such that:

1. the set of literals in $M$ is consistent or $M = M'l$, where the set of literals in $M'$ is consistent and contains $\bar{l}$, and
2. if $M = M'l^\Delta M''$, then $l$ is unassigned in $M'$.

For instance, if $\delta = \{a, b\}$, then $\emptyset$, $a$, $\neg a^\Delta b$, $\neg a\, b^\Delta a$ and $\perp$ are examples of states over $\delta$. If $M$ is a state, by $[M]$ we denote the *set* of the literals in $M$ (that is, we drop annotations and ignore the order). Our definition of a state allows for inconsistent states. However, inconsistent states are of a very specific form — the inconsistence arises because of the last literal in the state. There is also a restriction on annotated (decision) literals. A decision literal must not appear in a state following another occurrence of that literal or its dual (annotated or not). Intuitively, a literal annotated by $\Delta$ denotes a current assumption: thus once a literal is assigned in a state, there is no point of later making an assumption concerning whether it holds or not.

Each module $S$ determines its *transition graph* $AM_S$. The set of nodes of $AM_S$ consists of all states relative to $\sigma(S)$. The edges of the graph $AM_S$ are specified by the *transition rules* listed in Figure 4. The first rule depends on the module, the last three do not. They have the same form no matter what module we consider. Hence, we omit the reference to the module from its notation.

$$Propagate_S: \quad M \longrightarrow Ml \text{ if } \begin{cases} [M] \text{ is consistent, } l \notin [M], \text{ and} \\ \text{for some } M' \subseteq [M], (M', l) \text{ is an inference of } S \end{cases}$$

$$Fail: \quad M \longrightarrow \perp \text{ if } [M] \text{ is inconsistent and } M \text{ contains no decision literals}$$

$$Backtrack: \quad P\, l^\Delta\, Q \longrightarrow P\, \bar{l} \text{ if } \begin{cases} [P\, l^\Delta\, Q] \text{ is inconsistent, and} \\ Q \text{ contains no decision literals} \end{cases}$$

$$Decide: \quad M \longrightarrow M\, l^\Delta \text{ if } [M] \text{ is consistent and } l \text{ is unassigned by } [M]$$

**Fig. 4.** The transition rules of the graph $AM_S$

The graph $AM_S$ can be used to decide whether a module $S$ has a model. The following properties are essential.

**Theorem 1.** *For every module $S$,*

*(a) graph $AM_S$ is finite and acyclic,*
*(b) for any terminal state $M$ of $AM_S$ other than $\perp$, $[M]^+$ is a model of $S$,*
*(c) state $\perp$ is reachable from $\emptyset$ in $AM_S$ if and only if $S$ is unsatisfiable (has no models).*

Thus, to decide whether a module $S$ has a model it is enough to find in the graph $\text{AM}_S$ a path leading from node $\emptyset$ to a terminal node $M$. If $M = \bot$, $S$ is unsatisfiable. Otherwise, $[M]^+$ is a model of $S$. For instance, let $S$ be a module in Figure 2. Below we show a path in the transition graph $\text{AM}_S$ with every edge annotated by the corresponding transition rule:

$$\emptyset \quad \overset{Decide}{\longrightarrow} \quad b^\Delta \quad \overset{Propagate_S}{\longrightarrow} \quad b^\Delta \, \neg a. \tag{5}$$

The state $b^\Delta \, \neg a$ is terminal. Thus, Theorem 1(b) asserts that $\{b\}$ is a model of $S$. There may be several paths determining the same model. For instance, the path

$$\emptyset \quad \overset{Decide}{\longrightarrow} \quad \neg a^\Delta \quad \overset{Decide}{\longrightarrow} \quad \neg a^\Delta \, b^\Delta. \tag{6}$$

leads to the terminal node $\neg a^\Delta \, b^\Delta$, which is different from $b^\Delta \, \neg a$ but corresponds to the same model.

We can view a path in the graph $\text{AM}_S$ starting in $\emptyset$ and ending in a terminal node as a description of a specific way to search for a model of module $S$. Each such path is determined by a function (strategy) selecting for each non-terminal state exactly one of its outgoing edges (exactly one applicable transition). Therefore, solvers based on the transition graph $\text{AM}_S$ are uniquely determined by the "select-edge-to-follow" function. Such a function can be based, in particular, on assigning strict priorities to inferences in $S$. Below we describe an algorithm that captures "classical" DPLL strategy. Assuming $M$ is the current state and it is not terminal, the algorithm proceeds as follows :

> if $M$ is inconsistent and has no decision literals, follow the *Fail* edge (this is the only applicable transition); if $M$ is inconsistent and has decision literals, follow the *Backtrack* edge (this is the only applicable transition); if $M$ is consistent and *Propagate*$_S$ applies, follow the edge implied by the highest priority inference of the form $(M', l)$ in $S$ such that $M' \subseteq [M]$; otherwise, follow the *Decide* edge.

This is still not a complete specification of a solver, as it offers no specification on how to select a decision literal (which of many possible *Decide* transitions to apply). Much of research on SAT solvers design, for example, has focused on this particular aspect and several heuristics were proposed over the years. Each such heuristics for selecting a decision literal when the *Decide* transition applies yields an algorithm.

Additional algorithms can be obtained by switching the preference over *Propagate* and *Decide* rules. Earlier, we selected a *Propagate* edge and only if impossible, we would select a *Decide* edge. But that order can be reversed resulting in another class of algorithms. Finally, we could even consider a more complicated selection functions that, when both *Decide* and *Propagate* edges are available, in some cases select a *Propagate* edge and in others a *Decide* one.

We now show how the approaches proposed by Nieuwenhuis et al. [20] and Lierler [12] to describe and analyze SAT and ASP solvers, respectively, fit in our abstract framework. Let $F$ be a CNF formula that contains no empty clause. Nieuwenhuis et al. [20], defined the transition graph DP$_F$ to capture the computation of the DPLL algorithm. We now review this graph in the form convenient for our purposes. All states over the vocabulary of $F$ form the vertices of $\text{DP}_F$. The edges of $\text{DP}_F$ are specified by the three "generic" transition rules *Fail*, *Backtrack* and *Decide* of the graph $\text{AM}_S$, and the *Unit Propagate* rule below:

$$Unit\ Propagate_F : \quad M \longrightarrow Ml \ if \ \begin{cases} [M] \text{ is consistent}, l \notin [M], \text{ and} \\ \text{there is } C \vee l \in F, \text{ such that} \\ \text{for every } u \in C, \overline{u} \in [M] \end{cases}$$

For example, let $F$ be the theory consisting of a single clause $a$. Figure 5 presents $\text{DP}_F$.

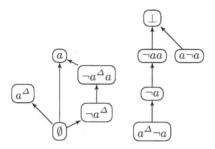

**Fig. 5.** The $\text{DP}_F$ graph where $F = a$

It turns out that we can see the graph $\text{DP}_F$ as the transition graph of the abstract module $UP(F)$.

**Proposition 6.** *For every CNF formula $F$ with no empty clause,* $\text{DP}_F = \text{AM}_{UP(F)}$.

Theorem 1, Proposition 6, and the fact that a CNF formula $F$ and the module $UP(F)$ are equivalent (Proposition 4) imply the following result.

**Corollary 1.** *For any CNF formula $F$,*

*(a) graph $\text{DP}_F$ is finite and acyclic,*
*(b) for any terminal state $M$ of $\text{DP}_F$ other than $\bot$, $[M]^+$ is a model of $F$,*
*(c) state $\bot$ is reachable from $\emptyset$ in $\text{DP}_F$ if and only if $F$ is unsatisfiable (has no models).*

This is precisely the result stated by Nieuwenhuis et al. [20] and used to argue that the graph $\text{DP}_F$ is an abstraction of the DPLL method. To decide the satisfiability of $F$ (and to find a model, if one exists), it is enough to find a path leading from the state $\emptyset$ to a terminal state $M$. If $M = \bot$ then $F$ is unsatisfiable; otherwise, $[M]^+$ is a model of $F$. For instance, the only terminal states reachable from the state $\emptyset$ in $\text{DP}_F$ are $a$ and $a^\Delta$. This translates into the fact that $\{a\}$ is a model of $F$. Specific algorithm encapsulated by the graph $\text{DP}_F$ (equivalently, $\text{AM}_{UP(F)}$) can be obtained by deciding on a way to select an edge while in a consistent state. Typical implementations of basic backtracking SAT solvers follow a *Unit Propagate$_F$* edge whenever possible, choosing *Decide* edges only if nothing else applies. These algorithms differ from each other in the heuristics they use for the selection of a decision literal.

Next, we show that our abstract approach to model generation in logics applies to answer-set programming [8,16,18]. Lierler [12] introduced a transition system $\text{SM}_\Pi$ to describe and study the SMODELS solver. We first review the graph $\mathrm{SM}_\Pi$ and then show that Lierler's approach can be viewed as an instantiation of our general theory.

The set of nodes of the graph $\mathrm{SM}_\Pi$ consists of all states relative to the vocabulary of program $\Pi$. The edges of $\mathrm{SM}_\Pi$ are specified by the transition rules of the graph $\mathrm{DP}_{\Pi^{cl}}$ and the rules presented in Figure 6.

$Unfounded_\Pi:$     $M \longrightarrow M\neg a$ if $[M]$ is consistent, $\neg a \notin [M]$, and $a \in U([M], \Pi)$

$All\ Rule\ Cancelled:$     $M \longrightarrow M\neg a$ if $\begin{cases} [M] \text{ is consistent, } \neg a \notin [M], \text{ and} \\ \text{for every } B \in Bodies(\Pi, a), \\ \text{there is } u \in s(B) \text{ such that } \overline{u} \in [M] \end{cases}$

$Backchain\ True:$     $M \longrightarrow Ml$ if $\begin{cases} [M] \text{ is consistent, } l \notin [M] \\ \text{for some } a \leftarrow B \in \Pi, a \in [M], l \in s(B), \text{ and} \\ \text{for every } B' \in Bodies(\Pi, a) \setminus \{B\}, \\ \text{there is } u \in s(B') \text{ such that } \overline{u} \in [M] \end{cases}$

Fig. 6. Transition rules of the graph $\mathrm{SM}_\Pi$

The following result shows that Lierler's approach can be viewed as an instantiation of our general theory.

**Proposition 7.** *For every logic program* $\Pi$, $\mathrm{SM}_\Pi = \mathrm{AM}_{smodels(\Pi)}$.

Indeed, this proposition, Theorem 1 and the fact that $\Pi$ is equivalent to the module $smodels(\Pi)$ (Proposition 5) imply the result stemming from Lierler [12].

**Corollary 2.** *For every logic program* $\Pi$,

(a) *graph* $\mathrm{SM}_\Pi$ ($\mathrm{AM}_{smodels(\Pi)}$) *is finite and acyclic,*
(b) *for any terminal state* $M$ *of* $\mathrm{SM}_\Pi$ ($\mathrm{AM}_{smodels(\Pi)}$) *other than* $\bot$, $M^+$ *is an answer set of* $\Pi$,
(c) *state* $\bot$ *is reachable from* $\emptyset$ *in* $\mathrm{SM}_\Pi$ ($\mathrm{AM}_{smodels(\Pi)}$) *if and only if* $\Pi$ *has no answer sets.*

Since $UPUF(\Pi)$ is also equivalent to $\Pi$, we obtain a similar corollary for the transition graph $\mathrm{AM}_{UPUF(\Pi)}$. Intuitively, this graph is characterized by the transition rules of the graph $\mathrm{DP}_{\Pi^{cl}}$ as well as the rule *Unfounded* presented in Figure 6. Thus, $\mathrm{AM}_{UPUF(\Pi)}$ is a model of another correct algorithm for finding answer sets of programs. In fact, it is so for any module $S$ such that $UPUF(\Pi) \subseteq S \subseteq smodels(\Pi)$.

Also the graph $\mathrm{SM}_\Pi$ describes a whole family of backtracking search algorithms for finding answer sets of programs. They differ from each other by the way we select an edge while in a consistent state. The selection function could be based on priorities of the propagation rules.

Our discussion of SAT and ASP solvers shows that the framework of modules uniformly encompasses different logics. Furthermore, it uniformly models diverse reasoning mechanisms (the logical entailment, reasoning under specific inference rules). Our results also show that transition graphs proposed earlier to represent and analyze SAT and ASP solvers are special cases of transition graphs for abstract inference modules.

## 4 Abstract Modular System and Solver AMS$_{\mathcal{A}}$

By capturing diverse logics in a single framework, abstract modules are well suited for studying modularity in declarative formalisms and for analyzing solvers for such modular formalisms. As illustrated by our examples, abstract inference modules can capture reasoning of various logics including classical reasoning with propositional theories and reasoning with programs under the answer-set semantics. Putting modules together provides an abstract uniform way to represent hybrid modular systems, in which modules represent theories from different logics.

We now define an abstract modular declarative framework that uses the concept of a module as its basic element. We then show how abstract transition graphs for modules generalize to the new formalism.

**Definition 2.** *An* abstract modular inference system *(AMS) is a finite set of abstract inference modules. The vocabulary of an AMS $\mathcal{A}$ is the union of the vocabularies of modules of $\mathcal{A}$ (they do not have to have the same vocabulary); we denote it by $\sigma(\mathcal{A})$. A set $X \subseteq \sigma$ is a* model *of $\mathcal{A}$, if $X$ is a model of every module $S \in \mathcal{A}$.*

Let $S_1$ be a module presented in Figure 1(b) and $S_2$ be a module in Figure 2. The vocabulary of the AMS $\mathcal{A} = \{S_1, S_2\}$ consists of the atoms $a$ and $b$. It is easy to see that the set $\{a\}$ is the only model of $\mathcal{A}$ contained in $\sigma(\mathcal{A})$ (more generally, a set $X$ is a model of $\mathcal{A}$ if and only if $X$ contains $a$). In Section 2, we observed that $S_1 = Ent(T)$ (and also $= UP(T)$), for a propositional theory $T$, and that $S_2 = smodels(\Pi)$, where $\Pi$ is the program given by (4). This illustrates how abstract modular systems can serve as an abstraction for heterogeneous multi-logic systems.

For a general example of a modular declarative formalism that can be cast as an abstract modular system we now discuss the case of modular logic programs [15]. The semantics of modular logic programs relies on the notion of an input answer set of a program [14]. A set $X$ of atoms is an *input answer set* of a logic program $\Pi$ if $X$ is an answer set of the program $\Pi \cup (X \setminus Head(\Pi))$, where $Head(\Pi)$ denotes the set of all head atoms of $\Pi$. Informally, input answer sets treat all atoms *not occurring* in the heads of program rules as *open* so that they can assume any logical value. These atoms are viewed as the "input." To capture the semantics of input answer sets in terms of inferences, we introduce a modified version of the propagation rule *Unfounded*:

*Unfounded'*: derive $l$ if $l = \neg a$, $a \in U(M, \Pi)$ and $a \in Head(\Pi)$.

This rule gives rise to an inference module $UF'(\Pi)$ defined by taking the condition of the rule as defining when $(M, l)$ is to be an inference of the module. With the module $UF'(\Pi)$ in hand, we define $UPUF'(\Pi) = UP(\Pi) \cup UF'(\Pi)$.

An inference module $S$ is *input-equivalent* to a logic program $\Pi$ if input answer sets of $\Pi$ coincide with models of $S$. We now restate Proposition 5 for the case of input-equivalence.

**Proposition 8.** *Every program $\Pi$ is input-equivalent to the module $UPUF'(\Pi)$.*

A *modular (logic) program* is a set of logic programs [15]. For a modular program $\mathcal{P}$, a set $X$ of atoms is an *answer set* of $\mathcal{P}$ if $X$ is an input answer set of every program $\Pi$ in $\mathcal{P}$. An AMS $\mathcal{A}$ is *equivalent* to a modular program $\mathcal{P}$ if answer sets of $\mathcal{P}$ coincide with models of $\mathcal{A}$.

**Proposition 9.** *Every modular program* $\{\Pi_1, \dots, \Pi_n\}$ *is equivalent to the abstract modular system* $\{UPUF'(\Pi_1), \dots, UPUF'(\Pi_n)\}$.

Theories in the logics SM(ASP) [15] and PC(ID) [17] can be cast as abstract modular systems in the same manner.

We now resume our study of general properties of abstract modular systems. For an AMS $\mathcal{A} = \{S_1, \dots, S_n\}$, we define $\mathcal{A}^\cup = S_1 \cup \dots \cup S_n$. We can now state the result showing that modular systems can be expressed in terms of a single abstract inference module.

**Theorem 2.** *Every abstract modular inference system* $\mathcal{A}$ *is equivalent to the abstract inference module* $\mathcal{A}^\cup$.

Each AMS $\mathcal{A}$ determines its *transition graph* AMS$_\mathcal{A}$, which we define by setting AMS$_\mathcal{A}$ = AM$_{\mathcal{A}^\cup}$. Theorem 1 implies the following result.

**Theorem 3.** *For every AMS* $\mathcal{A}$,

*(a) the graph* AMS$_\mathcal{A}$ *is finite and acyclic,*
*(b) any terminal state* $M$ *of* AMS$_\mathcal{A}$ *other than* $\perp [M]^+$ *is a model of* $\mathcal{A}$,
*(c) the state* $\perp$ *is reachable from* $\emptyset$ *in* AMS$_\mathcal{A}$ *if and only if* $\mathcal{A}$ *is unsatisfiable.*

As in other cases, Theorem 3 shows that the graph AMS$_\mathcal{A}$ is an abstract representation of an algorithm to decide satisfiability of a modular system $\mathcal{A}$. Such algorithm searches in AMS$_\mathcal{A}$ for a path leading from node $\emptyset$ to a terminal node by moving from a node to node, selecting any edge originating in the current node. Theorem 3 guarantees that the method terminates, the other two parts of that component ensure correctness.

For instance, let $\mathcal{A}$ be the AMS $\{S_1, S_2\}$ where $S_1$ is a module in Figure 1(b) and $S_2$ is a module in Figure 2. Below is a valid path in the transition graph AMS$_\mathcal{A}$ with every edge annotated by the corresponding transition rule:

$$\emptyset \xrightarrow{Decide} \neg a^\Delta \xrightarrow{Propagate\, S_2} \neg a^\Delta\, b \xrightarrow{Propagate\, S_1} \neg a^\Delta\, b\, a \xrightarrow{Backtrack} a \xrightarrow{Decide} a\, \neg b^\Delta.$$

The state $a\, \neg b^\Delta$ is terminal. Thus, Theorem 3 (b) asserts that $\{a, \neg b\}$ is a model of $\mathcal{A}$. Let us interpret this example. Earlier we demonstrated that module $S_1$ can be regarded as a representation of a propositional theory consisting of a single clause $a$ whereas $S_2$ corresponds to the logic program (4) under the semantics of answer sets. We then illustrated how modules $S_1$ and $S_2$ give rise to particular algorithms for implementing search procedures. The graph AMS$_\mathcal{A}$ represents the algorithm obtained by *integrating* the algorithms supported by the modules $S_1$ and $S_2$ separately.

We will now discuss some classes of algorithms captured by the graph AMS$_\mathcal{A}$. As before, they are more specifically determined by a strategy of selecting an outgoing edge from the current state. Let us assume that such a strategy is available for each module $S \in \mathcal{A}$. Let us also assume that the modules in $\mathcal{A}$ are prioritized. This leads to an algorithm that proceeds as follows (assuming $M$ is the current state and it is not terminal):

> if $M$ is inconsistent, we always select the *Fail* or *Backtrack* edge (whichever is applicable); if $M$ is consistent then we select an edge determined by the highest priority inference from the highest priority module.

Assuming that modules in $\mathcal{A}$ are enumerated $S_1, \ldots, S_k$ from the highest priority one to the lowest, the described algorithm works as follows. It starts by moving along edges implied by inferences of the module $S_1$ (according to the selection strategy for that module). If we reach $\perp$, the entire search is over with failure. Otherwise, we reach a consistent state, in which no inference from module $S_1$ is applicable (that state represents a model of $S_1$). The phase of search involving module $S_1$ gets suspended and we continue in the same way but now following edges determined by inferences in module $S_2$. In other words, we start the phase of the search involving module $S_2$. If we reach $\perp$, the search is over with failure. If we reach an inconsistent state that contains decision literals, we apply the *Backtrack* rule. If that rule backtracks to a literal introduced after we moved to module $S_2$, we remain in the module $S_2$ phase and continue. If the backtrack takes us back to a literal introduced while a higher priority module was considered (in this case, that must be module $S_1$), we resume the module $S_1$ phase of the search suspended earlier. If *Propagate* or *Decide* edges in module $S_2$ are available, we select one of them following the strategy for module $S_2$. If we reach a consistent state with no outgoing edges implied by inferences of $S_2$ (that state represents a model of both $S_1$ and $S_2$) we suspend the module $S_2$ phase and start the module $S_3$ phase, and continue in that way until a terminal state is reached.

The main advantage of such an algorithm is that each phase is concerned only with inferences coming from a single module and state changes involve only literals from the vocabulary of that module. The literals established during phases involving higher priority modules remain fixed. Thus, the search space in each phase is effectively limited to that of the module involved in that phase.

Clearly, other specializations of the graph $\text{AMS}_\mathcal{A}$ are possible. For instance, we may alternate between modules in a more arbitrary way, possibly switching from the current module to another even in situations when the current state has outgoing edges implied by the inferences of the current module. However, such algorithms may have to work with search spaces that are larger than the search space for a single module.

**DLVHEX:** Our results apply to a version of the DLVHEX[3] solver [5] restricted to logic programs. DLVHEX computes models of *HEX-programs* by exploiting their modularity, that is, representing programs as an equivalent modular program. Answer set programs consisting of rules of the form (2) form a special class of HEX-programs. Therefore, DLVHEX restricted to such programs can be seen as an answer-set solver that exploits their modularity. Given a program $\Pi$, DLVHEX starts its operation by constructing a modular program $\mathcal{P} = \{\Pi_1, \ldots, \Pi_n\}$ so that (i) $\Pi = \Pi_1 \cup \cdots \cup \Pi_n$ and (ii) answer sets of $\mathcal{P}$ coincide with answer sets of $\Pi$. It then processes modules one after another according to an order determined by the structure of a program. That process can be modeled in abstract terms described above. In particular, the graph $\text{AMS}_{\{UPUF'(\Pi_1), \ldots, UPUF'(\Pi_n)\}}$ can be seen as an abstraction capturing the family of DLVHEX-like algorithms based on *Unit Propagate* and *Unfounded'* inferences.

---

[3] http://www.kr.tuwien.ac.at/research/systems/dlvhex/

## 5   Related Work and Conclusions

In an important development, Brewka and Eiter [3] introduced an abstract notion of a *heterogeneous nonmonotonic multi-context system* (MCS). One of the key aspects of that proposal is its abstract representation of a logic that allows one to study MCSs without regard to syntactic details. The independence of contexts from syntax promoted focus on semantic aspect of modularity in multi-context systems. Since their inception, multi-context systems have received substantial attention and inspired implementations of hybrid reasoning systems including DLVHEX [5] and DMCS [1]. There are some similarities between AMSs and MCSs. However, there is also a key difference. MCSs provide an abstract framework to define semantics of hybrid systems. In contrast, AMSs explicitly represent inferences of a logic and provide an abstract framework for studying model-generation algorithms. On a more technical level, another notable difference concerns information sharing among modules. MCSs use to this end the so-called "bridge rules." In AMS information sharing is implemented by a simple notion of sharing parts of the vocabulary between the modules.

Modularity is one of the key techniques in principled software development. This has been a major trigger inspiring research on modularity in declarative programming paradigms rooting in KR languages such as answer-set programming, for instance. Oikarinen and Janhunen [21] proposed a modular version of answer-set programs called lp-modules. In that work, the authors were primarily concerned with the decomposition of lp-modules into sets of simpler ones. They proved that under some assumptions such decompositions are possible. Järvisalo, Oikarinen, Janhunen, and Niemelä [11], and Tasharrofi and Ternovska [23] studied the generalizations of lp-modules. In their work the main focus was to abstract lp-modules formalism away from any particular syntax or semantics. They then study properties of the modules such as "joinability" and analyze *different ways* to join modules together and the semantics of such a join. We are interested in building simple modular systems using abstract modules – the only composition mechanism that we study is based on conjunction of modules. Also in contrast to the work by Järvisalo et al. [11] and Tasharrofi and Ternovska [23], we define such conjunction for any modules disregarding their internal structure and interdependencies between each other.

Tasharrofi, Wu, and Ternovska [24] developed and studied an algorithm for processing modular model expansion tasks in the abstract multi-logic system concept developed by Tasharrofi and Ternovska [23]. They use the traditional pseudocode method to present the developed algorithm. In this work we adapt the graph-based framework for designing backtrack search algorithms for abstract modular systems. The benefits of that approach for modeling families of backtrack search procedures employed in SAT, ASP, and PC(ID) solvers were demonstrated by Nieuwenhuis et al. [20], Lierler [12], and Lierler and Truszczynski [14]. Our work provides additional support for the generality and flexibility of the graph-based framework as a finer abstraction of backtrack search algorithms than direct pseudocode representations, allowing for convenient means to prove correctness and study relationships between the families of the algorithms.

Gebser and Schaub [7] describe a form of a tableaux system to describe inferences involved in computing answer sets. Several rules used in their approach are closely related to those we discussed in the context of modules designed to represent reasoning on logic programs. However, the two approaches are formally different. Most notably, the concepts of states in a tableaux and in an abstract module are different. Still, there seems to be a connection between them, which we plan to investigate in our future work.

We introduced abstract modules and abstract modular systems and showed that they provide a framework capable of capturing diverse logics and inference mechanisms integrated into modular knowledge representation systems. In particular, we showed that transition graphs determined by modules and modular systems provide a unifying representation of model-generating algorithms, or solvers, and simplify reasoning about such issues as correctness or termination. We believe they can be useful in theoretical comparisons of solver effectiveness and in the development of new solvers.

# References

1. Bairakdar, S.E.-D., Dao-Tran, M., Eiter, T., Fink, M., Krennwallner, T.: The DMCS solver for distributed nonmonotonic multi-context systems. In: Janhunen, T., Niemelä, I. (eds.) JELIA 2010. LNCS, vol. 6341, pp. 352–355. Springer, Heidelberg (2010)
2. Barrett, C., Sebastiani, R., Seshia, S., Tinelli, C.: Satisfiability modulo theories. In: Biere, A., Heule, M., van Maaren, H., Walsch, T. (eds.) Handbook of Satisfiability, pp. 737–797. IOS Press (2008)
3. Brewka, G., Eiter, T.: Equilibria in heterogeneous nonmonotonic multi-context systems. In: Proceedings of National Conference on Artificial Intelligence (AAAI), pp. 385–390 (2007)
4. Denecker, M., Lierler, Y., Truszczynski, M., Vennekens, J.: A Tarskian informal semantics for answer set programming. In: Dovier, A., Costa, V.S. (eds.) International Conference on Logic Programming (ICLP). LIPIcs, vol. 17. Schloss Dagstuhl - Leibniz-Zentrum fuer Informatik (2012)
5. Eiter, T., Ianni, G., Schindlauer, R., Tompits, H.: A uniform integration of higher-order reasoning and external evaluations in answer set programming. In: Proceedings of International Joint Conference on Artificial Intelligence (IJCAI), pp. 90–96. Professional Book Center (2005)
6. Gebser, M., Kaufmann, B., Neumann, A., Schaub, T.: Conflict-driven answer set solving. In: Proceedings of 20th International Joint Conference on Artificial Intelligence (IJCAI 2007), pp. 386–392. MIT Press, Cambridge (2007)
7. Gebser, M., Schaub, T.: Tableau calculi for answer set programming. In: Etalle, S., Truszczyński, M. (eds.) ICLP 2006. LNCS, vol. 4079, pp. 11–25. Springer, Heidelberg (2006)
8. Gelfond, M., Lifschitz, V.: The stable model semantics for logic programming. In: Kowalski, R., Bowen, K. (eds.) Proceedings of International Logic Programming Conference and Symposium, pp. 1070–1080. MIT Press (1988)
9. Giunchiglia, E., Lierler, Y., Maratea, M.: Answer set programming based on propositional satisfiability. Journal of Automated Reasoning 36, 345–377 (2006)
10. Jaffar, J., Maher, M.: Constraint logic programming: A survey. Journal of Logic Programming 19(20), 503–581 (1994)
11. Järvisalo, M., Oikarinen, E., Janhunen, T., Niemelä, I.: A module-based framework for multi-language constraint modeling. In: Erdem, E., Lin, F., Schaub, T. (eds.) LPNMR 2009. LNCS, vol. 5753, pp. 155–168. Springer, Heidelberg (2009),
http://dx.doi.org/10.1007/978-3-642-04238-6_15

12. Lierler, Y.: Abstract answer set solvers with backjumping and learning. Theory and Practice of Logic Programming 11, 135–169 (2011)
13. Lierler, Y.: On the relation of constraint answer set programming languages and algorithms. In: Proceedings of the AAAI Conference on Artificial Intelligence. MIT Press (2012)
14. Lierler, Y., Truszczynski, M.: Transition systems for model generators — a unifying approach. In: Theory and Practice of Logic Programming, 27th Int'l. Conference on Logic Programming (ICLP 2011), Special Issue 11(4-5) (2011)
15. Lierler, Y., Truszczynski, M.: Modular answer set solving. In: Proceedings of Twenty-Seventh AAAI Conference on Artificial Intelligence (AAAI 2013) (2013)
16. Marek, V., Truszczyński, M.: Stable models and an alternative logic programming paradigm. In: The Logic Programming Paradigm: a 25-Year Perspective, pp. 375–398. Springer (1999)
17. Mariën, M., Wittocx, J., Denecker, M., Bruynooghe, M.: SAT(ID): Satisfiability of propositional logic extended with inductive definitions. In: Kleine Büning, H., Zhao, X. (eds.) SAT 2008. LNCS, vol. 4996, pp. 211–224. Springer, Heidelberg (2008)
18. Niemelä, I.: Logic programs with stable model semantics as a constraint programming paradigm. Annals of Mathematics and Artificial Intelligence 25, 241–273 (1999)
19. Niemelä, I., Simons, P.: Extending the Smodels system with cardinality and weight constraints. In: Minker, J. (ed.) Logic-Based Artificial Intelligence, pp. 491–521. Kluwer (2000)
20. Nieuwenhuis, R., Oliveras, A., Tinelli, C.: Solving SAT and SAT modulo theories: From an abstract Davis-Putnam-Logemann-Loveland procedure to DPLL(T). Journal of the ACM 53(6), 937–977 (2006)
21. Oikarinen, E., Janhunen, T.: Modular equivalence for normal logic programs. In: 17th European Conference on Artificial Intelligence (ECAI), pp. 412–416 (2006)
22. Rossi, F., van Beek, P., Walsh, T.: Constraint programming. In: van Harmelen, F., Lifschitz, V., Porter, B. (eds.) Handbook of Knowledge Representation, pp. 181–212. Elsevier (2008)
23. Tasharrofi, S., Ternovska, E.: A semantic account for modularity in multi-language modelling of search problems. In: Tinelli, C., Sofronie-Stokkermans, V. (eds.) FroCoS 2011. LNCS, vol. 6989, pp. 259–274. Springer, Heidelberg (2011)
24. Tasharrofi, S., Wu, X.N., Ternovska, E.: Solving modular model expansion tasks. CoRR abs/1109.0583 (2011)
25. Van Gelder, A., Ross, K., Schlipf, J.: The well-founded semantics for general logic programs. Journal of ACM 38(3), 620–650 (1991)

# Sunroof: A Monadic DSL for Generating JavaScript

Jan Bracker[1] and Andy Gill[2]

[1] Institut für Informatik
Christian-Albrechts-Universität, Kiel, Germany
[2] ITTC / EECS
The University of Kansas, Lawrence, KS 66045

**Abstract.** Sunroof is a Haskell-hosted Domain Specific Language (DSL) for generating JavaScript. The central feature of Sunroof is a JavaScript monad, which, like the Haskell IO-monad, allows access to external resources, but specifically JavaScript resources. As such, Sunroof is primarily a feature-rich foreign-function API to the browser's JavaScript engine, and all the browser-specific functionality, including HTML-based rendering, event handling, and drawing to the HTML5 canvas element.

In this paper, we give the design and implementation of Sunroof. Using monadic reification, we generate JavaScript from a deep embedding of the JavaScript monad. The Sunroof DSL has the feel of native Haskell, with a simple Haskell-based type schema to guide the Sunroof programmer. Furthermore, because we are generating code, we can offer Haskell-style concurrency patterns, such as MVars and Channels. In combination with a web-services package, the Sunroof DSL offers a robust platform to build interactive web applications.

**Keywords:** DSLs, JavaScript, Web Technologies, Cloud Computing.

## 1 Introduction

There are many reasons to want to program in a functional language: efficiency of development, formal and informal reasoning, and high-level control- and concurrency-structures, such as monads [27]. However, mainstream languages often have better environmental support than what is provided by functional language compilers, for example the Objective C and the iOS ecosystem, or JavaScript and HTML5 web browsers. This paper examines the challenges of providing an intentionally blurred interface between Haskell and JavaScript, to support the development of web-based applications.

JavaScript is an imperative language with access to a wide range of established and useful services like graphical canvases and event handling of browser events. We want to express JavaScript in Haskell, adding use of Haskell's static typing, and gaining access to JavaScript services in the browser directly from Haskell.

M. Flatt and H.-F. Guo (Eds.): PADL 2014, LNCS 8324, pp. 65–80, 2014.

One way of providing access to non-native services, such as the HTML5 canvas, is to provide, in Haskell, foreign function "hooks" to key JavaScript functionality, and compile Haskell to JavaScript by rewriting the compiler backend. Haskell already provides many similar hooks into the C RTS, so why not into JavaScript? There are already a number of systems attempting this [36,29]. If executed well, this would be ideal, but there are engineering shortcomings: many standard libraries and Hackage packages are not supported directly, the generated code is not as efficiently executed as native Haskell, and the runtime system is often incomplete. These compilers will continue to improve, and with initiatives like asm.js [1] and Emscripten [40], the efficiency gap will close.

Rather than rewrite the compiler and runtime system, an alternative approach is to keep the existing runtime system, and provide the same foreign function "hooks" to key JavaScript functionality, but instead the executed Haskell becomes a server that JavaScript, and the browser, interact with. Unfortunately, every JavaScript call becomes an expensive proposition: a Remote Procedure Call (RPC) to a browser. Though some straight-line calls can be batched together — our own `blank-canvas` Hackage package [19] was built on this idea — the granularity of interaction through JavaScript calls is just too fine for this idea to scale well.

Another approach, and the one we investigate, is to use a deeply embedded Domain Specific Language (DSL), and the recently discovered monad reification technique [30,16,34,37]. A Haskell-hosted deeply embedded DSL is where Haskell combinators are used to build syntactical forms in the target language, in this case JavaScript. Historically, these embeddings have worked well for dataflow, for example generating combinatorial hardware, but had serious challenges with capturing binding and control flow. Monad reification, where a monadic computation is representable in the deep embedding, partially mitigates this shortcoming, allowing statements and effectful bindings to be expressed directly.

Sunroof is an exercise in scaling up the use of monad reification, and other domain-specific language techniques, to a full-scale JavaScript DSL. With Sunroof bindings being regular Haskell monadic bindings, the language fits with what would be expected from a monadic API. In a previous paper, we showed, using a prototype, that reification of a JavaScript-like language is possible [16]. In this paper, we expand on this observation, and show that monadic-reification is useful in practice.

Building on this DSL, we also investigate providing JavaScript control flow and function abstraction mechanisms to the Haskell programmer interested in using the browser API. Though for technical reasons we cannot directly compile pattern matching and let-binding to JavaScript without committing to a full Haskell to JavaScript compiler, both control flow and function abstraction can be provided with a small syntactical overhead, and reifiable fix-points can be provided with a modest syntactical overhead. With these capabilities, a programmer can start programming using the JavaScript API directly, and refine their program to migrate more and more computation from the server into the browser.

## 2   Calling JavaScript from Haskell

From a programmers' point of view, calling JavaScript functions appears straight-forward. We as a community know how to reflect an API into Haskell, using the IO monad. Furthermore, objects in the target API become handles in Haskell.

As a first example, consider this simplified example of Sunroof code, and corresponding JavaScript.

```
-- Haskell                          // JavaScript
ioCode :: IO ()
ioCode = send jsCode

jsCode :: JS ()
jsCode = do                         function jsCode() {
    name <- prompt "Name?"              var name = prompt("Name?");
    alert ("Your name: " <> name)       alert("Your name: " + name);
                                    }
```

Here, we use a new monad, the JS monad, our JavaScript analog of the IO monad, and an explicit **send** command that sends the JavaScript to the browser. This reversal of control, where the server sends the client commands, follows the Comet AJAX application model. Comet is a push technology that allows a server to push messages to a client. In our case, the Comet interaction is implemented by *long polling* on behalf of the client. For the above example, this interface bundles the **prompt** and **alert** commands into a single interaction. It is this flavor of interface we want to support in our Sunroof DSL and web server.

To make Sunroof a viable interface to JavaScript, we need to resolve the following issues:

- JavaScript is an object-based, imperative, dynamically typed language. Haskell is a pure, function-based, statically typed language. In Section 3, we introduce expressions and statements in Sunroof, and show how they jointly form an object model, mapping these two worlds together. The Sunroof DSL does not support laziness; the DSL expresses monadic Sunroof code strictly, reflecting the JavaScript target.
- We need to select a concurrency model for Sunroof. Natively, JavaScript only supports non-blockable threads. In Section 4, we give the Sunroof interface for providing both non-blocking and blocking cooperative threads, using the type system to delimit the two concurrency models.
- We choose to provide a way of defining functions in Sunroof such that they are first-class functions in JavaScript. In Section 5, we show how we support both functions and continuations.
- We need to provide a foreign function interface, to allow us to call specific JavaScript-native functions, such as **prompt** and **alert**. In Section 6 we present this interface.
- Critically, we need to be able to compile our Sunroof DSL into JavaScript. We examine this in Section 7.

**Table 1.** Sunroof types and their Haskell analogs

| Constraint | Haskell Type $\tau_\uparrow$ | Sunroof Type $\tau$ | js |
|---|---|---|---|
| | () | () | ✓ |
| | Bool | JSBool | ✓ |
| | Double | JSNumber | ✓ |
| | String | JSString | ✓ |
| Sunroof $\alpha$ | $[\alpha_\uparrow]$ | JSArray $\alpha$ | |
| SunroofKey $\alpha$<br>Sunroof $\beta$ | Map $\alpha_\uparrow$ $\beta_\uparrow$ | JSMap $\alpha$ $\beta$ | |
| SunroofArgument $\alpha$<br>Sunroof $\beta$ | $\alpha_\uparrow \rightarrow$ JS$_A$ $\beta_\uparrow$ | JSFunction $\alpha$ $\beta$ | |
| SunroofArgument $\alpha$ | $\alpha_\uparrow \rightarrow$ JS$_B$ $\beta$ | JSContinuation $\alpha$ | |
| SunroofArgument $\alpha$ | MVar $\alpha_\uparrow$ | JSMVar $\alpha$ | |
| SunroofArgument $\alpha$ | Chan $\alpha_\uparrow$ | JSChan $\alpha$ | |

- To enable the compiled code to dynamically interact with a web browser, we provide an expansion of the **send** idea above, which we discuss in Section 8.

We close with related work and our conclusions. The underlying ideas used here are not new, though the use of monadic reification for JavaScript generation is original. What we demonstrate is how far the practical aspects of DSL capture have come, using the full scale example of Haskell to JavaScript translation.

## 3  Sunroof Expressions and Statements

JavaScript makes a distinction between expressions and statements. Sunroof is a typed version of JavaScript, so therefore also makes this distinction, and does so using Haskell types.

### 3.1  Sunroof Expressions

In JavaScript, there are a small number of core types, such as `object`, `array`, and `string`. In our JavaScript object model, there is a reflection of this family of core types, all prefixed with JS. There is support for booleans, strings, numbers, functions, arrays, and other common programming structures. The use of JSNumber, rather than (say) `Double`, explicitly reminds us of the enforced diminished capabilities of being within an embedded language. All of the JS- types are representable in our target language. Table 1 enumerates the major JS- types used in Sunroof. The left-hand column of Table 1 gives constraints, implemented via Haskell type classes.

- All our core types are brought together with the Sunroof class. If a type is an instance of Sunroof, then that type can be realized inside JavaScript. All the JS- types are instances of Sunroof.

- Instances of the `SunroofArgument` class are values that can be passed to JavaScript functions and methods, including tuples of values which are used for representing multi-argument function calls. The asymmetry here is a reflection of the JavaScript asymmetry inherited from C: you can pass multiple arguments to a function, but only get a single thing back.
- Finally, there is a third class, `SunroofKey`, which is a JavaScript version of the Haskell `Show` class, but specifically for generating JavaScript object keys, which are realized as JavaScript strings.

Using our JS-types, we can build expressions using the traditional Haskell expression-building mechanisms. `JSNumber` is overloaded, and thus can be used directly for arithmetic. `JSBool` is an instance of the relevant classes in the Hackage package `boolean`. `boolean` provides the capability to express control-flow in an embedded DSL, as needed by Sunroof. Further, `JSString` is a `Monoid`, which is only possible because JavaScript strings are immutable values, providing a neat and standard string-concatenation operator for Sunroof.

To help the conversion between classical Haskell values and Sunroof values, we provide the overloaded function `js`. The second column of Table 1 shows what types can be converted, using `js`. The full types of `js` is:

```
js :: (SunroofValue a, Sunroof (ValueOf a)) => a -> ValueOf a
```

`SunroofValue` and the type function [8] `ValueOf` represent the mapping given in the table. Putting the expression-building capability together, along with a show function called `toString`, we can write:

```
alert ("n=" <> js (n::Int) <> " m=" <> toString (m::JSNumber))
```

Here, `n` is a Haskell `Int`, and `m` is a Sunroof number, presumably the result of a previous computation. Given that we are bundling expressions to send to a browser for execution, `n` is a static value, and `m` is a dynamic value, unobservable until inside our browser's execution. Finally, `toString` has type:

```
toString :: Sunroof a => a -> JSString
```

One design decision in Sunroof is that we enforce a stronger typing than JavaScript itself would. Specifically, there are restrictions on the type arguments of our container types, like `JSArray`. What can be seen from this is that we enforce a Hindley-Milner style thinking to our containers, which is distinct from JavaScript dynamic typing. Some types involve phantom types to enforce this imposed type safety [23]. Thus, `JSArray` is a restricted type of JavaScript `array`, that, like Haskell, only supports collections of the same type.

From experience with using Sunroof, the mis-match in typing between Haskell and Sunroof/JavaScript is not a large problem in practice. However, sometimes casting between types, which is implicit in JavaScript, is needed. So we provide an explicit dynamic `cast`, for use where the type-systems differ, and both sides of the `cast` are instances of `Sunroof`.

```
cast :: (Sunroof a, Sunroof b) => a -> b
```

## 3.2   Sunroof Statements

The building block of object-oriented programing is calling an object's method. This is almost universally done using the dot (.) operator. JavaScript, our target language, follows this trend, with the method-call syntax being as follows:

```
object.method(a1,a2,a3,...,aN)    // JavaScript method call
```

For our Sunroof object model, we want to follow this as closely as possible.

We, have our method calls use a monad because method calls are (in general) effectful. By convention, we take the object as the *last* argument.

```
// Shape of a Sunroof method
(SunroofArgument args, Sunroof res) => args -> (JSObject -> JS res)
```

A neat way of writing method calls in Haskell is transcribing the JavaScript dot, which is already use for both namespace resolution and function composition in Haskell, with the # combinator [33,35].

```
// Sunroof
(#) :: a -> (a -> JS b) -> JS b
(#) obj act = act obj
```

This gives the following fragment for a Sunroof call to `method` on `object`.

```
object # method (a1,a2,a3,...,aN)
```

In this way, JavaScript can be transliterated into Haskell where needed, native JavaScript call idioms can be used, while other Haskell abstraction mechanisms can be used for the interface that calls Sunroof code.

We piece together our Sunroof method calls using do-notation, Haskell's syntactic support for monads.

```
do r1 <- obj # method1 (a1,a2,a3,...,aN)
   r2 <- obj # method2 ({-... can use r1 ...-})
   ....
```

In this fragment, `r1` is bound to the result of the `method1` call, and can be used as an argument to `method2`.

Sometimes, a JavaScript API requires direct access to object attributes. We do so using a typed `JSSelector`.

```
label :: JSString -> JSSelector a
(!)   :: (Sunroof o, Sunroof a) => o -> JSSelector a -> a
(:=)  :: (Sunroof a, Sunroof o) => JSSelector a -> a -> (o -> JS t ())
```

We can build a selector (`label`), use a selector to access an attribute in a specific object (`!`), or update an attribute in a specific object (`:=`). The update is in our object-normal-form, that is the object is the final argument. Sunroof is, in essence, a strict functional language, with monads for effect. We choose to support direct (non-monadic) reading of attributes, but all updating of objects requires the monad. This is a design decision we may return to in the future. The net effect is that assignments to fields can be neatly expressed.

```
// JavaScript                       // Sunroof
c.fillStyle = "red";                c # fillStyle := "red"
```

Notice that ':=' binds tighter than '#'; the 'fillStyle := "red"' is effectively building and calling a setter method for 'c', on the fly.

# 4   Threading Models

JavaScript uses a callback-centric model of computation. There is no support for concurrency, only a single central loop that executes callbacks, which should be non-blocking, as events occur. In contrast, Haskell has robust concurrency and wide-spread abstractions for synchronization, e.g. MVars and Chans [21]. So the question arises: do we generate non-blocking JavaScript code, and keep the callback centric model, or do we add concurrency support as value-added by our transliteration to JavaScript?

In our earlier work [16], we prototyped both blocking and non-blocking translations, and observed that both choices had poor consequences.

- Existing JavaScript APIs assume atomic, non-blocking semantics. Therefore, if we compile a higher-order function for a callback, it must not block. Further, if this higher-order function returns a result, the function must respect this non-blocking requirement.
- The lure of threads, and the abstractions they allow, is strong. Threaded code is — from experience — cleaner if directly used, rather that being faked in JavaScript itself. There are new libraries in JavaScript that encode some cooperative concurrency abstractions, like promises [2]; Sunroof is a chance to translate using cooperative concurrency directly when generating JavaScript.

In our full-scale implementation of Sunroof, we decided to explicitly support both blocking and non-blocking threads,and use types to denote which threading *strategies* should be used. This means that the programmer can choose which concurrency model fits the given situation.

In terms of user-interface, we parameterize the JS-monad with a phantom type that represents the threading model used, with A for Atomic, and B for Blocking threads. Atomic threads are classical JavaScript computations that cannot be interrupted and actively use the callback mechanism. Blocking threads can support suspending operations and cooperative concurrency abstractions as known from Haskell. By using phantom types, we can express the necessary restrictions on specific combinators, as well as provide combinators to allow both types of threads to cooperate.

The blocking model hides the callback mechanism behind abstractions. This implies that every atomic computation can be converted into a potentially blocking computation. liftJS achieves this.

```
liftJS :: Sunroof a => JS A a -> JS t a
```

When suspending, we register our current continuation as a callback to resume later. This gives other threads (registered continuations) a chance to run. Of course, this model depends on cooperation between the threads, because a non-terminating or suspending thread will keep others from running.

There are two main primitives for the blocking model:

```
forkJS      :: SunroofThread t1 => JS t1 () -> JS t2 ()
threadDelay :: JSNumber -> JS B ()
```

They can both be seen as analogs of their IO counterparts. forkJS resembles forkIO; it registers the given computation as a callback. In forkJS, the SunroofThread constraint allows the DSL compiler to know if this callback should be blocking or non-blocking, based on the type of t1. Both blocking and non-blocking threads can fork new threads, so t2 is unconstrained. threadDelay sets a continuation callback to be called after a certain amount of time. We rely on the JavaScript function window.setTimeout [3] to register our callbacks.

This parameterization of JS allows us to use types to capture the blocking semantics of our primitives. Furthermore, the Haskell type system automatically propagates the thread semantics. In this way, Sunroof can offer concurrency as an additional, first class, abstraction. As an example of what is possible, based on these primitive threading combinators, consider Sunroof's versions of Haskell's Chan, called JSChan. The Sunroof API for JSChan is as follows.

```
newChan    :: (SunroofArgument a) => JS t (JSChan a)
writeChan  :: (SunroofArgument a) => a -> JSChan a -> JS t ()
readChan   :: (SunroofArgument a) => JSChan a -> JS B a
```

Note that the types reflect if a specific operation can block. Both newChan and writeChan can never block, so you can use either threading model, but readChan may block, so uses the B threading model.

## 5   Functions and Continuations

Functions are first-class values in Haskell and JavaScript. Sunroof represents function *values* with the type JSFunction $\alpha$ $\beta$, which corresponds to a function of type $\alpha \rightarrow \beta$ in JavaScript. In Sunroof, we create function objects with the function combinator.

```
function :: (SunroofArgument a, Sunroof b)
         => (a -> JS A b)  -> JS t (JSFunction a b)
```

As a function can have side-effects, its computation and result have to be expressed in the JS-monad. The creation of a function is considered a side-effect, due to observable allocation. To see an example of usage, consider defining a double function.

```
double <- function $ \ (n :: JSNumber) -> return (n + n)
```

Now `double`, which has type `JSFunction JSNumber JSNumber`, can be stored in structures, passed to JavaScript functions, and enjoys all the privileges of first-class JavaScript function objects. `function` acts as a staging combinator, converting a monadic Haskell function into a JavaScript-level function.

Function application of `JSFunction` objects is done through the `apply/$$` combinator; they are synonyms. Functions can only be applied in the JS-monad, since they can have side-effects.

```
apply, ($$) :: (SunroofArgument a, Sunroof b)
            => JSFunction a b -> a -> JS t b
```

Together, `function` and `apply` give a way of getting into and back from the abstract `JSFunction` object.

Sunroof also can express recursive functions, using a version of the fixpoint combinator.

```
fixJS :: (SunroofArgument a) => (a -> JS A a) -> JS t a
```

There is a restriction that the higher-order function be atomic, but the usage of `fixJS` is straightforward, if verbose.

```
fib <- fixJS $ \ (fib :: JSFunction JSNumber JSNumber) ->
       function $ \ (n :: JSNumber) ->
         ifB (n <* 2)
           (return 1)
           (liftM2 (+) (fib $$ (n - 1)) (fib $$ (n - 2)))
```

The 'fib' type is a `JSFunction` object, and we also need to use the JS monad, because JavaScript functions are assumed to be effectful. `<*` is the lifted version of `<`, as provided by the `boolean` package.

Continuations are functions that never return. JavaScript uses them; for example many callbacks are actually continuations. We can express continuation objects (continuations in object form), using the type `JSContinuation` $\alpha$. Technically, `JSContinuation` $\alpha$ are only specializations of functions, but restricted to a specific threading model. Continuations are meant to be a representation of side effects — ongoing computations inside the JS-monad — and might not terminate, so they do not return a value. As with functions, there is a combinator to create and apply a continuation.

```
continuation :: (SunroofArgument a)
             => (a -> JS B ()) -> JS t (JSContinuation a)
goto         :: (SunroofArgument a)
             => JSContinuation a -> a -> JS B ()
```

The presented `goto` should not be considered harmful [11]. It calls a continuation, as `apply` calls functions. The difference is that a call to `goto` will never return, as it executes the given continuation and abandons the current one — the () result is never returned.

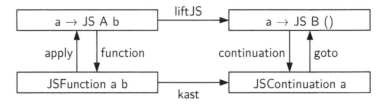

**Fig. 1.** How functions and continuations relate between the Haskell and Sunroof

Access to the current continuation is given through the powerful call-with-current-continuation combinator `callcc`.

```
callcc :: SunroofArgument a
       => (JSContinuation a -> JS B a) -> JS B a
```

Functions and continuations, and their JS-analogs, are connected to each other, as can be seen in Fig. 1. We can go back and forth between the Haskell and the Sunroof representation of a function or continuation. But once a function is specialized to a continuation, it is not possible to go back, because continuations only model the side effect, but do not return anything. `kast` is just a specialized version of `cast`.

## 6    Foreign Function Interface

Sunroof also offers a simple foreign function interface, which enables us to easily access predefined JavaScript. There are four core functions:

```
fun    :: (SunroofArgument a, Sunroof r)
       => String -> JSFunction a r
object :: String -> JSObject
new    :: (SunroofArgument a)
       => String -> a -> JS t JSObject
invoke :: (SunroofArgument a, Sunroof o, Sunroof r)
       => String -> a -> o -> JS t r
```

`fun` is used to create Sunroof functions from their names in JavaScript. This can happen in two ways: either to call a function inline, or to create a real binding for that function. As an example, the `alert` function can be called in line through `fun "alert" $$ "text"`, or you can provide a binding in form of a Haskell function for it.

```
alert :: JSString -> JS t ()
alert s = fun "alert" $$ s
```

Existing objects can be bound through the `object` function, e.g. the `document` object is bound through `object "document"`. Constructors can be called using `new`. To create a new object you would call `new "Object" ()`.

We can call methods of objects through `invoke`. Again, this can be used inline and to create a real binding. An inline use of this to produce `document.getElementById("id")` would look like this:

```
object "document" # invoke "getElementById" "id"
```

To provide a binding to the `getElementById` method, one can write:

```
getElementById :: JSString -> JSObject -> JS t JSObject
getElementById s = invoke "getElementById" s
```

Providing actual bindings ensures that everything is typed correctly and prevents the need to resolve ambiguities through large type annotations inside of code. The current release of Sunroof on Hackage provides bindings for most of the core browser API, the HTML5 canvas element, and some of the JQuery API.

# 7   Compiling Sunroof

Our domain-specific language, embedded in Haskell, is useless unless we can actually compile the DSL to JavaScript. We apply four main techniques. We believe Sunroof is the first time all four have been used simultaneously in a full-scale embedded DSL.

*Expression Reification:* The first technique we use is capturing Sunroof expressions as expression trees. This is a classical use of a deeply-embedded language. Every expression/JS-type is a Haskell `newtype` wrapper around an expression syntax tree. This internal expression syntax is simple, with only five constructors: literals, variable names, JavaScript 'dot', application, and anonymous functions. When compiling expressions, we use IO-based observable sharing [18] internally. We preserve a simple and monomorphic representation of our expression type to allow our generated code to optionally contain types in comments — this was especially useful for debugging. Overall, this aspect of the Sunroof DSL compiler is straightforward and unsurprising.

*Function Reification:* The second technique is we use is capturing functions, as delimited by the `function` combinator. Again, existing techniques can be used. Consider this simple example: '`Plus`' is the infix application of the `Plus` combinator.

```
data Expr = Plus Expr Expr | Lit Int | Var String

f :: Expr -> Expr
f x = x `Plus` (Lit 1)
```

We can reify `f` by applying it to `(Var "x")`, where `"x"` is a fresh name, giving `Plus (Var "x") (Lit 1)`. By overloading the literals and arithmetic — a common trick — we can write a clean Haskell function that can still be reified:

```
f x = x + 1
```

The Sunroof `function` combinator reifies functions in exactly this way. The type of the argument is constrained by the `SunroofArgument` class, and each instance of the class has a mechanism for generating a prototypical argument, like (`Var "x"`) above. For example, a 2-tuple argument would generate (`Var "x",Var "y"`) as the template argument.

*Monadic Reification:* Monadic reification is the capture of monadic statements, including the bindings, as an abstract syntax tree. A GADT-based deep embedding of the specific monadic operations (bind, return), and all the primitives (method call, etc.), allows the capture of the operations as abstract syntax trees. The trick is normalizing the monadic bind [34], both in the GADT, and in a smart instance of the monadic bind.

```
data JS :: * -> * -> * where
  Return :: a -> JS t a
  Bind :: (Sunroof a) => JSPrim t a -> (a -> JS t b) -> JS t b

instance Monad (JS t) where
  return = Return
  (Return a)  >>= k = k a                          -- left id
  (Bind ma h) >>= k = Bind ma (\ a -> h a >>= k)  -- assoc
```

Because `Bind` is pre-normalized, constraints from the `JSPrim` GADT (not shown) can discharge the `Sunroof` constraint. Simplified, this is the DSL compiler; `JSCode` is a simple (and unsurprising) AST for JavaScript.

```
compileJS :: Sunroof a => JS t a -> M (JSCode, a)
compileJS (Return a) = return ("",a)
compileJS (Bind jx k) = do
  (c1,x)  <- compileJSPrim jx -- typechecks
  (c2,a)  <- compileJS (k x)
  return (c1 ++ c2,a)

compileJSPrim :: Sunroof a => JSPrim t a -> M (JSCode, a)
-- Implementation of compileJSPrim not given
```

Counterintuitively, there can be a constraint on the GADT `Bind` constructor which is not needed in the monad instance; indeed it was thought to be impossible to have GADT constraints on `Bind` and still use the standard monad infrastructure. For the technical details, including why it works, and what generalizations are possible, see [34].

*CPS translation:* Finally, we compile JS A and JS B differently with respect to control flow. The compilation of JA A is straightforward, and a transliteration. The compilation of JS B uses CPS internally, to give CPS-style JavaScript for control flow. This compilation, though involved in the presence of the other generalizations in Sunroof, is straightforward.

# 8    The Sunroof Server

The Sunroof server provides infrastructure to send arbitrary pieces of JavaScript to a web client for execution. It is thus possible to interleave Haskell and JavaScript computations as needed. The three major functions provided are sunroofServer, syncJS and asyncJS.

```
sunroofServer :: SunroofServerOptions
                 -> (SunroofEngine -> IO ()) -> IO ()

syncJS  :: SunroofResult a
        => SunroofEngine -> JS t a -> IO (ResultOf a)
asyncJS :: SunroofEngine -> JS t () -> IO ()
```

SunroofEngine is a handle into our specific web session, one per web application instance. sunroofServer starts a server that will call the given callback function for each request. syncJS and asyncJS allow the server to run Sunroof code inside the requesting website. asyncJS executes it asynchronously without waiting for a return value. In contrast, syncJS waits until the execution is complete and then sends the result back to the server. It is converted into a Haskell value that can be processed further. Values that can be converted to a Haskell type after a synchronous call use the type function ResultOf to allow JSString to return a Haskell String, JSNumber to return Double, etc.

# 9    Related Work

There have been several attempts to compile Haskell to JavaScript. Prominent ones are the compiler backends for UHC [10,36] and GHCJS [29]. The functional language Clean has also used JavaScript as a backend [12], and there has been an attempt to use Clean's Core to support the translation of Haskell to JavaScript [13]. There is also Fay [14] that compile subsets of Haskell to JavaScript and JMacro [7] which use quasiquotation [26] to embed a custom-tailored language into Haskell code. At the same time there are also projects like CoffeeScript [6] or LiveScript [28] to build custom languages that are very similar to JavaScript but add convenient syntax and support for missing features.

Our approach to cooperative concurrency through continuations in JavaScript has been used before [9,31]. To our knowledge, creating a direct connection between Haskell and JavaScript continuations has not been attempted before.

Deep embeddings of monads based on data structures have been used before in Unimo [24] and Operational [5,4]. The specific approach Sunroof takes to monadic reification, and alternative implementation techniques, are discussed in Sculthorpe et al. [34] in detail.

Another effort to map a functional embedding to JavaScript is the JavaScript DSL embedded inside Scala [22]. Rather than using a deep embedding, they use Lightweight Modular Staging (LMS) [32]. Though the language-specific challenges are different, the two systems are comparable in capability.

The Sunroof server does not aim to provide a full-featured web framework, as HAppS, Snap or Yesod do. It only provides the infrastructure to communicate with the currently calling website through the Kansas comet [20] push mechanism [25].

To our knowledge, Sunroof is the only library that supports generation of JavaScript inside of Haskell using pure Haskell in a type-safe manner. All other approaches discussed above either require a separate compilation step or introduce new syntax inside of Haskell. There also is an effort to generalize Active [38], a library for animations, by implementing a backend based on Sunroof [17].

## 10    Conclusion

Sunroof takes the key idea of monad reification and successfully creates a typed JavaScript language, based around the JS-monad, to describe computations intended for a JavaScript interpreter. This paper documents our investigations since our initial prototype. With pervasive use of types in Sunroof, and the concepts of JSFunction and JSContinuation, there now is a clearer connection between functions in the JavaScript and Sunroof language spaces (Fig. 1). It is possible to go back and forth between both worlds.

We were also able to create a two internal translations of our JS monad, one a direct transliteration, and one based on on the translation of continuations from Haskell to JavaScript. This enabled us to build applications that use a blocking threading model on top of JavaScript that resembles the model already known from Haskell. Based on this model and the provided abstraction over continuations, we can construct primitives such as forkJS or threadDelay, and higher-level abstractions like JSMVar and JSChan.

We believe this is the first Haskell-to-JavaScript DSL that makes use of monadic reification. We think that this form of reification gives a useful DSL, and we expect many future DSLs to re-use this design pattern.

The Sunroof DSL compiler, server, and several examples, including our web-based    unit    tests,    are    available    on    github.com/ku-fpg    and hackage.haskell.org. We plan to build a number of abstraction on top of Sunroof: a port of diagrams [39], an animation DSL [38], and a simple GUI toolkit for teaching functional programming.

**Acknowledgments.** We want to thank Conal Elliott for his support in adapting the boolean package [15] and helping us to extend it with support for deeply embedded numbers. We would also like to thank both the TFP'13 and PADL'14 referees for their useful and constructive feedback. This material is based upon work supported by the National Science Foundation under Grant No. 1117569.

## References

1. http://asmjs.org/
2. http://taskjs.org/

3. HTML Living Standard - Timers, `http://www.whatwg.org/specs/web-apps/current-work/multipage/timers.html#timers`
4. Apfelmus, H.: (2010), `http://hackage.haskell.org/package/operational`
5. Apfelmus, H.: The Operational Monad Tutorial. The Monad. Reader 15, 37–55 (2010)
6. Ashkenas, J.: CoffeeScript, `http://coffeescript.org/`
7. Bazerman, G.: JMacro, `http://www.haskell.org/haskellwiki/Jmacro`
8. Chakravarty, M.M.T., Keller, G., Peyton Jones, S.: Associated type synonyms. In: International Conference on Functional Programming, pp. 241–253. ACM (2005)
9. Cooper, E., Lindley, S., Wadler, P., Yallop, J.: Links: Web Programming Without Tiers. In: de Boer, F.S., Bonsangue, M.M., Graf, S., de Roever, W.-P. (eds.) FMCO 2006. LNCS, vol. 4709, pp. 266–296. Springer, Heidelberg (2007)
10. Dijkstra, A., Stutterheim, J., Vermeulen, A., Swierstra, S.: Building JavaScript applications with Haskell. In: Hinze, R. (ed.) IFL 2012. LNCS, vol. 8241, pp. 37–52. Springer, Heidelberg (2013)
11. Dijkstra, E.W.: Letters to the editor: go to statement considered harmful. Communications of the ACM 11(3), 147–148 (1968)
12. Domoszlai, L., Bruël, E., Jansen, J.M.: Implementing a non-strict purely functional language in JavaScript. Acta Universitatis Sapientiae 3, 76–98 (2011)
13. Domoszlai, L., Plasmeijer, R.: Compiling Haskell to JavaScript through Clean's core. In: Selected papers of 9th Joint Conference on Mathematics and Computer Science (February 2012)
14. Done, C., Bergmark, A.: Fay, `https://github.com/faylang/fay/wiki`
15. Elliott, C.: Boolean, `http://hackage.haskell.org/package/Boolean`
16. Farmer, A., Gill, A.: Haskell DSLs for Interactive Web Services. In: First Workshop on Cross-model Language Design and Implementation (2012)
17. Gill, A.: Sunroof-active, `https://github.com/ku-fpg/sunroof-active`
18. Gill, A.: Type-Safe Observable Sharing in Haskell. In: Proceedings of the Second ACM SIGPLAN Haskell Symposium, Haskell 2009, pp. 117–128 (September 2009)
19. Gill, A.: (2013), `http://hackage.haskell.org/package/blank-canvas`
20. Gill, A., Farmer, A.: Kansas Comet, `http://hackage.haskell.org/package/kansas-comet`
21. Jones, S.P., Gordon, A., Finne, S.: Concurrent Haskell. In: Proceedings of the 23rd ACM SIGPLAN-SIGACT Symposium on Principles of Programming Languages, vol. 21, pp. 295–308 (1996)
22. Kossakowski, G., Amin, N., Rompf, T., Odersky, M.: JavaScript as an Embedded DSL. In: Noble, J. (ed.) ECOOP 2012. LNCS, vol. 7313, pp. 409–434. Springer, Heidelberg (2012)
23. Leijen, D., Meijer, E.: Domain Specific Embedded Compilers. In: Domain-Specific Languages, pp. 109–122. ACM (1999)
24. Lin, C.: Programming Monads Operationally with Unimo. In: International Conference on Functional Programming, pp. 274–285. ACM (2006)
25. Mahemoff, M.: HTTP Streaming, `http://ajaxpatterns.org/Comet`
26. Mainland, G.: Why It's Nice to be Quoted: Quasiquoting for Haskell. In: Proceedings of the ACM SIGPLAN Haskell Workshop, Haskell 2007, New York, NY, USA, pp. 73–82 (2007)
27. Moggi, E.: Computational lambda-calculus and monads. In: Logic in Computer Science, pp. 14–23. IEEE Press (1989)
28. Murakami, S., Ashkenas, J.: LiveScript, `http://livescript.net/`

29. Nazarov, V.: GHCJS Haskell to Javascript Compiler,
    `https://github.com/ghcjs/ghcjs`
30. Persson, A., Axelsson, E., Svenningsson, J.: Generic monadic constructs for embedded languages. In: Gill, A., Hage, J. (eds.) IFL 2011. LNCS, vol. 7257, pp. 85–99. Springer, Heidelberg (2012)
31. Predescu, O.: Model-View-Controller in Cocoon using continuations-based control flow (2002),
    `http://www.webweavertech.com/ovidiu/weblog/archives/000042.html`
32. Rompf, T., Odersky, M.: Lightweight modular staging: a pragmatic approach to runtime code generation and compiled DSLs. In: Proceedings of the Ninth International Conference on Generative Programming and Component Engineering, GPCE 2010, pp. 127–136. ACM, New York (2010)
33. Finne, S., et al.: Calling hell from heaven and heaven from hell (1999)
34. Sculthorpe, N., Bracker, J., Giorgidze, G., Gill, A.: The Constrained-Monad Problem. In: International Conference on Functional Programming, pp. 287–298. ACM (2013)
35. Shields, M., Peyton Jones, S.: Object-oriented style overloading for Haskell. In: First Workshop on Multi-Language Inferastructure and Interoperability (BABEL 2001), Firenze, Italy (September 2001)
36. Stutterheim, J.: Improving the UHC JavaScript backend. Tech. rep., Utrecht University (2012), `http://www.norm2782.com/improving-uhc-js-report.pdf`
37. Svenningsson, J., Svensson, B.J.: Simple and compositional reification of monadic embedded languages. In: International Conference on Functional Programming, pp. 299–304. ACM (2013)
38. Yorgey, B.: Active, `https://github.com/diagrams/active`
39. Yorgey, B.: Active, `https://github.com/diagrams`
40. Zakai, A.: Emscripten: An LLVM-to-Javascript Compiler,
    `http://emscripten.org/`

# Compiling DNA Strand Displacement Reactions Using a Functional Programming Language

Matthew R. Lakin[1,2] and Andrew Phillips[1]

[1] Biological Computation Group, Microsoft Research, Cambridge, CB1 2FB, UK
[2] Department of Computer Science, University of New Mexico, NM 87131, USA
mlakin@cs.unm.edu, andrew.phillips@microsoft.com

**Abstract.** DNA nanotechnology is a rapidly-growing field, with many potential applications in nanoscale manufacturing and autonomous *in vivo* diagnostic and therapeutic devices. As experimental techniques improve it will become increasingly important to develop software tools and programming abstractions, to enable rapid and correct design of increasingly sophisticated computational circuits. This is analogous to the need for hardware description languages for VLSI. In this paper we discuss our experience implementing a domain-specific language for DNA nanotechnology using a functional programming language. The ability to use abstract data types to describe molecular structures and to recurse over these types to derive the various interactions between structures was a major reason for the use of a functional language in this project.

**Keywords:** DNA strand displacement, process calculus, biological modelling.

## 1 Introduction

DNA is an attractive engineering material for controlling matter at the nanoscale, as it is robust and undergoes predictable, sequence-specific, programmable interactions. Previous work has shown that synthetic DNA circuits can be used to implement computational systems including digital logic circuits [1], neural networks [2] and game-playing automata [3]. In this setting, DNA is used both as an information carrier *and* as an engineering material, simultaneously. Furthermore, DNA is inherently biocompatible, meaning that DNA-based computing devices could feasibly operate in living cells, autonomously monitoring the cell state and administering appropriate treatment for diseases at the cellular level [4].

As the scale and complexity of DNA-based computing devices continues to grow, tool support will become ever more important. A key goal is to formalize the structures and interactions of DNA molecules, so that their behaviour may be analyzed [5]. To this end we developed a domain-specific language known as DSD [6], which is a process calculus for describing a particular class of DNA circuits that interact via *strand displacement* reactions [7]. Prior to the development of the DSD language, strand displacement circuits were largely designed by hand, which was time-consuming and not scalable. The key aspects of the DSD language design are its syntax for representing a particular class of DNA structures, and the operational semantics which models the real-world interactions between those structures. We implemented a compiler,

M. Flatt and H.-F. Guo (Eds.): PADL 2014, LNCS 8324, pp. 81–86, 2014.

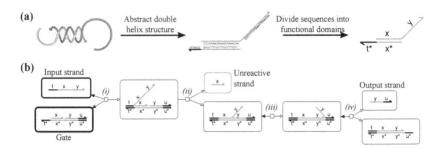

**Fig. 1.** (a) DNA secondary structure abstraction. (b) Basic strand displacement reactions.

stochastic and deterministic simulators and state space analysis tools for the DSD language in F# [8], and in this paper we describe the experience of modelling and compiling DNA reactions in a functional language.

## 2    DNA Strand Displacement

DNA strand displacement [7] is a robust mechanism for engineering sequence-specific interactions between DNA molecules. As shown in Figure 1a, we use the *secondary structure* abstraction of DNA structure, which ignores the double helical structure and absolute positions of the molecules and represents the relative positions of the strands by parallel lines, with arrowheads denoting strand orientations. Instead of dealing with nucleotide sequences ($G, A, T, C$) we define *domains* as shorthands for particular finite sequences. We write $x^*$ for the *complement* of the domain $x$, which is the domain that binds to $x$. This is defined by the standard Watson-Crick base-pairing rules for DNA ($G \leftrightarrow C, A \leftrightarrow T$). We assume that domains have been chosen to be non-interfering, so that each domain only binds to its complement. Domains are divided into *toeholds* (drawn in black in figures and denoted by a caret in the text), which are sufficiently short that they bind reversibly to their complements, and *long domains* (drawn in grey in figures), which are sufficiently long that they do not spontaneously unbind from their complements. Toeholds are identified by a caret, for example $t^\wedge$ and $t^{\wedge *}$.

Figure 1b illustrates the fundamental reactions involved in DNA strand displacement, in which a single strand of DNA interacts with a multi-strand complex, which we call a *gate*. In reaction *(i)*, the input strand binds reversibly to the gate via the toehold $t^\wedge$. The next long domain on the input strand matches the neighbouring domain on the gate structure, which allows the remainder of the input strand to continue binding to the gate across the $x$ reaction, as in the *strand displacement* reaction *(ii)*. In this reaction, the input strand completely displaces another strand from the gate. (We refer to this displaced strand as *unreactive* because it contains no toeholds, and we require that the only exposed complementary domains are toeholds.) Since the remaining domains also match, the input strand can displace the $y$ domain from the input gate, in a reversible *branch migration* reaction *(iii)*. Finally, when the output strand is only bound to the gate by the toehold $u^\wedge$, the output strand may unbind, as in reaction *(iv)*, which is reversible because the output strand may rebind to the gate via the exposed toehold $u^\wedge$.

**(a)**  4   5   `Upper([Long("4",false), Toe("5",false)]) : strand`

**(b)**

```
LowerJoin(Seg([Long("1",false)],[],[Long("2",false)],[],[]),
          Seg([Long("6",false)],[],[Toe("3",false),Long("4",false)],
              [],[Toe("5",true)])) : gate
```

**Fig. 2.** DNA strand and gate structures, and their translation to abstract data types. Examples are from [9]. (a) An upper strand. (b) A gate made by joining two segments along their lower strand.

Despite their apparent simplicity, strand displacement reactions like those outlined in Figure 1b are capable of rich behavior. Since the output strand produced by one strand displacement reaction may serve as the input to another reaction, strand displacement systems may be scaled up to produce more complex circuits. Our goal is to formalize these structures and their reactions, at various levels of detail.

## 3 Modelling DNA Structures

We consider the class of DNA structures introduced in [6]: either single *strands* or multi-strand *gates*. For user convenience, we distinguish between *upper* and *lower* strands. A gate is made up of one or more *segments*, which consist of a double-stranded section of one or more complementary domains and possible single-stranded overhanging regions. A segment is connected to its neighbour by joining *either* the upper or the lower strand. These structures are translated to the following ML data types:

```
type domain = Toe of (string * bool) | Long of (string * bool)
type strand = Upper of domain list | Lower of domain list
type segment = Seg of domain list * domain list * domain list
                     * domain list * domain list
type gate = Single of segment
          | LowerJoin of segment * gate
          | UpperJoin of segment * gate
```

In the case of domains, the `string` represents the name of the domain and the `bool` represents whether that domain is complemented. The translation of DNA structures into these data types is illustrated in Figure 2. Note that if two segments are joined across an overhang, then there are multiple ways to express the resulting structure: hence the representation is not unique. Therefore, we normalize structures to a common representation by gathering overhangs on joining strands, using the following functions

```
let normLower Seg(L1,L1',S1,R1,R1') Seg(L2,L2',S1,R2,R2')
        = (Seg(L1,L1',S1,R1,(R1'@L2')),Seg(L2,[],S1,R2,R2'))
```

of type `segment -> segment -> (segment * segment)`, and a corresponding function `normUpper` for upper strand joins. By applying the appropriate normalization function to each segment join in the gate structure, we obtain a canonical gate representation.

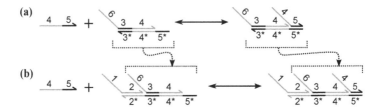

**Fig. 3.** Enumerating DNA reactions, using the example species from Figure 2. (a) An upper strand binding to a single segment. (b) An upper strand binding to a multi-segment gate, which is inferred from the segment-level interaction.

## 4 Compiling DNA Reactions

To analyze the dynamic behavior of DNA strand displacement systems it is necessary to enumerate the interactions between the species. We achieve this by defining a compiler that takes a set of initial DNA species as input and produces the set of all possible generated species and all possible reactions that could occur. This enables the dynamic behaviour of a strand displacement system to be simulated before one attempts a laboratory implementation. We begin by defining a type for reactions:

```
type species = Strand of strand | Gate of gate
type reaction = Reac of species list * float * species list
```

The structures of the abstract syntax trees for the DNA strands and gates guide the definition of the functions that enumerate reactions—consider the problem of enumerating all possible reactions between a strand and a gate. A free upper strand will only bind to the exposed lower single-stranded parts of a gate, and only then if a complementary pair of toeholds are present. As in the definition of the structure normalization function described above, the basic approach here is to write a "segment-level" compilation function that enumerates all possible ways that a strand can interact with a particular segment:

```
strandBindsToSegment : strand -> segment -> segment list
```

This function returns a list of all segments that could result from the binding of the strand in question to the segment, as shown in Figure 3a. Using a custom map-like functional that collects all the segments that result from the binding of a particular strand at any point along the gate struture, we can define a compilation function that produces all possible reactions between the strand and the gate, as shown in Figure 3b:

```
strandBindsToGate : strand -> gate -> reaction list
```

Note that these reactions will produce a new gate in which the incoming strand is just bound by the toehold, since this function only considers the binding reaction.

The unimolecular reactions are strand unbinding, branch migration and strand displacement. These can be enumerated similarly, using segment-level compilation functions that are then mapped across the gate structure.

```
strandUnbindings : segment -> (strand * segment) list
branchMignUpper : segment -> segment -> (segment * segment) option
strandDispUpper : segment -> segment -> (segment * segment) option
```

Strand unbinding reactions can be identified at the single segment level, but branch migration and strand displacement reactions occur across the boundary between two neighbouring segments, hence the `branchMignUpper` and `strandDispUpper` functions require two segments as arguments. Note that we have only presented signatures for functions to calculate branch migration and strand displacement reactions on the upper strand of a gate. This is because the set of possible DNA reactions is closed under a "mirror" operation which swaps the top and bottom strands, so we only need to define enumeration functions for the top strand and use mirroring to check for possible reactions on the bottom strand.

To enable modelling at various levels of detail it is desirable to compile reactions at different levels of abstraction, defined in [6]:

```
type absLevel = Detailed | Finite | Default | Infinite
```

We achieve this by categorizing the classes of reactions as *fast* or *slow*, depending on the desired level of abstraction. Strand binding is always a slow reaction, and any fast reactions that may occur after a slow reaction are simply merged with the slow reaction to produce a single reaction. In all but the most detailed levels of abstraction, *branch migration* reactions (reaction *(iii)* from Figure 1b) are assumed to happen so quickly that we use a structural congruence that identifies gates up to branch migration.

In addition, we have implemented reaction rules to enable two gates to interact end to end, forming linear heteropolymers that may be used to design DNA strand displacement stack machines [10,11], and to allow modelling of "crosstalk" reactions to study failure modes of DNA circuits [6].

## 5   Discussion

While the use of domain-specific languages for formal modelling of biological processes is a well-established technique [12], the design of engineered biochemical systems can also benefit from domain-specific languages for specification and simulation. In addition to DSD, other such languages include GEC [13] and gro [14]. We believe that this is a fruitful new direction for research in programming languages.

Our experience developing the DSD compiler in F# convinced us that functional languages are an ideal implementation vehicle for this kind of domain-specific language, since in DNA nanotechnology, structure and function are closely linked. Base-level representations of DNA secondary structure based on strings [15] or numeric encodings [16] are often too detailed, meaning that some abstraction of structures into high-level features is typically required. Abstract data types provide a convenient means of representing DNA secondary structures at the level of domains, since each DNA structure is reflected in the structure of the abstract syntax tree of the corresponding value. Furthermore, the ability to pattern-match on these values and recurse over them allows concise definitions of the structure-function relationship.

The DSD language has been used to develop a number of DNA strand displacement systems [1,2,17]. In particular, the strand displacement digital logic circuit that was used to compute the square roots of four-bit binary numbers [1] consists of 74 initial species (a total of 130 DNA strands). This illustrates the scale of systems that can be modelled using the DSD language and constructed in the laboratory. Our implementation can be used online via the Visual DSD web server [18], which is accessible at http://research.microsoft.com/dna/ with accompanying documentation.

## References

1. Qian, L., Winfree, E.: Scaling up digital circuit computation with DNA strand displacement cascades. Science 332, 1196–1201 (2011)
2. Qian, L., Winfree, E., Bruck, J.: Neural network computation with DNA strand displacement cascades. Nature 475, 368–372 (2011)
3. Stojanovic, M.N., Stefanovic, D.: A deoxyribozyme-based molecular automaton. Nat. Biotechnol. 21(9), 1069–1074 (2003)
4. Benenson, Y., Gil, B., Ben-Dor, U., Adar, R., Shapiro, E.: An autonomous molecular computer for logical control of gene expression. Nature 429, 423–429 (2004)
5. Lakin, M.R., Parker, D., Cardelli, L., Kwiatkowska, M., Phillips, A.: Design and analysis of DNA strand displacement devices using probabilistic model checking. JRS Interface 9(72), 1470–1485 (2012)
6. Lakin, M.R., Youssef, S., Cardelli, L., Phillips, A.: Abstractions for DNA circuit design. JRS Interface 9(68), 470–486 (2012)
7. Zhang, D.Y., Seelig, G.: Dynamic DNA nanotechnology using strand-displacement reactions. Nat. Chem. 3(2), 103–113 (2011)
8. Syme, D., Granicz, A., Cisternino, A.: Expert F#. Springer (2008)
9. Zhang, D.Y., Turberfield, A.J., Yurke, B., Winfree, E.: Engineering entropy-driven reactions and networks catalyzed by DNA. Science 318, 1121–1125 (2007)
10. Qian, L., Soloveichik, D., Winfree, E.: Efficient Turing-universal computation with DNA polymers. In: Sakakibara, Y., Mi, Y. (eds.) DNA 16. LNCS, vol. 6518, pp. 123–140. Springer, Heidelberg (2011)
11. Lakin, M.R., Phillips, A.: Modelling, simulating and verifying Turing-powerful strand displacement systems. In: Cardelli, L., Shih, W. (eds.) DNA 17. LNCS, vol. 6937, pp. 130–144. Springer, Heidelberg (2011)
12. Priami, C., Regev, A., Shapiro, E., Silverman, W.: Application of a stochastic name-passing calculus to representation and simulation of molecular processes. Information Processing Letters 80, 25–31 (2001)
13. Pedersen, M., Phillips, A.: Towards programming languages for genetic engineering of living cells. JRS Interface 6(suppl. 4), S437–S450 (2009)
14. Jang, S.S., Oishi, K.T., Egbert, R.G., Klavins, E.: Specification and simulation of synthetic multicelled behaviors. ACS Synthetic Biology 1, 365–374 (2012)
15. Hogeweg, P., Hesper, B.: Energy directed folding of RNA sequences. Nucleic Acids Res. 12(1), 67–74 (1984)
16. Fanning, M.L., Macdonald, J., Stefanovic, D.: ISO: numeric representation of nucleic acid form. In: Proceedings of ACM-BCB 2011. ACM (2011)
17. Chen, Y.-J., Dalchau, N., Srinivas, N., Phillips, A., Cardelli, L., Soloveichik, D., Seelig, G.: Programmable chemical controllers made from DNA. Nat. Nanotechnol. 41(1), e33 (2013)
18. Lakin, M.R., Youssef, S., Polo, F., Emmott, S., Phillips, A.: Visual DSD: a design and analysis tool for DNA strand displacement systems. Bioinformatics 27(22), 3211–3213 (2011)

# Two Applications of the ASP-Prolog System: Decomposable Programs and Multi-context Systems

Tran Cao Son, Enrico Pontelli, and Tiep Le

Department of Computer Science, New Mexico State University
{tson,epontell,tile}@cs.nmsu.edu

**Abstract.** This paper presents two applications of the *ASP-Prolog* system, one of the earliest modular logic programming frameworks for integrating ASP and traditional Prolog/CLP reasoning. Both applications represent significant challenges to existing ASP technologies and share some common traits—mostly related to the inadequacy of the *ground-and-solve* approach. The first application stems from several practical experiences in using state-of-the-art Answer Set Programming (ASP) solvers to tackle combinatorial problems in different domains (e.g., bioinformatics, distributed constraint problem solving). A recurrent issue is the presence of computationally tractable subproblems that turn out to be challenging, or even practically infeasible, for current ASP technologies. The second application of ASP-Prolog is its use to compute the equilibrium semantics of *Multi-Context Systems (MCS)*.

## 1 Introduction and Motivation

*Answer Set Programming (ASP)* [15,13] is a declarative programming paradigm that has gained a prominent role in a variety of application domains, especially in domains with knowledge-intensive applications and combinatorial problems in high complexity classes. An important driving force behind the success of ASP is the continuous development and improvement of state-of-the-art ASP solvers, that has led to several highly competitive ASP solvers (e.g., CLASP[1]). The majority of ASP solvers employ heuristic search in computing answer sets. To facilitate the use of variables in ASP programs, ASP solvers use a two-stage approach, referred to as *ground-and-solve*, in computing answer sets of programs with variables. The program is first grounded—by replacing variables with all possible variable-free terms—and the ground program is used for the computation of solutions. ASP solvers require the program resulting from grounding to be finite. In order to accomplish this, ASP solvers impose different syntactical restrictions on programs with variables. These restrictions may disallow certain problem encodings: such encodings might represent natural ASP representations of problems, but violate some of the syntactical restrictions imposed by the ASP solvers.

There have been attempts to integrate ASP with other programming environments for different purposes (see [7] for a discussion), including early attempts to integrate ASP and Prolog (e.g., [7,4]). The ASP-Prolog system [7,17] represents one of the first

---

[1] http://potassco.sourceforge.net/

M. Flatt and H.-F. Guo (Eds.): PADL 2014, LNCS 8324, pp. 87–103, 2014.

systems proposed to provide an embedding of ASP within Prolog. ASP-Prolog is an extension of a modular Prolog system, which enables the integration of Prolog-style reasoning with ASP. The overarching goal of ASP-Prolog is to provide a platform for the integration of heterogeneous knowledge bases and an alternative computation paradigm to ASP (goal-oriented computation vs. model computation). In general, an ASP-Prolog program is a collection of modules, where each module can be declared to contain either Prolog code or ASP code. Each module provides an interface which allows the module to export predicate definitions and import definitions from other modules. In the current implementation, the root of the module hierarchy is expected to be a Prolog module, that can be interacted with using the traditional Prolog-style query-answering mechanism. ASP-Prolog has been used in several applications (e.g., [14,21]).

The objective of this paper is twofold. On one hand, we intend to identify a class of interesting problems that are challenging for existing ASP systems—and ASP-Prolog is used to illustrate a technique that can address such problems. On the other hand, the paper shows how the relatively simple features of ASP-Prolog can provide elegant and effective solutions in challenging domains.

## 2   Background: Logic Programming, ASP-Prolog, and MCS

**Logic Programming.** A logic program $\Pi$ is a set of rules of the form
$$c \leftarrow a_1, \ldots, a_m, not\ a_{m+1}, \ldots, not\ a_n$$
where $0 \leq m \leq n$, each $a_i$ is a literal of a propositional language[2] and $not\ a_j$, $m < j \leq n$, is called a negation-as-failure literal (or naf-literal). $c$ can be a literal or omitted. When $n = 0$, the rule is called a *fact*. When $c$ is omitted, the rule is a *constraint*. For a rule $r$, $pos(r)$ denotes the set $\{a_1, \ldots, a_m\}$ and $neg(r)$ is the set $\{a_{m+1}, \ldots, a_n\}$. A set of literals $X$ is consistent if there is no atom $a$ s.t. $\{a, \neg a\} \subseteq X$. A rule $r$ is *satisfied* by $X$ if (i) $neg(r) \cap X \neq \emptyset$, (ii) $pos(r) \setminus X \neq \emptyset$, or (iii) $c \in X$.

Let $\Pi$ be a program. For a consistent set of literals $S$, the *reduct* of $\Pi$ w.r.t. $S$, denoted by $\Pi^S$, is the program obtained from the set of all rules of $\Pi$ by deleting (i) each rule that has a naf-literal $not\ a$ in its body with $a \in S$, and (ii) all naf-literals in the bodies of the remaining rules. $S$ is an *answer set* of $\Pi$ [10] if it satisfies the following conditions: (i) If $\Pi$ does not contain any naf-literal then $S$ is the minimal set of literals satisfying all rules in $\Pi$; and (ii) If $\Pi$ contains some naf-literal then $S$ is an answer set of $\Pi$ if $S$ is the answer set of $\Pi^S$. For convenience of notation, we will use some extensions of ASP that have been proposed—such as choice atoms as defined in [20], that can occur in a rule wherever a literal can, and aggregate literals.

We will focus on programs that admit a splitting sequence[3] [11]. For a program $\Pi$, a set of literals $S$ is a *splitting set* of $\Pi$ if for every rule $r$ of $\Pi$, if $head(r) \in S$ then $pos(r) \cup neg(r) \subseteq S$. A sequence of splitting sets $\langle S_i \rangle_{i=0}^{\infty}$ of $\Pi$ is a splitting sequence of $\Pi$, if $S_i \subseteq S_j$ for $i \leq j$ and $\bigcup_{i=0}^{\infty} S_i$ is the set of literals occurring in $\Pi$.

**ASP-Prolog.** The ASP-Prolog system, used in this paper, has been originally described in [7,17]. It provides a modular structure and a set of predicates to enable the interaction

---

[2] A rule with variables is viewed as a shorthand of the set of its ground instances.

[3] For simplicity of the presentation, we consider only splitting sequences with ordinal $\omega$.

between Prolog modules and ASP modules. Among the various components (see [17]), ASP-Prolog's interface includes:

- use_asp(+ASPModule, +PModule, +Parameters): The Prolog module PModule is created, providing predicates to access the answer sets of the ASP program ASPModule with the parameters specified in Parameters. The new module contains the literals entailed by the skeptical semantics of ASPModule and has sub-modules which encode the answer sets of ASPModule. PModule provides the names of the models containing the answer sets through atoms of the form model/1. PModule and the Parameters arguments are optional.
- assertnb(ASPModule, Progs) and retractnb(ASPModule, Progs): these two predicates are extended versions of the assert and retract predicates of Prolog, designed to operate on modules associated to ASP programs. Their effects are to add and remove, respectively, the clauses specified in Progs to the ASPModule and create new modules analogously to use_asp(ASPModule).

**Multi-context Systems (MCS).** *Heterogeneous nonmonotonic multi-context systems* (MCS) have been introduced in [3]. A *logic* is a tuple $L = (KB_L, BS_L, ACC_L)$ where $KB_L$ is the set of well-formed knowledge bases of L—each being a set of formulae. $BS_L$ is the set of possible belief sets; each element of $BS_L$ is a set of syntactic elements representing the beliefs L may adopt. Finally, $ACC_L : KB_L \to 2^{BS_L}$ is a function specifying the *"semantics"* of L by assigning to each element of $KB_L$ a set of acceptable sets of beliefs.

Using the concept of logic, we can introduce the notion of multi-context system. A *Multi-Context System (MCS)* $M = (C_1, \cdots, C_n)$ consists of contexts $C_i = (L_i, kb_i, br_i)$, $(1 \le i \le n)$, where $L_i = (KB_i, BS_i, ACC_i)$ is a logic, $kb_i \in KB_i$ is a knowledge base, and $br_i$ is a set of $L_i$-bridge rules of the form:

$$s \leftarrow (c_1 : p_1), \cdots, (c_j : p_j), not\ (c_{j+1} : p_{j+1}), \cdots, not\ (c_m : p_m)$$

where $1 \le c_k \le n$, $p_k$ is an element of some belief set of $L_{c_k}$, $1 \le k \le m$, and $kb \cup \{s\} \in KB_i$ for each $kb \in KB_i$. Intuitively, a bridge rule $r$ allows us to add $s$ to a context, depending on the beliefs in the other contexts. Given a bridge rule $r$, we will denote by $head(r)$ the part $s$ of $r$. The semantics of MCS is described by the notion of belief states. Let $M = (C_1, \cdots, C_n)$ be a MCS. A *belief state* is a sequence $S = (S_1, \cdots, S_n)$ where each $S_i$ is an element of $BS_i$.

Given a belief state $S = (S_1, \cdots, S_n)$ and a bridge rule $r$, we say that $r$ is *applicable* in $S$ if $p_i \in S_{c_i}$ for each $1 \le i \le j$ and $p_k \notin S_{c_k}$ for each $j + 1 \le k \le m$.

The semantic of a MCS $M$ is defined in terms of particular belief states $(S_1, \cdots, S_n)$ that take into account the bridge rules that are applicable with respect to the given belief sets. A belief state $S = (S_1, \cdots, S_n)$ of $M$ is an *equilibrium* if, for all $1 \le i \le n$, we have that $S_i \in ACC_i(kb_i \cup \{head(r) | r \in br_i \text{ is applicable in } S\})$.

*Example 2.1.* Let $M_1 = (C_1, C_2)$ where $C_i = (L_i, kb_i, br_i)$ for $i = 1, 2$, where $L_i$ is the logic of programming under answer set semantics with $kb_1 = \{a \leftarrow not\ b; b \leftarrow not\ a\}$ and $br_1 = \{a \leftarrow (2 : d)\}$; and $kb_2 = \{c \leftarrow not\ d; d \leftarrow not\ c\}$ and $br_2 = \{d \leftarrow (1 : b)\}$. It is possible to show that $M_1$ has two equilibria $(\{a\}, \{c\})$ and $(\{a\}, \{d\})$.

## 3 Decomposable Programs

### 3.1 Use Cases

**Use Case #1: Optimal Communication Orders between Constraint Nodes.** Let us consider a *distributed constraint satisfaction problem (DisCSP)* [22]. A DisCSP is a tuple $(\mathcal{X}, \mathcal{D}, \mathcal{C}, \mathcal{A})$, where $\mathcal{X} = \{x_1, \ldots, x_n\}$ is a finite set of variables, $\mathcal{D} = \{D_1, \ldots, D_n\}$ is a corresponding set of finite domains, $\mathcal{C}$ is a set of binary constraints $C_{i,j}$ (on the variables $x_i$ and $x_j$) and $\mathcal{A} = \{A_1, \ldots, A_k\}$ is a set of agents. Each agent $A_i$ owns a subset $\mathcal{X}_{A_i}$ of the variables of $\mathcal{X}$, s.t. $\mathcal{X}_{A_1}, \ldots, \mathcal{X}_{A_k}$ is a partition of $\mathcal{X}$. A solution to a DisCSP is a complete variable assignment satisfying all constraints.

A large number of DisCSP algorithms rely on implementing an asynchronous depth-first search (DFS). Each agent is placed in an ordering relation; the DFS is reproduced by having each agent communicate their variable instantiations towards the children agents, and in case of failure propagate backtracking to their parent agent. This assumes an ordering $\prec$ among agents—where $A_u \prec A_v$ denotes that agent $A_u$ is the parent of $A_v$ in the DFS tree. The ordering should ensure that if there is a constraint $C_{i,j}$ such that $x_i \in \mathcal{X}_{A_u}$ and $x_j \in \mathcal{X}_{A_v}$, then either $A_u \prec^* A_v$ or $A_v \prec^* A_u$ ($\prec^*$ is the transitive closure of $\prec$). Algorithms (e.g., [23]) have been proposed to compute such orderings.

A more complex, but realistic, scenario originates from the assumption that the communications among agents have non-uniform costs. Let us denote with $\omega(A_u, A_v)$ the communication cost between agents $A_u$ and $A_v$. In this case, the goal is to determine an ordering that will minimize the maximum communication cost among agents. The communication cost between agents $A_u$ and $A_v$ with respect to an agent order $\prec$, denoted by $\zeta_{\prec}(A_u, A_v)$, such that $\zeta_{\prec}(A_u, A_u) = 0$ for any agent $A_u$, and $\zeta_{\prec}(A_u, A_v) = \max\{\omega(A_u, x) + \zeta_{\prec}(x, A_v) \mid A_u \prec x, x \prec^* A_v\}$ for any two agents $A_u \neq A_v$ such that $A_u \prec^* A_v$. The overall cost is $\zeta(\prec) = \max\{\zeta_{\prec}(A_u, A_v) \mid A_u \prec^* A_v\}$.

The problem admits an elegant encoding in ASP. Let us assume that the facts of the form $edge(X, Y)$ are used to describe the constraint graph of a DisCSP—where $edge(X, Y)$ states that there exists a constraint containing variables owned by $X$ and $Y$. Similarly, let $comm(X, Y, C)$ denote that the non-negative cost of communication between agents $X, Y$ is $C$. The ordering $\prec$ and the DFS tree can be generated by:[4]

$$1\{root(X) : node(X)\}1. \qquad\qquad \{order(X, Y)\} \leftarrow node(X), node(Y), X \neq Y, not\ root(Y).$$

The $\prec^*$ relation can be described by a simple transitive closure:

$$order\_s(X, Y) \leftarrow order(X, Y). \qquad order\_s(X, Z) \leftarrow order(X, Y), order\_s(Y, Z).$$

The following constraints guarantee the DFS conditions:

$$\leftarrow order(X, Y), order(Y, X). \qquad\qquad \leftarrow node(Y), 2\{order(X, Y) : node(X)\}.$$
$$\leftarrow node(X), not\ root(X), not\ has\_ancestor(X).$$
$$\leftarrow edge(X, Y), \{order\_s(X, Y), order\_s(Y, X)\}0.$$

We can associate costs to agents based on their distance from the root of the DFS:

$$cost\_node(X, 0) \leftarrow root(X).$$
$$cost\_node(Y, C1 + C2) \leftarrow not\ root(Y), order(X, Y), comm(X, Y, C1), cost\_node(X, C2).$$
$$leaf\_cost(X, C) \leftarrow cost\_node(X, C), leaf(X).$$

---

[4] We omit the definition of trivial predicates like `leaf`.

and the cost of the resulting DFS tree is

$$tree\_cost(C1) \leftarrow C1 = \#\max[leaf\_cost(\_, C) = C], C1 > 0.$$

Note that the definition of *tree_cost* makes use of an aggregate (#max). Our objective is to determine DFSs with certain properties, e.g., with minimal cost. Observe that this program has a splitting sequence $S_0, S_1, S_2$ where:

*(i)* $S_0$ consists of literals of the form $node(X)$, $edge(X, Y)$, $leaf(X)$, $root(X)$, $order(X, Y)$, and $order\_s(X, Y)$;
*(ii)* $S_1$ consists of $S_0$ and the literals relating to the cost $(cost\_node(X, Y)$ and $leaf\_cost(X, Y))$; and
*(iii)* $S_3$ consists of $S_2$ and the other literals.

Intuitively, this splitting sequence represents the steps involved in the process of solving the problem: *(i)* create an ordering among the nodes; *(ii)* compute the cost of each leaf of the specified order; *(iii)* compute the cost of the tree as the maximal cost of the leaves.

The difficulty posed to ASP solvers by the above program lies in the rules defining the cost of the nodes. Without bounding the cost C2 of the rule, the grounding process does not terminate in any reasonable amount of time. Limiting the cost C2 to be the sum of all (positive) costs allows CLASP to solve instances that have a small overall communication cost between nodes (e.g., when the the bound to C2 is smaller than $1,000$). The grounder needs to ground all combinations of the second rule in this group and this number increases with the bound. We observe that the system ASP{f} [2] could be useful in this situation. An alternative approach to using functions is to *inform the grounder* about the steps in computing the answer sets of the program via an extra parameter (i.e., effectively exposing the stratification to the grounder):

$$cost(X, 0, 1) \leftarrow root(X).$$
$$cost(X, C1 + C2, T + 1) \leftarrow level(T), not\ root(X), order(Y, X), comm(Y, X, C1),$$
$$cost(Y, C2, T).$$
$$leaf\_cost(Y, C) \leftarrow leaf(Y), cost(Y, C, T + 1), level(T).$$

where level is a predicate defining the level in a tree, which can be at most the number of nodes in the graph. With this change, CLASP is able to identify that C2 can only take a small set of possible values and has no problem with the value of the weights. The potential cyclic dependency between cost(X,C1+C2) and cost(Y,C2) is now a single way dependency (i.e., first depends on the second). Although the method of breaking dependencies works in this problem, it does not work in the next example.

**Use Case #2: Approximated Supertree Computation.** We consider *phylogenies* [12] as trees where each internal node has at least two children. We will assume the traditional terminology for trees. For a tree $T$, let $L(T)$ denote the set of leaves of $T$. An *internal edge* is an edge connecting two internal nodes, one of which can be the root. A *cluster* is the set of all the leaves that are descendants of the same internal node. Let us denote with $MRCA(S)$ the most recent common ancestor of the set of leaves $S$.

For two sets of leaves $A, B \subseteq L(T)$, $A <_T B$ if $MRCA(A)$ is a descendant of $MRCA(B)$. A tree $T'$ is obtained from $T$ by *contraction* if $T'$ can be obtained from $T$ by contracting some internal edges. Let $A \subseteq L(T)$. The subtree of $T$ with the leaf set $A$ is the subtree of $T$ whose root has $A$ as its cluster; we refer to it as the *subtree of*

$T$ *induced by* $A$, and denote it with $T|A$. A tree $T$ *displays* a tree $t$ if $t$ is an induced subtree of $T$, or can be obtained from an induced subtree by contraction.

Let $\mathcal{T}$ be a collection of trees and $S = \bigcup_{T \in \mathcal{T}} L(T)$. A *supertree method* takes $\mathcal{T}$ as input and returns a tree $T$ with the leaf set $S$ such that $T$ displays each element of $\mathcal{T}$ [18]. Several popular algorithms to compute supertrees have been proposed; in this section, we consider a rough approximation of the method in [19]. The approximation has been developed to quickly generate putative supertrees as part of the CDAOStore project [16]. For a tree $T$ and a set of leaves $S$, $pruned(T, S)$ denotes the tree obtained from $T$ by: **(1)** Deleting all the subtrees of internal nodes whose set of leaves is a subset of $S$, and the edges coming into these internal nodes; **(2)** Deleting all the remaining leaves appearing in $S$ and the edges leading to such leaves; and **(3)** Simplifying the remaining tree by removing all internal nodes which have only one child. A *weighted tree* $T$ is a tree with an associated weight $w$. Given $\mathcal{T}$, a weighted graph $S_{\mathcal{T}}$ is defined as follows: **(1)** The nodes of $S_{\mathcal{T}}$ are the leaves of $\mathcal{T}$; **(2)** Nodes $a$ and $b$ are connected if $a$ and $b$ are in a proper cluster in one of the trees in $\mathcal{T}$ (i.e., if there is a tree in $\mathcal{T}$ where $MRCA(a, b)$ is not the root of the tree); **(3)** The weight of an edge $(a, b)$ in the graph $S_{\mathcal{T}}$ is the total weight of all trees in which $a$ and $b$ are in a proper cluster.

The APPROXSUPERTREE algorithm is described in Algorithm 1. This program runs in polynomial time in the size of the trees. The APPROXSUPERTREE algorithm can be

---

**Algorithm 1.** APPROXSUPERTREE($\mathcal{T}$)

---

**Require:** a set of $k$ trees $\mathcal{T}$, with leaves set $S = \bigcup_{T \in \mathcal{T}} L(T) = \{x_1, \dots, x_n\}$.
1: **if** n = 1 or n = 2 **then**
2:     **return** a single node labeled by $x_1$ or $x_1$ and $x_2$
3: **end if**
4: construct $S_{\mathcal{T}}$
5: **if** $S_{\mathcal{T}}$ is connected **then**
6:     Let $E^{cut}$ be the set edges of minimal weight of $S_{\mathcal{T}}$
7:     $S_{\mathcal{T}}/E^{cut}$ is obtained from $S_{\mathcal{T}}$ by deleting all edges in $E^{cut}$
8:     Replace $S_{\mathcal{T}}$ with $S_{\mathcal{T}}/E^{cut}$
9: **end if**
10: Let $S_1, \dots, S_k$ be the components of $S_{\mathcal{T}}$
11: **for** each component $S_i$ **do**
12:     $T_i =$ APPROXSUPERTREE($\mathcal{T}|S_i$), where $\mathcal{T}|S_i = \{pruned(T, L(T) \setminus S_i) \mid T \in \mathcal{T}\}$
13:     Construct a new tree $T'$ by connecting the roots of the trees $T_i$ to a new root $r$
14: **end for**
15: **return** $T$

---

implemented by an ASP program with the following basic components that implement one iteration of the algorithm. To fully implement this algorithm, the predicates need to be extended with an extra parameter denoting the iteration step.

- *Encoding trees:* a tree is described by a set of atoms of the form $edge(t, n_1, n_2)$ and a fact $tree(tree\_name, weight)$. Rules for defining node, root, leaf, ancestor (*anc*), etc. can be easily defined based on these predicates and are omitted to save space.
- *Code for computing the pruned tree:* this code computes the tree $pruned(T, L(T) \setminus S_i)$ (Line 12, Algorithm 1). We assume that the tree $T$ and the pruned set of

leaves $S$ are given. Elements of $S$ are specified by $member(X, S)$. First, we define $some\_descendants\_out(T, S, N)$ which is true whenever $N$—a non-leaf in the tree $T$—has a descendant that does not belong to the pruned set $S$.

$$some\_descendants\_out(T, S, N) \leftarrow pruned\_set(S), node(T, N), leaf(T, N_1),$$
$$not\ member(N_1, S), ancestor(T, N, N_1).$$

We then identify the nodes that should be deleted. These are the nodes whose leaf-descendants belong to the pruned set.

$$delete\_node(T, S, N) \leftarrow pruned\_set(S), node(T, N), not\ leaf(T, N),$$
$$not\ some\_descendants\_out(T, S, N).$$

The above predicates are used to define the predicate $simplify\_node(T, S, N)$, which says that a non-leaf node that has not been deleted should be simplified if it has only one child that is not deleted.

$$simplify\_node(T, S, N) \leftarrow pruned\_set(S), node(T, N), not\ leaf(T, N),$$
$$not\ delete\_node(T, S, N),$$
$$NC = \#count\{edge(T, N, N_1) : not\ delete\_node(T, S, N_1)$$
$$: not\ member(N_1, S)\}, NC < 2$$

A node remains after pruning if it is not deleted, not a member of the pruned set, and not simplified. This is defined by the following predicate.

$$is\_new\_node(T, S, N) \leftarrow pruned\_set(S), node(T, N), not\ member(N, S),$$
$$not\ delete\_node(T, S, N), not\ simplify\_node(T, S, N).$$

This allows us to define the new tree $pruned(T, S)$, that is the result of pruning $S$ from the tree by identifying the edges of the tree.

$$ptree\_edge(pruned(T, S), N_1, N_2) \leftarrow pruned\_set(S), tree(T, W), ancestor(T, N_1, N_2),$$
$$is\_new\_node(T, S, N_1), is\_new\_node(T, S, N_2), NA < 1,$$
$$NA = \#count\{ancestor(T, NM, N_2) : ancestor(T, N_1, NM)$$
$$: not\ simplify\_node(T, S, NM)\}.$$

This rule says that there is an edge between two nodes $N_1$ and $N_2$ in the tree, after pruning, if $N_1$ is an ancestor of $N_2$ and all the ancestors of $N_2$ which are descendants of $N_1$ have been simplified.

- *Code for computing the connected graph of leaves of a set of trees*: this code creates the weighted graph $\mathcal{S}_T$ (Line 4, Algorithm 1). We first identify the cluster of a tree. Two leaves $A$ and $B$ of the tree $T$ with the weight $W$ are in a proper cluster if they share the same ancestor which is not the root.

$$in\_cluster(T, A, B, W) \leftarrow tree(T, W), leaf(T, A), leaf(T, B), node(T, N),$$
$$not\ root(T, N), ancestor(T, N, A), ancestor(T, N, B).$$

Next we define the edge of the graph. An edge of the graph is an edge between two nodes in the same cluster. The weight of the edge is the sum of all the weights of the corresponding trees in which the nodes appear in the same cluster.

$$graph(A, B, WG) \leftarrow leaf(T, A), leaf(T, B),$$
$$1\{in\_cluster(T_1, A, B, W):tree(T_1, \_)\}, WG=\#sum[in\_cluster(\_, A, B, W) = W].$$

- *Code for constructing the supertree after one iteration:* this code accomplishes the task of computing $T_i$ (Line 12, Algorithm 1). This starts with the construction of the reduced graph by eliminating edges with minimal weight. To achieve this, we compute the minimal weight ($WM$).

$$min\_edge(WM) \leftarrow WM = \#min[graph(\_, \_, W_1) = W_1].$$

The reduced graph will contain edges whose weight is greater than the minimal weight. We also introduce the predicate $not\_reduced(A)$, to indicate that $A$ is the vertex of at least one edge that is not eliminated.

$$3\{not\_reduced(A), not\_reduced(B), reduced\_graph(A, B, W)\}3 \leftarrow$$
$$graph(A, B, W), min\_edge(WMin), WMin < W.$$

If all edges going out from a vertex are eliminated then the vertex is itself a component of the reduced graph. We have the following rule to characterize this.

$$reduced\_graph(A, A, 0) \leftarrow graph(A, B, W),$$
$$min\_edge(WMin), WMin == W, not\ not\_reduced(A).$$

The next step in computing the supertree is to identify the components of the reduced graph and select a representative for each component. The rule

$$\{representative(A)\} \leftarrow leaf(T, A).$$

defines that only leaves could be selected to be representatives. Since each component has one and only one representative, we add the following rules:

$$connected(A, B) \leftarrow 1\{reduced\_graph(A, B, \_), reduced\_graph(B, A, \_)\}.$$
$$connected(A, B) \leftarrow reduced\_graph(A, C, \_), connected(C, B).$$
$$is\_connected(A) \leftarrow representative(B), leaf(T, A), connected(A, B).$$
$$is\_connected(A) \leftarrow representative(B), leaf(T, A), connected(B, A).$$
$$\leftarrow leaf(T, A), not\ is\_connected(A).$$
$$\leftarrow representative(A), representative(B), A \neq B, connected(B, A).$$

The first four rules define the connectivity relationship, based on the edges of the reduced graph. The next rules guarantee that exactly one representative is selected for each component. Having computed the components and their representatives, the supertree can be derived using the following rules. To identify the number of nodes in a component, we define the degree of a node using the rule:

$$degree(A, D) \leftarrow representative(A), D = \#count\{connected(A, \_)\}.$$

If the component is a singleton then it will be connected to the root, which is represented by the name of the pruned set.

$$edge\_s(S, A) \leftarrow representative(A), degree(A, 1), pruned\_set(S).$$

If the component has exactly two elements, then a new root will be created and connected to the root. The new root is connected to the two leaves. In the next rule, $@newName(S, A)$ creates a new constant that is a direct descendant of the pruned set and is the parent of the two leaves.

$$3\{edge\_s(S, N), edge\_s(N, A), edge\_s(N, B)\} \leftarrow representative(A), degree(A, 2),$$
$$connected(A, B), A \neq B, pruned\_set(S), N := @newName(S, A).$$

If the component has more than two elements then a new root is created and the algorithm computes the pruned set for the next iteration.

$$2\{edge\_s(root, N), generated\_pruned\_set(N, A)\} \leftarrow representative(A),$$
$$degree(A, D), D > 2, pruned\_set(S), N := @newName(S, A).$$

Here, $generated\_pruned\_set(N, A)$ records a new pruned set, named $N$, related to the representative $A$. The pruned set and its members are defined in the next rules.

$$new\_pruned\_set(N) \leftarrow generated\_pruned\_set(N, A).$$
$$new\_member(B, N) \leftarrow generated\_pruned\_set(N, A), ptree\_leaf(T, B),$$
$$not\ connected(A, B).$$

Observe that $ptree\_leaf$ is defined in a similar fashion as $leaf$.

Let us point out the following aspects that prevent an effective use of ASP for this algorithm. The algorithm needs to be repeated until all components contain either one or two leaves. In each iteration, the computation needs to identify the set of leaves that will be pruned for the computation of the pruned trees. Given the set of leaves that will be pruned, the pruned trees are uniquely identified. On the other hand, if the set of leaves is unknown, the ASP solver will need to guess, i.e., it will have to ground *all possible combinations* of the leaves of the trees. Thus, the proposed encoding can only deal with problems with very few leaves (e.g., less than 10). A simple example commonly encountered in the literature (12 leaves) cannot be solved. We observe that the full ASP implementation of this algorithm also possesses a splitting sequence corresponding to the iteration steps that the algorithm must go through in order to compute the supertree.

**Use Case #3: Union of All MinCut Sets of a Weighted Graph.** A MinCut of a weighted graph is a set of edges of minimal weight that disconnects the graph. The problem we consider is to compute the union of all MinCuts of a graph (useful, e.g., for supertree computations). Unlike the previous problems, this problem has a polynomial time algorithm but does not seem to have a straightforward ASP encoding.

If we only need to compute one MinCut, the ASP encoding is simple: generate a cut and minimize its weight. The problem is no longer trivial when we need to generate the union of all MinCuts. One can try to index the possible MinCuts and use multiple minimization statements. Since the minimal weight is unique, one would have to add a constraint that the weight of the cuts is unique. This encoding faces several problems, e.g., it requires the number of MinCuts and the solver will try to find an answer set where all weights are equal—which is not necessarily the minimal weight.

An alternative approach relies on the observation that, given a graph $G = (V, E)$, an edge $e \in E$ is in at least one MinCut of $G$ iff $c(G) = c((V, E \backslash \{e\})) + w(e)$, where $c(G)$ is the cost of the MinCut of $G$ and $w(e)$ is the weight of edge $e$. This can be captured by distinct sets of rules that compute one MinCut for $G$ and for each $(V, E \backslash \{e\})$, plus a final rule that checks which edges have the above property. In this case, grounding is not an issue, the repeated minimizations required to compute MinCuts lead to a very large computation time (no results after 2 hours), while the individual sets of rules can be executed in less than one second. Also in these cases, an interleaved grounding and solving would help, by allowing the accumulation of MinCuts from iteration to iteration, and combining the weights of MinCuts at the end to determine relevant edges.

### 3.2   ASP-Prolog for Decomposable Programs

**Interleaving Grounding and Computation.** The above three examples highlight a real limitation of ASP solvers that employ the traditional ground-and-solve approach. All three problems share a property that each program possesses a splitting sequence corresponding to the steps that can be used in computing the answer of the problem. This is characterized by the splitting sequence theorem in [11]. The theorem shows that, for each answer set $A$ of a program $\Pi$ that has a splitting sequence $\langle S_i \rangle_{i \geq 0}$, there exists a decomposition of $A$ in a sequence of sets $\langle A_i \rangle_{i \geq 0}$, such that $A_i$'s can be computed step-by-step in the following fashion: **(1)** Compute an answer set $A_0$ of the bottom program $b_{S_0}(\Pi)$ that consists of all rules in $\Pi$ whose atoms belong to $S_0$; **(2)** For each

$i \geq 0$, compute an answer set $A_{i+1}$ of the program $e_{S_i}(b_{S_{i+1}}(\Pi) \setminus b_{S_i}(\Pi), \bigcup_{j \leq i} A_j)$. In this definition, $e_S(\Pi, X)$ is a program containing rules determined as follows: (a) remove all rules $r \in \Pi$ such that either there is a positive atom in the body belonging to $S$ but not $X$ or a negative atom belonging to $S$ and $X$; and (b) removing all occurrence of $a$ or $not \; a$ for $a \in S$ from the remaining rules. We refer to programs that admit a splitting sequence as *decomposable programs*.

Decomposable programs can be seen as a sequence of *lp-functions* [9] $\langle \Pi_i \rangle_{i \geq 0}$ where each lp-function $\Pi_i$ accepts a set of input predicates $In_i$ and defines a set of output predicates $Out_i$, such that $In_i \subseteq \bigcup_{j < i} Out_j$ for every $i$. Under this view, decomposable programs are well-suited to encode iterative algorithms or dynamic programming algorithms, that frequently occur in a variety of application domains.

Observe that every stratified program, whose answer sets can be computed in polynomial time in the size of the program, is decomposable—while the converse does not necessarily hold. Thus, computing answer sets of a decomposable program is not necessarily a simple task. However, the computation of an answer set of a decomposable program could potentially be done more efficiently, if the splitting theorem was applied in the process. This is because the size of the program $\Pi_i$ depends not only on the original program $\Pi$, but also on the answer sets computed up to that point (i.e., $\bigcup_{j < i} A_j$). This requires the interleaving of grounding and solving. By interleaving grounding and solving, some problems that cannot be solved with current ASP solvers may become efficiently solvable—as the examples illustrated earlier in this paper.

This type of computation is quite natural to encode in the context of ASP-Prolog. Assume that the program $\Pi$ has been decomposed into a list $L$ of components. The following Prolog predicate can be used in ASP-Prolog to compute answer sets of $\Pi$.

$solve([], Out, Out).$
$solve([H|T], In, A) \leftarrow use\_asp(H, H, In), H : model(M), collect\_facts(M, F),$
$\qquad solve(T, F, A).$

To compute answer sets of the program $\Pi$ with the list of components $L$, the goal `solve(L, [], A)` should be issued. The predicate `collect_facts(M,F)` collects in a list F all elements of the answer set named M. Observe that the above implementation requires a prior decomposition of the program. The implementation could be improved by introducing a module that analyzes the program and automatically identifies the splitting sequence—a topic of future work.

**Computing Iterative Algorithms.** We will continue with a general methodology for the implementation of iterative algorithms such as the supertree computation algorithm detailed earlier. Observe that this type of algorithm can be characterized by a sequence of values $F(0), F(1), \ldots, F(n), \ldots$. The computation stops when a boolean condition, denoted by $H$, is satisfied. A generic procedure for computing iterative algorithms can be roughly described as follows: **(1)** initialize settings and initialize counter $i$ to 0; **(2)** while the halting condition $H$ is not satisfied, compute $F^i(v)$ using input $F^{i-1}(v)$ and increment $i$; and **(3)** return $F^i(v)$.

Assume that the initialization (step **(1)** and the body of the loop in **(2)** can be implemented by the ASP programs $R$ and $Q$, such that $Q$ has a splitting set $S$. This assumption is, for example, met in the supertree computation problem—thus, we can view algorithm 1 as a typical iterative algorithm and its implementation satisfies this condition—where the splitting set $S$ of $Q$ contains all but the atoms of the form $new\_pruned\_set(n)$, $new\_member(b, n)$, and $generated\_pruned\_set(n, a)$ in $Q$. Under the above assumptions, we can use the following steps to implement the iterative algorithm in ASP: **(a)** add $t$ as the last parameter for every predicate in $S$; **(b)** add $t + 1$ as the last parameter for every predicate not in $S$; and **(c)** add the declaration that $t$ is a constant in $Q$. The following pseudo code realizes the algorithm in ASP-Prolog:

$solve(Q, R, A) \leftarrow solve(Q, R, A, 0).$

$solve(Q, R, A, 0) \leftarrow use\_asp(R, R, []), R : model(M), create\_file(M, File),$
$\qquad\qquad (satisfied(M, H) \rightarrow A = File; solve(Q, A, File, 1)).$

$solve(Q, A, Prev, T) \leftarrow T > 0, create\_string(Paras, T, Prev),$
$\qquad\qquad use\_asp(Q, Q, [Paras]), Q : model(M), create\_file(M, File),$
$\qquad\qquad (satisfied(M, H) \rightarrow A = File; solve(Q, A, File, T + 1)).$

In the above code, `create_string(Paras,T,Prev)` creates a string of the form '-c t=@T @M' where @T (@M) is replaced by the value of $T$ ($Prev$) respectively; and the predicate `satisfied(M,H)` indicates whether the current answer set (described by module named M) satisfies the halting condition $H$ on Line 3. This code is problem specific and needs to be instantiated by the programmer. A simple way to achieve this can be realized by adding a rule of the following form

$incomplete \leftarrow not\ H.$

to the program $Q$. For instance, for the program computing the supertree, the rule

$incomplete \leftarrow new\_pruned\_set(N).$

can be used. In this case, the test `satisfied(M,H)` is equivalent to checking the membership of $incomplete$ in M. We have applied this method in solving the problem of computing the approximated supertree. We should note that, with this method, we were able to compute the solutions for all three problems described in the three use cases. In particular, we can solve the largest problem for computing the supertree that was discussed in the literature (two trees, with 41 leaves and 31 leaves, respectively).

Before we conclude this section, we would like to point out that there are easy ways to facilitate an interleaving between grounding and solving using current ASP solvers (e.g., using a scripting language). However, we believe that an off-the-shelf ASP solver with this feature would have a much larger impact, as it would open ASP to other types of applications that have not been considered so far. Furthermore, we observe that this feature could be implemented in a similar fashion as the ICLINGO system (as a matter of fact, it could be a minor modification of ICLINGO).

## 4  Computing Equilibria

In this section, we will present another challenging application of ASP-Prolog. We describe a system, called ASP-Prolog$^{MCS}$, for computing the equilibrium semantics of multi-context systems (MCS). Observe that the previous applications are concerned with one program that can be decomposed into a sequence of programs, whose answer sets can be computed sequentially. The second application is concerned with a set of inter-connected programs whose semantics (an equilibrium) is a sequence of models. In many cases, these models might not be computed sequentially as in the first application. Before we detail the implementation of ASP-Prolog$^{MCS}$ let us discuss the algorithms that can be used in computing the equilibrium semantics of a MCS.

Let $M = (C_1, \ldots, C_n)$ be a MCS, where the logic for each context is logic programming under answer set semantics [10]. For each context $C_i = (L_i, kb_i, br_i)$ and for each bridge rule $r$ in $br_i$, we introduce a new set of "tagged" atoms in the language of $L_i$, of the form $t(c_k, p_k)$, for $k = 1, \ldots, m$ and $c_k \neq i$. We define the program $R(r)$ that consists of the following rules (for $k = 1, \ldots, m$ and $c_k \neq i$):

$$0 \{t(c_k, p_k)\} 1 \leftarrow$$
$$s \leftarrow t(c_1, p_1), \ldots, t(c_j, p_j), \text{ not } t(c_{j+1}, p_{j+1}), \ldots, \text{ not } t(c_m, p_m).$$

where $(c_i, p_i)$ is replaced by $t(c_i, p_i)$. We denote the second rule above by $t(r)$. Let $P_i = kb_i \cup \bigcup_{r \in br_i} R(r)$ and $MP = (P_1, \ldots, P_n)$. The set of literals of the form $t(k, p)$ occurring in $P_i$ is denoted by $T_i$. For the MCS $M_1$ in Example 2.1, we have that $T_1 = \{t(2, d)\}$ and $T_2 = \{t(1, b)\}$.

For a belief state $S = (S_1, \ldots, S_n)$ of $M$, we define $t(i, S) = \{t(j, p) | t(j, p) \in T_i \text{ and } p \in S_j\}$. We can show that a belief state $S = (S_1, \ldots, S_n)$ is an equilibrium of $M$ if $S_i \cup t(i, S)$ is an answer set of $P_i$. Continuing with the MCS $M_1$ in Example 2.1, $S = (\{a\}, \{d\})$ is an equilibrium of $M_1$ because we have that $t(1, S) = \{t(2, d)\}$ and $t(2, S) = \emptyset$; in this case, $\{a\} \cup t(1, S)$ is an answer set of $P_1$, and $\{d\} \cup t(2, S) = \{d\}$ is an answer set of $P_2$. On the other hand, $S = (\{b\}, \{d\})$ is not an equilibrium of $M_1$. We can observe that $t(1, S) = \{t(2, d)\}$ and $t(2, S) = \{t(1, b)\}$; thus, $\{d\} \cup t(2, S) = \{d, t(1, b)\}$ is an answer set of $P_2$, but $\{b\} \cup t(1, S) = \{b, t(2, d)\}$ is not an answer set of $P_1$.

Two answer sets $Z_i$ and $Z_j$ of $P_i$ and $P_j$ are *compatible* if: $t(i, p) \in Z_j$ iff $p \in Z_i$ and $t(i, p) \in T_j$, and $t(j, p) \in Z_i$ iff $p \in Z_j$ and $t(j, p) \in T_i$. Again, consider the MCS $M_1$ in Example 2.1, $\{a\}$ is compatible with $\{c\}$; $\{a, t(2, d)\}$ is compatible with $\{d\}$; however, $\{a\}$ is not compatible with $\{d\}$.

We can show that for a sequence of answer sets $Z = (Z_1, \ldots, Z_n)$ of $(P_1, \ldots, P_n)$, $Z' = (Z_1 \setminus T_1, \ldots, Z_n \setminus T_n)$ is an equilibrium of $M$ if $Z_i$ is compatible with $Z_j$ for every pair of $i \neq j$. This enables a naive computation of the equilibrium in a generate-and-test fashion: *(i)* Generate a belief state $Z = (Z_1, \ldots, Z_n)$ of $(P_1, \ldots, P_n)$; *(ii)* Check for compatibility of $Z$. This is the first algorithm that we implemented in ASP-Prolog$^{MCS}$.

The naive algorithm, however, requires an excessive amount of memory when dealing with programs that have a large number of answer sets. We can exploit the compatibility between answer sets of the programs $P_i$'s in the construction of an equilibrium $S = (S_1, \ldots, S_n)$ of $M$ in an incremental fashion.[5] Given a MCS $M = (C_1, \ldots, C_n)$, the algorithm needs to first compute $MP = (P_1, \ldots, P_n)$ and then compute a sequence of compatible answer sets $Z = \text{compatible}(MP)$. If $Z$ is not a failure, then the result will be $S = (Z_1 \setminus T_1, \ldots, Z_n \setminus T_n)$. The function that computes a sequence of compatible answer sets (compatible) is given in Algorithm 2. Observe that the algorithm has two non-deterministic choices.

Both the naive and the incremental algorithms can compute MCS with arbitrary topologies, and they can be easily implemented in ASP-Prolog. Before discussing this, we consider some enhancements that take into consideration the topology of MCS. We define the *dependency graph* $G_M = (V_M, E_M)$ of a MCS $M = (C_1, \ldots, C_n)$ as follows:

○ The set of vertices is $V_M = \{1, \ldots, n\}$;
○ $(i, j) \in E_M$ if $(i : p)$ appears in the body of some bridge rule in $br_j$ and $i \neq j$.

---

[5] This is possible since $M$ is reducible [3].

---

**Algorithm 2.** `compatible(MP)`

---

1: **Input:** $MP = (P_1, \ldots, P_n)$
2: Nondeterministically select $Z$ in `compatible`$(P_1, \ldots, P_{n-1})$
3: Assume that $Z = (Z_1, \ldots, Z_{n-1})$
4: **if** $Z \neq$ **fail then**
5:    Let $Q_i^1 = \{\leftarrow not\ p \mid t(n, p) \in Z_i\}$ for $i < n$
6:    Let $Q_i^2 = \{t(i, p) \leftarrow \mid t(i, p) \in T_n$ and $p \in Z_i\}$ for $i < n$
7:    Let $Q_i^3 = \{\leftarrow t(i, p) \mid t(i, p) \in T_n$ and $p \notin Z_i\}$ for $i < n$
8:    $P_n = P_n \cup \bigcup_{i=1}^{n-1}(Q_i^1 \cup Q_i^2 \cup Q_i^3)$
9:    Select an answer set $Z_n$ of $P_n$, $Z_n$ compatible with $Z_j$ for $j \leq n - 1$
10:   **return** $Z = (Z_1, \ldots, Z_{n-1}, Z_n)$
11: **end if**
12: **return fail**

---

Intuitively, an edge $(i, j)$ in $E_M$ indicates that if $S = (S_1, \ldots, S_n)$ is an equilibrium of $M$ then the applicability of a bridge rule in $br_j$ depends on the belief set $S_i$. It is well-known that the graph $G_M$ specifies a topology that can be used in computing equilibria of $M$. For instance, if $(i, j)$ is an edge in $G_M$ and $G_M$ does not contain the edge $(j, i)$, it is sensible to compute the $i^{th}$ belief set before computing the $j^{th}$ belief set. This has been utilized in the systems DMCS and DMCSOPT [6,1].[6]

Let us define an ordering $\prec_M$ between the contexts, where $i \prec_M j$ if there exists a path from $i$ to $j$ in $G_M$. We consider the following cases:

- $\prec_M$ is a partial order: it can be extended to a total order $\prec_M^*$ over the set $\{1, \ldots, n\}$.
- $\prec_M$ contains a cycle: let $SCC_1, \ldots, SCC_t$ be a set of strongly connected components (SCC) of $G_M$, $SCC_i = (V_i, E_i)$, such that $V_M = \bigcup_{i=1}^t V_i$ and $E_M = \bigcup_{i=1}^t E_i$. Furthermore, the following induced order is a partial order over the SCCs: $SCC_i \prec_M SCC_j$ iff there exists some $s_i \in SCC_i$ and $s_j \in SCC_j$ such that $s_i \prec_M s_j$.

The order $\prec_M$ can be used for computing the equilibria of $M$ as follows:

- Add the computation of the dependency graph $G_M$, the SCCs of $G_M$, and the ordering $\prec_M$ before the computation of $MP$.
- Sort $P_1, \ldots, P_n$ using $\prec_M$ on the SCCs of $G_M$ and provide Algorithm 2 with the ordering $\prec_M$ (for programs in the same SCC, an arbitrary order is used).
- Modify Algorithm 2 to eliminate the compatibility checking between $Z_n$ and $Z_i$ if $n \prec_M i$ does not hold (Line 9).

The next section discusses the implementation.

## 4.1 ASP-Prolog$^{MCS}$

The current implementation of ASP-Prolog$^{MCS}$ computes equilibria for MCS of the form $M = (C_1, \ldots, C_n)$ where the logic underlying each context is logic programming

---

[6] In these systems, the dependency graph is defined in reverse order and used somewhat differently from our proposal.

under answer set semantics [10]. Extending ASP-Prolog$^{MCS}$ to allow different seman-tics can easily be introduced since ASP-Prolog can support different types of semantics for different modules. We assume that each $C_i = (L_i, kb_i, br_i)$ is stored in a file named $p_i$ containing $p_i = kb_i \cup br_i$. The main predicates of ASP-Prolog$^{MCS}$ are:

- `load_MCS(Input)`: this predicate prepares the computation of the equilibrium of the MCS whose contexts are specified by the list `Input`. Its execution will:
  - Create a Prolog module named $p_i$, for each $p_i \in$ `Input`, and compute $P_i = kb_i \cup \bigcup_{r \in br_i} R(r)$ (as defined earlier);
  - Create a dependency graph between contexts. This is achieved by defining a pred-icate $dependency/4$ where, for each literal $(c_k : p_k)$ in a bridge rule $r$ of the context $c_i$ such that $c_k \neq c_i$, we assert the atom $dependency(c_i, s, c_k, p_k)$. Intu-itively, the atom $dependency(i, a, j, p)$ states that there is a dependence of atom $a$ in the context $i$ to atom $p$ in the context $j$.

- `compute_equilibrium(Input, Answer)`: two versions of this predicate have been implemented. The first one implements the naive generate-and-test algorithm and the second one implements the modified algorithm discussed above. The imple-mentation of this predicate makes use of the infrastructure provided by ASP-Prolog. Execution of this predicate will: load the files in `Input`, which is a list of files rep-resenting the MCS, compute the answer sets of each program in `Input` (via the predicate `use_asp/3`), and call the predicate that implements the naive algorithm or the Algorithm 2 to obtain the equilibrium.

- `generate_and_test(Input, Answer)`: this predicate implements the generate and test algorithm and returns the answer.

- `compatible(Input, Answer)`: this implements the algorithm `compatible` and returns the answer.

### 4.2    Experiments

We experimented ASP-Prolog$^{MCS}$ with the set of benchmarks downloaded from the DMCS system website.[7] The benchmarks include five domains (`Diamond`, `Ring`, `Zig-zag`, `House` and `Binary tree`). The name of each domain characterizes the topology of the MCS, for example, in an instance of the `Diamond` domain, the contexts are combined by multiple diamonds in a row.

Both algorithms were used in testing this set of problems. The experiments were successful, showing a competitive performance. The only limitation encountered was in problems where selected contexts have a large number of answer sets—e.g., sev-eral thousands—in which case the answer sets occasionally saturated the streams cre-ated by the underlying Prolog system—SICStus Prolog, used in the current imple-mentation, imposes limitations on the number of concurrent open streams (around 200 streams). Only the generate-and-test algorithm can successfully solve all problems, due to the limitations on the numbers of opened streams; the second algorithm cannot be used for MCS with more than 200 contexts. However, whenever possible both algo-rithms performed well. Overall, ASP-Prolog$^{MCS}$ performs well in the search for an

---

[7] www.kr.tuwien.ac.at/research/systems/dmcs/experiments.html

equilibrium after the contexts have been loaded. The complete evaluation can be found at www.cs.nmsu.edu/~tile/aspmcs/experiment.html.

## 4.3  Application of ASP-Prolog$^{MCS}$

Although ASP-Prolog$^{MCS}$ was developed for MCSs, an interesting by-product of the system is that it can be used to compute answer sets of decomposable logic programs.

Let $\Pi$ be a decomposable logic program. For simplicity, let us assume that $\Pi$ has a splitting set $S$. Let us consider a partition $(\Pi_1, \Pi_2)$ of $\Pi$, such that $\Pi_1$ is the bottom of $\Pi$ with respect to $S$, i.e., $\Pi_1 = b_S(\Pi)$ and $\Pi_2 = \Pi \setminus \Pi_1$. Let $M = (C_1, C_2)$ where $C_i = (L_i, \Pi_i, br_i)$, $L_i$ is the logic of logic programming under answer set semantics, $br_1 = \emptyset$ and $br_2 = \{l \leftarrow c_1 : l \mid l \in S\}$. It is easy to see that $X$ is an answer set of $\Pi$ iff $X = X_1 \cup X_2$ such that $(X_1, X_2)$ is an equilibrium of $M$. This means that the equilibrium of the MCS $(C_1, C_2)$ can be computed by Algorithm 2 without backtracking, i.e., ASP-Prolog$^{MCS}$ could provide an alternative platform for the implementation of decomposable programs and iterative algorithms, as the above observation can be generalized to a splitting sequence of $\Pi$. We will show next that ASP-Prolog$^{MCS}$ could be used to explore heuristics in answer set programming.

Let us consider the well-known graph coloring problem. Given a undirected graph $(V, E)$, we would like to know whether the graph has a 3-coloring solution. The ASP encoding for computing a 3-coloring solution of a graph $(V, E)$, denoted by $\Pi(V, E)$, is well-known and is omitted here to save space.

**Table 1.** ASP-Prolog$^{MCS}$ in 3-coloring

| Instance | colorable | ASP-Prolog$^{MCS}$ | | | Instance | colorable | ASP-Prolog$^{MCS}$ | | |
|---|---|---|---|---|---|---|---|---|---|
| | | Load | MCS | total | | | Load | MCS | total |
| p10000e10000 | y | 20.63 | 10.16 | 30.79 | p10000e11000 | y | 22.75 | 12.56 | 35.31 |
| p10000e12000 | y | 24.99 | 13.53 | 38.52 | p10000e13000 | y | 25.74 | 17.87 | 43.61 |
| p10000e14000 | y | 27.42 | 14.93 | 42.35 | p10000e15000 | y | 31.93 | 16.68 | 48.61 |
| p10000e16000 | y | 37.37 | 20.93 | 58.30 | p10000e17000 | y | 52.71 | 18.99 | 71.70 |
| p10000e18000 | y | 50.73 | 12.51 | 63.24 | p10000e19000 | y | 50.46 | 11.79 | 62.25 |
| p10000e20000 | y | 53.57 | 10.80 | 64.37 | p10000e21000 | n | 59.02 | 4.51 | 63.53 |

A well-known heuristic for solving the 3-coloring problem is as follows. Let the degree of a node $X$, denoted by $degree(X)$, be the number of edges that have one endpoint in $X$. Let $R(V, E) = (V', E')$ be the graph obtained from $(V, E)$ by removing all vertices whose degree is less than 3 and all the edges to/from these vertices. It is easy to see that $\Pi(V, E)$ has an answer set iff $\Pi(V', E')$ does. This process can be repeated until the degree of all vertices in the graph is at least three (including the possibility of the graph becoming empty). This can be used to create a partition $(V_1, \ldots, V_n)$ of $V$, where $V_i$ is the set of vertices with degree less than 3 in the graph consisting of the vertices $\bigcup_{j=1}^{i} V_j$ and the edges among them that belong to $E$. Intuitively, $V_i$ is the set of nodes removed at the $i^{th}$ iteration of the process described above. Using this partition, we can define a MCS $M = (C_1, \ldots, C_n)$ where, for each $i$, **(i)** $kb_i$ contains the rules

$\Pi(V_i, E_i)$, where $E_i$ is the set of edges from $E$ between nodes in $V_i$; **(ii)** $br_i$ contains the following constraints: for each $(p, q) \in E$ such that $q \in V_i$ and $p \in V_k$ with $k < i$:

$$\leftarrow (k : color(p, C)), color(q, C).$$

The Prolog code for computing the above partition is straightforward. We experimented this idea using the instances of the graph coloring problems obtained from `assat.cs.ust.hk/Assat-2.0/coloring-2.0.html`. The results of this experiment are presented in Table 1. In this table, each instance is of the form p*nem*, where $n$ is the number of vertices and $m$ is the number of edges in the graph. All the reported problems are randomly generated. The results show the simplicity of adding heuristics in the process. The execution times are relatively high compared to optimized ASP solvers (e.g., CLASP), due to the relative cost of decomposing the graph into MCS, but show success where other systems (e.g., standard Prolog or CLP(FD)) would fail.

## 5   Conclusions

In this paper, we presented two applications of the ASP-Prolog system. The first application deals with a large class of logic programs that are computationally easy, yet sometimes unsolvable for current ASP solvers. We showed how answer sets of this type of programs can be computed using the ASP-Prolog platform. The experimental results with the use cases highlight the potential of ASP-Prolog as a viable platform for the use of ASP in practical problems.

The second application is a centralized MCS system, ASP-Prolog$^{MCS}$, built using the facilities provided by ASP-Prolog. We described the implementation of the computation of equilibria semantics and encouraging experimental results. The system implements various algorithms that are required for the computation of equilibria of MCS systems; these are made possible by the specific capabilities of ASP-Prolog. The system can be used in applications that can be formulated as MCSs. The experimental evaluation is promising. Nevertheless, it also highlighted a need for improving the performance of ASP-Prolog$^{MCS}$. We believe that this can be achieved via targeted optimizations. In particular, we propose to explore mechanisms to optimize backtracking among modules (e.g., through caching mechanisms) and communication. This will be one of our goals in the nearest future.

As another future work of both applications, we propose to explore the role that the specific capabilities of ASP-Prolog (e.g., constraint solving capabilities) can have.

## References

1. Bairakdar, S.E.-D., Dao-Tran, M., Eiter, T., Fink, M., Krennwallner, T.: The DMCS Solver for Distributed Nonmonotonic Multi-Context Systems. In: Janhunen, T., Niemelä, I. (eds.) JELIA 2010. LNCS, vol. 6341, pp. 352–355. Springer, Heidelberg (2010)
2. Balduccini, M., Gelfond, M.: The Language ASP{f} with arithmetic expressions and consistency-restoring rules. CoRR, abs/1301.1387 (2013)
3. Brewka, G., Eiter, T.: Equilibria in Heterogeneous Nonmonotonic Multi-Context Systems. In: AAAI, pp. 385–390 (2007)

4. Castro, L., Swift, T., Warren, D.: XASP: Answer Set Programming with XSB and Smodels. SUNY Stony Brook (2002), xsb.sourceforge.net/packages/xasp.pdf
5. Citrigno, S., et al.: The DLV system: Model generator and application frontends. In: WLP, pp. 128–137 (1997)
6. Dao-Tran, M., et al.: Distributed nonmonotonic multi-context systems. In: KR. AAAI Press (2010)
7. Elkhatib, O., Pontelli, E., Son, T.C.: ASP-Prolog: A System for Reasoning about Answer Set Programs in Prolog. In: Jayaraman, B. (ed.) PADL 2004. LNCS, vol. 3057, pp. 148–162. Springer, Heidelberg (2004)
8. Gebser, M., Kaufmann, B., Neumann, A., Schaub, T.: *clasp*: A conflict-driven answer set solver. In: Baral, C., Brewka, G., Schlipf, J. (eds.) LPNMR 2007. LNCS (LNAI), vol. 4483, pp. 260–265. Springer, Heidelberg (2007)
9. Gelfond, M., Gabaldon, A.: From functional specifications to logic programs. In: ILPS, pp. 355–370. MIT Press (1997)
10. Gelfond, M., Lifschitz, V.: Logic programs with classical negation. In: ICLP, pp. 579–597 (1990)
11. Lifschitz, V., Turner, H.: Splitting a logic program. In: ICLP, pp. 23–38. MIT Press (1994)
12. Maddison, W., Maddison, D.: MacClade 4: Analysis of Phylogeny and Character Evolution. Sinauer (2000)
13. Marek, V., Truszczyński, M.: Stable models and an alternative logic programming paradigm. In: The Logic Programming Paradigm, pp. 375–398. Springer (1999)
14. Nguyen, N.-H., Son, T.C., Pontelli, E., Sakama, C.: ASP-prolog for negotiation among dishonest agents. In: Delgrande, J.P., Faber, W. (eds.) LPNMR 2011. LNCS, vol. 6645, pp. 331–344. Springer, Heidelberg (2011)
15. Niemelä, I.: Logic programming with stable model semantics as a constraint programming paradigm. Annals of Mathematics and Artificial Intelligence 25(3,4), 241–273 (1999)
16. Pontelli, E., et al.: ASP at Work: An ASP Implementation of PhyloWS. In: ICLP. LIPICs (2012)
17. Pontelli, E., Son, T.C., Nguyen, N.-H.: Combining Answer Set Programming and Prolog: the ASP-Prolog System. In: Balduccini, M., Son, T.C. (eds.) Logic Programming, Knowledge Representation, and Nonmonotonic Reasoning. LNCS, vol. 6565, pp. 452–472. Springer, Heidelberg (2011)
18. Sanderson, M., Purvis, A., Henze, C.: Phylogenetic Supertrees: Assembling the Trees of Life. Trends Ecol. Evol. 13, 105–109 (1998)
19. Semple, C., Steel, M.: A Supertree Method for Rooted Trees. Di. Ap. Math. 105, 147–158 (2000)
20. Simons, P., Niemelä, N., Soininen, T.: Extending and implementing the stable model semantics. Artificial Intelligence 138(1-2), 181–234 (2002)
21. Son, T.C., Pontelli, E., Nguyen, N.-H.: Planning for multiagent using ASP-Prolog. In: Dix, J., Fisher, M., Novák, P. (eds.) CLIMA X. LNCS, vol. 6214, pp. 1–21. Springer, Heidelberg (2010)
22. Yokoo, M., et al.: The Distributed Constraint Satisfaction Problem: Formalization and Algorithms. IEEE Transactions on Knowledge and Data Engineering 10(5), 673–685 (1998)
23. Yokoo, M., Hirayama, K.: Algorithms for Distributed Constraint Satisfaction: A Review. Autonomous Agents and Multi-Agent Systems 3(2), 185–207 (2000)

# Towards Modeling Morality Computationally with Logic Programming

Ari Saptawijaya* and Luís Moniz Pereira

Centro de Inteligência Artificial (CENTRIA), Departamento de Informática
Faculdade de Ciências e Tecnologia, Univ. Nova de Lisboa, 2829-516 Caparica, Portugal
ar.saptawijaya@campus.fct.unl.pt, lmp@fct.unl.pt

**Abstract.** We investigate the potential of logic programming (LP) to model morality aspects studied in philosophy and psychology. We do so by identifying three morality aspects that appear in our view amenable to computational modeling by appropriately exploiting LP features: dual-process model (reactive and deliberative) in moral judgments; justification of moral judgments by contractualism; and intention in moral permissibility. The research aims at developing an LP-based system with features needed in modeling moral settings, putting emphasis on modeling these above mentioned morality aspects. We have currently co-developed two essential ingredients of the LP system, i.e., abduction and logic program updates, by exploiting the benefits of tabling features in logic programs. They serve as the basis for our whole system, into which other reasoning facets will be integrated, to model the surmised morality aspects. Moreover, we touch upon the potential of our ongoing studies of LP based cognitive features for the emergence of computational morality, in populations of agents enabled with the capacity for intention recognition, commitment and apology.

**Keywords:** abduction, program updates, argumentation, reactive behavior, deliberative reasoning, morality, emergence.

## 1 Introduction

The importance of imbuing agents more or less autonomous, with some capacity for moral decision making has recently gained a resurgence of interest from the artificial intelligence community, bringing together perspectives from philosophy and psychology. A new field of enquiry, *computational morality* (also known as machine ethics, machine morality, artificial morality and computational ethics) has emerged from their interaction, as emphasized e.g., in [5, 17, 65]. Research in artificial intelligence particularly focuses on how to employ various techniques, namely from computational logic, machine learning and multi-agent systems, in order to computationally model moral decision making (to some improved extent). The overall result is therefore not only important for equipping agents with the capacity for moral decision making, but also for helping us better understand morality, through the creation and testing of computational models of ethical theories.

---

\* Affiliated with Faculty of Computer Science at University of Indonesia, Depok, Indonesia.

M. Flatt and H.-F. Guo (Eds.): PADL 2014, LNCS 8324, pp. 104–119, 2014.

Recent results in computational morality have mainly focused on equipping agents with particular ethical theories, cf. [6] and [51] for modeling utilitarianism and deontological ethics, respectively. Another line of work attempts to provide a general framework to encode moral rules, in favor of deontological ethics, without resorting to a set of specific moral rules, e.g., [11]. The techniques employed include machine learning techniques, e.g., case-based reasoning [39], artificial neural networks [21], inductive logic programming [3, 7], and logic-based formalisms e.g., deontic logic [11] and nonmonotonic logics [51]. The use of these latter formalisms has only been proposed rather abstractly, with no further investigation on its use pursued in detail and implemented.

Apart from the use of inductive logic programming in [3, 7], there has not much been a serious attempt to employ the Logic Programming (LP) paradigm in computational morality. Notwithstanding, we have preliminarily shown in [24, 44–48] that LP, with its currently available ingredients and features, lends itself well to the modeling of moral decision making. In these works, we particularly benefited from abduction [30], stable model [19] and well-founded model [64] semantics, preferences [15], and probability [9], on top of evolving logic programs [1], amenable to both self and external updating. LP-based modeling of morality is addressed at length, e.g., in [33].

Our research further investigates the appropriateness of LP to model morality, emphasizing morality aspects studied in philosophy and psychology, thereby providing an improved LP-based system as a testing ground for understanding and experimentation of such aspects and their applications. We particularly consider only some – rather than tackle all morality aspects – namely those pertinent to moral decision making, and, in our view, those particularly amenable to computational modeling by exploring and exploiting the appropriate LP features. Our research does not aim to propose some new moral theory, the task naturally belonging to philosophers and psychologists, but we simply uptake their known results off-the-shelf. We identify henceforth three morality aspects for the purpose of our work: dual-process model (reactive and deliberative) in moral judgments [13, 38], justification of moral judgments by contractualism [58, 59], and the significance of intention in regard to moral permissibility [60].

The remainder of the paper is organized as follows. Section 2 discusses the state-of-the-art of approaches that have been sought in computational morality. In Section 3 we detail the potential of LP for computational morality in the context of our research goal, and give a direction on how LP can be exploited to model the three chosen morality aspects. Section 4 presents two novel implementation techniques for abduction and knowledge updates, which serve as basic ingredients of the system being developed. Section 5 summarizes an application concerning a princess-saving moral robot. We conclude, in Section 6, by pointing out the importance of cognitive abilities in what regards the emergence of cooperation and morality in populations of individuals, as fostered in our own work, and mention directions for the future in this respect.

# 2   State of the Art

The field of computational morality, known too as machine ethics [5], has started growing, motivated by various objectives, e.g., to equip machines with the capability of moral decision making in certain domains, to aid (or even train) humans in moral decision making, to provide a general modeling framework for moral decision making, and to understand morality better by experimental model simulation.

The purpose of 'artificial morality' in [14] is somewhat different. The aim is to show that moral agents successfully solve social problems that amoral agents cannot. This work is based on the techniques from game theory and evolutionary game theory, where social problems are abstracted into social dilemmas, such as Prisoner's Dilemma and Chicken, and interactions of agents in games are implemented using Prolog.

The systems TruthTeller and SIROCCO were developed based on case-based reasoning [39]. Both systems implement the ethical approach casuistry [29]. TruthTeller is designed to accept a pair of ethical dilemmas and describe the salient similarities and differences between the cases, from both an ethical and a pragmatic perspective. On the other hand, SIROCCO is constructed to accept an ethical dilemma and to retrieve similar cases and ethical principles relevant to the ethical dilemma presented.

In [21], artificial neural networks, i.e., simple recurrent networks, are used with the main purpose of understanding morality from the philosophy of ethics viewpoint, and in particular to explore the dispute between moral particularism and generalism. The learning mechanism of neural networks is used to classify moral situations by training such networks with a number of cases, involving actions concerning killing and allowing to die, and then using the trained networks to classify test cases.

Besides case-based reasoning and artificial neural networks, another machine learning technique that is also utilised in the field is inductive logic programming, as evidenced by two systems: MedEthEx [7] and EthEl [3]. These are advisor systems in the domain of biomedicine, based on prima facie duty theory [53] from biomedical ethics. MedEthEx is dedicated to give advice for dilemmas in biomedical fields, while EthEl serves as a medication-reminder system for the elderly and as a notifier to an overseer if the patient refuses to take the medication. The latter system has been implemented in a real robot, the Nao robot, being capable to find and walk toward a patient who needs to be reminded of medication, to bring the medication to the patient, to engage in a natural-language exchange, and to notify an overseer by email when necessary [4].

Jeremy is another advisor system [6], which is based upon Jeremy Bentham's act utilitarianism. The moral decision is made in a straightforward manner. For each possible decision $d$, there are three components to consider with respect to each person $p$ affected: the intensity of pleasure/displeasure ($I_p$), the duration of the pleasure/displeasure ($D_p$) and the probability that this pleasure/displeasure will occur ($P_p$). Total net pleasure for each decision is then computed: $total_d = \Sigma_{p \in Person}(I_p \times D_p \times P_p)$. The right decision is the one giving the highest total net pleasure.

Apart from the adoption of utilitarianism, like in the Jeremy system, in [51] the deontological tradition is considered having modeling potential, where the first formulation of Kant's categorical imperative [32] is concerned. Three views are taken into account in reformulating Kant's categorical imperative for the purpose of machine ethics: mere consistency, common-sense practical reasoning, and coherency. To realize the first view, a form of deontic logic is adopted. The second view benefits from nonmonotonic logic, and the third view presumes ethical deliberation to follow a logic similar to that of belief revision. All of them are considered abstractly and there seems to exist no implementation on top of these formalisms.

Deontic logic is envisaged in [11], as a framework to encode moral rules. The work resorts to Murakami's axiomatized deontic logic, an axiomatized utilitarian formulation of multiagent deontic logic, that is used to decide operative moral rule to attempt to arrive at an expected moral decision. This is achieved by seeking a proof for the expected moral outcome that follows from candidate operative moral rules.

The use of category theory appears in [12], where it is used as the formal framework to reason over logical systems, taking the view that logical systems are being deployed to formalize ethical codes. The work is strongly based on Piaget's position [28]. As argued in [12], this idea of reasoning *over* – instead of reasoning *in* – logical systems, favors post-formal Piaget's stages beyond his well-known fourth stage. In other words, category theory is used as the meta-level of moral reasoning.

Belief-Desire-Intention (BDI) model [10] is adopted in SophoLab [66], a framework for experimental computational philosophy, which is implemented with JACK agent programming language. In this framework, the BDI model is extended with the deontic-epistemic-action logic [63] to make it suitable for modeling moral agents. SophoLab is used, for example, to study negative moral commands and two different utilitarian theories, viz. act and rule utilitarianism.

We have preliminarily shown, in [44, 45], the use of integrated LP features to model the classic trolley problem[1] [18] and the double effect[2] as the basis of moral decisions on these dilemmas. In particular, possible decisions in a moral dilemma are modeled as abducibles, and abductive stable models are computed to capture abduced decisions and their consequences. Models violating integrity constraints, i.e., those that contain actions violating the double effect principle, are ruled out. A posteriori preferences, including the use of utility functions, are eventually applied to prefer models that characterize more preferred moral decisions. The computational models, based on the prospective logic agent architecture (shown in Figure 1) and developed on top of XSB Prolog, successfully deliver moral decisions in accordance with the double effect principle. They conform to the results of empirical experiments conducted in cognitive science [27] and law [40]. In [46–48], the computational models of the trolley problem dilemmas are extended, using the same LP system, by considering another moral principle, viz. the triple effect principle [31]. The work was extended further, in [24], by

---

[1] The trolley dilemmas, adapted from [27]: "There is a trolley and its conductor has fainted. The trolley is headed toward five people walking on the track. The banks of the track are so steep that they will not be able to get off the track in time." The two main cases of the trolley dilemmas:

**Bystander:** Hank is standing next to a switch that can turn the trolley onto a side track, thereby preventing it from killing the five people. However, there is a man standing on the side track. Hank can throw the switch, killing him; or he can refrain from doing so, letting the five die. Is it morally permissible for Hank to throw the switch?

**Footbridge.** Ian is on the bridge over the trolley track, next to a heavy man, which he can shove onto the track in the path of the trolley to stop it, preventing the killing of five people. Ian can shove the man onto the track, resulting in death; or he can refrain from doing so, letting the five die. Is it morally permissible for Ian to shove the man?

[2] The doctrine of double effect states that doing harms to another individual is permissible if it is the foreseen consequence of an action that will lead to a greater good, but is impermissible as an intended means to such greater good [27].

introducing various aspects of uncertainty, achieved using P-log [9], into trolley problem dilemmas, both from the view of oneself and from that of others. The latter by tackling the case of jury trials to proffer rulings beyond reasonable doubt.

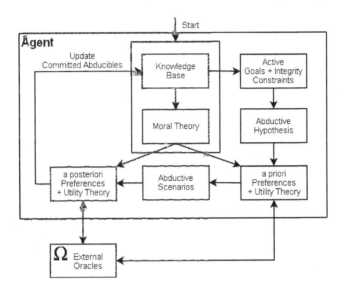

**Fig. 1.** Prospective logic agent architecture

## 3    Potential of Logic Programming for Computational Morality

Logic programming (LP) offers a formalism for declarative knowledge representation and reasoning. It thus has been used to solve problems in diverse areas of artificial intelligence (AI), e.g., planning, diagnosis, decision making, hypothetical reasoning, natural language processing, machine learning, etc.

Our research aims at developing an LP-based system with features needed in modeling moral settings, to represent agents' knowledge in those settings, and to allow moral reasoning under morality aspects studied in philosophy and moral psychology.

The choice of the LP paradigm is due to its potentials to model morality. For one thing, it allows moral rules, being employed when modeling some particular aspects, to be specified declaratively. For another, research in LP has provided us with necessary ingredients that are promising enough at being adept to model morality, e.g. default negation is suitable for expressing exception in moral rules, abductive logic programming [30] and (say) stable model semantics [19] can be used to generate possible decisions along with their moral consequences, and preferences [15] are appropriate for enabling to choose among moral decisions or moral rules.

We have identified three important morality aspects, from the fields of philosophy and psychology, that in our view are amenable to computational model by exploiting appropriate LP features: (1) the dual-process of moral judgments [13, 38], (2) justification of moral judgments [58, 59], and (3) the significance of intention in regard to moral permissibility [60]. The choice of these aspects is made due to their conceptual closeness with existing logic-based formalisms under available LP approaches as explained below. The choice is not meant to be exhaustive (as morality is itself a complex subject), in the sense that there may be other aspects that can be modeled computationally, particularly in LP. On the other hand, some aspects are not directly amenable to model in LP (at least for now), e.g., to model the role of emotions in moral decision making.

The development of the system is driven by the above three important morality aspects. The following LP features, being an integral part of the agent's observe-think-decide-act life cycle, serve as basic ingredients for the system to bring about moral reasoning:

1. **Knowledge updates, be they external or internal.** This is important due to constantly changing environment, and also particularly relevant in moral settings where an agent's moral rules are susceptible to updating, including when considering judgments about others, which are often made in spite of incomplete, or even contradictory, information.
2. **Deliberative and reactive decision making.** These two modes of decision making correspond to the dual-process model of moral judgments. Furthermore, reactive behavior can be employed for fast and frugal decision making with pre-compiled moral rules, thereby avoiding costly deliberative reasoning performed every time.

Given these basic ingredients, the whole process of moral decision making are particularly supported with the following capabilities of the system, justified by our need of modeling morality:

- To exclude undesirable actions. This is important when we must rule out actions that are morally impermissible under the moral rules being considered.
- To recognize intentions behind available actions, particularly in cases where intention is considered a significant aspect when addressing permissibility of actions.
- To generate alternatives of actions along with their consequences. In moral dilemmas agents are confronted with more than one course of action. They should be made available, along with their moral consequences, for an agent to ultimately decide about them.
- To prefer amongst alternatives of actions based on some measures. Preferences are relevant in moral settings, e.g. in case of several actions being permissible, preferences can be exercised to prefer one of them on the grounds of some criteria. Moreover, it is realistic to consider uncertainty of intentions, actions or consequences, including to perform counterfactual reasoning, in which cases preferences based on probability measures play a role.
- To inspect consequences of an action without deliberate imposition of the action itself as a goal. This is needed for instance to distinguish moral consequences of actions performed by an agent to satisfy its goals from those of its actions and side-effects performed unwittingly, not being part of the agent's goals.
- To provide an action with reasons for it (not) to be done. Reasons are used to justify permissibility of an action on grounds that one expects others to accept. In other words, morality in this way is viewed as striving towards argumentative consensus.

With respect to the first morality aspect, we look into recent approaches in combining deliberative and reactive logic-based systems [34, 35]. Inspired by these approaches, we have proposed two implementation techniques which are the basis for our system. First, we have improved the abduction system ABDUAL [2], employed for deliberative moral decision making in our previous work [24, 44–48]. We particularly explored the benefit of LP tabling mechanisms in abduction, to table abductive solutions for future reuse, resulting in a tabled abduction system TABDUAL [54]. Second, we have adapted evolving logic programs (EVOLP) [1], a formalism to model evolving agents, i.e., agents whose knowledge may dynamically change due to some (internal or external) updates. In EVOLP, updates are made possible by introducing the reserved predicate $assert/1$ into its language, whether in rule heads or rule bodies, which updates the program by the rule $R$, appearing in its only argument, whenever the assertion $assert(R)$ is true in a model; or retracts $R$ in case $assert(not\ R)$ obtains in the model under consideration. We simplified EVOLP, in an approach termed EVOLP/R [55, 56], by restricting assertions to fluents only, whether internal or external world ones. We discuss both TABDUAL and EVOLP/R in Section 4.

The second morality aspect views moral judgments as those about the adequacy of justification and reasons for accepting or rejecting the situated employment of broad consensual principles, whilst allowing for exceptions. This view is supported by *contractualism* [58], one of the major schools in moral philosophy. Contractualism provides flexibility on the set of principles to justify moral judgments so long as no one could reasonably reject them, i.e., reasoning becomes an important feature [59]. Thus, morality can be viewed as (possibly defeasible) argumentative consensus, which is why contractualism is interesting from a computational and AI perspective. We are researching the applicability of argumentative frameworks, such as [16, 52, 62], to deal with this aspect.

Finally, we shall employ results on intention recognition, e.g., [23] for the third morality aspect, about intention in regard to moral permissibility. Counterfactuals will also play some role in uncovering possible implicit intentions, and "What if?" questions in order to reason retrospectively about past decisions. With regard to counterfactuals, both causal models [8, 41] and the extension of inspection points [43] to examine contextual side effects of counterfactual abduction may be considered, meaning foreseeable extraneous consequences in future or past hypothetical scenarios.

The lighter conceptual and implementation advantages of EVOLP/R will help in combining with TABDUAL, to model both reactive and deliberative reasoning. Their combination also provides the basis for other reasoning facets needed in modeling other morality aspects, notably: argumentative frameworks and intention recognition to deal with the second and the third aspects, respectively.

## 4    TABDUAL and EVOLP/R

We recently proposed novel implementation techniques, both in abduction and logic program updates, by employing tabling mechanisms in LP. Tabling mechanisms in LP, known as the tabled logic programming paradigm, is currently supported by a number of Prolog systems, to different extent. Tabling affords solutions reuse, rather than recomputing them, by keeping in tables subgoals and their answers obtained by query evaluation. Our techniques are realized in XSB Prolog [61], one of the most advanced tabled LP systems, with features such as tabling over default negation, incremental tabling, answer subsumption, call subsumption, and threads with shared tables.

## 4.1 Tabled Abduction (TABDUAL)

The basic idea behind tabled abduction (its prototype is termed TABDUAL) is to employ tabling mechanisms in logic programs in order to reuse priorly obtained abductive solutions, from one abductive context to another. It is realized via a program transformation of abductive normal logic programs. Abduction is subsequently enacted on the transformed program.

The core transformation of TABDUAL consists of an innovative re-uptake of prior abductive solution entries in tabled predicates and relies on the dual transformation [2]. The dual transformation, initially employed in ABDUAL [2], allows to more efficiently handle the problem of abduction under negative goals, by introducing their positive dual counterparts. It does not concern itself with programs having variables. In TABDUAL, the dual transformation is refined, to allow it dealing with such programs. The first refinement helps ground (dualized) negative subgoals. The second one allows to deal with non-ground negative goals.

As TABDUAL is implemented in XSB, it employs XSB's tabling as much as possible to deal with loops. Nevertheless, tabled abduction introduces a complication concerning some varieties of loops. Therefore, the core TABDUAL transformation has been adapted, resorting to a pragmatic approach, to cater to all varieties of loops in normal logic programs, which are now complicated by abduction.

From the implementation viewpoint, several pragmatic aspects have been examined. First, because TABDUAL allows for modular mixes between abductive and non-abductive program parts, one can benefit in the latter part by enacting a simpler translation of predicates in the program comprised just of facts. It particularly helps avoid superfluous transformation of facts, which would hinder the use of large factual data. Second, we address the issue of potentially heavy transformation load due to producing the *complete* dual rules (i.e., all dual rules regardless of their need), if these are constructed in advance by the transformation (which is the case in ABDUAL). Such a heavy dual transformation makes it a bottleneck of the whole abduction process. Two approaches are provided to realizing the dual transformation *by-need*: creating and tabling all dual rules for a predicate only on the first invocation of its negation, or, in contrast, lazily generating and storing its dual rules in a trie (instead of tabling), only as new alternatives are required. The former leads to an eager (albeit by-need) tabling of dual rules construction (under local table scheduling), whereas the latter permits a by-need-driven lazy one (in lieu of batched table scheduling). Third, TABDUAL provides a system predicate that permits accessing ongoing abductive solutions. This is a useful feature and extends TABDUAL's flexibility, as it allows manipulating abductive solutions dynamically, e.g., preferring or filtering ongoing abductive solutions, e.g., checking them explicitly against nogoods at predefined program points.

We conducted evaluations of TABDUAL with various objectives, where we examine five TABDUAL variants of the same underlying implementation by separately factoring out TABDUAL's most important distinguishing features. They include the evaluations of: (1) the benefit of tabling abductive solutions, where we employ an example from declarative debugging, now characterized as abduction [57], to debug incorrect solutions of logic programs; (2) the three dual transformation variants: complete, eager by-need, and lazy by-need, where the other case of declarative debugging, that of debugging missing solutions, is employed; (3) tabling so-called *nogoods* of subproblems in the context of abduction (i.e., abductive solution candidates that violate constraints), where it can be shown that tabling abductive solutions can be appropriate for tabling nogoods of subproblems; (4) programs with loops, where the results are compared with ABDUAL, showing that TABDUAL provides more correct and complete results. Additionally, we show how TABDUAL can be applied in action decision making under hypothetical reasoning, and in a real medical diagnosis case [57].

## 4.2  Restricted Evolving Logic Programs (EVOLP/R)

We have defined the language of EVOLP/R in [56], adapted from that of Evolving Logic Programs (EVOLP) [1], by restricting updates at first to fluents only. More precisely, every fluent $F$ is accompanied by its fluent complement $\sim F$. Retraction of $F$ is thus achieved by asserting its complement $\sim F$ at the next timestamp, which renders $F$ supervened by $\sim F$ at later time; thereby making $F$ false. Nevertheless, it allows paraconsistency, i.e., both $F$ and $\sim F$ may hold at the same timestamp, to be dealt with by the user as desired, e.g., with integrity constraints or preferences.

In order to update the program with rules, special fluents (termed *rule name fluents*) are introduced to identify rules uniquely. Such a fluent is placed in the body of a rule, allowing to turn the rule on and off, cf. Poole's "naming device" [50]; this being achieved by asserting or retracting the rule name fluent. The restriction thus requires that all rules be known at the start.

EVOLP/R is realized by a program transformation and a library of system predicates. The transformation adds some extra information, e.g., timestamps, for internal processing. Rule name fluents are also system generated and added in the transform. System predicates are defined to operate on the transform by combining the usage of two features of tabling in XSB Prolog: incremental and answer subsumption tabling.

Incremental tabling of fluents allows to automatically maintain the consistency of program states, analogously to assumption based truth-maintenance system in artificial intelligence, due to assertion and retraction of fluents, by relevantly propagating their consequences. Answer subsumption of fluents, on the other hand, allows to address the frame problem by automatically keeping track of their latest assertion or retraction, whether obtained as updated facts or concluded by rules. Despite being pragmatic, employing these tabling features has profound consequences in modeling agents, i.e., it permits separating higher-level declarative representation and reasoning, as a mechanism pertinent to agents, from a world's inbuilt reactive laws of operation. The latter are relegated to engine-level enacted tabling features (in this case, the incremental and answer subsumption tabling); they are of no operational concern to the problem representation level.

Recently, in [55], we refined the implementation technique by fostering further incremental tabling, but leaving out the problematic use of the answer subsumption feature. The main idea is the perspective that knowledge updates (either self or world wrought changes) occur whether or not they are queried, i.e., the former take place independently of the latter. That is, when a fluent is true at a particular time, its truth lingers on independently of when it is queried. Fluent updates are initially kept pending in the database, and on the initiative of top-goal queries, i.e., by need only, incremental assertions make these pending updates become active (if not already so), but only those with timestamps up to an actual query time. Such assertions automatically trigger system-implemented incremental upwards propagation and tabling of fluent updates. In order to delimit answers in the table, which in some cases could lead to iterative non-termination, the propagation is bounded by some given predefined upper global time limit. Though foregoing answer subsumption, recursion through the frame axiom can thus still be avoided, and a direct access to the latest time a fluent is true is made possible by means of existing table inspection predicates. Benefiting from the automatic upwards propagation of fluent updates, the program transformation in the new implementation technique becomes simpler than our previous one, in [56]. Moreover, it demonstrates how the dual program transformation, introduced in the context of abduction and used in TABDUAL, is employed for helping propagate the dual negation complement of a fluent incrementally, in order to establish whether the fluent is still true at some time point or if rather its complement is. In summary, the refinement affords us a form of controlled, though automatic, system level truth-maintenance, up to the actual query time. It reconciles high-level top-down deliberative reasoning about a query, with autonomous low-level bottom-up world reactivity to ongoing updates.

### 4.3 LP Implementation Remarks: What's Still Left to Be Done

Departing from the current state of our research, the integration of TABDUAL and EVOLP/R becomes naturally the next step. We shall define how reactive behavior (described as maintenance goals in [34, 35]) can be achieved in the integrated system. An idea would be to use integrity constraints as sketched below:

$$assert(trigger(conclusion)) \leftarrow condition$$
$$false \leftarrow trigger(conclusion), not\ do(conclusion)$$
$$do(conclusion) \leftarrow some\_actions$$

Accordingly, fluents of the form $trigger(conclusion)$ can enact the launch of maintenance goals, in the next program update state, by satisfying any corresponding integrity constraints. Fluents of the form $\sim trigger(conclusion)$, when asserted, will refrain any such launching, in the next program update state. In line with such reactive behavior, is fast and frugal moral decision making, which can be achieved via pre-compiled moral rules (cf. heuristics for decision making in law [20]).

Once TABDUAL and EVOLP/R are integrated, we are ready to model moral dilemmas, focusing on the first morality aspect, starting from easy scenarios (low-conflict) to difficult scenarios (high-conflict). In essence, moral dilemmas will serve as vehicles to model and to test this morality aspect (and also others). The inclusion of other ingredients into the system, notably argumentation and intention recognition (including counterfactuals), is in our research agenda. The choice of their appropriate formalisms still need to be defined, driven by the salient features of the second and the third morality aspects to model.

# 5   Application: A Princess Saviour Moral Robot

Apart from dealing with incomplete information, knowledge updates (as realized by EVOLP/R) are essential to account for moral updating and evolution. It concerns the adoption of new (possibly overriding) moral rules on top of those an agent currently follows. Such adoption is often necessary when the moral rules one follows have to be revised in the light of situations faced by the agent, e.g. when other moral rules are contextually imposed by an authority.

Moral updating is not only relevant in a real world setting, but also in imaginary ones, e.g., in interactive storytelling; cf. [37], where the robot in the story must save the princess in distress while it should also follow (possibly conflicting) moral rules that may change dynamically as imposed by the princess and may conflict with the robot's survival.

It does so by employing Prospective Logic Programming (PLP), a declarative framework supporting the specification of autonomous agents capable of anticipating and reasoning about hypothetical future scenarios. This capability for prediction is essential for proactive agents working with partial information in dynamically changing environments. The work explores the use of state-of-the-art declarative non-monotonic reasoning in the field of interactive storytelling and emergent narratives and is supported by a concrete graphics application prototype to enact the story of a princess saved by a robot imbued with moral reasoning. Note that ACORDA [36], an ad hoc abduction implementation on top of the updates system EVOLP [1], is used in the previous LP implementation for this application, without exploiting tabling features. From that experience, we now move on to a new single integrated system, as described in Section 4.3, that fully exploits tabling technology.

In order to test the PLP framework and the integration of a virtual environment for interactive storytelling, a simplified scenario was developed. In this fantasy setting, an archetypal princess is held in a castle awaiting rescue. The unlikely hero is an advanced robot, imbued with a set of declarative rules for decision making and moral reasoning. As the robot is asked to save the princess in distress, he is confronted with an ordeal. The path to the castle is blocked by a river, crossed by two bridges. Standing guard at each of the bridges are minions of the wizard which originally imprisoned the princess. In order to rescue the princess, he will have to defeat one of the minions to proceed.[3]

Prospective reasoning is the combination of pre-preference hypothetical scenario generation into the future plus post-preference choices taking into account the imagined consequences of each preferred scenario. By reasoning backwards from this goal, the agent generates three possible hypothetical scenarios for action. Either it crosses one of the bridges, or it does not cross the river at all, thus negating satisfaction of the rescue goal. In order to derive the consequences for each scenario, the agent has to reason forwards from each available hypothesis. As soon as these consequences are known, meta-reasoning techniques can be applied to prefer amongst the partial scenarios.

This simple scenario already illustrates the interplay between different LP techniques and demonstrates the advantages gained by combining their distinct strengths. Namely,

---

[3] More at online demo: http://centria.di.fct.unl.pt/~lmp/
publications/slides/padl10/quick_moral_robot.avi

the integration of top-down, bottom-up, hypothetical, moral and utility-based reasoning procedures results in a flexible framework for dynamic agent specification. The open nature of the framework embraces the possibility of expanding its use to yet other useful models of cognition such as counterfactual reasoning and theories of mind.

# 6  Emergence and Computational Morality

The mechanisms of emergence and evolution of cooperation in populations of abstract individuals with diverse behavioral strategies in co-presence have been undergoing mathematical study via Evolutionary Game Theory, inspired in part on Evolutionary Psychology. Their systematic study resorts as well to implementation and simulation techniques, thus enabling the study of aforesaid mechanisms under a variety of conditions, parameters, and alternative virtual games. The theoretical and experimental results have continually been surprising, rewarding, and promising.

Recently, in our own work we have initiated the introduction, in such groups of individuals, of cognitive abilities inspired on techniques and theories of Artificial Intelligence, namely those pertaining to both Intention Recognition and to Commitment (separately and jointly), encompassing errors in decision-making and communication noise. As a result, both the emergence and stability of cooperation become reinforced comparatively to the absence of such cognitive abilities. This holds separately for Intention Recognition and for Commitment, and even more when they are engaged jointly.

From the viewpoint of population morality, the modeling of morality in individuals using appropriate LP features (like abduction, knowledge updates, argumentation, counterfactual reasoning, and others touched upon our research) within a networked population shall allow them to dynamically choose their behavior rules, rather than to act from a predetermined set. That is, individuals will be able to hypothesize, to look at possible future consequences, to (probabilistically) prefer, to deliberate, to take into account history, to adopt and fine tune game strategies.

Indeed, the study of properties like the emergent cooperative and tolerant collective behavior in populations of complex networks, very much needs further investigation of the cognitive core in each of the social atoms of the individuals in such populations (albeit by appropriate LP features). See our own studies on intention recognition and commitments, such as in e.g. [22, 23, 25, 26, 49]). In particular, the references [42, 49] aim to sensitize the reader to these Evolutionary Game Theory based studies and issues, which are accruing in importance for the modeling of minds with machines, with impact on our understanding of the evolution of mutual tolerance, cooperation and commitment. In doing so, they also provide a coherent bird's-eye view of our own varied recent work, whose more technical details, references and results are spread throughout a number of publishing venues, to which the reader is referred therein for a fuller support of claims where felt necessary.

In those works we model intention recognition within the framework of repeated interactions. In the context of direct reciprocity, intention recognition is performed using the information about past *direct* interactions. We study this issue using the well-known repeated Prisoner's Dilemma (PD), i.e., so that intentions can be inferred from past individual experiences. Naturally, the same principles could be extended to cope with indirect information, as in indirect reciprocity. This eventually introduces moral judgment and concern for individual reputation, which constitutes "per se" an important area where intention recognition may play a pivotal role.

In our work too, agents make commitments towards others, they promise to enact their play moves in a given manner, in order to influence others in a certain way, often by dismissing more profitable options. Most commitments depend on some incentive that is necessary to ensure that the action is in the agent's interest and thus, may be carried out to avoid eventual penalties. The capacity for using commitment strategies effectively is so important that natural selection may have shaped specialized signaling capacities to make this possible. And it is believed to have an incidence on the emergence of morality. Not only bilaterally wise but also in public goods games, where in both cases we are presently researching into complementing commitment with apology.

Modeling such cognitive capabilities in individuals, and in populations, may well prove useful for the study and understanding of ethical robots and their emergent behavior in groups, so as to make them implementable in future robots and their swarms, and not just in the simulation domain but in the real world engineering one as well.

## 7  Message in a Bottle

In realm of the individual, Logic Programming is a vehicle for the computational study and teaching of morality, namely in its modeling of the dynamics of knowledge and cognition of agents.

In the collective realm, norms and moral emergence has been studied computationally in populations of rather simple-minded agents.

By bridging these realms, cognition affords improved emerged morals in populations of situated agents.

**Acknowledgements.** AS acknowledges the support of Fundação para a Ciência e a Tecnologia (FCT/MEC) Portugal, grant SFRH/BD/72795/2010.

## References

[1] Alferes, J.J., Brogi, A., Leite, J., Pereira, L.M.: Evolving logic programs. In: Flesca, S., Greco, S., Leone, N., Ianni, G. (eds.) JELIA 2002. LNCS (LNAI), vol. 2424, pp. 50–61. Springer, Heidelberg (2002)

[2] Alferes, J.J., Pereira, L.M., Swift, T.: Abduction in well-founded semantics and generalized stable models via tabled dual programs. Theory and Practice of Logic Programming 4(4), 383–428 (2004)

[3] Anderson, M., Anderson, S.L.: EthEl: Toward a principled ethical eldercare robot. In: Procs. AAAI Fall 2008 Symposium on AI in Eldercare (2008)

[4] Anderson, M., Anderson, S.L.: Robot be good: A call for ethical autonomous machines. Scientific American (October 2010)

[5] Anderson, M., Anderson, S.L. (eds.): Machine Ethics. Cambridge U. P. (2011)

[6] Anderson, M., Anderson, S.L., Armen, C.: Towards machine ethics: implementing two action-based ethical theories. In: Procs. AAAI 2005 Fall Symposium on Machine Ethics (2005)

[7] Anderson, M., Anderson, S., Armen, C.: MedEthEx: a prototype medical ethics advisor. In: IAAI 2006 (2006)

[8] Baral, C., Hunsaker, M.: Using the probabilistic logic programming language P-log for causal and counterfactual reasoning and non-naive conditioning. In: IJCAI 2007 (2007)

[9] Baral, C., Gelfond, M., Rushton, N.: Probabilistic reasoning with answer sets. Theory and Practice of Logic Programming 9(1), 57–144 (2009)

[10] Bratman, M.E.: Intention, Plans and Practical Reasoning. Harvard University Press (1987)

[11] Bringsjord, S., Arkoudas, K., Bello, P.: Toward a general logicist methodology for engineering ethically correct robots. IEEE Intelligent Systems 21(4), 38–44 (2006)

[12] Bringsjord, S., Taylor, J., van Heuveln, B., Arkoudas, K., Clark, M., Wojtowicz, R.: Piagetian roboethics via category theory: Moving beyond mere formal operations to engineer robots whose decisions are guaranteed to be ethically correct. In: Anderson, M., Anderson, S.L. (eds.) Machine Ethics. Cambridge U. P. (2011)

[13] Cushman, F., Young, L., Greene, J.D.: Multi-system moral psychology. In: Doris, J.M. (ed.) The Moral Psychology Handbook. Oxford University Press (2010)

[14] Danielson, P.: Artificial Morality: Virtuous Robots for Virtual Games. Routledge (1992)

[15] Dell'Acqua, P., Pereira, L.M.: Preferential theory revision. J. of Applied Logic 5(4), 586–601 (2007)

[16] Dung, P.M.: On the acceptability of arguments and its fundamental role in nonmonotonic reasoning, logic programming and n-person games. Artificial Intelligence 77(2), 321–357 (1995)

[17] Economist. Morals and the machine. Main Front Cover and Leaders, June 2-8, p. 13. The Economist (2012)

[18] Foot, P.: The problem of abortion and the doctrine of double effect. Oxford Review 5, 5–15 (1967)

[19] Gelfond, M., Lifschitz, V.: The stable model semantics for logic programming. In: 5th Intl. Logic Programming Conf. MIT Press (1988)

[20] Gigerenzer, G., Engel, C.: Heuristics and the Law. MIT Press (2006)

[21] Guarini, M.: Computational neural modeling and the philosophy of ethics: Reflections on the particularism-generalism debate. In: Anderson, M., Anderson, S.L. (eds.) Machine Ethics. Cambridge U. P. (2011)

[22] Han, T.A.: Intention Recognition, Commitments and Their Roles in the Evolution of Cooperation: From Artificial Intelligence Techniques to Evolutionary Game Theory Models. SAPERE, vol. 9. Springer (2013) ISBN 978-3-642-37511-8

[23] Han, T.A., Pereira, L.M.: State-of-the-art of intention recognition and its use in decision making. AI Communications 26(2), 237–246 (2013)

[24] Han, T.A., Saptawijaya, A., Pereira, L.M.: Moral reasoning under uncertainty. In: Bjørner, N., Voronkov, A. (eds.) LPAR-18. LNCS, vol. 7180, pp. 212–227. Springer, Heidelberg (2012)

[25] Han, T.A., Pereira, L.M., Santos, F.C., Lenearts, T.: Good agreements make good friends. Nature Scientific Reports 3(2695) (2013), doi:10.1038/srep02695

[26] Han, T.A., Pereira, L.M., Santos, F.C., Lenearts, T.: Why Is It So Hard to Say Sorry: The Evolution of Apology with Commitments in the Iterated Prisoner's Dilemma. In: IJCAI 2013, pp. 177–183. AAAI Press (2013)

[27] Hauser, M.D.: Moral Minds: How Nature Designed Our Universal Sense of Right and Wrong. Little Brown (2007)

[28] Inhelder, B., Piaget, J.: The Growth of Logical Thinking from Childhood to Adolescence. Basic Books (1958)

[29] Jonsen, A.R., Toulmin, S.: The Abuse of Casuistry: A History of Moral Reasoning. University of California Press (1988)

[30] Kakas, A., Kowalski, R., Toni, F.: The role of abduction in logic programming. In: Gabbay, D., Hogger, C., Robinson, J. (eds.) Handbook of Logic in Artificial Intelligence and Logic Programming, vol. 5. Oxford U. P. (1998)

[31] Kamm, F.M.: Intricate Ethics: Rights, Responsibilities, and Permissible Harm. Oxford U. P. (2006)

[32] Kant, I.: Grounding for the Metaphysics of Morals, translated by J. Ellington. Hackett (1981)

[33] Kowalski, R.: Computational Logic and Human Thinking: How to be Artificially Intelligent. Cambridge U. P. (2011)

[34] Kowalski, R., Sadri, F.: Abductive logic programming agents with destructive databases. Annals of Mathematics and Artificial Intelligence 62(1), 129–158 (2011)

[35] Kowalski, R., Sadri, F.: A logic-based framework for reactive systems. In: Bikakis, A., Giurca, A. (eds.) RuleML 2012. LNCS, vol. 7438, pp. 1–15. Springer, Heidelberg (2012)

[36] Lopes, G., Pereira, L.M.: Prospective programming with ACORDA. In: ESCoR 2006 Workshop, IJCAR 2006 (2006)

[37] Lopes, G., Pereira, L.M.: Prospective storytelling agents. In: Carro, M., Peña, R. (eds.) PADL 2010. LNCS, vol. 5937, pp. 294–296. Springer, Heidelberg (2010)

[38] Mallon, R., Nichols, S.: Rules. In: Doris, J.M. (ed.) The Moral Psychology Handbook. Oxford University Press (2010)

[39] McLaren, B.M.: Computational models of ethical reasoning: Challenges, initial steps, and future directions. IEEE Intelligent Systems, 29–37 (2006)

[40] Mikhail, J.: Universal moral grammar: Theory, evidence, and the future. Trends in Cognitive Sciences 11(4), 143–152 (2007)

[41] Pearl, J.: Causality: Models, Reasoning and Inference. Cambridge U. P. (2009)

[42] Pereira, L.M.: Evolutionary tolerance. In: Magnani, L., Ping, L. (eds.) PCS 2011. SAPERE, vol. 2, pp. 263–287. Springer (2012)

[43] Pereira, L.M., Pinto, A.M.: Inspection points and meta-abduction in logic programs. In: INAP 2009 (2009)

[44] Pereira, L.M., Saptawijaya, A.: Moral Decision Making with ACORDA. In: Local Procs. of LPAR 2007 (2007a)

[45] Pereira, L.M., Saptawijaya, A.: Modelling Morality with Prospective Logic. In: Neves, J., Santos, M.F., Machado, J.M. (eds.) EPIA 2007. LNCS (LNAI), vol. 4874, pp. 99–111. Springer, Heidelberg (2007)

[46] Pereira, L.M., Saptawijaya, A.: Modelling Morality with Prospective Logic. International Journal of Reasoning-based Intelligent Systems 1(3/4), 209–221 (2009)

[47] Pereira, L.M., Saptawijaya, A.: Computational Modelling of Morality. The Association for Logic Programming Newsletter 22(1) (2009)

[48] Pereira, L.M., Saptawijaya, A.: Modelling Morality with Prospective Logic. In: Anderson, M., Anderson, S.L. (eds.) Machine Ethics, pp. 398–421. Cambridge U. P. (2011)

[49] Pereira, L.M., Han, T.A., Santos, F.C.: Complex systems of mindful entities – on intention recognition and commitment. In: Magnani, L. (ed.) Model-Based Reasoning in Science and Technology: Theoretical and Cognitive Issues. SAPERE, vol. 8. Springer (2013)

[50] Poole, D.L.: A logical framework for default reasoning. Artificial Intelligence 36(1), 27–47 (1988)

[51] Powers, T.M.: Prospects for a Kantian machine. IEEE Intelligent Systems 21(4), 46–51 (2006)

[52] Rahwan, I., Simari, G. (eds.): Argumentation in Artificial Intelligence. Springer (2009)

[53] Ross, W.D.: The Right and the Good. Oxford University Press (1930)

[54] Saptawijaya, A., Pereira, L.M.: Tabled abduction in logic programs (technical communication of ICLP 2013). Theory and Practice of Logic Programming, Online Supplement 13(4-5) (2013)

[55] Saptawijaya, A., Pereira, L.M.: Incremental tabling for query-driven propagation of logic program updates. In: McMillan, K., Middeldorp, A., Voronkov, A. (eds.) LPAR-19. LNCS, vol. 8312, pp. 694–709. Springer, Heidelberg (2013)

[56] Saptawijaya, A., Pereira, L.M.: Program updating by incremental and answer subsumption tabling. In: Cabalar, P., Son, T.C. (eds.) LPNMR 2013. LNCS, vol. 8148, pp. 148–160. Springer, Heidelberg (2013)

[57] Saptawijaya, A., Pereira, L.M.: Towards practical tabled abduction usable in decision making. In: KES-IDT 2013, Frontiers of Artificial Intelligence and Applications (FAIA). IOS Press (2013)

[58] Scanlon, T.M.: Contractualism and utilitarianism. In: Sen, A., Williams, B. (eds.) Utilitarianism and Beyond. Cambridge U. P. (1982)

[59] Scanlon, T.M.: What We Owe to Each Other. Harvard University Press (1998)

[60] Scanlon, T.M.: Moral Dimensions: Permissibility, Meaning, Blame. Harvard University Press (2008)

[61] Swift, T., Warren, D.S.: XSB: Extending Prolog with tabled logic programming. Theory and Practice of Logic Programming 12(1-2), 157–187 (2012)

[62] Toni, F.: Argumentative agents. In: Procs. Intl. Multi Conference on Computer Science and Information Technology, vol. 5 (2010)

[63] van den Hoven, J., Lokhorst, G.-J.: Deontic logic and computer-supported computer ethics. Metaphilosophy 33(3), 376–386 (2002)

[64] van Gelder, A., Ross, K.A., Schlipf, J.S.: The well-founded semantics for general logic programs. Journal of ACM 38(3), 620–650 (1991)

[65] Wallach, W., Allen, C.: Moral Machines: Teaching Robots Right from Wrong. Oxford U. P. (2009)

[66] Wiegel, V.: SophoLab; Experimental Computational Philosophy. PhD thesis, Delft University of Technology (2007)

# A Declarative Specification of Giant Number Arithmetic

Paul Tarau

Department of Computer Science and Engineering
University of North Texas
tarau@cs.unt.edu

**Abstract.** The tree based representation described in this paper, *hereditarily binary numbers*, applies recursively a run-length compression mechanism that enables computations limited by the structural complexity of their operands rather than by their bitsizes. While within constant factors from their traditional counterparts for their average and worst case behavior, our arithmetic operations open the doors for interesting numerical computations, intractable with a traditional number representation.

We provide a complete specification of our algorithms in the form of a purely declarative Prolog program.

**Keywords:** hereditary numbering systems, compressed number representations, arithmetic computations with giant numbers, tree-based numbering systems, Prolog as a specification language.

## 1 Introduction

This paper is about a *hereditary number system* that supports computations with *giant numbers* and is based on a recursively applied *run-length* compression of a special bijective base-2 notation.

While *notations* like Knuth's "up-arrow" [1] or tetration are useful in describing very large numbers, they do not provide the ability to actually *compute* with them - as, for instance, addition or multiplication with a natural number results in a number that cannot be expressed with the notation anymore.

The novel contribution of this paper is a tree-based numbering system that *allows computations* with numbers comparable in size with Knuth's "arrow-up" notation. Moreover, these computations have an average and worst case complexity that is comparable with the traditional binary numbers, while their best case complexity outperforms binary numbers by an arbitrary tower of exponents factor. Simple operations like successor, multiplication by 2, exponent of 2 are practically constant time and a number of other operations of practical interest like addition, subtraction and comparison benefit from significant complexity reductions.

To facilitate cost analysis, a concept of structural complexity is introduced, based on the size of our tree representations. It provides estimates on worst

M. Flatt and H.-F. Guo (Eds.): PADL 2014, LNCS 8324, pp. 120–135, 2014.

and best cases for our algorithms and it serves as an indicator of the expected performance of our arithmetic operations.

We have adopted a *literate programming* style, i.e. the code contained in the paper forms a self-contained Prolog program (tested with SWI-Prolog, Lean Prolog and Styla), also available as a separate file at http://logic.cse.unt.edu/tarau/research/2013/hbn.pl . We hope that this will encourage the reader to experiment interactively and validate the technical correctness of our claims.

The paper is organized as follows. Section 2 gives some background on representing bijective base-2 numbers as iterated function application and section 3 introduces hereditarily binary numbers. Section 4 describes constant average time successor and predecessor operations on tree-represented numbers. Section 5 shows an emulation of bijective base-2 with hereditarily binary numbers and section 6 discusses some of their basic arithmetic operations. Section 7 defines a concept of structural complexity and studies best and worst cases and comparisons with bitsizes. Section 8 discusses related work and section 9 concludes the paper.

## 2 Bijective Base-2 Numbers as Iterated Function Applications

Natural numbers can be seen as represented by iterated applications of the functions $o(x) = 2x + 1$ and $i(x) = 2x + 2$ corresponding the so called *bijective base-2* representation [2] together with the convention that 0 is represented as the empty sequence. As each $n \in \mathbb{N}$ can be seen as a unique composition of these functions we can make this precise as follows:

**Definition 1.** *We call bijective base-2 representation of $n \in \mathbb{N}$ the unique sequence of applications of functions $o$ and $i$ to $\epsilon$ that evaluates to $n$.*

With this representation, and denoting the empty sequence $\epsilon$, one obtains $0 = \epsilon, 1 = o(\epsilon), 2 = i(\epsilon), 3 = o(o(\epsilon)), 4 = i(o(\epsilon)), 5 = o(i(\epsilon))$ etc. and the following holds:

$$i(x) = o(x) + 1 \tag{1}$$

### 2.1 Properties of the Iterated Functions $o^n$ and $i^n$

**Proposition 1.** *Let $f^n$ denote application of function $f$ $n$ times. Let $o(x) = 2x + 1$ and $i(x) = 2x + 2$, $s(x) = x + 1$ and $s'(x) = x - 1$. Then $k > 0 \Rightarrow s(o^n(s'(k))) = k2^n$ and $k > 1 \Rightarrow s(s(i^n(s'(s'(k))))) = k2^n$. In particular, $s(o^n(0)) = 2^n$ and $s(s(i^n(0))) = 2^{n+1}$.*

*Proof.* By induction. Observe that for $n = 0, k > 0, s(o^0(s'(k))) = k2^0$ because $s(s'(k)) = k$. Suppose that $P(n) : k > 0 \Rightarrow s(o^n(s'(k))) = k2^n$ holds. Then, assuming $k > 0$, P(n+1) follows, given that $s(o^{n+1}(s'(k))) = s(o^n(o(s'(k)))) = s(o^n(s'(2k))) = 2k2^n = k2^{n+1}$. Similarly, the second part of the proposition also follows by induction on $n$.

The underlying arithmetic identities are:

$$o^n(k) = 2^n(k+1) - 1 \tag{2}$$

$$i^n(k) = 2^n(k+2) - 2 \tag{3}$$

and in particular

$$o^n(0) = 2^n - 1 \tag{4}$$

$$i^n(0) = 2^{n+1} - 2 \tag{5}$$

# 3    Hereditarily Binary Numbers

## 3.1    Hereditary Number Systems

Let us observe that conventional number systems, as well as the bijective base-2 numeration system described so far, represent *blocks of contiguous 0 and 1 digits* appearing in the binary representation of a number somewhat naively - one digit for each element of the block. Alternatively, one might think that counting the blocks and representing the resulting counters as *binary numbers* would be also possible. But then, the same principle could be applied recursively. So instead of representing each block of 0 or 1 digits by as many symbols as the size of the block – essentially a *unary* representation – one could also encode the number of elements in such a block using a *binary* representation.

This brings us to the idea of hereditary number systems.

## 3.2    Hereditarily Binary Numbers as a Data Type

First, we define a data type for our tree represented natural numbers, that we call *hereditarily binary numbers* to emphasize that *binary* rather than *unary* encoding is recursively used in their representation.

**Definition 2.** *The data type* $\mathbb{T}$ *of the set of hereditarily binary numbers is defined inductively as the set of Prolog terms such that:*

$$X \in \mathbb{T} \text{ if and only if } X = e \text{ or } X \text{ is of the form } v(T, Ts) \text{ or } w(T, Ts) \tag{6}$$

where $T \in \mathbb{T}$ and $Ts$ stands for a finite sequence (list) of elements of $\mathbb{T}$.

The intuition behind the set $\mathbb{T}$ is the following:

- The term $e$ (empty leaf) corresponds to zero
- the term $v(T, Ts)$ counts the number $T+1$ (as counting starts at 0) of o applications followed by an *alternation* of similar counts of i and o applications in $Ts$
- the term $w(T, Ts)$ counts the number $T+1$ of i applications followed by an *alternation* of similar counts of o and i applications in $Ts$
- the same principle is applied recursively for the counters, until the empty sequence is reached

**Definition 3.** *The function* $n : \mathbb{T} \to \mathbb{N}$ *shown in equation* **7** *defines the unique natural number associated to a term of type* $\mathbb{T}$.

$$n(T) = \begin{cases} 0 & \text{if } T = \texttt{e}, \\ 2^{n(X)+1} - 1 & \text{if } T = \texttt{v(X,[])}, \\ (n(U) + 1)2^{n(X)+1} - 1 & \text{if } T = \texttt{v(X,[Y|Xs])} \text{ and } U = \texttt{w(Y,Xs)}, \\ 2^{n(X)+2} - 2 & \text{if } T = \texttt{w(X,[])}, \\ (n(U) + 2)2^{n(X)+1} - 2 & \text{if } T = \texttt{w(X,[Y|Xs])} \text{ and } U = \texttt{v(Y,Xs)}. \end{cases} \quad (7)$$

For instance, the computation of N in ?- n(w(v(e, []), [e, e, e]),N) expands to $(((2^{0+1} - 1 + 2)2^{0+1} - 2 + 1)2^{0+1} - 1 + 2)2^{2^{0+1}-1+1} - 2 = 42$. The Prolog equivalent of equation (7) (using bit-shifts for exponents of 2) is:

```
n(e,0).
n(v(X,[]),R)  :-n(X,Z),R is 1<<(1+Z)-1.
n(v(X,[Y|Xs]),R):-n(X,Z),n(w(Y,Xs),K),R is (K+1)*(1<<(1+Z))-1.
n(w(X,[]),R):-n(X,Z),R is 1<<(2+Z)-2.
n(w(X,[Y|Xs]),R):-n(X,Z),n(v(Y,Xs),K),R is (K+2)*(1<<(1+Z))-2.
```

The following example illustrates the values associated with the first few natural numbers.

```
0:e, 1:v(e,[]), 2:w(e,[]), 3:v(v(e,[]),[]), 4:w(e,[e]), 5:v(e,[e])
```

Note that a term of the form v(X,Xs) represents an odd number in $\mathbb{N}^+ = \mathbb{N} - \{0\}$ and a term of the form w(X,Xs) represents an even number in $\mathbb{N}^+$. The following holds:

**Proposition 2.** $n : \mathbb{T} \to \mathbb{N}$ *is a bijection, i.e., each term canonically represents the corresponding natural number.*

*Proof.* It follows from the identities (2) and (3) by replacing the power of 2 functions with the corresponding iterated applications of $o$ and $i$.

## 4   Successor and Predecessor

We will now specify successor and predecessor through a *reversible* Prolog predicate s(Pred,Succ) holding if Succ is the successor of Pred.

```
s(e,v(e,[])).
s(v(e,[]),w(e,[])).
s(v(e,[X|Xs]),w(SX,Xs)):-s(X,SX).
s(v(T,Xs),w(e,[P|Xs])):-s(P,T).
s(w(T,[]),v(ST,[])):-s(T,ST).
s(w(Z,[e]),v(Z,[e])).
s(w(Z,[e,Y|Ys]),v(Z,[SY|Ys])):-s(Y,SY).
s(w(Z,[X|Xs]),v(Z, [e,SX|Xs])):-s(SX,X).
```

It can be proved by structural induction that Peano's axioms hold, and consequently, $< \mathbb{T}, e, s >$ is a Peano algebra.

**Proposition 3.** *The predicate s works in constant time, on the average, when computing the successor or the predecessor.*

*Proof.* Observe that the average size of a contiguous block of 0s or 1s in a number of bitsize $n$ has the upper bound 2 as $\sum_{k=0}^{n} \frac{1}{2^k} = 2 - \frac{1}{2^n} < 2$. As on 2-bit numbers we have an average of 0.25 more calls, we can conclude that the total average number of calls is constant, with upper bound $2 + 0.25 = 2.25$.

A quick empirical evaluation confirms this. When computing the successor on the first $2^{30} = 1073741824$ natural numbers, there are in total 2381889348 calls to s averaging to 2.2183 per computation. The same average for 100 successor computations on very large 100000 bit random numbers oscillates around 2.22. The worst case (a deep linear tree) is bounded by the very slowly growing iterated logarithm.

Note also that by using a single reversible predicate s for both successor and predecessor, while the solution is always unique, some backtracking occurs in the latest case. One can eliminate this by using two specialized predicates for successor and predecessor.

## 5    Emulating the Bijective Base-2 Operations o, *i*

To be of any practical interest, we will need to ensure that our data type $\mathbb{T}$ emulates also binary arithmetic. We will first show that it does, and next we will show that on a number of operations like exponent of 2 or multiplication by an exponent of 2, it significantly lowers complexity.

Intuitively, the first step should be easy, as we need to express single applications or "un-applications" of o and i in terms of their iterated applications encapsulated in the terms of type $\mathbb{T}$.

First we emulate single applications of o and i seen in terms of s. Note that o/2 and i/2 are also *reversible* predicates.

```
o(e,v(e,[])).
o(w(X,Xs),v(e,[X|Xs])).
o(v(X,Xs),v(SX,Xs)):-s(X,SX).

i(e,w(e,[])).
i(v(X,Xs),w(e,[X|Xs])).
i(w(X,Xs),w(SX,Xs)):-s(X,SX).
```

Finally the "recognizers" o_ and i_ simply detect v and w corresponding to o (and respectively i) being the last operation applied and s_ detects that the number is a successor, i.e., not the empty term e.

```
s_(v(_,_)).    s_(w(_,_)).

o_(v(_,_)).    i_(w(_,_)).
```

Note that each of the predicates o and i calls s exactly once, therefore:

**Proposition 4.** o *and* i *are constant time, on the average.*

**Definition 4.** *The function* $t : \mathbb{N} \to \mathbb{T}$ *defines the unique tree of type* $\mathbb{T}$ *associated to a natural number as follows:*

$$t(x) = \begin{cases} \text{e} & \text{if } x = 0, \\ \text{o}(t(\frac{x-1}{2})) & \text{if } x > 0 \text{ and } x \text{ is odd}, \\ \text{i}(t(\frac{x}{2} - 1)) & \text{if } x > 0 \text{ and } x \text{ is even} \end{cases} \tag{8}$$

We can now define the corresponding Prolog predicate that converts from terms of type $\mathbb{T}$ to natural numbers. Note that we use bit-shifts (>>) for division by 2.

```
t(0,e).
t(X,R):-X>0, X mod 2=:=1,Y is (X-1)>>1, t(Y,A),o(A,R).
t(X,R):-X>0, X mod 2=:=0,Y is (X>>1)-1, t(Y,A),i(A,R).
```

The following holds:

**Proposition 5.** *Let* id *denote* $\lambda x.x$ *and* "∘" *function composition. Then, on their respective domains*

$$t \circ n = id, \quad n \circ t = id \tag{9}$$

*Proof.* By induction, using the arithmetic formulas defining the two functions.

Note also that the cost of $t$ is proportional to the bitsize of its input and the cost of $n$ is proportional to the bitsize of its output.

## 6   Arithmetic Operations

### 6.1   A Few Low Complexity Operations

Doubling a number db and reversing the db operation (hf) are quite simple, once one remembers that the arithmetic equivalent of function o is $\lambda x.2x + 1$.

```
db(X,Db):-o(X,OX),s(Db,OX).
hf(Db,X):-s(Db,OX),o(X,OX).
```

Note that efficient implementations follow directly from our number theoretic observations in section 2. For instance, as a consequence of proposition 1, the operation exp2 computing an exponent of 2 , has the following simple definition in terms of s:

```
exp2(e,v(e,[])).
exp2(X,R):-s(PX,X),s(v(PX,[]),R).
```

**Proposition 6.** *The operations* db, hf *and* exp2 *are constant time, on the average.*

*Proof.* It follows by observing that at most 2 calls to s , o are made in each.

## 6.2 Addition and Subtraction Favoring Numbers with Large Contiguous Blocks of 0s and 1s

We now derive efficient addition and subtraction operations similar to the successor/predecessor s, that *work on one run-length encoded bloc at a time*, rather than by individual o and i steps.

We first define the predicates otimes corresponding to $o^n(k)$ and itimes corresponding to $i^n(k)$.

```
otimes(e,Y,Y).
otimes(N,e,v(PN,[])):-s(PN,N).
otimes(N,v(Y,Ys),v(S,Ys)):-add(N,Y,S).
otimes(N,w(Y,Ys),v(PN,[Y|Ys])):-s(PN,N).

itimes(e,Y,Y).
itimes(N,e,w(PN,[])):- s(PN,N).
itimes(N,w(Y,Ys),w(S,Ys)):-add(N,Y,S).
itimes(N,v(Y,Ys),w(PN,[Y|Ys])):-s(PN,N).
```

They are part of a chain of *mutually recursive predicates* as they are already referring to the add predicate, to be implemented later. Note also that instead of naively iterating, they implement a more efficient "one bloc at a time" algorithm. For instance, when detecting that its argument counts a number of applications of o, otimes just increments that count. On the other hand, when the last predicate applied was i, otimes simply inserts a new count for o operations. A similar process corresponds to itimes. As a result these algorithms favor numbers composed of large blocks of 0s and 1s.

We also need a number of arithmetic identities on $\mathbb{N}$ involving iterated applications of o and i.

**Proposition 7.** *The following hold:*

$$o^k(x) + o^k(y) = i^k(x+y) \tag{10}$$

$$o^k(x) + i^k(y) = i^k(x) + o^k(y) = i^k(x+y+1) - 1 \tag{11}$$

$$i^k(x) + i^k(y) = i^k(x+y+2) - 2 \tag{12}$$

*Proof.* By (2) and (3), we substitute the $2^k$-based equivalents of $o^k$ and $i^k$, then observe that the same reduced forms appear on both sides.

The corresponding Prolog code is:

```
oplus(K,X,Y,R):-add(X,Y,S),itimes(K,S,R).

oiplus(K,X,Y,R):-add(X,Y,S),s(S,S1),itimes(K,S1,T),s(R,T).

iplus(K,X,Y,R):-add(X,Y,S),s(S,S1),s(S1,S2),itimes(K,S2,T),s(P,T),s(R,P).
```

Note that the code uses the predicate add that we will define later and that it is part of a chain of mutually recursive predicate calls, that together will provide an intricate but efficient implementation of the intuitively simple idea: *we want to work on one run-length encoded block at a time.*

The corresponding identities for subtraction are:

**Proposition 8.**

$$x > y \;\Rightarrow\; o^k(x) - o^k(y) = o^k(x - y - 1) + 1 \tag{13}$$

$$x > y + 1 \;\Rightarrow\; o^k(x) - i^k(y) = o^k(x - y - 2) + 2 \tag{14}$$

$$x \geq y \;\Rightarrow\; i^k(x) - o^k(y) = o^k(x - y) \tag{15}$$

$$x > y \;\Rightarrow\; i^k(x) - i^k(y) = o^k(x - y - 1) + 1 \tag{16}$$

*Proof.* By (2) and (3), we substitute the $2^k$-based equivalents of $o^k$ and $i^k$, then observe that the same reduced forms appear on both sides. Note that special cases are handled separately to ensure that subtraction is defined.

The Prolog code, also covering the special cases, is:

```
ominus(_,X,X,e).
ominus(K,X,Y,R):-sub(X,Y,S1),s(S2,S1),otimes(K,S2,S3),s(S3,R).

iminus(_,X,X,e).
iminus(K,X,Y,R):-sub(X,Y,S1),s(S2,S1),otimes(K,S2,S3),s(S3,R).

oiminus(_,X,Y,v(e,[])):-s(Y,X).
oiminus(K,X,Y,R):-s(Y,SY),s(SY,X),exp2(K,P),s(P,R).
oiminus(K,X,Y,R):-
  sub(X,Y,S1),s(S2,S1),s(S3,S2),s_(S3), % S3 <> e
  otimes(K,S3,S4),s(S4,S5),s(S5,R).

iominus(K,X,Y,R):-sub(X,Y,S),otimes(K,S,R).
```

Note the use of the predicate sub, to be defined later, which is also part of the mutually recursive chain of operations.

The next two predicates extract the iterated applications of $o^n$ and respectively $i^n$ from v and w terms:

```
osplit(v(X,[]), X,e).
osplit(v(X,[Y|Xs]),X,w(Y,Xs)).

isplit(w(X,[]), X,e).
isplit(w(X,[Y|Xs]),X,v(Y,Xs)).
```

We are now ready for defining addition. The base cases are:

```
add(e,Y,Y).
add(X,e,X):-s_(X).
```

In the case when both terms represent odd numbers, we apply with `auxAdd1` the identity (10), after extracting the iterated applications of $o$ as A and B with the predicate `osplit`. Note also the reference to the comparison operation `cmp`, to be defined later, also part of our chain of mutually recursive operations.

```
add(X,Y,R):-o_(X),o_(Y),osplit(X,A,As),osplit(Y,B,Bs),cmp(A,B,R1),
  auxAdd1(R1,A,As,B,Bs,R).
```

In the case when the first term is odd and the second even, we apply with `auxAdd2` the identity (11), after extracting the iterated application of $o$ and $i$ as A and B.

```
add(X,Y,R):-o_(X),i_(Y),osplit(X,A,As),isplit(Y,B,Bs),cmp(A,B,R1),
  auxAdd2(R1,A,As,B,Bs,R).
```

In the case when the first term is even and the second odd, we apply with `auxAdd3` the identity (11), after extracting the iterated applications of $i$ and $o$ as, respectively, A and B.

```
add(X,Y,R):-i_(X),o_(Y),isplit(X,A,As),osplit(Y,B,Bs),cmp(A,B,R1),
  auxAdd3(R1,A,As,B,Bs,R).
```

In the case when both terms represent even numbers, we apply with `auxAdd4` the identity (12), after extracting the iterated application of $i$ as A and B.

```
add(X,Y,R):-i_(X),i_(Y),isplit(X,A,As),isplit(Y,B,Bs),cmp(A,B,R1),
  auxAdd4(R1,A,As,B,Bs,R).
```

Note that in each case we ensure that a block of the same size is extracted, depending on which of the two operands A or B is larger. Beside that, the auxiliary predicates `auxAdd1`, `auxAdd2`, `auxAdd3` and `auxAdd4` implement the equations of Prop. 7.

```
auxAdd1('=',A,As,_B,Bs,R):- s(A,SA),oplus(SA,As,Bs,R).
auxAdd1('>',A,As,B,Bs,R):-
  s(B,SB),sub(A,B,S),otimes(S,As,R1),oplus(SB,R1,Bs,R).
auxAdd1('<',A,As,B,Bs,R):-
  s(A,SA),sub(B,A,S),otimes(S,Bs,R1),oplus(SA,As,R1,R).

auxAdd2('=',A,As,_B,Bs,R):- s(A,SA),oiplus(SA,As,Bs,R).
auxAdd2('>',A,As,B,Bs,R):-
  s(B,SB),sub(A,B,S),otimes(S,As,R1),oiplus(SB,R1,Bs,R).
auxAdd2('<',A,As,B,Bs,R):-
  s(A,SA),sub(B,A,S),itimes(S,Bs,R1),oiplus(SA,As,R1,R).

auxAdd3('=',A,As,_B,Bs,R):- s(A,SA),oiplus(SA,As,Bs,R).
auxAdd3('>',A,As,B,Bs,R):-
  s(B,SB),sub(A,B,S),itimes(S,As,R1),oiplus(SB,R1,Bs,R).
auxAdd3('<',A,As,B,Bs,R):-
  s(A,SA),sub(B,A,S),otimes(S,Bs,R1),oiplus(SA,As,R1,R).
```

```
auxAdd4('=',A,As,_B,Bs,R):- s(A,SA),iplus(SA,As,Bs,R).
auxAdd4('>',A,As,B,Bs,R):-
  s(B,SB),sub(A,B,S),itimes(S,As,R1),iplus(SB,R1,Bs,R).
auxAdd4('<',A,As,B,Bs,R):-
  s(A,SA),sub(B,A,S),itimes(S,Bs,R1),iplus(SA,As,R1,R).
```

The code for the subtraction predicate sub is similar:

```
sub(X,e,X).
sub(X,Y,R):-o_(X),o_(Y),osplit(X,A,As),osplit(Y,B,Bs),cmp(A,B,R1),
  auxSub1(R1,A,As,B,Bs,R).
```

In the case when both terms represent odd numbers, we apply the identity (13), after extracting the iterated applications of o as A and B. For the other cases, we use, respectively, the identities 14, 15 and 16:

```
sub(X,Y,R):-o_(X),i_(Y),osplit(X,A,As),isplit(Y,B,Bs),cmp(A,B,R1),
  auxSub2(R1,A,As,B,Bs,R).
```

```
sub(X,Y,R):-i_(X),o_(Y),isplit(X,A,As),osplit(Y,B,Bs),cmp(A,B,R1),
  auxSub3(R1,A,As,B,Bs,R).
```

```
sub(X,Y,R):-i_(X),i_(Y),isplit(X,A,As),isplit(Y,B,Bs),cmp(A,B,R1),
  auxSub4(R1,A,As,B,Bs,R).
```

Note also the auxiliary predicates auxSub1, auxSub2, auxSub3 and auxSub4 that implement the equations of Prop. 8.

```
auxSub1('=',A,As,_B,Bs,R):- s(A,SA),ominus(SA,As,Bs,R).
auxSub1('>',A,As,B,Bs,R):-
  s(B,SB),sub(A,B,S),otimes(S,As,R1),ominus(SB,R1,Bs,R).
auxSub1('<',A,As,B,Bs,R):-
  s(A,SA),sub(B,A,S),otimes(S,Bs,R1),ominus(SA,As,R1,R).
```

```
auxSub2('=',A,As,_B,Bs,R):- s(A,SA),oiminus(SA,As,Bs,R).
auxSub2('>',A,As,B,Bs,R):-
  s(B,SB),sub(A,B,S),otimes(S,As,R1),oiminus(SB,R1,Bs,R).
auxSub2('<',A,As,B,Bs,R):-
  s(A,SA),sub(B,A,S),itimes(S,Bs,R1),oiminus(SA,As,R1,R).
```

```
auxSub3('=',A,As,_B,Bs,R):- s(A,SA),iominus(SA,As,Bs,R).
auxSub3('>',A,As,B,Bs,R):-
  s(B,SB),sub(A,B,S),itimes(S,As,R1),iominus(SB,R1,Bs,R).
auxSub3('<',A,As,B,Bs,R):-
  s(A,SA),sub(B,A,S),otimes(S,Bs,R1),iominus(SA,As,R1,R).
```

```
auxSub4('=',A,As,_B,Bs,R):- s(A,SA),iminus(SA,As,Bs,R).
auxSub4('>',A,As,B,Bs,R):-
  s(B,SB),sub(A,B,S),itimes(S,As,R1),iminus(SB,R1,Bs,R).
auxSub4('<',A,As,B,Bs,R):-
  s(A,SA),sub(B,A,S),itimes(S,Bs,R1),iminus(SA,As,R1,R).
```

### 6.3    A Comparison Operation Optimized for Numbers with Large Contiguous Blocks of 0s and 1s

The comparison operation `cmp` provides a total order (isomorphic to that on $\mathbb{N}$) on our type $\mathbb{T}$. It relies on `bitsize` computing the number of applications of $o$ and $i$ that build a term in $\mathbb{T}$, which is also part of our mutually recursive predicates, to be defined later.

We first observe that only terms of the same bitsize need detailed comparison, otherwise the relation between their bitsizes is enough, *recursively*. More precisely, the following holds:

**Proposition 9.** *Let* `bitsize` *count the number of applications of $o$ or $i$ operations on a bijective base-2 number. Then* `bitsize`$(x) <$ `bitsize`$(y) \Rightarrow x < y$.

*Proof.* Observe that, given their lexicographic ordering in "big digit first" form, the bitsize of bijective base-2 numbers is a non-decreasing function.

```
cmp(e,e,'=').
cmp(e,Y,('<')):-s_(Y).
cmp(X,e,('>')):-s_(X).
cmp(X,Y,R):-s_(X),s_(Y),bitsize(X,X1),bitsize(Y,Y1),cmp1(X1,Y1,X,Y,R).

cmp1(X1,Y1,_,_,R):- \+(X1=Y1),cmp(X1,Y1,R).
cmp1(X1,X1,X,Y,R):-reversedDual(X,RX),reversedDual(Y,RY),
   compBigFirst(RX,RY,R).
```

The predicate `compBigFirst` compares two terms known to have the same `bitsize`. It works on reversed (big digit first) variants, computed by `reversedDual` and it takes advantage of the block structure using the following proposition:

**Proposition 10.** *Assuming two terms of the same bitsizes, the one starting with $i$ is larger than one starting with $o$.*

*Proof.* Observe that "big digit first" numbers are lexicographically ordered with $o < i$.

As a consequence, `cmp` only recurses when *identical* blocks head the sequence of blocks, otherwise it infers the "<" or ">" relation.

```
compBigFirst(e,e,'=').
compBigFirst(X,Y,R):- o_(X),o_(Y),
   osplit(X,A,C),osplit(Y,B,D),cmp(A,B,R1),fcomp1(R1,C,D,R).
compBigFirst(X,Y,R):-i_(X),i_(Y),
   isplit(X,A,C),isplit(Y,B,D),cmp(A,B,R1),fcomp2(R1,C,D,R).
compBigFirst(X,Y,('<')):-o_(X),i_(Y).
compBigFirst(X,Y,('>')):-i_(X),o_(Y).

fcomp1('=',C,D,R):-compBigFirst(C,D,R).
fcomp1('<',_,_,'>').
fcomp1('>',_,_,'<').
```

```
fcomp2('=',C,D,R):-compBigFirst(C,D,R).
fcomp2('<',_,_,'<').
fcomp2('>',_,_,'>').
```

The predicate `reversedDual` reverses the order of application of the $o$ and $i$ operations to a "biggest digit first" order. For this, it only needs to reverse the order of the alternative blocks of $o^k$ and $i^k$. It uses the predicate `len` to compute with `auxRev1` and `auxRev2` the number of these blocks. Then, it infers that if the number of blocks is odd, the last block is of the same kind as the first; otherwise it is of its alternate kind (`w` for `v` and vice versa).

```
reversedDual(e,e).
reversedDual(v(X,Xs),R):-reverse([X|Xs],[Y|Ys]),len([X|Xs],L),
  auxRev1(L,Y,Ys,R).
reversedDual(w(X,Xs),R):-reverse([X|Xs],[Y|Ys]),len([X|Xs],L),
  auxRev2(L,Y,Ys,R).

auxRev1(L,Y,Ys,R):-o_(L),R=v(Y,Ys).
auxRev1(L,Y,Ys,R):-i_(L),R=w(Y,Ys).

auxRev2(L,Y,Ys,R):-o_(L),R=w(Y,Ys).
auxRev2(L,Y,Ys,R):-i_(L),R=v(Y,Ys).

len([],e).
len([_|Xs],L):- len(Xs,L1),s(L1,L).
```

## 6.4   Computing `bitsize`

The predicate `bitsize` computes the number of applications of the `o` and `i` operations. It works by summing up the *counts* of `o` and `i` operations composing a tree-represented natural number of type $\mathbb{T}$.

```
bitsize(e,e).
bitsize(v(X,Xs),R):-tsum([X|Xs],e,R).
bitsize(w(X,Xs),R):-tsum([X|Xs],e,R).

tsum([],S,S).
tsum([X|Xs],S1,S3):-add(S1,X,S),s(S,S2),tsum(Xs,S2,S3).
```

Bitsize concludes our chain of *mutually recursive* predicates. Note that it also provides an efficient implementation of the integer $log_2$ operation `ilog2`.

```
ilog2(X,R):-s(PX,X),bitsize(PX,R).
```

## 6.5   Multiplication by an Exponent of 2

The predicate `leftshiftBy` uses the fact that repeated application of the `o` operation (`otimes`) provides an efficient implementation of multiplication with an exponent of 2 for numbers composed of large blocks of 0s or 1s.

```
leftShiftBy(_,e,e).
leftShiftBy(N,K,R):-s(PK,K),otimes(N,PK,M),s(M,R).
```

### 6.6    General Multiplication One Block at a Time

**Proposition 11.** *The following holds:*

$$o^n(a)o^m(b) = o^{n+m}(ab + a + b) - o^n(a) - o^m(b) \qquad (17)$$

*Proof.* By 2, we can expand and then reduce as follows: $o^n(a)o^m(b) = (2^n(a + 1) - 1)(2^m(b + 1) - 1) = 2^{n+m}(a + 1)(b + 1) - (2^n(a + 1) + 2^m(b + 1)) + 1 = 2^{n+m}(a + 1)(b + 1) - 1 - (2^n(a + 1) - 1 + 2^m(b + 1) - 1 + 2) + 2 = o^{n+m}(ab + a + b + 1) - (o^n(a) + o^m(b)) - 2 + 2 = o^{n+m}(ab + a + b) - o^n(a) - o^m(b)$

The corresponding Prolog code starts with the obvious base cases:

```
mul(_,e,e).
mul(e,Y,e):-s_(Y).
```

When both terms represent odd numbers we apply the identity (17):

```
mul(X,Y,R):-o_(X),o_(Y),osplit(X,N,A),osplit(Y,M,B),
   add(A,B,S),mul(A,B,P),add(S,P,P1),s(N,SN),s(M,SM),
   add(SN,SM,K),otimes(K,P1,P2),sub(P2,X,R1),sub(R1,Y,R).
```

The other cases are reduced to the previous one by the identity $i = s \circ o$.

```
mul(X,Y,R):-o_(X),i_(Y),s(PY,Y),mul(X,PY,Z),add(X,Z,R).
mul(X,Y,R):-i_(X),o_(Y),s(PX,X),mul(PX,Y,Z),add(Y,Z,R).
mul(X,Y,R):-i_(X),i_(Y),
   s(PX,X),s(PY,Y),add(PX,PY,S),mul(PX,PY,P),add(S,P,R1),s(R1,R).
```

Note that when the operands are composed of large blocks of alternating $o^n$ and $i^m$ applications, the algorithm works (roughly) in time proportional to the number of blocks rather than the number of digits.

## 7    Structural Complexity as Size of Our Tree Representation

As a measure of structural complexity we define the predicate `tsize` that counts the nodes of a tree of type $\mathbb{T}$ (except the root).

```
tsize(e,e).
tsize(v(X,Xs),R):- tsizes([X|Xs],e,R).
tsize(w(X,Xs),R):- tsizes([X|Xs],e,R).

tsizes([],S,S).
tsizes([X|Xs],S1,S4):-tsize(X,N),add(S1,N,S2),s(S2,S3),tsizes(Xs,S3,S4).
```

It corresponds to the function $c : \mathbb{T} \to \mathbb{N}$ defined by equation (18):

$$c(T) = \begin{cases} 0 & \text{if } T = \text{e}, \\ \sum_{Y \in [X|Xs]} (1 + c(Y)) & \text{if } T = \text{v(X,Xs)}, \\ \sum_{Y \in [X|Xs]} (1 + c(Y)) & \text{if } T = \text{w(X,Xs)}. \end{cases} \qquad (18)$$

The following holds:

**Proposition 12.** *For all terms $T \in \mathbb{T}$,* tsize(T) $\leq$ bitsize(T).

*Proof.* By induction on the structure of $T$, by observing that the two predicates have similar definitions and corresponding calls to tsize return terms assumed smaller than those of bitsize.

Note that the while the actual heap representation size of the tree is larger in terms of bits used, it is within a constant factor of tsize and therefore within a constant factor of bitsize. The following example illustrates their use:

```
?- t(123456,T),tsize(T,S1),n(S1,TSize),bitsize(T,S2),n(S2,BSize).
T = w(e, [w(e, [e]), e, v(e, []), e, w(e, []), w(e, [])]),
S1 = w(e, [e, e]), TSize = 12,
S2 = w(e, [w(e, [])]), BSize = 16 .
```

Figure 1 shows compares of structural complexity with bitsize.

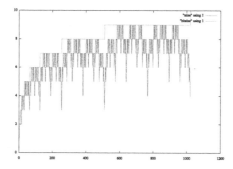

**Fig. 1.** Structural complexity bounded by bitsize from 0 to $2^{10} - 1$

After defining the predicate iterated, that applies K times the predicate F

```
iterated(_,e,X,X).
iterated(F,K,X,R):-s(PK,K),iterated(F,PK,X,R1),call(F,R1,R).
```

we can exhibit a best case, of minimal structural complexity for its size

```
bestCase(K,Best):-iterated(wtree,K,e,Best).
wtree(X,w(X,[])).
```

and a worst case, of maximal structural complexity for its size

```
worstCase(K,Worst):-iterated(io,K,e,Worst).
io(X,Z):-o(X,Y),i(Y,Z).
```

The following examples illustrate these predicates:

```
?- t(3,T),bestCase(T,Best),n(Best,N).
T = v(v(e, []), []), Best = w(w(w(e, []), []), []), N = 65534 .
?- t(3,T),worstCase(T,Worst),n(Worst,N).
T = v(v(e, []), []), Worst = w(e, [e, e, e, e, e]), N = 84 .
```

It follows from identity (5) that the predicate `bestCase` computes the iterated exponent of 2 (tetration) and then applies the predecessor to it twice, i.e., it computes $2^{2^{\cdot^{\cdot^{\cdot 2}}}} - 2$. A simple closed formula (easy to prove by induction) can also be found for `worstCase`, the predicate `worstCase` k computes the value in $\mathbb{T}$ corresponding to the value $\frac{4(4^k-1)}{3} \in \mathbb{N}$.

The average space-complexity of our number representation is related to the average length of the *integer compositions of the bitsize of a number*. Intuitively, the shorter the partition in alternative blocks of $o$ and $i$ applications, the more significant the compression is.

The following example shows that computations with towers of exponents 20 and 30 levels tall become possible with our number representation.

```
?- t(20,X),bestCase(X,A),t(30,Y),bestCase(Y,B),add(A,B,C),
|       tsize(C,S),n(S,TSize),write(TSize),nl,fail.
314
```

Note that the structural complexity of the result (that we did not print out) is still quite manageable: **314**. *This opens the door to a new world where tractability of computations is not limited by the size of the operands but only by their structural complexity.*

# 8   Related Work

A draft version of this paper has been presented at CICLOPS'13 with informal proceedings at the arxiv.org repository [3].

Natural numbers in word array-based systems like GMP, OpenSSL's BigNum or Java's BigInteger, given that on a 64-bit architecture array sizes cannot exceed $2^{64}$ words, are limited by the corresponding $0..2^{2^{64}}$ range. On the other hand, our tree numbers are limited only by a measure of structural complexity, defined as the size of the trees representing them.

More closely, several notations for very large numbers accommodating "towers of exponents" have been invented in the past. Examples include Knuth's *arrow-up* notation [1] covering operations like the *tetration* (a notation for towers of exponents). In contrast to our tree-based natural numbers, such notations are not closed under addition and multiplication, and consequently they cannot be used as a replacement for ordinary binary or decimal numbers.

The first instance of a hereditary number system, at our best knowledge, occurs in the proof of Goodstein's theorem [4]. Another hereditary number system is Knuth's TCALC program [5] that decomposes $n = 2^a + b$ with $0 \le b < 2^a$ and then recurses on a and b with the same decomposition. While hereditary, given the constraint on $a$ and $b$, the TCALC system is not based on a bijection between $\mathbb{N}$ and $\mathbb{N} \times \mathbb{N}$ and therefore the representation is not canonical. Moreover, the literate C-program that defines it only implements successor, addition, comparison and multiplication and does not provide similar constant time exponent of 2 and low complexity left-shift / nightshift operations like our tree representation does. In [6] a similar (non-canonical) exponential-based notation called "integer decision diagrams" is introduced, providing a compressed representation for sparse integers, sets and various other data types.

Our first take on a hereditary number system is described in [2]. Like [5], it uses a binary tree-based representation derived from the bijection $f : \mathbb{N} \times \mathbb{N} \to \mathbb{N}^+, f(x, y) = 2^x(2y + 1)$. The representation is canonical, it provides constant time exponent of 2 and left-shift operation and, like the proposal in this paper, it implements all the basic arithmetic operations. However, by contrast with this paper, it does not handle well arbitrary linear combinations of towers of exponent numbers, as for instance, numbers of the form $2^x - 1$ expand to large unbalanced binary trees.

## 9 Conclusion

We have provided a declarative specification of a tree-based number system. Our emphasis here was on the correctness and the theoretical complexity bounds of our operations. We have also ensured that our algorithms are as simple as possible and we have closely correlated our Prolog code with the formulas describing the corresponding arithmetical properties. Our algorithms rely on properties of blocks of iterated applications of functions rather than the "digits as coefficients of polynomials" view of traditional numbering systems. They favor numbers with large contiguous blocks of 0s and 1s, allowing computations with with giant numbers (e.g. towers of exponents) provided that they have a tractable representation size. While the rules for our operations are often more complex, restricting our code to a purely declarative subset of Prolog made managing a fairly intricate network of mutually recursive dependencies much easier.

## References

1. Knuth, D.E.: Mathematics and Computer Science: Coping with Finiteness. Science 194(4271), 1235–1242 (1976)
2. Tarau, P., Haraburda, D.: On Computing with Types. In: Proceedings of SAC 2012, ACM Symposium on Applied Computing, PL track, Riva del Garda (Trento), Italy, pp. 1889–1896 (March 2012)
3. Tarau, P.: A Prolog Specification of Giant Number Arithmetic. In: Rocha, R., Have, C.T. (eds.) Proceedings of the 13th International Colloquium on Implementation of Constraint Logic Programming Systems (CICLOPS 2013), Istanbul, Turkey (August 2013), http://arxiv.org/abs/1307.8389
4. Goodstein, R.: On the restricted ordinal theorem. Journal of Symbolic Logic (9), 33–41 (1944)
5. Knuth, D.E.: TCALC program (December 1994)
6. Vuillemin, J.: Efficient Data Structure and Algorithms for Sparse Integers, Sets and Predicates. In: 19th IEEE Symposium on Computer Arithmetic, ARITH 2009, pp. 7–14 (June 2009)

# Embedding Foreign Code

Robert Clifton-Everest, Trevor L. McDonell,
Manuel M.T. Chakravarty, and Gabriele Keller

University of New South Wales,
School of Computer Science and Engineering
{robertce,tmcdonell,chak,keller}@cse.unsw.edu.au

**Abstract.** Special purpose embedded languages facilitate generating high-performance code from purely functional high-level code; for example, we want to program highly parallel GPUs without the usual high barrier to entry and the time-consuming development process. We previously demonstrated the feasibility of a skeleton-based, generative approach to compiling such embedded languages.

In this paper, we (a) describe our solution to some of the practical problems with skeleton-based code generation and (b) introduce our approach to enabling interoperability with native code. In particular, we show, in the context of a functional embedded language for GPU programming, how template meta programming simplifies code generation and optimisation. Furthermore, we present our design for a foreign function interface for an embedded language.

## 1 Introduction

*Accelerate* is an *embedded language* for general-purpose GPU programming. It is implemented in Haskell, which also serves as its host language, and generates optimised CUDA code [14] from regular, multi-dimensional array programs [2,13]. Accelerate is an example of a class of embedded languages aiming at simplifing the programming of specialised high-performance architectures by offering a restricted high-level language with a specialised code generator. Other recent examples are Nikola [12], Obsidian [4], Delight/LMS [19], as well as embedded hardware description languages [1,10]. These embedded languages reuse part of the language infrastructure of their host language, while supplying a dedicated and specialised code generator. This reuse is in contrast to standalone languages with similar aims, such as StreamIT [22], Halide [18], and NOVA [7].

Among those languages, Accelerate's implementation is unique by being based on a generative, template-based code generator, in the spirit of Cole's algorithmic skeletons [6]. The main advantage of this approach to code generation is the simplicity with which code idioms of the target architecture can be adopted — this is crucial for GPU programs as GPUs only deliver high performance if both control structures and data access patterns are suitably constrained [20]. The approach's main challenges are two: (1) we need a mechanism to express, instantiate, and compose code skeletons and (2) we need a fusion framework that

M. Flatt and H.-F. Guo (Eds.): PADL 2014, LNCS 8324, pp. 136–151, 2014.
© Springer International Publishing Switzerland 2014

eliminates intermediate structures at skeleton boundaries. In previous work [13], we addressed the second challenge by a novel fusion framework for SIMD languages. In the present paper, we address the first challenge and also explain the interplay between our fusion framework and skeleton instantiation.

Moreover, the use of any special-purpose language in practice needs to address interoperability with native code. In particular, we need to be able to use existing, third-party library code from embedded code as well as enable the use of embedded code from native applications. To this end, we present the design of a *foreign function interface* for embedded array code.

In summary, this paper discusses the generation of high-performance foreign code by way of code skeletons as well as a foreign function interface for embedded programs to leverage native libraries and applications. It makes the following main contributions:

- We discuss how to implement skeleton-based code generation with template meta programming (Section 2).
- We explain how to implement consumer-producer fusion as skeleton instantiation (Section 3).
- We introduce the, to our knowledge, first foreign function interface for an embedded language (Section 4).
- We explain how to integrate embedded Haskell GPU code in a CUDA C program (Section 5).

We discuss benchmarks in Section 6 and related work in Section 7. All code is available from `https://github.com/AccelerateHS/accelerate`.

## 2   Embedding GPU Programs as Skeletons

Accelerate offers a range of aggregate operations on multi-dimensional arrays. They include operations modelled after Haskell's list library, such as `map` and `fold`, but also array-oriented operations, such as `permute` and stencil convolutions.

As a simple example, consider the dot product of two vectors:

```
dotp :: Acc (Vector Float) -> Acc (Vector Float) -> Acc (Scalar Float)
dotp xs ys = fold (+) 0 (zipWith (*) xs ys)
```

The crucial difference to vanilla Haskell is the `Acc` type constructor representing *embedded array-valued computations*. The types `Vector e` and `Scalar e` represent one-dimensional and zero-dimensional (singleton) arrays, respectively.

The expression `zipwith (*) xs ys` implements pointwise multiplication of the two argument vectors, and `fold (+) 0` sums the resulting products up to yield the final, scalar result, wrapped into a singleton array. The type of `fold` is

```
fold :: (Shape sh, Elt a) => (Exp a -> Exp a -> Exp a)
     -> Exp a -> Acc (Array (sh:.Int) a) -> Acc (Array sh a)
```

It uses a binary folding function operating on *embedded scalar computations* of type `Exp a` to implement a parallel reduction along the innermost dimension of an *n*-dimensional, embedded array of type `Array (sh:.Int) a`. The *shape* `sh:.Int` consist of a polymorphic shape `sh` with one added (innermost) dimension, which is missing from the shape of the result array.

## 2.1 Array Operations as Skeletons

Accelerate's CUDA[1] backend is based around the idea of *algorithmic skeletons* [6]. In other words, the backend implements each of the aggregate array operations, such as `map`, by way of a CUDA C *code template* that is parameterised with array types and worker functions, such as the mapped function.

This generative approach is attractive for specialised hardware, such as GPUs, as the CUDA C code templates are hand-tuned to avoid expensive control flow, ensure efficient global-memory access, and use fast on-chip shared memory for local communication, all of which is required for high-performance GPU code [14]. It is much more difficult —and subject to open research questions— to generate the corresponding code idioms with a synthetic code generator.

In the first version of Accelerate, we implemented CUDA C code templates and template instantiation with a mixture of C++ templates and C preprocessor macros — see [2] for details. While workable, this approach turned out to have a number of problems. Firstly, the use of CPP is fragile and hard to maintain. Template instantiation by inlining of CPP macros required the use of fixed variables with no static checking to ensure the consistent use of names or that used names where defined before their use. Moreover, it was easy to generate code that wasn't even syntactically valid. All this seriously complicated maintenance and further extension of the code generator. Secondly, the approach led to the generation of dead code whenever specific template instances didn't use some of their parameters or fields of structured data. (The CUDA compiler was not able to remove most of this dead code.) Finally, and most importantly, the use of CPP did not scale to support the implementation of producer-consumer skeleton fusion, which is a crucial optimisation, even for code as simple as dot product.

Next, we discuss a new approach to template definition avoiding these problems. Then, we will discuss the implementation of producer-consumer skeleton fusion and general template instantiation in the following section.

## 2.2 Skeletons as Template Meta Programs

Due to the shortcomings of C++ templates and CPP, we explored the use of template meta programming to implement CUDA skeletons. More specifically, we use Mainland's *quasiquotation* extensions [11] to Template Haskell to define skeletons as quoted CUDA C templates with splices for the template parameters.

---

[1] CUDA is NVIDIA's C/C++-based framework for general-purpose GPU programming: `http://www.nvidia.com/object/cuda_home_new.html`

```
[cunit|
  __global__ void map( $params:argIn, $params:argOut )                — (3)
  {
      const int shapeSize    = size(shOut);
      const int gridSize     = $exp:(gridSize dev);

      for (int ix = $exp:(threadIdx dev); ix < shapeSize; ix += gridSize)
      {
          $items:(dce x         .=. get ix)                          — (2)
          $items:(setOut "ix" .=. f x)                               — (1)
      }
  }
|]
```

**Listing 1.** Accelerate CUDA skeleton for the `map` operation

Listing 1 displays the skeleton template for the map family of functions (which also includes `zipWith`). The [cunit|···|] brackets enclose CUDA C definitions. CUDA uses the `__global__` keyword to indicate that `map` is a *GPU kernel*: a single data-parallel computation launched on the GPU by the CPU. *Antiquotations* $params:e, $exp:e, $items:e, and $stms:e denote template parameters using a Haskell expression e to splice CUDA C parameters, expressions, items, and statements, respectively, into the skeleton.

The map skeleton is parameterised by a function f that gets applied to the individual array elements in the line marked *(1)*. The arguments to f are extracted from the input arrays in the line marked *(2)*, and we will explain the meaning of the auxiliary combinators `get`, `setOut`, `dce`, and (`.=.`) in the next section. Finally, the arguments to a specific instantiation of the `map` template are computed and spliced in the function head marked *(3)*.

As the quasiquoter [cunit|···|] executes at Haskell compile time, syntactic errors in the quotations and antiquotations as well as in their composition are flagged at compile time; i.e., we can be sure that the generated code is syntactically correct if we can compile our backend. See [11] for more details on quasiquoters.

## 3   Instantiating Skeletons

In the first, pre-template meta programming, version of Accelerate we generated one or more CUDA GPU kernels for each aggregate array operation. This scheme led to superfluous intermediate arrays and array traversals. Recall the body of the definition of the dot product: `fold (+) 0 (zipWith (*) xs ys)`. The function `zipWith` compiles to an instance of the `map` template that we discussed in the previous section. Similarly, `fold` compiles to an instance of the `fold` template. As a result, the execution of `zipWith` produces an array that the `fold` kernels consume.

This is not what a CUDA programmer would manually implement; it is more efficient to inline the zipWith computation into the kernel of the fold. This strategy eliminates one GPU kernel and an intermediate array that is of the same size as the two input arrays. To achieve the same performance as handwritten CUDA code, we developed the array fusion system described in [13].

Our fusion system distinguishes producer-producer and consumer-producer fusion. The former combines two skeletons that produce complex arrays, whereas the latter combines an array producer (such as map) with a skeleton reducing an array (such as fold). Central to our approach is a representation of arrays as functions, which we call *delayed arrays* (in contrast to *manifest arrays*) and represent as follows:

```
data DelayedAcc a where
  Delayed :: (Shape sh, Elt e)
          => Exp sh                  — array extent
          -> Fun (sh  -> e)          — generate element at index
          -> Fun (Int -> e)          — ...at linear index
          -> DelayedAcc (Array sh e)
```

Instead of generating a map skeleton instance for zipWith straight away, we represent the computation implemented by zipWith as a function —actually, a pair of functions— together with the extent (domain) of the array as a value of type DelayedAcc. For more details on this representation, see [13].

As far as skeleton template instantiation goes, the crucial step in Accelerate's CUDA backend is the function codegenAcc, which turns an Accelerate array operation (of type Acc a) into the AST of instantiated skeleton CUDA code CUSkeleton a:

```
codegenAcc :: DeviceProperties -> Acc a -> CUSkeleton a
codegenAcc dev (Fold f z a)
  = mkFold dev (codegenFun dev f) (codegenExp dev z) (codegenDelayed dev a)
codegenAcc dev (Map f a)
  = mkMap ...
```

Here we see that mkFold, which generates an instance of the fold template, gets the code generated from a delayed array as its last argument from the call to codegenDelayed. In the case of the dot product code, that delayed array will be a delayed representation of zipWith whose code —as an AST— will be passed to mkFold. In the following, we will discuss template instantiation by our skeleton constructors such as mkFold and mkMap.

### 3.1   Consumer Producer Fusion by Template Instantiation

The use of template meta programming to implement CUDA skeletons is crucial to enable consumer-producer fusion by way of template instantiation. In the dot product example, the delayed producer is equivalent to the scalar function $\lambda ix \rightarrow$ (xs!ix) * (ys!ix). The call to mkFold in codegenAcc passes a CUDA version of this function, which is bound to the argument get in the mkFold definition given in Listing 2. This delayed producer function is used in the line marked *(1)*, where it expands to the following C code:

```
mkFold :: DeviceProperties -> CUFun (e -> e -> e) -> CUExp e
  -> CUDelayedAcc (Array (sh :. Int) e) -> CUSkeleton (Array sh e)
mkFold dev combine seed (CUDelayed shape _ get)
  = CUSkeleton [cunit|
      __global__ void foldAll( $params:argIn, $params:argOut )
      {   // omitted variable declarations
          if ( ix < shapeSize ) {
              $items:(y .=. get ix)

              for ( ix += gridSize; ix < shapeSize; ix += gridSize ) {
                  $items:(x .=. get ix)                            — (1)
                  $items:(y .=. combine x y)
              }
          }
          $items:(sdata "threadIdx.x" .=. y)
          __syncthreads();                                        — (2)
          $stms:(treeReduce dev combine sdata)
          // first thread writes the result to memory
      }
    |]
```

**Listing 2.** Accelerate CUDA skeleton for the `foldAll` operation

```
const Int64 v2 = ix;
const int v3 = toIndex(shIn0, shape(v2));
const int v4 = toIndex(shIn1, shape(v2));
y0 = arrIn0_a0[v3] * arrIn1_a0[v4];
```

The functions `shape` and `toIndex` map multi-dimensional indices to linear array representations. In this example these functions do not contribute anything as dot product consumes two vectors, and the CUDA compiler is able to remove the superfluous assignments in this case.

In contrast to the `map` skeleton, the code generated by `mkFold` proceeds in two phases of parallel activities. The first phase is the sequential `for` loop including the use of `get`. The second phase starts after the CUDA `__syncthreads()` statement at the line marked *(2)* and implements a parallel tree reduction [3].

## 3.2   Instantiating Skeletons with Scalar Code

Most aggregate array operations in Accelerate are parameterised by scalar functions, such as the mapping function for `map` and the binary operator for `fold`. Hence, a crucial part of template instantiation is the inlining of CUDA code implementing scalar Accelerate functions into template code. Inlining of scalar functions is always possible as the scalar sublanguage of Accelerate is first-order and does not support recursion. These restrictions are necessary to generate GPU code as GPU hardware neither supports large stacks (for recursion) nor closures (for higher-order functions).

To splice scalar code fragments into the skeleton code of array operations, we define a typeclass of l-values and r-values to define a generic assignment operator (.=.), which is, for example, used in the lines marked *(1)* and *(2)* in Listing 1. This representation abstracts over whether our skeleton uses l-values in single static assignment-style to const declarations or as a statement updating a mutable variable. The class declarations are the following:

```
class Lvalue a where
  lvalue :: a -> C.Exp -> C.BlockItem

class Rvalue a where
  rvalue :: a -> C.Exp

class Assign l r where
  (.=.) :: l -> r -> [C.BlockItem]

instance (Lvalue l, Rvalue r) => Assign l r
  -- method definition omitted
```

Furthermore, we can also bring any additional terms into scope before evaluating an r-value. As an example, see the **get** code fragment in Section 3.1 in the calculations of **toIndex**. We enable this by way of the following class instance:

```
instance Assign l r => Assign l ([C.BlockItem], r)
  -- method definition omitted
```

### 3.3   Eliminating Dead Code

As mentioned before, one problem of the original code generator based on CPP and C++ templates was its inability to remove some forms of dead code. As an example, consider the following Accelerate function that projects the first component of each element of a vector of quadruples:

```
fst4 :: Acc (Vector (a,b,c,d)) -> Acc (Vector a)
fst4 = map (\v -> let (x,_,_,_) = unlift v in x)
```

The function **unlift** turns an embedded scalar expression that yields a quadruple into a quadruple comprising four embedded scalar expressions — hence, we can pattern match on the quadruple in the let-binding. The use of **fst4** can lead to serious inefficiencies as Accelerate uses a *non-parametric* array representation: arrays of tuples are represented as tuples of arrays. This helps us to maintain the strict memory access rules that CUDA requires for best performance. Clearly, an efficient implementation of this operation should simply select the first tuple component of the representation, only taking constant time.

If a value of type Vector (a,b,c,d) is represented as a tuple of arrays, an application of **fst4** should execute in constant time (independent of the size of the array). As explained in [2], to keep the number of skeletons reasonable, our CPP/C++-template code generator represented scalar tuples as C-structs and resorted, during skeleton instantiation, to a family of getter and setter functions consuming these structs to read and write the elements from the non-parametric array representation.

As a consequence, in `fst4`, array elements are copied into a struct, only for the first element to be extracted again and the struct to be discarded. One might hope that the CUDA compiler spots (1) the redundant copying of array elements and (2) that the elements of three of the four arrays are never used. Alas, it does not and as a result `fst4` does not run in constant time, and it generates considerable memory traffic.

With template meta programming and the `Assign` type class introduced previously, we fare much better. Template instantiation inlines the scalar computations, including all array accesses, directly into the AST representing the skeleton. Instead of packaging the tuple into a `struct`, we represent it by a set of individuals values, one per component. During code generation, we keep track of the values constituting a tuple by maintaining a list of expressions, one for each component of the tuple. Moreover, a generalised version of the (`.=.`) operator allows us to assign all values making up a tuple with one assignment in our meta programming system — i.e., we use lists of l- and r-values:

```
instance Assign l r => Assign [l] [r]
  -- method definition omitted
```

Unfortunately, the CUDA compiler doesn't always eliminate memory reads, as it does not always detect if the values are not used. Hence, rather than rely on the CUDA compiler, we explicitly keep track of which values are used at all in generated scalar code, and when splicing assignments into a skeleton template, we elide dead statement; i.e., those whose results are not used. The following instance of the `Assign`-class uses a flag that is `False` whenever the assigned value of an assignment is not used:

```
instance Assign l r => Assign (Bool,l) r where
  (.=.) (used,lhs) rhs
    | used      = lhs .=. rhs
    | otherwise = []
```

The `map` skeleton of Listing 1 exploits this: when generating code for the mapped function `f`, the function `dce :: [a] -> [(Bool,a)]` —on the line marked *(2)*— determines for each term whether it is being used. Thus, when the code generated by `get` reads data from the input array, it doesn't read unused values. Consequently, `fst4` only touches the array representing the first component of the quadruple of arrays. In combination with fusion, we completely avoid any unnecessary memory traffic.

In summary, the use of template meta programming for skeleton definition and instantiation enables us to combine the advantages of conventional synthetic code generators (such as def-use analysis for dead code elimination) with those of generative skeleton-based code generators (such as handwritten idiomatic code for special-purpose architectures).

# 4   Using Foreign Libraries

Accelerate is a high-level language framework capturing idioms suitable for massively parallel GPU architectures, without requiring the expert knowledge needed to achieve good performance at the level of CUDA. However, there are existing highly optimised CUDA libraries, for example, for high performance linear algebra and fast Fourier transforms. For Accelerate to be practically useful, we need to provide a means to use those libraries. Moreover, access to native CUDA code also provides a developer the opportunity to drop down to raw CUDA C in those parts of an application where the code generated by Accelerate is not sufficiently efficient. We achieve access to CUDA libraries and native CUDA components with the *Accelerate Foreign Function Interface* (or FFI).

The Accelerate FFI is a two-way street: (1) it enables calling native CUDA C code from embedded Accelerate computations and (2) it facilitates calling Accelerate computations from non-Haskell code. Overall, a developer can implement an application in a mixture of Accelerate and other languages in a manner that the source code is portable across multiple Accelerate backends.

Given that Accelerate is embedded in Haskell, it might seem that Haskell's standard FFI should be sufficient to enable interoperability with foreign code. Unfortunately, this is not the case. With Haskell's standard FFI, we can call C functions that in turn invoke GPU computations from Haskell host code. However, we want to call GPU computations from within embedded Accelerate code and pass data structures located in GPU memory directly to native CUDA code and vice versa. The latter is crucial, as transferring data from CPU memory to GPU memory and back is very expensive.

## 4.1   Importing Foreign Functions

Calling foreign code in an embedded Accelerate computation requires two steps: (1) the foreign function must be made accessible to the host Haskell program and (2) the foreign function must be lifted into an Accelerate computation to be available to embedded code. For the first step, we use the standard Haskell FFI. The second step requires an extension to Accelerate.

As a concrete example, let us use the vector dot product of the highly optimised *CUDA Basic Linear Algebra Subprograms (CUBLAS)* library [15]. This CUBLAS function is called `cublasSDot()`; it computes the vector dot product of two arrays of 32-bit floating point values. To access it from Haskell, we use this Haskell FFI import declaration:

```
foreign import ccall "cublas_v2.h cublasSdot_v2" cublasSdot
  :: Handle
  -> Int                            — Number of array elements
  -> DevicePtr Float -> Int         — The two input arrays, and...
  -> DevicePtr Float -> Int         — ...element stride
  -> DevicePtr Float                — Result array
  -> IO ()
```

The `Handle` argument is required by the foreign library and created on initialisation. The `DevicePtr` arguments are pointers into GPU memory. As mentioned before, the primary aim of the Accelerate FFI is to ensure that we do not unnecessarily transfer data between GPU and CPU memory.

To manage device pointers, the Accelerate FFI provides a GPU memory allocation function `allocateArray` and a function `devicePtrsOfArray` to extract the device pointers of an Accelerate array. We can use these functions to invoke `cublasSdot` with GPU-side data:

```
dotp_cublas :: Handle
            -> (Vector Float, Vector Float)
            -> CIO (Scalar Float)
dotp_cublas handle (xs, ys) = do
  let n = arraySize (arrayShape xs)     — number of input elements
  result     <- allocateArray Z         — allocate a new Scalar array
  ((),xptr) <- devicePtrsOfArray xs     — get device memory pointers
  ((),yptr) <- devicePtrsOfArray ys
  ((),rptr) <- devicePtrsOfArray result
  liftIO $ cublasSdot handle n xptr 1 yptr 1 rptr
  return result
```

The result of `devicePtrsOfArray` is a nested tuple of pointers, as we represent arrays of tuples as tuples of arrays; hence, we can have multiple CUDA arrays for one Accelerate array. In the above example, there is only one, though. The `CIO` monad is simply the `IO` monad enriched with some information used by the CUDA backend to manage devices, memory, and caches.

## 4.2   Executing Foreign Functions with Accelerate

The function `dotp_cublas` invokes native CUDA code in such a manner that it directly uses arrays in GPU memory. This leaves us with two challenges: (1) we need to enable calling functions, such as `dotp_cublas`, in embedded code and (2) we need to account for Accelerate supporting multiple backends, while Accelerate programs should be portable across backends.

To discuss these issues, we need to briefly recap some of the Accelerate internals described in [2]. Accelerate reifies embedded programs into an abstract syntax tree (AST) encoded as a generalised abstract data type (GADT) to track types of the embedded language in the host language — i.e., the AST can only represent well-typed embedded programs. Accelerate compiles fused collections of array operations into GPU kernels and orchestrates the execution of those kernels CPU-side by a tree traversal of the AST.

Returning to the two remaining challenges, we address the challenge of enabling calling functions, such as `dotp_cublas`, by extending the AST with a new node type `Aforeign` representing foreign calls. One instance of an `Aforeign` node encodes the code for one backend, but it also contains a fallback implementation in case a different backend is being used. The AST data constructor is defined as follows:

```
Aforeign :: (Arrays as, Arrays bs, Foreign f)
            => f as bs                    — foreign function
            -> (Acc as -> Acc bs)         — fallback implementation
            -> Acc as                     — input array
            -> Acc bs
```

When the tree walk during code execution encounters an `Aforeign` AST node, it dynamically checks whether it can execute the foreign function. If it can't, it instead executes the fallback implementation. A fallback implementation might be another `Aforeign` node with native code for a different backend (e.g., for OpenCL instead of CUDA), or it can simply be a vanilla Accelerate implementation of the same functionality that is provided by the foreign code. With a cascade of `Aforeign` nodes, we can provide an optimised native implementation of a function for a range of backends and still maintain a vanilla Accelerate version of the same functionality for execution in the Accelerate interpreter.

The dynamic check for the suitability of a foreign function is facilitated by the class constraint `Foreign f` in the context of `Aforeign`. The class `Foreign` is a subclass of `Typeable` with instances for data types that represent foreign functions for specific backends. For the CUDA backend, we have the following:

```
class Typeable2 f => Foreign f where ...
instance Foreign CUDAForeignAcc where ...
data CUDAForeignAcc as bs where
  CUDAForeignAcc :: as -> CIO bs
```

`CUDAForeignAcc` wraps calls to foreign CUDA code executed in the `CIO` monad. When the CUDA backend encounters an AST node `Aforeign foreignFun alt arg`, it attempts to `cast`[2] the value of `foreignFun` to type `CUDAForeignAcc as bs`. If that `cast` succeeds, it can unwrap the `CUDAForeignAcc` and invoke the function it contains. Otherwise, it needs to execute the alternative implementation `alt`.

Finally, we can define an embedded vector dot product that uses CUBLAS when possible and, otherwise, falls back to the version defined in Section 3.1:

```
dotp' :: Acc (Vector Float) -> Acc (Vector Float)
      -> Acc (Scalar Float)
dotp' xs ys = Aforeign (CUDAForeignAcc (dotp_cublas handle))
                       (uncurry dotp)
                       (lift (xs, ys))
```

Foreign calls are not curried; hence, they only have got one argument, which is an instance of the class `Arrays` of tuples of Accelerate arrays.

### 4.3  Embedding Foreign Scalar Functions

So far, we discussed the use of foreign array computations from Accelerate. However, we also wish to be able to use foreign scalar operations in embedded array computations. For example, CUDA provides fused floating-point multiply-add intrinsics with a variety of rounding modes.

_____

[2] See Haskell's `Data.Typeable` library for details on `cast`.

We import foreign scalar functions similarly to foreign array computations. In particular, the AST type `Exp` for scalar embedded computations includes a data constructor `Foreign` that serves the same purpose as `Aforeign` for `Acc`:

```
Foreign :: (Elt x, Elt y, Foreign f)
        => f x y -> (Exp x -> Exp y) -> Exp x -> Exp y
```

Where we used `CUDAForeignAcc` to wrap CUDA array computations for use with `Aforeign`, we use `CUDAForeignExp` to wrap scalar CUDA functions for use with `Foreign`. However, instead of wrapping a Haskell FFI call, the scalar case simply encodes the textual representation of the CUDA function in CUDA code. As discussed in Section 2, scalar code is used to instantiate skeleton templates. The skeleton code is a template for CUDA code; so, a Haskell function invocation wouldn't be appropriate. As in the array case, functions are uncurried, but in the scalar case, they can only return a single scalar argument:

```
data CUDAForeignExp x y where
  CUDAForeignExp :: IsScalar y
               => [String] -> String -> CUDAForeignExp x y
```

The first argument is a list of header files that need to be included when compiling an instantiated skeleton template including this specific foreign function.

Overall, we define a foreign function based on CUDA's explicitly fused floating-point multiply-add intrinsics as follows (using IEEE rounding towards zero):

```
fmaf :: Exp Float -> Exp Float -> Exp Float -> Exp Float
fmaf x y z = Foreign (CUDAForeignExp [] "__fmaf_rz")
                    (\v -> let (x,y,z) = unlift v in x * y + z)
                    (lift (x, y, z))
```

## 5    Embedding Embedded Programs

Accelerate simplifies writing GPU code as it obviates the need to understand most low-level details of GPU programming. Hence, we would like to use Accelerate from other languages. As with importing foreign code into Accelerate, the foreign export functionality of the standard Haskell FFI is not sufficient for efficiently using Accelerate from languages, such as C. In the following, we describe how the Accelerate FFI supports exporting Accelerate code as standard C calls.

### 5.1    Exporting Accelerate Programs

To export Accelerate functions as C functions, we make use of Template Haskell [21]. For example, we might export our Accelerate dot product:

```
dotp :: Acc (Vector Float, Vector Float) -> Acc (Scalar Float)
dotp = uncurry $ \xs ys -> fold (+) 0 (zipWith (*) xs ys)

exportAfun 'dotp "dotp_compile"
```

The function `exportAfun` is defined in Template Haskell and takes the name of an Accelerate function, here `dotp`, as an argument. It generates the necessary export declarations by inspecting the properties of the name it has been passed, such as its type.

Compiling a module that exports Accelerate computations in this way (say, `M.hs`) generates the additional file `M_stub.h` containing the C prototype for the foreign exported function. For the dot product example, this header contains:

```
#include "HsFFI.h"
extern AccProgram dotp_compile(AccContext a1);
```

A C program needs to include this header to call the Accelerate dot product.

## 5.2  Running Embedded Accelerate Programs

One of the functions to execute an Accelerate computation in Haskell is:

```
run1In :: (Arrays as, Arrays bs)
          => Context -> (Acc as -> Acc bs) -> as -> bs
```

This function comprises two phases: (1) program optimisation and instantiation of skeleton templates of its second argument and (2) execution of the compiled code in a given CUDA context (first argument). The implementation of `run1In` is structured such that, partially applying it to only its first and second argument, yields a new function of type `as -> bs`, where Phase (1) has been executed already — in other words, it precompiles the Accelerate code. Repeated application of this function of type `as -> bs` executes the CUDA code without any of the overheads associated with just-in-time compilation.

The Accelerate export API retains the ability to precompile Accelerate code. The C function provided by `exportAfun` compiles the Accelerate code, returning a reference to the compiled code. Then, in a second step, `runProgram` marshals input arrays, executes the compiled program, and marshals output arrays:

```
OutputArray    out;
InputArray     in[2]   = { ... };
AccProgram     dotp    = dotp_compile( context );

runProgram( dotp, in, &out );
```

The function `dotp_compile` was generated by `exportAfun 'dotp "dotp_compile"`.

## 5.3  Marshalling Input and Output Arrays

Accelerate uses a non-parametric representation of multi-dimensional arrays: an array of tuples is represented as a tuple of arrays. The type `InputArray` follows this convention. It is a C struct comprising an array of integers indicating the extent of the array in each dimension together with an array of pointers to each underlying GPU array of primitive data.

```
typedef struct { int* shape; void** adata; } InputArray;
```

**Table 1.** General performance of Accelerate (in ms) — c.f., [13]

| Benchmark | Input Size | Contender | Accelerate |
|---|---|---|---|
| Black Scholes | 20M | 6.70 (CUDA) | 6.19 (0.92×) |
| Dot Product | 20M | 1.88 (CUBLAS) | 2.35 (1.25×) |
| N-Body | 32k | 54.42 (CUDA) | 102.47 (1.88×) |
| SMVM (protein) | 4M | 0.641 (CUSP) | 0.637 (0.99×) |

**Table 2.** Fast Fourier Transform based benchmarks (in ms)

| Benchmark | Input Size | Contender | Accelerate full | Accelerate no fusion | Accelerate no FFI |
|---|---|---|---|---|---|
| FFT | 512×512 | 43 (FFTW) | 4.36 (0.1×) | 5.9 (0.14×) | 3658 (8.5×) |
| High pass | 512×512 | 65 (FFTW) | 14.97 (0.23×) | 27.82 (0.43×) | 21936 (34×) |
| SmoothLife | 128×128 | 16.21 (MATLAB) | 4.01 (0.25×) | 6.38 (0.39×) | 6829 (42×) |

OutputArray includes an extra field, a stable pointer, that maintains a reference to the associated Haskell-side Array. This keeps the array from being garbage collected until the OutputArray is explicitly released with freeOutput.

```
typedef struct { int* shape; void** adata;
                 HsStablePtr stable_ptr; } OutputArray;
```

# 6   Applications and Benchmarks

We conducted benchmarks on a single Tesla T10 processor (compute capability 1.3, 30 multiprocessors = 240 cores at 1.3GHz, 4GB RAM) backed by two quad-core Xenon E5405 CPUs (64-bit, 2GHz, 8GB RAM) running GNU/Linux (Ubuntu 12.04 LTS). The reported runtimes are the average of 100 runs.

Table 1 establishes baseline Accelerate performance, showing a comparison of kernel runtimes for a selection of Accelerate programs compared to native CUDA implementations. Accelerate is clearly competitive.

## 6.1   Fast Fourier Transform (FFT) — Foreign Import

The column "Accelerate, no FFI" in Table 2 measures a pure Accelerate implementation of an out-of-place Cooley-Tukey FFT algorithm [8], whereas "Accelerate, full" uses the FFI to access NVIDIA's highly optimised CUFFT library [16]. "Accelerate, no fusion" also uses the FFI, but without fusion.

The row labelled "FFT" measures a single forward Fourier transform of a greyscale image. The row labelled "High pass" is a high-pass filter of an RGB image, which for each component performs a forward transform, zeros out the centre (high) frequencies, then performs the inverse transform. Finally, the row "SmoothLife" measures a generalisation of Conway's *Game of Life* to a continuous domain [17], which is based on Fourier transforms.

We compare the single FFT and the high-pass filter to the highly regarded FFTW library [9] (multithreaded, estimate mode). We compare the Accelerate implementation of SmoothLife to SmoothLife's reference implementation in MATLAB (version R2012B). FFTW and MATLAB execute on multicore CPUs.

In all cases, our out-of-place Cooley-Tukey implementation of FFT in pure Accelerate is much slower than the highly optimised FFTW and MATLAB multicore implementations. However, once we use the Accelerate FFI to utilise CUFFT, the Accelerate code clearly outperforms the FFTW and MATLAB implementations. This is although we incur significant overhead due to a mismatch of complex number representations. CUFFT represents complex numbers in a packed AoS format, requiring marshalling to and from Accelerate's SoA representation. Array fusion allows this additional overhead to be integrated into surrounding operations, amortizing the cost of this impedance mismatch when calling foreign libraries. This is particularly noticeable in the high-pass filter benchmark. We leave native support of packed vector types to future work.

### 6.2  N-Body — Foreign Export

To demonstrate the use of Accelerate code from C, we use an $n$-body example that simulates Newtonian gravitational forces on a set of massive bodies in 3D space, using the naive $O(n^2)$ algorithm. We export the Accelerate $n$-body implementation into an OpenGL program that visualises the positions of the particles at each step of the simulation. The visualisation program — part of the $n$-body example from the NVIDIA CUDA distribution — uses a packed AoS representation for which we had to introduce additional marshalling. We did not note any performance difference between executing the Accelerate program from Haskell compared to execution via the C-based visualisation program. This is because the $O(n)$ additional marshalling is dominated by the $O(n^2)$ $n$-body calculations.

## 7  Related Work

Our work is based on the quasiquotation extension to Template Haskell described in [11] to instantiate the skeletons by splicing in parameters and customised code. The flexibility of this approach is essential for many of our optimisations.

Nikola [12] and Obsidian [5] also embed GPU computations in Haskell, but are not based on skeletons. Obsidian offers no FFI. Nikola does not have an FFI as such, but it allows to embed CUDA code blocks in Nikola programs. Since it only supports single kernel programs, it only deals with limited interactions between the imported code and the rest of the EDSL program.

Delite/LMS [19] is a framework for parallel DSLs in Scala using library-based multi-pass staging. It is not based on skeletons and doesn't seem to have an FFI.

NOVA [7] is a *standalone* functional language for GPU programming, which unlike Accelerate supports nested parallel computations. It also allows importing foreign functions, but not for exporting NOVA computations.

**Acknowledgements.** We thank Serge Le Huitouze for helpful comments.

# References

1. Bjesse, P., Claessen, K., Sheeran, M., Singh, S.: Lava: hardware design in Haskell. In: Proceedings of the Third ACM SIGPLAN International Conference on Functional Programming. ACM (1998)
2. Chakravarty, M.M.T., Keller, G., Lee, S., McDonell, T.L., Grover, V.: Accelerating Haskell array codes with multicore GPUs. In: DAMP: Declarative Aspects of Multicore Programming. ACM (2011)
3. Chatterjee, S., Prins, J.: COMP663: Parallel Computing Algorithms. Department of Computer Science, University of North Carolina at Chapel Hill (2009)
4. Claessen, K., Sheeran, M., Svensson, B.J.: Expressive array constructs in an embedded GPU kernel programming language. In: DAMP: Declarative Aspects and Applications of Multicore Programming. ACM (2012)
5. Claessen, K., Sheeran, M., Svensson, J.: Obsidian: GPU programming in Haskell. In: IFL: Implementation and Application of Functional Languages (2008)
6. Cole, M.I.: Algorithmic Skeletons: Structured Management of Parallel Computation. The MIT Press (1989)
7. Collins, A., Grewe, D., Grover, V., Lee, S., Susnea, A.: Nova: A functional language for data parallelism. Tech. rep., NVIDIA (2013)
8. Cooley, J.W., Tukey, J.W.: An algorithm for the machine calculation of complex Fourier series. Mathematics of Computation (90) (1965)
9. Frigo, M., Johnson, S.G.: The design and implementation of FFTW3. Proceedings of the IEEE 93(2), 216–231 (2005); Special issue on "Program Generation, Optimization, and Platform Adaptation"
10. Gill, A., Bull, T., Kimmell, G., Perrins, E., Komp, E., Werling, B.: Introducing Kansas Lava. In: Morazán, M.T., Scholz, S.-B. (eds.) IFL 2009. LNCS, vol. 6041, pp. 18–35. Springer, Heidelberg (2010)
11. Mainland, G.: Why it's nice to be quoted. In: Haskell Symposium, p. 73. ACM Press, New York (2007)
12. Mainland, G., Morrisett, G.: Nikola: Embedding compiled GPU functions in Haskell. In: Haskell Symposium. ACM (2010)
13. McDonell, T.L., Chakravarty, M.M.T., Keller, G., Lippmeier, B.: Optimising Purely Functional GPU Programs. In: ICFP: International Conference on Functional Programming (September 2013)
14. NVIDIA: CUDA C Programming Guide (2012)
15. NVIDIA: CUBLAS Library (2013)
16. NVIDIA: CUFFT Library (2013)
17. Rafler, S.: Generalization of Conway's "Game of Life" to a continuous domain–SmoothLife (2011)
18. Ragan-Kelley, J., Barnes, C., Adams, A., Paris, S., Durand, F., Amarasinghe, S.: Halide: a language and compiler for optimizing parallelism, locality, and recomputation in image processing pipelines. In: PLDI 2013. ACM (2013)
19. Rompf, T., Sujeeth, A.K., Amin, N., Brown, K.J., Jovanovic, V., Lee, H., Odersky, M., Olukotun, K.: Optimizing data structures in high-level programs: New directions for extensible compilers based on staging. In: POPL 2013. ACM (2013)
20. Sengupta, S., Harris, M., Zhang, Y., Owens, J.D.: Scan primitives for GPU computing. In: Symposium on Graphics Hardware. Eurographics Association (2007)
21. Sheard, T., Peyton Jones, S.: Template meta-programming for Haskell. In: Proceedings of the 2002 ACM SIGPLAN Workshop on Haskell, pp. 1–16. ACM (2002)
22. Thies, W., Karczmarek, M., Amarasinghe, S.: StreamIt: A language for streaming applications. In: Nigel Horspool, R. (ed.) CC 2002. LNCS, vol. 2304, pp. 179–196. Springer, Heidelberg (2002)

# Exploring the Use of GPUs in Constraint Solving

Federico Campeotto[1,2], Alessandro Dal Palù[3], Agostino Dovier[1],
Ferdinando Fioretto[1,2], and Enrico Pontelli[2]

[1] Dept. Mathematics & Computer Science, Univ. of Udine
[2] Dept. Computer Science, New Mexico State Univ.
[3] Dept. Mathematics, Univ. of Parma

**Abstract.** This paper presents an experimental study aimed at assessing the feasibility of parallelizing *constraint propagation*—with particular focus on arc-consistency—using *Graphical Processing Units (GPUs)*. GPUs support a form of data parallelism that appears to be suitable to the type of processing required to cycle through constraints and domain values during consistency checking and propagation. The paper illustrates an implementation of a constraint solver capable of hybrid propagations (i.e., alternating CPU and GPU), and demonstrates the potential for competitiveness against sequential implementations.

## 1 Introduction

Constraint programming has gained prominence as an effective paradigm for problem modeling and solving, with applications to such diverse domains as scheduling, satisfiability testing, optimization, and verification. A typical *Constraint Satisfaction Problem (CSP)* consists of a set of variables, each taking values from an associated finite domain, along with a set of constraints. The constraints are used to restrict the values that different variables can simultaneously assume. Resolving a CSP consists of determining complete assignments of values to the variables that satisfy all the constraints. Constraint programming is frequently used to address combinatorial problems, which are, in general, NP-hard. Solving CSPs is usually achieved by combining backtracking search with forms of consistency checking, to prune values from the variables' domains that are inconsistent with the constraints. Polynomial time techniques like node, arc, path and bound consistency have been developed for this purpose.

The cost of solving complex CSPs has motivated the exploration of techniques to improve the exploration of the search space; parallelism has been recognized as a strong contender, especially with the wider availability of multicore and cluster platforms. A large body of research has been developed to address parallelization of backtracking search on a variety of parallel and distributed platforms.

The research presented in this paper makes a contribution to the domain of parallel constraint solving, by exploring ways of using *Single-Instruction Multiple-Threads (SIMT)* parallelism to reduce the cost of constraint propagation. The choice of SIMT parallelism has two driving motivations. First of all, it is our belief that this form of parallelism is suitable to the type of processing that constraints are subjected to during consistency checking. Second, SIMT is the style

M. Flatt and H.-F. Guo (Eds.): PADL 2014, LNCS 8324, pp. 152–167, 2014.

of parallelism that is natively supported by modern *General Purpose Graphical Processing Units (GPGPUs)*. GPGPUs are massive parallel architectures, that are available in the form of graphic cards in most modern computers; they provide hundreds of computing cores at an affordable cost. Exploiting the parallelism offered by GPUs is not trivial—the cores are often significantly slower than CPU cores, they impose restrictions on branching, and provide a complex memory hierarchy with differences in speed, size, and concurrency of accesses.

The contribution of this paper is a feasibility study that demonstrates the potential for using GPGPUs to speedup a constraint propagation engine, based on the notion of events [23]. We propose a methodology to map constraints, variables, and domain elements to threads running on GPU cores, thus enabling the concurrent analysis of arc and bound-consistency and removal of inconsistent domain values. The methodology is implemented in an experimental solver, and shown to produce performance enhancements even in its simple and unoptimized form. The prototype demonstrates also the strengths and weaknesses of GPU parallelism in constraint solving. This is, to the best of our knowledge, the first study investigating the use of GPGPUs in constraint propagation; this study opens the doors to an alternative way to enhance performance of constraint solvers, through the unexploited computational power offered by GPUs.

## 2 Background

A *Constraint Satisfaction Problem (CSP)* [19] is defined as $\mathcal{P} = (X, D, C)$ where:
- $X = \langle x_1, \dots, x_n \rangle$ is a $n$-tuple of variables;
- $D = \langle D^{x_1}, \dots, D^{x_n} \rangle$ is a $n$-tuple of *finite* domains, each associated to a distinct variable in $X$. We assume each $D^{x_i} \subseteq \mathbb{N}$; min $D^x$ and max $D^x$ denote the minimum and maximum element of $D^x$, respectively.
- $C$ is a finite set of constraints on variables in $X$, where a constraint $c$ on the $m$ variables $x_{i_1}, \dots, x_{i_m}$, denoted as $c(x_{i_1}, \dots, x_{i_m})$, is a relation $c(x_{i_1}, \dots, x_{i_m}) \subseteq \times_{j=i_1}^{i_m} D^{x_j}$. The variables $x_{i_1}, \dots, x_{i_m}$ are referred to as the *scope* of $c$ (denoted by scp($c$)).

A *solution* of a CSP is a tuple $\langle s_1, \dots, s_n \rangle \in \times_{i=1}^{n} D^{x_i}$ s.t. for each $c(x_{i_1}, \dots, x_{i_m}) \in C$, we have $\langle s_{i_1}, \dots, s_{i_m} \rangle \in c$. $\mathcal{P}$ is (in)consistent if it has (no) solutions.

CSP solvers (e.g., Algorithm 1) alternate two steps: (1) Selection of a variable and non-deterministic assignment of a value from its domain (*labeling*), and (2) Propagation of the assignment through the constraints, to reduce the admissible values of the variables and possibly detect inconsistencies (*constraint propagation*). Thus, at the core of a CSP solver there is a constraint propagation engine, that repeatedly propagates information based on the available constraints; its basic component is a function, from domains to domains, referred to as *propagator* [23]. Given two $n$-tuples of domains $D_1$ and $D_2$, we say that $D_1 \sqsubseteq D_2$ if, $\forall x \in X$, we have that $D_1^x \subseteq D_2^x$. A *propagator* $f$ is a monotonically decreasing function: $f(D) \sqsubseteq D$ and $f(D_1) \sqsubseteq f(D_2)$ whenever $D_1 \sqsubseteq D_2$. Each constraint $c \in C$ is implemented by a set of propagators prop($c$) that operate on the $m$-tuple of domains of the variables in scp($p$). In the paper we denote by $\mathcal{F}$ the set of all propagators considered. If $f(D) = D$ for all $f \in \mathcal{F}$ then $D$ is a *fixpoint* of $\mathcal{F}$. A *propagation solver* **i-solv** for a set of propagators $\mathcal{F}$ and an initial domain $D$ finds the greatest fixpoint of $\mathcal{F}$. **i-solv** start its computation from a subset $F_0 \subseteq \mathcal{F}$ of propagators and the current domains that will be, in general, reduced.

---

**Algorithm 1. search$(X, D, C, \ell)$**

1: **if** $\ell > |X|$ **then**
2:     output $D$; **return true**;
3: **end if**
4: **for all** $d$ **in** $D^{x_\ell}$ **do**
5:     $D' \leftarrow \langle D^{x_1}, \ldots, D^{x_{\ell-1}}, \{d\}, D^{x_{\ell+1}}, \ldots, D^{x_{|X|}} \rangle$;
6:     $F_0 \leftarrow \{\text{prop}(c) : c \in C \land x_\ell \in \text{scp}(c)\}$;
7:     **if** i-solv$(F_0, D') \land$ search$(X, D', C, \ell + 1)$ **then**
8:         **return   true**;
9:     **end if**
10: **end for**
11: **return false**;

---

The procedure **i-solv** (Algorithm 2) iteratively invokes the propagators until the greatest fixpoint is reached. Two general decisions have to be made in order to reach the fixpoint: *(1)* Which propagators should execute, and *(2)* In which order they should execute. These decisions are based on the notion of *events:* an event is a change in the domain of a variable. We distinguish five types of events: (1) *failed_event*: there is a variable $x$ such that $D'^x = \emptyset$. (2) *empty_event*: no event happened, i.e., $D'^x = D^x$ for all variables considered. (3) *sing_event*: there is a variable $x$ such that $|D'^x| = 1$. (4) *bc_event*: there is a variable $x$ such that $\min D'^x > \min D^x$ or $\max D'^x < \max D^x$. (5) *dmc_event*: there is a variable $x$ such that $D'^x \subset D^x$. These events are used to invoke the necessary propagators only, based on the changes to the variables' domains that occurred.

---

**Algorithm 2. i-solv$(Q,D)$**

1: $D' \leftarrow D$;
2: **while** $Q \neq \emptyset$ **do**
3:     **for all** $f \in Q$ **do**
4:         $D'' \leftarrow f(D)$;
5:         **if** *failed_event* **then return false; end if**
6:         $D \leftarrow D''$;
7:     **end for**
8:     $Q \leftarrow$ **new**$(Q, D', D'')$;
9: **end while**
10: **return   true**;

---

The pseudo code in Algorithm 2 is similar to the well-known *AC3* algorithm (c.f., e.g., [19]): the **while** loop (lines 2–9) propagates the constraints in the queue of propagators $Q$ until no changes happen in the domains, i.e., $D$ is a fixpoint for the propagators invoked, or some domain is empty. The procedure **new**$(Q, D', D'')$ chooses the new propagators to be inserted in the queue, based on the changes between the original domain $D'$ and the final domain $D''$ and on the propagators already in $Q$. As a side-effect, the procedure modifies the values of the calling domain variable in the **search** procedure.

# 3    GPU Computing

Modern graphic cards (*Graphics Processing Units*) are multiprocessor devices, offering hundreds of computing cores and a rich memory hierarchy for graphical processing (e.g., DirectX and OpenGL). Efforts like NVIDIA's *CUDA—Compute Unified Device Architecture* [21] aim at enabling the use of the multicores of a GPU to accelerate general applications—by providing programming models and APIs that enable the full programmability of the GPU. In this paper, we consider the CUDA programming model. The underlying conceptual model of parallelism supported by CUDA is *Single-Instruction Multiple-Thread (SIMT)*, a variant of the popular SIMD model. In SIMT, the same instruction is executed by different threads that run on identical cores, while data and operands may differ from thread to thread. CUDA's architectural model is represented in Figure 1.

Different NVIDIA GPUs provide different numbers of cores, organized in a different way, and with different amounts of memory. The GPU consists of a series of *Streaming MultiProcessors (SMs)*; the number of SMs depends on the specific characteristics of each class of GPU—e.g., the Fermi architecture provides 16 SMs. In turn, each SM contains a collection of computing cores (containing a fully pipelined ALU and floating-point unit); the number of cores per SM may range from 8 (in the older G80 platforms) to 32 (e.g., in the Fermi platforms). Each GPU provides access to on-chip memory (for thread registers and shared memory) and off-chip memory (L2 cache, global memory and constant memory)—see Fig. 1.

A logical view of computations is introduced by CUDA, in order to define abstract parallel work and to schedule it among different hardware configurations. A typical CUDA program is a C/C++ program that includes parts meant for execution on the CPU (referred to as the *host*) and parts meant for parallel execution on the GPU (referred to as the *device*). A parallel computation is described by a collection of *kernels*—each kernel is a function to be executed by several threads. Threads spawned on the device to execute a kernel are hierarchically organized to facilitate the mapping of the threads to the (possibly multi-dimensional) data structures being processed: threads are organized in a 3-dimensional structure (called *block*), and blocks themselves are organized in 2-dimensional tables (called *grids*). CUDA maps blocks (coarse-grain parallelism) on the SMs for execution; each SM schedules the threads in a block (fine-grain parallelism) on its computing cores in chunks of 32 threads at a time (called *warps*), thus allowing a group of threads in a block to use the computing resources while other

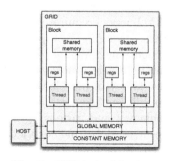

**Fig. 1.** CUDA Architecture

threads of the same block might be waiting for information (e.g., completing a slow memory request). Threads have access to several memory levels, each with different properties in terms of speed, organization (e.g., banks that can be concurrently accessed) and capacity. Each thread stores its private variables in very fast registers (anywhere from 8K to 64K per SM); threads within a block can communicate by reading and writing a common area of memory (called *shared memory*). On the other side, communication between blocks is not supported and it can be accomplished after the completion of the whole kernel. Nevertheless, global memory (up to several GBytes) can be used to store information that can be used by subsequent kernels.

The kernel, invoked by the host, is executed by the device and it is written in standard C-code. The number of running blocks (gridDim) and the number of threads of each block (blockDim) is specified by the kernel call that is invoked on the host code with the following syntax:

$$\text{Kernel} \lll \text{gridDim, blockDim} \ggg (\text{param}_1, \ldots, \text{param}_n);$$

In order to perform a computation on the GPU, it is possible to move data between the host memory and the device memory. By using the specific identifier of each block (blockIdx—providing $x, y$ coordinates of the block in the grid), its dimension (blockDim) and the identifier of each thread (threadIdx—providing $x, y, z$ coordinates for the thread within the block), it is possible to differentiate the data accessed by each thread and code to be executed. For example, the following code fragment shows a kernel and the corresponding call from the host. Each element of a two dimensional matrix is squared, and each thread is in charge of one element of the matrix. The matrix $A$ is represented by a pointer in the device's global memory; CUDA provides functions (e.g., cudaMemCopy) to transfer data between the host and the device's global memory.

```
int main() {   ...                    __global__ sqMatrix(float *Mat){
    dim3 thrsBlock(n,n);                 int i=threadIdx.x;
    sqMatrix<<<1,thrsBlock>>>(A);        int j=threadIdx.y;
    ...                                  Mat[i][j] = Mat[i][j]*Mat[i][j]; }
```

While it is relatively simple to develop correct CUDA programs (e.g., by incrementally modifying an existing sequential program), it is challenging to design an efficient solution. Several factors are critical in gaining performance. The SIMT model requires active threads in a warp to execute the same instruction—thus, diverging flow paths among threads may reduce the amount of actual concurrency. Memory levels have significantly different sizes (e.g., registers are in the order of dozens per thread, while shared memory is in the order of a few kilobytes per block) and access times; different cache behaviors are applied to different memory levels (e.g., constant memory is a cached read-only global memory) and various optimization techniques are used (e.g., accesses to consecutive global memory locations by contiguous threads can be *coalesced* into a single memory transaction). Thus, optimization of CUDA programs require a thorough understanding of the hardware characteristics of the GPU being used.

## 4    Parallelizing the Constraint Engine

In this section we describe our approach to GPU-based execution of the **i-solv** procedure presented in Section 2. The corresponding pseudo-code is reported in Algorithm 3.

Our model encodes three different types of parallelism for constraint propagation. Recall that constraint propagation is monotonic, therefore the order in which the data is analyzed does not influence the result (while it might affect the number of operations performed to reach the fixpoint).

Constraints: Given a set $C$ of constraints for which propagation and consistency checks are to be performed, a natural form of parallelism is to delegate the processing of each constraint $c \in C$ to a different parallel computation. In particular, it is convenient to map a block of threads $(B_c)$ to the handling of each $c$, in order to exploit the various parallel GPU's SM.
A kernel with a number of blocks of the size of the current constraint queue $C$ is invoked. Up to $2^{32}$ blocks can be used on NVIDIA 2.x cards, which is adequate for most CSPs.

Variables: A second level of parallelism is applied to the processing of a constraint $c$ assigned to a block $B_c$. Domain reductions for the variables involved in the constraint (namely $x \in scp(c)$) can be performed in parallel fashion. In particular, each variable can be handled by a different thread that executes the domain filtering. Moreover, the type of operations is executed in a SIMT fashion, since the code for propagation usually repeats identically for each variable. This level of parallelization is suitable to global constraints, such as *element*, *inverse*, or *table* constraint—while it would not bring benefit to constraints that admit efficient propagation algorithms.

CPU and GPU: Host and device are capable of independent and parallel work, that can be synchronized by specific programming constructs. We designed a third level of parallelism for constraint propagation, by partitioning the set of propagators in two queues: one to be processed by the CPU and another one by the GPU. Constraints with efficient propagators (e.g. few variables), remains on the host, while the others are delegated to the GPU. During the evolution of the propagation, exchanges of information between host and device ensure to reach the fixpoint faster.

Let us describe the main components of Algorithm 3. At each invocation of the **i-solv** procedure, the set of initial propagators $F_0$ is split between host and device by the function **split** that initializes the queues of constraints $Q_{host}$ and $Q_{dev}$ (host and device constraints), based on the type of constraints to be propagated in line 2. The default distribution, based uniquely on the type, can be changed by the **split** function according to two internal thresholds: **(1)** If the number of CPU-propagators is higher than a given *upper bound*, they are all moved to $Q_{dev}$; **(2)** If the number of GPU-propagators is lower than a given *lower bound*, they are moved to $Q_{host}$.

By varying these bounds, it is possible to force the computation completely on the CPU (huge lower bound) or completely on the GPU (upper bound =

**Algorithm 3.** i-solv$(F_0, D)$

```
1:  T ← max{|scp(c)| : c ∈ C};
2:  ⟨Q_host, Q_dev ⟩ ← split(F_0);
3:  while Q_host ∪ Q_dev ≠ ∅ do
4:      if Q_dev ≠ ∅ then
5:          cudaMemcpy(D_dev, D);
6:          gpu_propagate<<< |Q_dev|, T >>> (Q_dev, D_dev);
7:          cudaMemcpy(D', D_dev);
8:          if failed_event then return false; end if
9:      end if
10:     if Q_host ≠ ∅ then
11:         for f ∈ Q_host do
12:             D'' ← cpu_propagate(f, D);
13:             if failed_event then return false; end if
14:         end for
15:     end if
16:     D_aux ← D; D ← D' ∩ D'';
17:     ⟨Q_host, Q_dev ⟩ ← split(props(D, D_aux, Q_host ∪ Q_dev));
18: end while
19: return  true;
```

0). These bounds are used to handle the cases where a large number of efficient propagators are assigned to the CPU, while they could take advantage of parallel propagation or, vice-versa, very few expensive propagators are assigned to the GPU, where the time required by memory transactions between host and device would likely offset the advantages of a parallel propagation. The only exception to these rules is for complex constraints (such as the *table* constraint) that are always delegated to the GPU.

Every loop iteration analyzes and modifies the propagators in $Q_{host}$ and in $Q_{dev}$. If $Q_{dev}$ is not empty, parallel propagation is performed by invoking the kernel **gpu_propagate** (line 6), with as many blocks as the size of $Q_{dev}$, and as many threads per block as the maximum scope size among all constraints. The kernel function **gpu_propagate** is sketched in Algorithm 4 and explained later. If $Q_{host}$ is not empty sequential propagation is performed by invoking the function **cpu_propagate** (line 12). If both propagations succeed, the new states $D'$ and $D''$, produced respectively by the GPU and the CPU, are merged (line 16) and the function **props**() determines the minimal sets of propagators that are not at their fixpoint for the domain $D$ (line 17). The function **props**() is based on the notion of *events*. It calculates the events based on status $D_{aux}$ of the previous iteration and the current status $D$ ($evts(D, D_{aux})$), and updates the queue of propagators accordingly:

**props**$(D, D_{aux}, Q) = \{f \in \mathcal{F} : evt\_set(f) \cap evts(D, D_{aux}) \neq \emptyset\} \setminus$ fix$(Q, D)$

where the set $evt\_set(f)$ is the set of events related to the propagator $f$, and fix$(Q, D) = \{f \in Q : f(D) = D\}$. This set of events is computed by analyzing the differences between $D$ and $D_{aux}$.

Let us briefly discuss Algorithm 4. This kernel invokes a propagator per block. The identifier of the block (*blockIdx*) is used as index on the queue $Q$ to retrieve

**Algorithm 4. gpu_propagate($Q, D$)**

1: $c\_id \leftarrow Q[blockIdx]$;
2: **get_propagators**[**get_type**($c\_id$)]($c\_id, D$);

the identifier $c\_id$ of the constraint to propagate. The function **get_propagators** returns a pointer to the device function that implements the (set of) propagators for the constraint $c$ indexed by its type **get_type**($c\_id$). The constraint identifier $c\_id$ is also used by the propagator to identify the scope and any parameters of the constraint to propagate.[1] A **failed_event** is generated when there is an empty domain. If this is the case, then the propagation will fail and the **i-solve** procedure will return **false**; this will cause the search to backtrack (line 9).

The propagation on the host is similar; the kernel invocation is replaced by a *for* loop that iterates over all the propagators in $Q_{host}$ (lines 12-15). Let us note that, differently from the propagation on the device, the **failed_event** is checked every time a propagator has been considered. Let us discuss some details related to the CPU and GPU implementations of these algorithms.

**Domain Representation.** Domains are represented using *bit-masks* stored in $k$ *unsigned int* 32-bit variables. Precisely, considering $D \subseteq \{0, \ldots, 32k-1\}$ viewing the $k$ variables as a unique string, the domain $D$ is represented by $\sum_{i=0}^{32k-1} 2^i b_i$, where if $i \in D$ then $b_i = 1$, else $b_i = 0$. Negative numbers can be implemented using an appropriate offset value. The use of bit-wise operators on domains reduces the differences between the GPU cores and the CPU cores, since access to data in the former is much slower than in the latter. Three extra variables are used: two for storing the domain bounds ($\min D$ and $\max D$) and one for storing the current event associated to $D$. We denote with $M = k+3$ the number of variables used. For instance, for storing domains included in $[0..927]$ we use $M = 32$ unsigned int variables.

**Status Representation.** The status of the computation at every node of the search tree is represented by a vector of $M \cdot |V|$ where $M$ is as described above. This representation of the status reduces the total number of accesses to the global memory, since every consecutive 32 domain values are grouped together in a single *integer* value. The choice of $M$ as a multiple of 32 *integers* allows us to take advantage of the device cache, since global memory accesses are cached and served as part of 128-byte memory transactions. Moreover, using the same array of data for both the bit-mask and the domain bounds increases the *coalesced* memory accesses, i.e., the accesses to the global memory are coalesced for contiguous locations in global memory, increasing access performance.

**Data Transfers.** The memory dataflow is designed in order to optimize memory throughput. Since applications should strive to minimize data transfers between the host and the device (i.e., data transfers with low bandwidth), at each parallel propagation step we transfer the minimum information needed to represent the current state in the search tree. Namely, we copy into the global memory of the GPU the previous decisions performed in the current exploration of the search

---

[1] The relationships between constraints and variables (constraint graph) is stored in the device memory, to limit the information exchange between CPU and GPU.

tree, and only the domains of the variables not labeled yet. These domains still ensure a correct execution of the propagation algorithm, as we are interested in reducing only the domains of the variables that are still to be labeled. In order to allow concurrent computations on the host and the device, every **cudaMemcpy** is performed as an asynchronous data transfer. A call to the CUDA function **cudaDeviceSynchronize()**, used to synchronize the host and the device, is requested only when the CPU has finished its sequential propagation.

**MiniZinc Constraints Encoding.** In this work we considered the finite domain constraints that are available in the *MiniZinc/FlatZinc* modeling language [15]. Given a MiniZinc model, we translate it and produce an input for our solver in three steps: *(1)* first, we read the MiniZinc file to identify the global constraints being used; *(2)* we translate the model into a FlatZinc model without considering the global constraints (we use the compiler available in the MiniZinc distribution [15]); and *(3)* the FlatZinc translation is given as input to a parser that produces the input for the solver.

**Propagators.** We have implemented the propagators for the FlatZinc constraints plus specific propagators for some *global* constraints that take advantage of GPU parallelism. As described earlier, every propagator is implemented as a specific device function invoked by a single block. For example, let us consider an *all_different* constraint $c$ on the variables $x_1, \ldots, x_n$, naively encoded as a quadratic number of binary $\neq$ constraints. It can be implemented by a set of $n$ propagators $p_1, \ldots, p_n$, such that the propagator $p_i$ takes care of the constraints $x_i \neq x_j$ where $j \neq i$ (see Algorithm 5). The propagator is typically activated for one $i$ at a time. A sequential implementation of this propagator requires time $\mathcal{O}(n)$, while the parallel version requires $\mathcal{O}(1)$.

---

**Algorithm 5.** $p_i(c\_id, D)$

---

1: $x_i \leftarrow \mathbf{scp}(c\_id)[i]$;
2: $label \leftarrow min\ D^{x_i}$; {$min\ D^{x_i} = max\ D^{x_i}$ since $x_i$ is the current labeled variable}
3: $n \leftarrow \mathbf{scp}(c\_id).\mathbf{size}()$; {Constraints information on device global memory}
4: **if** $threadIdx < n \wedge threadIdx \neq i$ **then**
5:     $temp \leftarrow \mathbf{scp}(c\_id)[threadIdx]$;
6:     $D^{temp}[label] \leftarrow 0$;
7: **end if**

---

Some other constraints require more than one block to fully exploit the parallel computation. This is the case, for example, of the *table* constraint (see Sec. 5). To handle these cases, we modified Algorithm 3 in order to further split the queue $Q_{\mathrm{dev}}$ in two queues: one for constraints that are propagated using one block per propagator, and one for constraints that use more than one block.

## 5   Results

We experimentally evaluated our solver using several classical benchmarks. Benchmarks are encoded in MiniZinc and compiled automatically in the solver. In particular, we compare the performance of our solver (in terms of execution time) with that of two state-of-the-art solvers, namely *Gecode* [24] and

*JaCoP* [10]. Our solver does not include advanced search strategies at this time—therefore, for a fair comparison, we use Gecode and JaCoP with a naive "leftmost" strategy with increasing value assignment. In order to measure parallel performance, we analyze the speed-ups and limitations of the GPU version against a purely CPU execution of our code—as mentioned earlier, this can be realized by modifying the bounds used to manage the constraint queues. Thus, while the first set of comparisons gives us an idea about the baseline performance of our core solver (including an indication of the overhead introduced to support parallelism), the second set of data measures the improvements gained by using parallelism. We have aimed at creating a core solver that is efficient and competitive with the state-of-the-art, containing overhead to the minimum. All tests have been performed on the following hardware: the *Host* is an AMD Opteron 270, 2.01GHz, RAM 4GB, while the *Device* is an NVIDIA GeForce GTS 450, 192 cores (4MP), Processor Clock 1.566GHz, OS Linux.

**Comparison with Gecode and JaCoP.** We start by evaluating the performance of our solver w.r.t. the solvers Gecode and JaCoP on some classical benchmarks, specifically *nQueens*, *Schur* (numbers $1, \ldots, N$ in $B$ blocks), and the *propagation stress* benchmarks (see, e.g., the MiniZinc benchmarks folder [15]). Let us remark that the *all_different* constraints is implemented in a "quadratic way" in all these problem instances—this explains the relatively slow running times for nQueens. As expected, there are instances that better fit one solver, and other instances that better fit others (see Table 1—running times in seconds). We report two columns for our solver (CPU and GPU). For this experiment, let us focus on the GPU column (the CPU column is used in the following experiments). or a fair comparison, we modified the hybrid and adaptive recomputation parameters of Gecode. In particular we switched off cloning by setting the value $c_d$ (*commit distance*) greater than the expected depth of the search tree.

The labeling strategy for our solver, Gecode and JaCoP is the naive "leftmost" strategy with increasing value assignment. We can observe that the solver we are proposing is, on average, comparable with the state-of-the-art.

**Comparing GPU vs. CPU.** In this section we compare the GPU parallel version of the solver w.r.t. a purely sequential version. The core of the propagators

**Table 1.** Comparison between **i-solv** (sequential CPU and parallel CPU versions), Gecode, and JaCoP for the *nQueens*, *Schur*, and *propagation stress* benchmarks

| N | CPU | GPU | Gecode | JaCoP | N | B | CPU | GPU | Gecode | JaCoP |
|---|-----|-----|--------|-------|---|---|-----|-----|--------|-------|
| 24 | 6.273 | 9.699 | 7.094 | 47.59 | 40 | 4 | 88.59 | 84.75 | 19.02 | 2.570 |
| 26 | 5.975 | 8.773 | 7.438 | 47.55 | 41 | 4 | 92.92 | 90.71 | 19.54 | 2.610 |
| 28 | 50.88 | 68.47 | 66.88 | 442.6 | 42 | 4 | 97.03 | 95.41 | 20.54 | 2.700 |
| 30 | 930.3 | 1278 | 1407 | 9600 | 43 | 4 | 108.4 | 98.75 | 21.35 | 2.850 |

| k | n | m | CPU | GPU | Gecode | JaCoP |
|---|---|---|-----|-----|--------|-------|
| 10 | 20 | 200 | 0.043 | 0.053 | 0.696 | 2.550 |
| 10 | 20 | 300 | 0.068 | 0.082 | 1.740 | 4.730 |
| 10 | 20 | 400 | 0.175 | 0.159 | 3.155 | 8.460 |
| 10 | 20 | 500 | 0.339 | 0.306 | 4.968 | 13.94 |

are implemented in the same way (i.e., they use the same C encoding). The main drawbacks of the GPU computations are primarily related to data transfers, due to the GPU memory latency and coalesced access patterns, and to the difference between the GPU clock and the CPU clock.

We have tested various benchmarks described in Table 1: the running times are comparable for the sequential and parallel executions. Similar considerations hold for other "small" instances. We used the upper bound (UB) parameter to move constraints from the host queue to the device queue. UB is calculated empirically, and it is automatically set by the solver in a preprocessing step, by considering the average numbers of global memory accesses w.r.t. the type of propagators involved in the model. For example, if there is an average of 3 memory accesses for each propagator, and each propagator requires $\mathcal{O}(1)$ time, then the upper bound will be set to at least 900, since each global memory access requires about 300 clock cycles. Table 2 shows how the UB affects the computational time on the *Golomb ruler* problem for a ruler of 20 integers. Notice that the solver with an appropriate upper bound performs better than both the CPU and the GPU without upper bound (UB = 0, all constraints propagated on device). The model comprise both $\mathcal{O}(1)$ and $\mathcal{O}(n)$ propagators.

**Table 2.** Influence of the upper bound parameter on the *Golomb ruler* problem

| CPU | UB = 0 | UB = 100 | UB = 500 | UB = 1000 | UB = 1500 | UB = 2000 |
|------|--------|----------|----------|-----------|-----------|-----------|
| 266.4 | 223.4 | 216.4 | 214.2 | 210.4 | 207.8 | 208.2 |

Significant performance improvements emerge when more complex constraints are considered. As explained in Section 4, the GPU is delegated to large sets of non trivial propagators. Using the CUDA framework, the CPU and the GPU can execute concurrently, since the kernels and the memory copy operations between host and device can be performed asynchronously. Let us focus on two "expensive" constraints, namely the *inverse* and the combinatorial *table* constraint.

**The *inverse* Constraint.** This constraint ties two arrays of variables using the global *inverse* property. Given two lists $X = [x_1, \ldots, x_n]$ and $Y = [y_1, \ldots, y_n]$ of integer variables, where $D^{x_i} = D^{y_i} = [1..n]$, the constraint $inverse(X, Y)$ holds iff $(\forall i \in [1..n])(\forall j \in [1..n])(x_i = j \leftrightarrow y_j = i)$. The FlatZinc implementation of this constraint uses $n^2$ Boolean variables and $2n^2$ *reified equality* constraints:

$$\bigwedge_{i,j} x_i = j \leftrightarrow B_{ij} \wedge \bigwedge_{i,j} y_j = i \leftrightarrow B_{ij}$$

The GPU version of this constraint is implemented by $2n$ propagators. Namely, $n$ propagators are used for the "$\rightarrow$" (resp., "$\leftarrow$") direction of the constraint, considering the labeling of one variable in $X$ (resp., in $Y$). Since we expand the relation $x_i = j \leftrightarrow y_j = i$ either on the left or the right side depending on the labeled variable, we do not need to explicitly use the Boolean variables $B_{ij}$ to link the binary equality constraints. These constraints are propagated by $n$ threads. For example, let us assume that $x_1 = 2$ after the labeling of $x_1$; the constraint engine invokes the propagator $inverse(x_1, Y)$ where the thread whose *threadIdx* = 2 propagates the constraint $y_2 = 1$ (i.e, $B_{12} = $ **true**), while the other threads propagate the constraints $y_i \neq 1$, where $i \in \{1, 3, 4, \ldots, n-1, n\}$.

Table 3 compares the sequential and the parallel implementations of the *inverse* constraints, by increasing the number $n$ of variables in its scope.

**Table 3.** Time comparison for the *inverse* constraint

| n | CPU | GPU | Speedup |
|---|---|---|---|
| 100 | 0.030 | 0.026 | 1.15 |
| 250 | 0.338 | 0.152 | 2.22 |
| 500 | 2.456 | 0.744 | 3.30 |
| 750 | 7.855 | 2.142 | 3.66 |

For $n = 100$ there is a poor speedup, since the CPU cores are faster than the GPU cores and the instance of the problem is small. The speedup increases for bigger instances (i.e., $n > 200$) where the parallel computations offset the difference of speed between CPU and GPU cores. We have verified that the FlatZinc encoding of the *inverse* constraint is sensibly slower; for instance, if $n = 100$, the CPU takes time 3.583 seconds, while the GPU 3.334 seconds.

The *inverse* constraint is employed in several encodings, such as the *black hole* problem, and it is also used to create the dual models of problems.

**The *table* Constraint.** A *table constraint* is an *extensional* constraint defined by explicitly listing (a set of $n$) $m$-tuples of values that are either allowed (*positive* table constraint) of disallowed (*negative* table constraint) for the variables in its scope. *Table* constraints arise naturally in configuration problems where they represent available combinations of options. For some applications, compatibility between resources, e.g., persons or machines, can be expressed by tables. Tabular data may also come from databases: the results of database queries are sometimes expressed as tables that have large arity.

A table constraint $c$ represented by a $n \times m$ matrix and the *Generalized Arc Consistency* (*GAC*) [19] is maintained through propagation. Precisely, focusing on a variable $x_i \in \{x_1, \ldots, x_m\} = \mathrm{scp}(c)$ a *support* for all the values in $D^{x_i}$ is searched. This is realized by iterating over the $n$ allowed tuples until a valid one is found. This algorithm ensures consistency in time $\mathcal{O}(n^m)$ (a faster, but more complex, algorithm is presented in [12]).

Using the GPU, it is possible to reduce this time to (parallel) time $\mathcal{O}(1)$, by performing the GAC test as follows: we assign each row to a kernel block, and each column to a different thread within the block. For table constraints with scope size larger than 1024, we split the computation among multiple kernels. For $1 \leq i \leq n$ and $1 \leq j \leq m$, thread $t_{ij}$ checks whether the value contained in the cell $c_{ij}$ is valid w.r.t. the domain $D_{x_j}$. The domains of the variables involved in the constraint are then replaced with the (new) domains, containing only those values that still might lead to a solution, as determined by each block.

We impose a specific ordering among propagated constraints: we first propagate binary constraints and constraints that have a fast propagator, that may eventually lead to a failure; more expensive propagators are executed last.

Table 4 compares the times for the propagation of the *table* constraint varying the number of rows $n$, the number of columns $m$, and the size of the domains of the variables. The tables are filled with random values, where $|D|$ is the size of the domain; note that larger domains produce fewer valid tuples after the labeling of a variable involved in the constraint.

**Table 4.** Time comparison for the *table* constraint with random values.

| $n \times m$ | $D$ | CPU | GPU | Speedup | $n \times m$ | $D$ | CPU | GPU | Speedup |
|---|---|---|---|---|---|---|---|---|---|
| $100 \times 100$ | 2 | 0.002 | 0.001 | 2.00 | $100 \times 100$ | 50 | 0.001 | 0.001 | 1.00 |
| $250 \times 250$ | 2 | 0.007 | 0.003 | 2.30 | $250 \times 250$ | 50 | 0.003 | 0.001 | 3.00 |
| $500 \times 500$ | 2 | 0.026 | 0.010 | 2.60 | $500 \times 500$ | 50 | 0.013 | 0.004 | 3.25 |

**Examples Containing Table and Inverse Constraints.**
The *Three-barrels* problem is a planning problem, where the state of the world is represented by three barrels of wine, whose capacities are $n$ (even number), $n/2 + 1$, and $n/2 - 1$, respectively. At the beginning, the largest barrel is full of wine, while the other two are empty. The goal is to reach a state in which the two largest barrels contain the same amount of wine. Moreover, the only admissible action is to pour wine from one barrel to another, until the latter is full or the former is empty. We encoded this problem as a decision problem, by imposing an upper bound $\ell$ on the number of actions and evaluating whether the goal state can be reached in $\ell$ steps. In this setting, we have $3(\ell + 1)$ variables, with domains $\{1, \ldots, n\}$, representing the sequence of states, and $\ell$ variables with domains $\{0, \ldots, 5\}$, representing the 6 possible "pouring" actions. The labeling is done on the action variables, and $\ell$ table constraints tie the $i^{th}$ state with the successor $i + 1^{th}$ state. Table 6 (left) shows the results for the *Three-barrels* problem considering a number of actions $\ell$ equal to $n$, that was experimentally found to be the length of the shortest successful plan. The speedup is slowly increasing due to the size of the tables ($r \times 7$, with $r$ proportional to $n$) and the number of valid rows at each labeling (at most 6 given the current state), that reduce the propagation time to $\mathcal{O}(r)$.

The *Black-hole* is a card game problem derived from [4]. A MiniZinc model is also present in the benchmark folder of the MiniZinc distribution [15], using both the global constraints *inverse* and *table*. The former is used to relate card values and positions in the sequence, while the latter is used to impose matching constraints among consecutive cards. The $<$ constraints impose an order between played cards, and are always propagated on the host. Table 6 (right) shows the results for the *Black-hole* game problem. Since the game is devised for 52 cards, the set of order constraints for instances 104 and 208 are artificially introduced. The table shows an increasing speedup. The GPU is faster even on small instances, since the two expensive constraints are propagated in parallel on the GPU.

*Positive* table *constraint benchmarks.* The following benchmark problems are defined using only positive table constraints.[2] They include some well-known

---

[2] These benchmarks can be downloaded from http://becool.info.ucl.ac.be/resources/positive-table-constraints-benchmarks.

**Table 5.** Time comparison for the *Three-barrels* problem and the *Black-hole* game

| Three-Barrels Problem | | | |
|---|---|---|---|
| n | CPU | GPU | Speedup |
| 100 | 176.5 | 160.8 | 1.09 |
| 120 | 364.9 | 324.3 | 1.12 |
| 140 | 679.6 | 588.8 | 1.15 |

| Black-hole Problem | | | |
|---|---|---|---|
| n. cards | CPU | GPU | Speedup |
| 52 | 7.637 | 7.694 | 0.99 |
| 104 | 68.14 | 51.08 | 1.33 |
| 208 | 73.77 | 42.66 | 1.72 |

problems, such as the *crossword* game, the *Langford* problem, several synthetic problems, and some other real-world problems, such as the *modified Renault* problem. A speedup of at least 2 is obtained in all the problem instances, showing that the use of the GPU pays off on large instances and real problems.

**Table 6.** Positive *table* constraint benchmarks.

| Instance | CPU | GPU | Speedup | Instance | CPU | GPU | Speedup |
|---|---|---|---|---|---|---|---|
| CW-m1c-lex-vg4-6 | 0.015 | 0.005 | 3.00 | langford-2-50 | 44.06 | 15.16 | 2.94 |
| CW-m1c-uk-vg16-20 | 1.488 | 0.225 | 6.61 | ModRen_0 | 0.381 | 0.154 | 2.74 |
| CW-m1c-lex-vg7-7 | 209.4 | 43.87 | 4.77 | ModRen_49 | 0.317 | 0.117 | 2.74 |
| langford-2-40 | 136.4 | 46.39 | 2.90 | RD_k5_n10_d10_m15 | 0.138 | 0.053 | 2.60 |

# 6  Related Work

Extensive research has been conducted focusing on parallelizing backtracking search, both in the context of CSP as well as in more general search-based scenarios (e.g., [28,9,11,25]). Some works in this direction include the foundational work of Van Hentenryck in parallelizing the Chip system [26], the follow-up work in various CLP systems (e.g., [6]), the work of Perron [17], Schulte [22], and the more recent explorations by Michel et al. [14].

The problem of parallelizing consistency techniques has been also explored in the literature. The seminal works of Nguyen and Deville [16] and Hamadi [7] present methods based on message passing and distributed memory platforms; these approaches rely on the partitioning of the set of constraints among processors, and the use of messages to exchange variable domains. More recent approaches shifted the focus to multicore platforms and multithreaded implementations — e.g., the proposals by Rolf and Kuchcinksi [18] and Ruiz-Andino et al. (focused on non-binary constraints [20]). Note that, following the results from Kasif [8], establishing arc-consistency is P-complete; this is an indication that extracting parallelism from AC is, in general, not an easy problem (and, in the worst case, may not lead to complexity improvements).

To the best of our knowledge, this is the first reported effort exploring the use of GPGPUs in constraint propagation; some related effort includes [2], that shows how to parallelize unit propagation on GPGPUs. Some preliminary studies have instead addressed the problem of parallelizing *search* on GPUs [2,5,13].

## 7  Future Work and Conclusions

In this paper, we presented a feasibility study exploring the potential for exploitation of fine-grained GPU-level parallelism from the process of constraint propagation. The investigation has been grounded in a prototype (with competitive performance with the state-of-the-art), demonstrating the potential for enhanced performance, especially in the context of complex global constraints. This is not an easy task, and the speedups proposed are in-line with results observed for parallelization of other classes of problems on GPUs.

This work complements preliminary studies [2,27], conducted by the authors, in the context of SAT and ASP solving—where we demonstrated performance improvement from the "orthogonal" direction of parallelizing the actual search process. The combination of these two aspects (parallel search and parallel propagation) provide a roadmap for the creation of a fully GPU-parallel constraint solver—which is the focus of our future effort. The performance improvements for complex constraints reflect also on the potential for effective exploitation of parallelism in the case of domain-specific constraints with complex propagation strategies. We experimented with an ad-hoc constraint-based implementation of protein structure prediction via fragment assembly, parallelized on GPUs using similar techniques, with excellent performance results, outperforming previous approaches [1,3]. We will continue along our current efforts of developing ad-hoc strategy to propagate complex constraints on GPUs.

Let us conclude with a final observation: the overall strategy for handling constraint propagation reported in Algorithm 2 is designed for efficient sequential implementation, and indeed is at the core of the state-of-the-art constraint solvers. Alternative schemes (e.g., AC-3), that can be found in several other implementations, provide a lower level of sequential performance, but they are also more amenable for GPU-level parallelization (as we demonstrated in a preliminary study). Unfortunately, the difference in sequential performance effectively defeats the advantages gained from parallelism.

**Acknowledgments.** The authors acknowledge Marco Meneghin for his support in the developing of the wrapper from FlatZinc.

## References

1. Campeotto, F., Dovier, A., Pontelli, E.: Protein structure prediction on GPU: a declarative approach in a multi-agent framework. In: Proc. of International Conference on Parallel Processing, pp. 474–479. IEEE (2013)
2. Dal Palú, A., Dovier, A., Formisano, A., Pontelli, E.: Exploiting unexploited computing resources for computational logics. In: 9th Italian Convention on Computational Logic, CEUR Workshop Proceedings, vol. 857, pp. 74–88 (2012)
3. Dal Palú, A., Dovier, A., Fogolari, F., Pontelli, E.: CLP-based protein fragment assembly. TPLP 10(4-6), 709–724 (2010)
4. Gent, I., et al.: Search in the Patience Game 'Black Hole'. AI Communications 20(3), 211–226 (2007)

5. Gulati, K., Khatri, S.P.: Boolean Satisfiability on a Graphic Processor. In: Great Lakes Symposium on VLSI, pp. 123–126. ACM (2010)
6. Gupta, G., Pontelli, E., Carlsson, M., Hermenegildo, M., Ali, K.M.: Parallel Execution of Prolog Programs: a Survey. ACM TOPLAS 23(4), 472–602 (2001)
7. Hamadi, Y.: Optimal Distributed Arc Consistency. Constraints 7(3-4) (2002)
8. Kasif, S.: On the Parallel Complexity of Discrete Relaxation in Constraint Satisfaction Networks. Artificial Intelligence 45(3), 275–286 (1990)
9. Kitano, H., Hendler, J.A. (eds.): Massive Parallel Artificial Intelligence. AAAI/MIT Press (1994)
10. Kuchcinski, K., Szymanek, R.: JaCoP Library User's Guide (2012), http://jacop.osolpro.com/
11. Le, H., Pontelli, E.: Dynamic Scheduling in Parallel Answer Set Programming Solvers. In: High Performance Computing Symposium. ACM Press (2007)
12. Lecoutre, C.: STR2 Optimized Simple Tabular Reduction for Table Constraints. Constraints 16(1) (2011)
13. Meyer, Q., Schonfeld, F., Stamminger, M., Wanka, R.: 3-SAT on CUDA: Towards a Massively Parallel SAT Solver. In: HPCS, pp. 306–313. IEEE (2010)
14. Michel, L., See, A., Van Hentenryck, P.: Transparent Parallelization of Constraint Programming. INFORMS Journal on Computing 21(3) (2009)
15. Nethercote, N., Stuckey, P.J., Becket, R., Brand, S., Duck, G.J., Tack, G.: MiniZinc: Towards a Standard CP Modelling Language. In: Bessière, C. (ed.) CP 2007. LNCS, vol. 4741, pp. 529–543. Springer, Heidelberg (2007), www.minizinc.org
16. Nguyen, T., Deville, Y.: A Distributed Arc-Consistency Algorithm. Science of Computer Programming 30(1-2), 227–250 (1998)
17. Perron, L.: Search Procedures and Parallelism in Constraint Programming. In: Jaffar, J. (ed.) CP 1999. LNCS, vol. 1713, pp. 346–361. Springer, Heidelberg (1999)
18. Rolf, C., Kuchcinski, K.: Parallel Consistency in Constraint Programming. In: Proc. of PDPTA, pp. 638–644. CSREA Press (2009)
19. Rossi, F., van Beek, P., Walsh, T.: Handbook of Constraint Programming (Foundations of Artificial Intelligence). Elsevier (2006)
20. Ruiz-Andino, A., Araujo, L., Saenz, F., Ruz, J.: Parallel Execution Models for Constraint Propagation. In: Maher, M.J., Puget, J.-F. (eds.) CP 1998. LNCS, vol. 1520, p. 473. Springer, Heidelberg (1998)
21. Sanders, J., Kandrot, E.: CUDA by Example. An Introduction to General-Purpose GPU Programming. Addison Wesley (2010)
22. Schulte, C.: Parallel Search Made Simple. In: Techniques for Implementing Constraint Programming Systems, TRA9/00, University of Singapore (2000)
23. Schulte, C., Stuckey, P.J.: Efficient constraint propagation engines. ACM TOPLAS 31(1) (2008)
24. Schulte, C., Tack, G., Lagerkvist, M.Z.: Modeling and Programming with Gecode (2013), http://www.gecode.org
25. Talbi, E.G.: Parallel Combinatorial Optimization. John Wiley and Sons (2006)
26. Van Hentenryck, P.: Parallel Constraint Satisfaction in Logic Programming. In: Proc. of ICLP, pp. 165–180. MIT Press (1989)
27. Vella, F., Dal Palù, A., Dovier, A., Formisano, A.: Enrico Pontelli. CUD@ASP: Experimenting with GPGPUs in ASP solving. In: 10th Italian Convention on Computational Logic, CEUR Workshop Proceedings, vol. 1068, pp. 163–177 (2013)
28. Zhang, H., Bonacina, M.P., Hsiang, J.: PSATO: a Distributed Propositional Prover and its Application to Quasigroup Problems. JSC 21(4), 543–560 (1996)

# On the Correctness and Efficiency of Lock-Free Expandable Tries for Tabled Logic Programs

Miguel Areias and Ricardo Rocha

CRACS & INESC TEC and Faculty of Sciences, University of Porto
Rua do Campo Alegre, 1021, 4169-007 Porto, Portugal
{miguel-areias,ricroc}@dcc.fc.up.pt

**Abstract.** Tabling is an implementation technique that improves the declarativeness and expressiveness of Prolog in dealing with recursion and redundant sub-computations. A critical component in the implementation of an efficient tabling framework is the design of the data structures and algorithms to access and manipulate tabled data. One of the most successful data structures for tabling is *tries*. In previous work, our initial approach to deal with concurrent table accesses, implemented on top of the Yap Prolog system, was to use *lock-based* trie data structures. In this work, we propose a new design based on *lock-free* data structures and, in particular, we focus our discussion on the correctness and efficiency of extending Yap's tabling framework to support lock-free expandable tries. Experimental results show that our new lock-free design can effectively reduce the execution time and scale better, when increasing the number of threads, than the original lock-based design.

**Keywords:** Lock-Free, Tries, Hash Tables, Tabling.

## 1 Introduction

Tabling [3] is a refinement of Prolog's standard resolution that can reduce the search space, avoid looping and have better termination properties. Work on tabling proved its viability for application areas such as natural language processing, knowledge based systems, model checking, program analysis, among others. Currently, tabling is widely available in systems like B-Prolog, Ciao, Mercury, XSB and Yap. Multithreading in Prolog is the ability to concurrently perform computations, in which each computation runs independently but shares the program clauses. When multithreading is combined with tabling, we have the best of both worlds, since we can exploit the combination of higher procedural control with higher declarative semantics.

A critical component in the implementation of an efficient concurrent tabling system is the design of the data structures and algorithms to access and manipulate tabled data. One of the most successful data structures for tabling is *tries* [13], a tree-based data structure in which common prefixes are represented only once. To deal with concurrent table accesses, our initial approach, implemented on top of the Yap Prolog system [15], was to use *lock-based data*

M. Flatt and H.-F. Guo (Eds.): PADL 2014, LNCS 8324, pp. 168–183, 2014.

*structures* [2]. However, lock-based data structures have their performance restrained by multiple problems, such as, convoying, low fault tolerance and delays occurred inside a critical region. Yap's framework supports the evaluation of tabled programs according to the semantics of SLG resolution [3]. The practical significance of this is that, in general, we know that a concurrent tabled program will only execute search and insert operations over the table space shared data structures. Yap's shared data structures are only removed when the last running thread abolishes the tables. Since no concurrent delete operations are performed, the size of the shared tries always grows monotonically during an evaluation.

The main motivation of this work is then to refine our lock-based tries in order to be as efficient as possible in the concurrent search and insert operations and to maintain an efficient average node access as the size of the tries increases, independently of the number of running threads. In order to achieve that, we propose a new design based on *lock-free data structures* and we focus our discussion on the correctness and efficiency of extending Yap's tabling framework to support lock-free expandable tries, but our new design can be easily generalized and applied to similar concurrent data structures. Lock-freedom allows individual threads to starve but guarantees system-wide throughput. As we will see, this is very important since it allows to avoid the bottlenecks and performance problems mentioned above without introducing significant overheads for multithreaded tabled evaluation.

Experimental results show that our new lock-free design can effectively reduce the execution time and scale better, when increasing the number of threads, than the original lock-based design. Several lock-free approaches do exist in the literature, such as Shalev and Shavit split-ordered lists [16] or Prokopec *et al.* *CTries* [12], however to the best of our knowledge none of them is specifically aimed for an environment with the characteristics of our tabling framework. By avoiding the node deletion complexity, we were able to produce a fresh and new approach to deal with concurrency inside the tries.

The remainder of the paper is organized as follows. First, we briefly introduce some background and discuss related work. Then, we describe our new lock-free expandable tries design and we present the relevant implementation details. Next, we prove the correctness of our implementation. Finally, we discuss experimental results and we end by outlining some conclusions.

## 2   Background

The trie data structure provides complete discrimination for terms and permits look up and possibly insertion to be performed in a single pass through a term, hence resulting in a very efficient and compact data structure for term representation. An essential property of the trie structure is that common prefixes are represented only once. Two terms with common prefixes will branch off from each other at the first distinguishing token. Figure 1 shows an example for the internal representation of the trie levels. For the sake of simplicity, we only show two levels (the same idea applies to all trie levels).

The first level represents a parent node $P$ and the second level represents how the trie is adapted to the insertion of distinguish child nodes with values $V1$, $V2$, $V3$ and $V4$. Figure 1(a) shows the trie representation

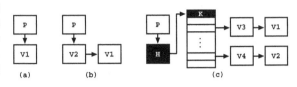

**Fig. 1.** Internal trie representation

after the insertion of $V1$ and Fig. 1(b) shows the trie representation after the insertion of $V2$. Note that new nodes are always inserted on the head for the level. Whenever the number of nodes in a level reaches a predefined threshold value, Yap's tries are expanded with a hash mechanism. Here, for the sake of simplicity, we will use a threshold value of 2. Figure 1(c) shows the hash representation after the insertion of values $V3$ and $V4$. The parent node $P$ now points to a special hash node $H$, which includes a pointer to a hash bucket array with $K$ entries, and the insert operation is now done on the head for the bucket entry corresponding to the hash key value $k$, $0 \leq k < K$. Whenever the hash bucket array becomes saturated, i.e., when the number of nodes in a bucket entry exceeds the threshold value and the total number of nodes exceeds $K$, then the bucket array is expanded to a new one with $2 * K$ entries (we will give more details about this expansion in the following sections).

To deal with concurrent table accesses, our initial approach was to use a lock-based scheme that allows a *single writer* per chain of sibling nodes that represent alternative paths from a common parent node, meaning that only one thread at a time can be inserting a new child node starting from the same parent node [2]. For locking, we used either a *locking field* per trie node or a *global array* of lock entries [1]. In order to reduce the lock duration, we also tried with *trylocks* instead of traditional locks. With trylocks, when a thread fails to get access to the lock, instead of waiting, it returns to the non-critical region, i.e., it traverses the newly inserted nodes, if any, searching if the value $V$ at hand was, in the meantime, inserted by another thread. If $V$ is not found, the process repeats until the thread gets access to the lock or until $V$ is found.

In this work, we are interested in taking advantage of the *CAS (Compare-and-Swap)* operation, that nowadays can be widely found on many common architectures. The CAS operation is an atomic instruction that compares the contents of a memory location to a given value and, if they are the same, modifies the contents of that memory location to a given new value. The atomicity guarantees that the new value is calculated based on up-to-date information, i.e., if the value had been updated by another thread in the meantime, the write would fail. The CAS result indicates whether it has successfully performed the substitution or not. Besides reducing the granularity of the synchronization, the CAS operation is at the heart of many *lock-free* objects [6]. An object is lock-free if it can be accessed by multiple threads concurrently without using any type of *locking mechanism*, such as spin-locks, mutexs or semaphores. For this work, we are most interested in lock-free linearizable objects as they permit greater concurrency since semantically consistent (non-interfering) operations may execute in parallel. Further, linearizability is a local property, and is therefore independent of any underlying scheduling policy or interaction between objects. Locality improves the portability and modularity of large concurrent systems, and can simplify reasoning about concurrent objects.

## 3   Related Work

Despite the availability of both threads and tabling in several Prolog systems, such as Ciao, XSB and Yap, the implementation of these two features such that they work together implies complex ties to one another and to the underlying engine. To the best of our knowledge, XSB and Yap are the unique Prolog systems combining tabling with multi-threading. XSB offers two types of models for supporting multi-threaded tabling: *private tables* and *shared tables* [8]. For private tables, each thread keeps its own copy of the table space. For shared tables, each tabled subgoal is computed independently by the first thread calling it, the *generator thread*, and each generator thread is the sole responsible for fully exploiting and obtaining the complete set of answers for the subgoal. Since both XSB models avoid concurrency over the table space, Yap is thus the single Prolog system that implements and supports concurrent table accesses.

We next briefly describe some of the state-of-the-art approaches for concurrent tries and lock-free hash tables using linked lists to deal with collisions. The first practical work about a lock-free algorithm for hash tables with linked lists was presented by Michael [10]. Experimental results showed that the lock-free implementation outperformed, by significant margins, the best lock-based implementations, both under high and low contention. Another lock-free algorithm for expandable hash tables was presented by Shalev and Shavit [16]. It is based in split-ordered lists and allows the number of hash buckets to vary dynamically according to the number of nodes inserted or deleted, preserving the read-parallelism. More recently, Triplett et al. presented a set of algorithms that allow concurrent wait-free, linear scalable searches while shrinking and expanding hash tables [17]. The experimental results showed a good performance even when the hash table is under resizing.

Regarding concurrent trie data structures, Prokopec et al. presented recently the *CTries* [12]. The CTries are trees composed of internal nodes (I-Nodes) and leaves, combined with the support for a snapshot operation, where the updates on the CTries are done on the I-Nodes. The work shows how the efficiency of the CTries is directly related with the efficiency of the snapshots and how to improve the efficiency of those snapshots.

## 4   Lock-Free Expandable Tries

This section presents our new lock-free design to support the concurrent search, insertion, hash creation and expansion inside the trie structures. We start with Fig. 2 showing a small example that illustrates how the concurrent insertion of

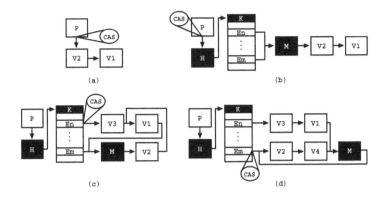

**Fig. 2.** Concurrent insertion of nodes in the new lock-free expandable trie structure

nodes in the new lock-free trie structure is done. Again, for the sake of simplicity, we are only considering two levels of the trie.

Figure 2(a) shows the trie configuration after the insertion of the child nodes $V1$ and $V2$ in the parent node $P$. At this stage, the search/insert operation for a node with a value $V$ is straightforward. Initially, a thread follows the pointer of $P$ to access the next level of the trie. Then, the chain of sibling nodes is searched for the value $V$ at hand. If no such node exists, the pointer of $P$ is used in a CAS operation to guarantee the synchronization of the insertion of $V$ in the chain. During the search, a local counter is used to count the number of nodes on the level which, in the case of a node insertion, is then used to verify if the trie level has reached the predefined threshold value required for hash creation. For this count, no synchronization is required, since only one thread will be able to have its local counter equal to the threshold value.

Figure 2(b) then shows the trie configuration in the case where a thread has started the hash creation process for a trie level. The thread first creates the special node $H$, the initial bucket array with size $K$ and initializes all entries in the bucket array pointing to a special marking node $M$. The node $M$ is then used to implement a synchronization point with the first child node $V$ of $P$ (node $V2$ in the figure) that, whenever both are synchronized, will correspond to a successful CAS operation on $P$ that updates $V$ to $H$. This means that, from this point on, the access to the trie level will be done through the new hash node $H$. If a thread has accessed the trie level before the hash creation, which means that it has not seen $H$, in such case, when trying to insert a new node, the CAS operation on $P$ will fail because $P$ is now pointing to $H$.

In the continuation, Fig. 2(c) and Fig. 2(d) show the adjustment process of placing the child nodes in the correct bucket entries. To ensure lock-free synchronization, we need to guarantee that, at any time, all threads are able to read the correct values (starting from any bucket entry) and insert new values without any delay from the adjustment process. To guarantee both properties, we use $M$ as a way to mark the beginning of the nodes not yet adjusted and we execute the adjustment process in reverse order. Figure 2(c) shows the case where node $V1$

is first adjusted to be in the bucket entry $En$ and Fig. 2(d) shows the case where node $V2$ is then adjusted to be in the bucket entry $Em$. Concurrently with the adjustment process, other threads can be inserting nodes in the same bucket entries. In Fig. 2(c), a new node $V3$ is inserted after $V1$ in entry $En$ and, in Fig. 2(d), a new node $V4$ is inserted before $V2$ in entry $Em$. To ensure that the nodes not yet adjusted (after $M$) can always be accessed from any bucket entry, the adjustment process may lead to cycles between the nodes. For example, in Fig. 2(c), node $V1$ is made to point to node $M$ and since $M$ is pointing to $V2$ and $V2$ is still pointing to $V1$, we have a temporary cycle between these nodes.

At the end of the adjustment process, all bucket entries still access $M$. To complete the hash creation process, the last operation is thus to remove $M$ from all entries. For each bucket entry $E$, if $M$ is on the head of $E$, then a CAS operation updating $M$ to $Null$ is necessary. Otherwise, if $M$ is not on the head of $E$, then we can simply mark as $Null$ the pointer of the node that is pointing to $M$ (nodes $V1$ and $V4$ in Fig. 2(d)). This can be safely done without any CAS operation since no other thread can write on those nodes.

We complete the presentation of our new lock-free design by describing how a hash table with a bucket array of size $K$ is expanded to a new one with size $2*K$. The decision of performing hash expansion is similar to the hash creation process. During the search, a local counter is used to count the number of nodes on a bucket entry which, in the case of a node insertion, is then used to verify the conditions for hash expansion (please refer to Section 2). In order to ensure that only one thread gains access to the hash expansion operation, we use a CAS operation to tag a specific field on $H$. Figure 3 illustrates the hash expansion of Fig. 2(d) after the insertion of a new node $V5$ on the bucket entry $En$.

The thread that gains access to the hash expansion operation starts by creating a new bucket array $B'$ of size $2*K$ entries. Next, for each old bucket entry $En$, it recomputes the hash function

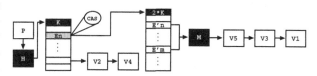

**Fig. 3.** Expanding the hash tables

tion for the nodes on $En$ and redistributes them on $B'$ accordingly to the new hash values. In particular, for our hash function, this means that a node on the $n$th entry of the old bucket array $B$ ($En$ on Fig. 3) will be assigned to the $n$th or $(n+K)$th entry of $B'$ (entries $E'n$ and $E'm$ on Fig. 3). As before, we use again a marking node $M$ to implement a synchronization point between the old bucket entry $En$ and the new bucket entries $E'n$ and $E'm$ that, whenever both are synchronized, will correspond to a successful CAS operation that updates $En$ to $B'$ (situation illustrated on Fig. 3). In the continuation, we follow the same adjustment process as before and, at the end, we remove $M$ from $E'n$ and $E'm$. At the end, when the process of bucket expansion is completed for all $K$ entries of $B$, we update $H$ to point to the new bucket array $B'$ (and remove simultaneously - same memory position - the tagging mark for hash expansion).

## 5    Implementation Details

We now present in more detail the algorithms that implement the key aspects of our new lock-free design. We start with Algorithm 1 that shows the pseudo-code for the search/insert operation of a new node $N$ in a given bucket entry $E$.

In a nutshell, the algorithm executes in a loop until one of the following situations occurs: (a) the search operation is successful, meaning that there is already a node in the trie level with the same value of $N$ (lines 14–15); or (b) $N$ is successfully inserted in the trie (lines 24–25).

In more detail, the algorithm starts by checking (lines 4–5) if the bucket entry $E$ is referencing another bucket array (this happens when another thread is doing hash expansion). In such case, it moves to the new bucket array (variable $B$ at line 6) and updates $E$ (by recomputing the hash function using the value on $N$), $markingNodeVisited$, $oldFirst$ and $first$ accordingly (lines 8–11). The aux-

---

**Algorithm 1.** $TrieSearchInsert(N, E)$

1:   $markingNodeVisited \leftarrow False$
2:   $oldFirst \leftarrow Null$
3:   **repeat**
4:     $first \leftarrow FirstNode(E)$
5:     **while** $IsBucketArray(first)$ **do**
6:       $B \leftarrow BucketArray(first)$
7:       $K \leftarrow Size(B)$
8:       $E \leftarrow BucketEntry(B, Hash(K, Val(N)))$
9:       $markingNodeVisited \leftarrow False$
10:      $oldFirst \leftarrow Null$
11:      $first \leftarrow FirstNode(E)$
12:     $chain \leftarrow first$
13:     **while** $chain \neq oldFirst$ **do**
14:      **if** $Val(chain) = Val(N)$ **then**
15:       **return** $chain$
16:      **else if** $IsMarkingNode(chain)$ **then**
17:       **if** $markingNodeVisited$ **then**
18:        **break**
19:       **else**
20:        $markingNodeVisited \leftarrow True$
21:      $chain \leftarrow NextNode(chain)$
22:     **if** not $IsMarkingNode(first)$ **then**
23:      $oldFirst \leftarrow first$
24:     $NextNode(N) \leftarrow first$
25:   **until** $CAS(E, first, N)$
26:   **return** $N$

---

iliary variable $markingNodeVisited$ denotes if the marking node was already visited and the auxiliary variable $oldFirst$ marks the beginning of the chain of nodes on $E$ that were already searched in a previous round.

On the second part of the algorithm, it then searches if there is a node with the same value of $N$ already in the chain (lines 12–21). Note that this search is done while the nodes in the chain were not yet searched in a previous round (while condition at line 13) and while the marking node was not visited twice (lines 16–20). This second condition allows to break any potential cycle between the nodes, as a result of a hash creation/expansion operation being done by another thread. Finally, if the value of $N$ is not found, the algorithm tries to insert $N$ on the bucket entry $E$ by using a CAS operation that updates $first$ to $N$ (line 25). In case of failure, this means that the head of $E$ has changed in the meantime, thus leading to a new round.

Next, Algorithm 2 shows the pseudo-code for the hash expansion operation given a hash node $H$ (due to the lack of space and since it is quite similar, we will leave aside the algorithm for hash creation). Please remember that to ensure that only one thread executes the hash expansion operation for $H$, we use a CAS operation to tag a specific field on $H$ (not shown here for the sake of simplicity).

The algorithm begins by initializing a set of local variables and by allocating a new bucket array (lines 1–5). Next, for each old bucket entry $oldE$, it redistributes the chain of nodes on $oldE$ to the corresponding bucket entries on the new bucket array $newB$ (lines 7–20). At line 9, it executes a CAS operation on $oldE$ trying to update a value of $Null$ to $newB$. A successful CAS operation means that $oldE$ was empty and thus no redistribution is necessary (it just becomes a pointer to the new bucket array). An unsuccessful CAS operation means that $oldE$ has nodes to be expanded. In such case, the algorithm then computes the

---

**Algorithm 2.** $HashExpansion(H)$

1: $M \leftarrow MarkingNode(H)$
2: $oldB \leftarrow BucketArray(H)$
3: $oldK \leftarrow Size(oldB)$
4: $newK \leftarrow 2 * oldK$
5: $newB \leftarrow AllocBucketArray(newK)$
6: $i \leftarrow 0$
7: **while** $i < oldK$ **do**
8:    $oldE \leftarrow BucketEntry(oldB, i)$
9:    **if not** $CAS(oldE, Null, newB)$ **then**
10:      $newE1 \leftarrow BucketEntry(newB, i)$
11:      $newE2 \leftarrow BucketEntry(newB, i + oldK)$
12:      $FirstNode(newE1) \leftarrow M$
13:      $FirstNode(newE2) \leftarrow M$
14:      **repeat**
15:        $NextNode(M) \leftarrow FirstNode(oldE)$
16:      **until** $CAS(oldE, NextNode(M), newB)$
17:      $AdjustNodes(M, newB)$
18:      $RemoveMarkingNode(M, newE1)$
19:      $RemoveMarkingNode(M, newE2)$
20:    $i + +$
21: $BucketArray(H) \leftarrow newB$
22: **return**

---

entries on $newB$ in which the nodes from $oldE$ will fall (entries $newE1$ and $newE2$) and initializes them to point to the marking node $M$ (lines 10–13). The marking node $M$ is then used to implement a synchronization point between the old bucket entry $oldE$ and the new bucket entries $newE1$ and $newE2$ that, whenever both are synchronized, will correspond to a successful CAS operation that updates $oldE$ to $newB$ (lines 14–16). In the continuation (lines 17–19), the algorithm proceeds by adjusting the nodes on the old chain (Algorithm 3 below) and by removing $M$ from the $newE1$ and $newE2$ chains (Algorithm 4 below). At the end, when the process of bucket expansion is completed for all entries in $oldB$, $H$ is updated to point to the new bucket array $newB$ (line 21).

Algorithm 3 shows the pseudo-code for the process of adjusting a chain of nodes, starting from a given node $N$, into a given new bucket array $B$. One can observe that the algorithm traverses the chain of nodes recursively and that the base case for recursion is the last node on the chain

---

**Algorithm 3.** $AdjustNodes(N, B)$

1: $chain \leftarrow NextNode(N)$
2: **if** $NextNode(chain) \neq Null$ **then**
3:    $AdjustNodes(chain, B)$
4: $K \leftarrow Size(B)$
5: $E \leftarrow BucketEntry(B, Hash(K, Val(chain)))$
6: **repeat**
7:    $NextNode(chain) \leftarrow FirstNode(E)$
8: **until** $CAS(E, NextNode(chain), chain)$
9: **return**

(lines 1–3). For each *chain* node, it then calculates the bucket entry $E$ in which it will fall (lines 4–5). The bucket entry $E$ is then used in repeated CAS operations until successfully insert the *chain* node on the head of $E$ (lines 6–8).

Finally, Algorithm 4 shows the pseudo-code for the operation of removing a given marking node $M$ from a given bucket entry $E$. Initially, it executes a CAS operation on $E$ trying to update an expected value $M$ to $Null$. A successful CAS operation means that no nodes were adjusted to be on $E$ (and $E$ just

---

**Algorithm 4.** *RemoveMarkingNode(M, E)*

1: **if not** $CAS(E, M, Null)$ **then**
2:     $chain \leftarrow FirstNode(E)$
3:     $next \leftarrow NextNode(chain)$
4:     **while** $(next \neq M)$ **do**
5:         $chain \leftarrow next$
6:         $next \leftarrow NextNode(chain)$
7:     $NextNode(chain) \leftarrow Null$
8: **return**

---

becomes a pointer to $Null$). An unsuccessful CAS operation means that at least one node was adjusted to be on $E$. In such case, the algorithm then follows the chain of nodes on $E$ until reaching $M$ and updates the node previous to $M$ to point to $Null$ (thus removing $M$ from the chain). This can be safely done without any CAS operation, because at this stage no other thread can be writing at this node.

## 6    Proof of Correctness

In this section, we discuss the correctness of our implementation.

### 6.1    Linearizability

Linearizability is an important correctness condition for the implementation of concurrent data structures [7]. A concurrent operation is linearizable if it appears to take effect instantaneously at some moment of time $I_{time}$ between its invocation and response. The literature often refers to $I_{time}$ as a *linearization point* and, for lock-free implementations, a linearization point is typically a single instant where its effects become visible to all the remaining operations. Linearizability guarantees that if all operations individually preserve an invariant, the system as a whole also will. Our new implementation is linearizable, since every trie manipulation operation takes effect in specific linearization points. The linearization points for our algorithms are the following:

- *TrieSearchInsert()* is linearizable at successful CAS in line 25.
- *HashExpansion()* is linearizable at successful CAS in lines 9 and 16 and at algorithms *AdjustNodes()* and *RemoveMarkingNode()* in lines 17–19:
    - *AdjustNodes()* is linearizable at successful CAS in line 8.
    - *RemoveMarkingNode()* is linearizable at successful CAS in line 1 and at line 7 when the node previous to the marking node is updated to $Null$.

Due to the lack of space, we do not show the full proof of correctness of the linearization points defined above. Instead, we focus on proving that our implementation is ABA-free.

## 6.2   The ABA Problem

We now discuss how we address the ABA problem. We use the fact that a memory location has not changed between two readings to assume that nothing has changed during the period of time from the first to the second reading. Although, this is a common technique when using the CAS operation, in some cases, it can lead to the ABA problem. An example of that would be: a thread $T$ reads a value $V1$ from a memory location $L$, uses $V1$ to do some work, updates $L$ to a new value $V2$ and, at the end of the work, changes the value of $L$ again to $V1$. In such case, if another thread has read the memory location $L$ before and after the work done by $T$, then it will be deceived by the fact that the memory location has not changed. In our implementation, a practical consequence of this would be to insert more than once the same value on the same level of the trie.

To address the ABA problem, several techniques already exist, such as *version tagging* [4], *hazard pointers* [11] or *value semantics* [5]. In general, these kind of techniques rely on the fact that a writing over a memory position always cause a transition from the current state of the system to a uniquely new different state. To prove that our algorithm is ABA-free, we prove that each concurrent memory location $L$ only points once to the same value $V1$, i.e., if $L$ is updated from $V1$ to $V2$ than $L$ will never point to $V1$ again. Our concurrent memory locations are defined by the pointers on the parent nodes $P$, on the hash nodes $H$ and on the bucket entries $E$ as described in the previous sections.

**Theorem 1.** *The new implementation is ABA-free.*

*Proof. Assume that $P$, $C$, $H$, $M$ and $E$ already exist in a trie $T$ and represent, respectively, a parent node, a child node, a hash node, a marking node and a bucket entry. Assume also that $NC$, $NH$ and $NB$ represent, respectively, a new child node, a new hash node and a new bucket array.*

*The following writing situations may occur: (i) if a write occurs in $P$ then a $NC$ or $NH$ was added to the trie $T$; (ii) if a write occurs in $H$ then a $NB$ was added to $T$; (iii) if a write occurs in $E$ then a $NC$ or $NB$ was added to $T$ or the node adjustment process adjusted $E$ to $Null$ or to a child node $C$.*

*In the latter situation, if $E$ is adjusted to $Null$ that means that before the write operation, $E$ was pointing to a marking node $M$. Otherwise, if $E$ is adjusted to a child node $C$, then before the write operation, $E$ was pointing to another node, say $N$. $N$ can be a new child node $NC$ added in the meantime, a marking node $M$, or another child node adjusted previously. In any case, $N$ is necessarily different from $C$ and $E$ will never point to $N$ again.*

*Thus, all concurrent memory locations always point once to the same value whenever a write operation occurs.*

## 6.3   Liveness

In this subsection, we prove that the insert and hash operations are lock-free and that the search operation is wait-free. For that, we begin by enumerating the following Lemmas.

**Lemma 1.** *If the CAS operation in TrieSearchInsert() at line 25 succeeds, then a new node was inserted in the trie.*

**Lemma 2.** *If the CAS operation in HashExpansion() at lines 9 or 16 succeeds, then the bucket entry was updated to point to a new bucket array.*

**Lemma 3.** *If the CAS operation in AdjustNodes() at line 8 succeeds, then the bucket entry was updated to point to a node that was already in the chain of the bucket entry.*

**Lemma 4.** *If the CAS operation in RemoveMarkingNode() at line 1 succeeds, then the bucket entry was updated to point to Null.*

To prove the property of lock-freedom, we prove that the insert and hash operations always lead to progress in the trie configuration. We start with Theorem 2 that proves that progress is always achieved for the insert operation. The proof is done on the point of the implementation where we try to insert new nodes in the trie, i.e., the CAS operation in *TrieSearchInsert()* at line 25. Note that, since we are assuming that the CAS operation was executed, this means that the given node $N$ was not found in the chain starting from *first* (lines 12 to 21) as otherwise the *return* at line 15 would have been executed.

**Theorem 2.** *In TrieSearchInsert(), everytime a thread executes the CAS operation at line 25, then the trie configuration has made progress when compared to the time at which the thread has entered the repeat loop at line 4.*

*Proof. If the CAS operation succeeds then, by Lemma 1, a new node was inserted in the trie thus leading to progress in the trie configuration.*

*Otherwise, if the CAS operation fails, then the value in the bucket entry $E$ is necessarily different from the initial one, as given by $first$ (initialized at lines 4 or 11). Thus, the new value of $E$ must be the result of one of the following situations: (i) a new node was inserted by another thread (Lemma 1); (ii) the current hash is being expanded by another thread (Lemma 2); or (iii) another thread is performing the adjustment process on $E$ (Lemmas 3 or 4). In either one of these three cases, another thread has lead to progress in the trie configuration.*

To prove that the hash creation/expansion operations progress even when other threads are inserting new nodes, we can use as sketch the proof for Theorem 2. Due to the lack of space, we are also omitting such proofs here.

**Theorem 3.** *The new implementation is lock-free.*

Next, we prove the wait-free property of the search operation and, for that, we show that any search operation is always completed in a bounded number of visited nodes. In particular, this bound is always lower or equal to the number of nodes in the chain being searched. Since the number of steps of the search operation is finite, the proof that the bound exists is sufficient to prove that the search operation is wait-free.

**Theorem 4.** *The search operation is completed within a bounded number of visited nodes.*

*Proof.* *Assume that $CN$ is a chain of nodes and that a search operation in $CN$ is executed between two instants of time, $I_{init}$ and $I_{final}$. This corresponds to the block of code between lines 12 and 21 in the $TrieSearchInsert()$ algorithm. Assume also that $N_{init}$ is the number of nodes at instant $I_{init}$, $N_{new}$ is the total number of new nodes inserted between $I_{init}$ and $I_{final}$, and that $N_{vis}$ is the number of nodes visited between $I_{init}$ and $I_{final}$.*

*The variable chain represents a node to be visited, the variable $first$ represents the first node visited, and variable $oldFirst$ represents the first node that was visited on the previous search operation. On the first search operation, $oldFirst$ is always $Null$. We begin now the proof that $N_{vis}$ is bounded for all the configurations of $CN$.*

*If $N_{init} = 0$, then $first$ and $oldFirst$ are both $Null$ and thus $N_{vis} = 0$.*

*If $N_{init} \neq 0$, then $first \neq Null$. Now, if $oldFirst = Null$ then two situations can occur. On the first situation, no concurrent hash expansion has interfered with the search, thus the variable chain visits all nodes until reaching $oldFirst$, and in such case $N_{vis} = N_{init}$. On the second situation, a concurrent hash expansion has interfered with the search, thus the variable chain may not visit all $N_{init}$ nodes (some nodes may be scheduled to a different bucket entry) but a node can be visited more than once (please remember that, during the adjustment process, we may have cycles between the nodes). In any case, it stops either when reaching $oldFirst$ (line 13) or when the marking node is visited twice (line 17). Thus, $N_{vis} \leq 2 * (N_{init} + N_{new})$.*

*Finally, if $N_{init} \neq 0$ and $oldFirst \neq Null$, then the variable chain will not visit all $N_{init}$ nodes (the ones after $oldFirst$) and thus $N_{vis} \leq N_{init}$.*

## 7   Experimental Results

We now present experimental results for the new lock-free design using the set of benchmarks from [1] which includes 19 different programs in total. We choose these benchmarks because they have characteristics that cover a wide number of scenarios in terms of trie usage. The benchmarks create different trie configurations with lower and higher number of nodes and depths, and also have different demands in terms of trie traversing. The environment for our experiments was a machine with 32 Core AMD Opteron (tm) Processor 6274 using 32 GBytes of memory and running the Linux kernel 3.6.6-1.fc17.x86_64 with Yap Prolog 6.3.

To compare our new design, which we named *Lock-Freedom (FD)*, we used the four lock-based strategies from the previous design, which we named *Local Locks (LL)*, *Global Locks (GL)*, *Local Trylocks (LT)* and *Global Trylocks (GT)*. All strategies use the Pthreads implementation for lock support. The LL and LT strategies use a lock field per trie node. The GL and GT strategies use a global array of 512 lock entries with a hash function that maps trie nodes to lock entries. Through experimentation, we observed that the number of trie nodes mapped by hash function to each lock entry shows a good balancing, thus reducing contention points. To put our results in perspective, we also make a comparison with XSB Prolog, version 3.4.0, using thread-private tables [8].

Note that our goal with these experiments is not to prove that we can speedup the execution of tabled programs, despite this is an obvious goal of having a concurrent implementation. Other works have already showed the parallel capabilities of the use of multithreaded tabling [8,9]. Since parallelism is highly dependent on the available concurrency that programs have and on the way synchronization is done, we can easily select/construct programs where linear speedups can be achieved or, on the other hand, where no speedups exist. Here, we are more interested in evaluating the robustness of our implementation when exposed to worst case scenarios. Note that if we are able to deal well with such scenarios, we will certainly have the conditions to better support parallelism. Moreover, by doing that, we avoid the peculiarities of the program at hand and we try to focus on measuring the real value of our new design.

Thus, we will follow a common approach to create worst case scenarios and we will run all threads starting with the same query goal. By doing this, it is expected that all threads will access the table space, to check/insert for subgoals and answers, at similar times, thus causing a huge stress on the same critical regions. To put the results in perspective, we experimented with intervals of 8 threads until 64 threads (two times the number of cores in our machine). Figure 4 shows the overhead ratios, comparing the execution time with 8, 16, 24, 32, 40, 48, 56 and 64 threads against the respective execution time with one thread, for the average of five runs, when running the set of benchmarks.

By observing Fig. 4, the results show that XSB achieves the best ratio for 8 threads but then, for more than 8 threads, XSB is noticeably worse than all Yap's strategies, showing a clear tendency to worsen as we increase the number of threads. For the sake of presentation, we are not showing the results for more than 24 threads (for 32, 40, 48, 56 and 64 threads, XSB is respectively 17.35, 22.35, 27.21, 32.41 and 36.60 times slower than the execution with one thread). On comparison with Yap, these results are even more important since XSB shows, on average, base execution times (with one thread) higher than Yap. Regarding Yap's synchronization strategies, the results show that FD is always the best strategy of all, regardless of the number of threads. The best lock-based strategy is LT, for 8 to 32 threads, and LL, for 40 to 64 threads. In general, the differences to the corresponding GT and GL strategies is meaningless, which confirms the low contention observed for the global lock array.

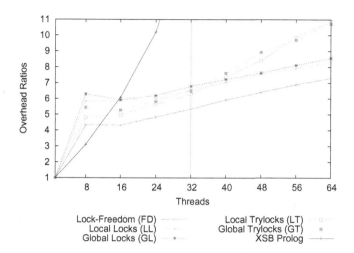

**Fig. 4.** Overhead ratios, comparing the execution time with 8, 16, 24, 32, 40, 48, 56 and 64 threads against the respective execution time with one thread

Starting from 32 threads, one can also observe that the LT and GT trylock strategies start to diverge and that the LL and GL strategies keep the difference to the FD design. This is explained by the fact that, in the Pthreads implementation, when a thread fails to get a lock it falls asleep, leaving the machine resources available to the remaining threads. In particular, for the LL and GL strategies, when the number of execution threads exceeds the number of cores, this leads to an inversion on the execution priorities, which results in having the machine resources always available to the threads inside the critical regions (i.e., holding the corresponding synchronization locks).

For a number of threads smaller than 32, the LT and GT trylock strategies perform better. This is due to the fact that, for fewer threads than the number of cores, they do not have to pay the cost of resuming the threads that fall asleep when failing to get a lock but, for more threads than the number of cores, they may have to pay the cost of not having machine resources always available to the threads holding the synchronization locks. Again, since the FD strategy is immune to the availability of machine resources, and since the CAS operation was a lower synchronization overhead when compared with a lock-based design, makes our new FD design clearly the best approach for both scenarios.

To better understand these results, we next show the overhead ratios, but now comparing the average *user time* (Fig. 5(a)) and the average *system time* (Fig. 5(b)) for 8, 16, 24, 32, 40, 48, 56 and 64 threads against the respective execution time (walltime) with one thread for Yap's synchronization strategies. The results on Fig. 5(a) show us how concurrency affects, on average, the execution of a thread, i.e., how much more user code, on average, a thread has to execute when compared with the base execution with one thread. One can observe that all strategies start to pay a huge cost for eight threads (between 2.32 (FD) and 3.04 (GL) times the execution time with one thread) and then this

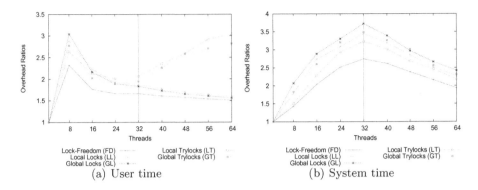

(a) User time                                      (b) System time

**Fig. 5.** Overhead ratios, comparing the average user/system time with 8, 16, 24, 32, 40, 48, 56 and 64 threads against the respective execution time with one thread

cost decreases gradually, except for the LT and GT trylock strategies that, for more than 32 threads, start paying the cost of not having machine resources always available (as explained before). The results on Fig. 5(b) show us how much more system (synchronization) code, on average, a thread has to execute when compared with the base execution with one thread. One can observe that all strategies show a similar tendency, with FD always showing the least overhead of all, which confirms the lower synchronization overhead of the CAS operation.

## 8   Conclusions

We have presented a novel, efficient and lock-free design for expandable trie data structures applied to the multithreaded tabled evaluation of logic programs. Our main motivation was to refine the previous lock-based design in order to be as efficient as possible in the concurrent search and insert operations and to maintain an efficient average node access as the size of the tries increases, independently of the number of running threads. We discussed the relevant implementation details and we proved the correctness of our implementation. Experimental results show that our new lock-free design can effectively reduce the execution time and scale better, when increasing the number of threads, than the original lock-based design. Further work will include extending our framework to support multithreaded mode-directed tabling [14], which includes studying how to extend our new lock-free design to allow the concurrent deletion of trie nodes.

**Acknowledgments.** This work is partially funded by the ERDF (European Regional Development Fund) through the COMPETE Programme and by FCT (Portuguese Foundation for Science and Technology) within projects LEAP (FCOMP-01-0124-FEDER-015008) and PEst (FCOMP-01-0124-FEDER-037281). Miguel Areias is funded by the FCT grant SFRH/BD/69673/2010.

# References

1. Areias, M., Rocha, R.: An Efficient and Scalable Memory Allocator for Multi-threaded Tabled Evaluation of Logic Programs. In: International Conference on Parallel and Distributed Systems, pp. 636–643. IEEE Computer Society (2012)
2. Areias, M., Rocha, R.: Towards Multi-Threaded Local Tabling Using a Common Table Space. Journal of Theory and Practice of Logic Programming, International Conference on Logic Programming, Special Issue 12(4 & 5), 427–443 (2012)
3. Chen, W., Warren, D.S.: Tabled Evaluation with Delaying for General Logic Programs. Journal of the ACM 43(1), 20–74 (1996)
4. Detlefs, D.L., Martin, P.A., Moir, M., Steele Jr., G.L.: Lock-Free Reference Counting. In: ACM Symposium on Principles of Distributed Computing, pp. 190–199. ACM (2001)
5. Hendler, D., Shavit, N., Yerushalmi, L.: A Scalable Lock-free Stack Algorithm. In: ACM Symposium on Parallelism in Algorithms and Architectures, pp. 206–215. ACM (2004)
6. Herlihy, M., Wing, J.M.: Axioms for Concurrent Objects. In: ACM SIGACT-SIGPLAN Symposium on Principles of Programming Languages, pp. 13–26. ACM (1987)
7. Herlihy, M., Wing, J.M.: Linearizability: a correctness condition for concurrent objects. ACM Transactions on Programming Languages and Systems 12(3), 463–492 (1990)
8. Marques, R., Swift, T.: Concurrent and Local Evaluation of Normal Programs. In: Garcia de la Banda, M., Pontelli, E. (eds.) ICLP 2008. LNCS, vol. 5366, pp. 206–222. Springer, Heidelberg (2008)
9. Marques, R., Swift, T., Cunha, J.: A Simple and Efficient Implementation of Concurrent Local Tabling. In: Carro, M., Peña, R. (eds.) PADL 2010. LNCS, vol. 5937, pp. 264–278. Springer, Heidelberg (2010)
10. Michael, M.M.: High Performance Dynamic Lock-Free Hash Tables and List-Based Sets. In: ACM Symposium on Parallel Algorithms and Architectures, pp. 73–82. ACM (2002)
11. Michael, M.M.: Hazard Pointers: Safe Memory Reclamation for Lock-Free Objects. IEEE Transactions on Parallel and Distributed Systems 15(6), 491–504 (2004)
12. Prokopec, A., Bronson, N.G., Bagwell, P., Odersky, M.: Concurrent Tries with Efficient Non-Blocking Snapshots. In: ACM SIGPLAN Symposium on Principles and Practice of Parallel Programming, pp. 151–160. ACM (2012)
13. Ramakrishnan, I.V., Rao, P., Sagonas, K., Swift, T., Warren, D.S.: Efficient Access Mechanisms for Tabled Logic Programs. Journal of Logic Programming 38(1), 31–54 (1999)
14. Santos, J., Rocha, R.: On the Efficient Implementation of Mode-Directed Tabling. In: Gupta, G. (ed.) PADL 2013. LNCS, vol. 7752, pp. 141–156. Springer, Heidelberg (2013)
15. Santos Costa, V., Rocha, R., Damas, L.: The YAP Prolog System. Journal of Theory and Practice of Logic Programming 12(1 & 2), 5–34 (2012)
16. Shalev, O., Shavit, N.: Split-Ordered Lists: Lock-Free Extensible Hash Tables. Journal of the ACM 53(3), 379–405 (2006)
17. Triplett, J., McKenney, P.E., Walpole, J.: Resizable, Scalable, Concurrent Hash Tables via Relativistic Programming. In: USENIX Annual Technical Conference, p. 11. USENIX Association (2011)

# Typelets — A Rule-Based Evaluation Model for Dynamic, Statically Typed User Interfaces

Martin Elsman[1] and Anders Schack-Nielsen[2]

[1] University of Copenhagen, Universitetsparken 5, DK-2100 Copenhagen, Denmark
mael@diku.dk
[2] SimCorp, Weidekampsgade 16, DK-2300 Copenhagen, Denmark
anders.schack-nielsen@simcorp.com

**Abstract.** We present the concept of *typelets*, a specification technique for dynamic graphical user interfaces (GUIs) based on types. The technique is implemented in a dialect of ML, called MLFi,[1] which supports dynamic types, for migrating type-level information into the object level, so-called type properties, allowing easy specification of, for instance, GUI control attributes, and type paths, which allows for type-safe access to type components at runtime. Through the use of Hindley-Milner style type-inference in MLFi, the features allow for type-level programming of user interfaces. The dynamic behavior of typelets are specified using declarative rules. The technique extends the flat spreadsheet programming model with higher-order rule composition techniques, extensive reuse, and type safety. A layout specification language allows layout programmers (e.g., end-users) to reorganize layouts in a type-safe way without being allowed to alter the rule machinery. The resulting framework is highly flexible and allows for creating highly maintainable modules. It is used with success in the context of SimCorp's high-end performance-critical financial asset-management system with screens containing several hundreds of GUI controls located in group-boxes, sub-tabs, and menu structures and with very complex dependency structures defined using declarative rule composition.

## 1   Introduction

Complex GUI applications are often developed using costly and error prone development procedures for which developers are required to design the precise static layout of GUI controls, using a so-called designer tool, and develop an excessive amount of boilerplate side-effecting event-handler functions for which the host language provides little (or no) type guarantees.

This paper presents a technique to obtain a dynamic GUI given a declarative description (in terms of a MLFi type declaration) that specifies the type of the different controls in the user interface as well as possible high-level layout properties such as relative positions and groupings of controls. The approach supports a large set of composable GUI controls, including ordinary value input fields (for integers, floats, amounts, etc.), buttons, select boxes, check boxes, date-picking

---

[1] MLFi is a derivative of OCaml, extended by LexiFi with extensions targeted at the financial industry.

M. Flatt and H.-F. Guo (Eds.): PADL 2014, LNCS 8324, pp. 184–199, 2014.
© Springer International Publishing Switzerland 2014

controls, grid controls, and various grouping controls, such as labeled groups, tab controls, and more.

For specifying the dynamic behavior of a typelet, the programmer writes rules, stating, for example, that a change in some fields influence the content of other fields. The rule-based approach is declarative in the sense that focus is on "what the end-user gets" instead of "how the end-user gets it".

Rules may be composed and attached to a typelet in a type-safe way. Moreover, rules are objects for analysis in the sense that it may statically be determined, for instance, that different rules target the same field or that a subset of rules form a cyclic dependency. The declarative nature of typelet rules is similar to the Functional Reactive Programming (FRP) approach, as seen in Fran [7], Fruit [6], and Flapjax [16].

The typelet implementation is augmented with a type-safe and rule-preserving layout specification mechanism, that allows for layout programmers (e.g., the end-user) to freely reorganize layouts using a set of layout combinators.

The contributions of this paper are the following:

1. We present a novel technique for programming dynamic graphical user interfaces, based on the notion of types and declarative rules for specifying how different parts of the GUI interact.
2. We show how the technique can be augmented with a technique for separating layout from functionality.
3. We describe how this novel declarative approach to programming graphical user interfaces with success is used in practice in SimCorp Dimension, a financial asset-management system with typelet-based trade screens containing several hundreds of inter-dependent fields and other controls, such as grids.
4. Finally, the paper also serves to demonstrate the usefulness of some of the dynamic type features of MLFi, including type properties, and type paths.

We first present a simple typelet and proceed by showing how MLFi type properties may be used to control details of layout and GUI behavior. In Sec. 4, we outline the dynamic type features of MLFi. We then cover the central concept of rules in Sec. 5 and discuss some details of the implementation in Sec. 6. The augmented type-safe layout specification mechanism is described in detail in Sec. 7. Related work is presented in Sec. 8 and Sec. 9 concludes.

## 2   Typelet Basics

We first demonstrate the typelet idea with a simple example that allows a user to enter some personal data and information about whether the user has passed an introductory programming course. Fig. 1(a) lists a typelet specification for the user interface. The result of displaying the specification as a GUI is shown in Fig. 1(b).

There are a series of points to be made here. First, notice that MLFi record field names are used as labels in the GUI; for localization purposes, the implementation allows these names to be overwritten by a resource file. Second,

```
type gender = Male | Female
type t = {
    name: string;
    address: string;
    age: int;
    gender: gender;
    passed_course: bool
}
```

(a)                                    (b)

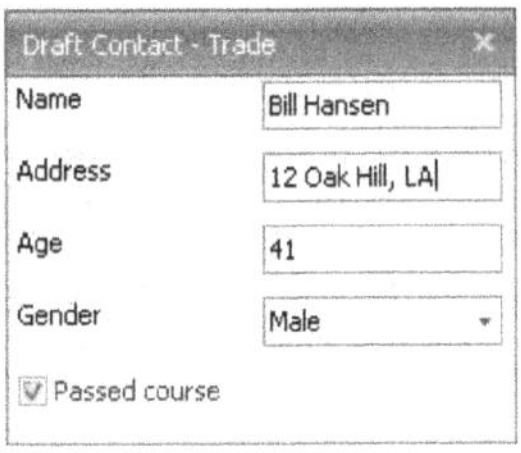

**Fig. 1.** A simple typelet with data entered by the end user

notice that default controls are selected based on the type of record field names in the typelet; for instance, a drop down selection box is chosen for the **gender** field. Third, the order the controls appear in the GUI matches closely the order of fields in the typelet. Finally, notice that default values are chosen for each control.

Typelets also support more dynamic behavior. For instance, if a typelet contains sum-types with data constructors that take arguments, a dynamic GUI is generated for which the GUI's representing the data constructor arguments are replaced and shown based on a left-positioned drop-down list with data constructor names.

There are many details to consider regarding the layout of even the simple typelet presented above. For instance, should all fields extend to the right if the GUI window is enlarged? How can it be specified that a radio button group is desired instead of a drop down selection box for the gender? How can it be specified that two controls should appear on the same row?

## 3   Increasing Control with Type Properties

MLFi supports the notion of type properties, which allows the programmer to attach arbitrary key-value properties (or key properties) to types. Fig. 2(a) lists the code for a small example typelet that makes use of type properties setting the width of controls and for specifying that a control should appear to the right of another control. The result of displaying the typelet is shown in Fig. 2(b).

A large number of type properties are supported for controlling the layout for various controls, including the number of digits for float fields, the caption field for a control, the height, width, and default value for a control, and so on. As demonstrated by the first two type declarations in the example, it is possible to make use of ML's type inference (and the fact that sets of type properties compose) to ease the annotation of types with type properties.

Whereas this possibility is great for getting a good initial layout for a user interface, we shall see in Sec. 7 how so-called typelet layouts allow for separation of layout specification from functionality.

```
type 'a r = 'a + [right]
type 'a fixed = 'a + [fixedwidth]
type t = {
  name: string; street: string;
  no: string r fixed
    + [width="50";
       nocaption];
  zip: string fixed
    + [width="100"];
  city: string r
}
```

(a)

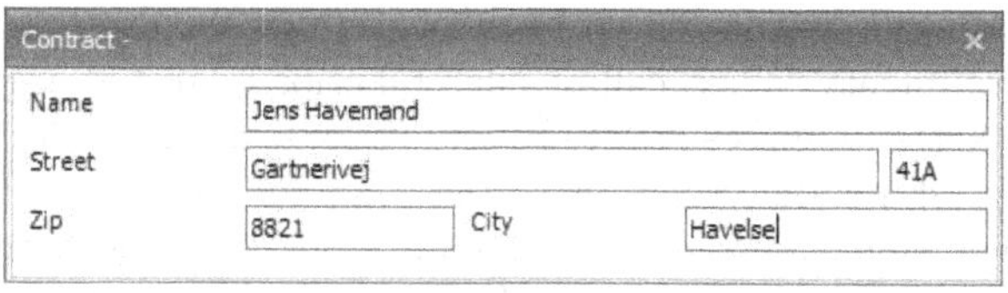

(b)

**Fig. 2.** Use of type properties to control layout

The typelet implementation makes use of special MLFi features (described in the next section) for computing a runtime representation for a type and for inspecting type properties in runtime representations of a type. Using these features, the typelet implementation allows for the typelet-programmer to make use of type properties for specifying details of how a control should be displayed and for specifying default values for controls, and so on.

## 4 Dynamic Types and Type Paths in MLFi

Before proceeding with presenting how a user may specify rules to give dynamic behavior to user interfaces, we summarize how MLFi extends OCaml with dynamic types and so-called type paths [11].

MLFi provides a universal datatype for representing static types at runtime:

```
type utype = Int | ...
           | List of utype | Option of utype
           | Record of (string * utype) list
           | Props of utype * (string * string) list
           | ...
```

Notice that the representation allows for the programmer to inspect the type properties for a type, inferred at compile time and provided to the programmer using the `Props` value constructor.

Further, MLFi supports an abstract notion of *typed dynamic types*, of type *t* ttype, for some concrete type *t*. Values of type *t* ttype can be constructed using the simple expression form (`ttype_of`:*t*) for injecting the static type *t* into a value of type *t* ttype. Values of type *t* ttype can easily be converted into values of type utype, with no computational overhead, using the function `to_utype`: 'a ttype -> utype. The type argument to the ttype type constructor is really just a phantom type, which provides for improved type-safe programming [2, 9, 10, 15]. In concert with the support for dynamic types, MLFi supports the notion of a universally tagged representation of values, called *variants*, which are useful for programming ad-hoc polymorphic functions, with a "pay-as-you-go" strategy (no overhead forced on ordinary code). MLFi has a built-in function `variantize: t:'a ttype -> 'a -> variant` and another built-in function `devariantize: t:'a ttype -> variant -> 'a`, which may fail by raising an exception. Notice here the so-called *labeled arguments* `t:'a ty`, a special feature of MLFi, which allows for the programmer to label particular arguments. When calling such functions, labeled arguments can be provided explicitly, as in `variantize ~t:(ttype_of:int) 5` or implicitly, in the case of typed dynamic types, with the compiler looking in the context for a value of the particular inferred type. In many cases, the programmer can then omit the typed dynamic type arguments. In the case above, the programmer may simply write `variantize 5`. Using the above features, it is straightforward to write pseudo-ad-hoc polymorphic functions, such as `print: t:'a ttype -> 'a -> string`.

MLFi also supports the notion *type paths*, which are values representing functions for pointing at a subcomponent of a value. Type paths have type `(t,s)tpath` where `t` is a type containing `s` as a subcomponent. A special type path is the identity type path of type `(t,t)tpath` for arbitrary `t`.

Syntactically, type paths are written using dot-notation (with a prefix dot). As an example, if `{a:{b:int;c:string}; d:bool}` is a MLFi type `t`, then `.a.b` is a type path of type `(t,int)tpath`. Type paths are a little more than selector functions on types. They compose, using a type path compose operator, but it is also possible to extract from a type path, at runtime, the sequence of labels that define the type path. The runtime representation works well together with dynamic types and variant values.

## 5   Rules for Specifying Typelet Dynamics

Before we describe the concept of typelet rules in detail, we demonstrate the concept with a simple temperature typelet:

```
type 'a ro = 'a + [readonly]
type temp = {celsius: float; fahrenheit: float ro; kelvin: float ro}
open Fields
let calc =
  Rule.update (value(.celsius)) (value(.fahrenheit) & value(.kelvin))
    (fun c -> (9.0 /. 5.0 *. c +. 32., c +. 273.15)
let low =
  Rule.validate (value(.celsius))
    (fun c -> if c <-273.15 then Some "Temperature too low" else None)
let () = typelet "Temperature" ~t:(ttype_of:temp) ~rules:[low;calc] ()
```

Notice first the load of the typelet using the `typelet` function in the last line. This function takes as argument a name, the type of the Typelet (i.e., the argument for `~t`), and a list of rules. Notice also that the Fahrenheit and Kelvin fields are marked `readonly` using type properties in the type declaration for `t`. The dynamic behavior of the typelet is specified using two rules, one that updates the Fahrenheit and Kelvin fields when there are changes to the Celsius field, and one that reports an error when a value in the Celsius field becomes invalid. The resulting typelet is shown in action in Fig. 3.

(a)                                                     (b)

**Fig. 3.** Temperature typelet. Image (a) shows the typelet after evaluation of the update rule (upon change of the Celsius field). Image (b) shows the typelet after evaluation of the validate rule on invalid input (Celsius below -273.15 degrees).

In principle, the `Rule.update` function takes three arguments, (1) a specification of which source fields the rule depends on, (2) a specification of which target fields the rule targets, and (3) a MLFi function that accepts a value corresponding to the source specification and computes a result corresponding to the target specification. The source and target specifications are specified using an algebra over type paths. The algebra over type paths allows for selection of multiple fields and for referring to basic properties of a field, such as its value or whether the field is read only or disabled.

The module type for the `Fields` module is presented in Fig. 4(a).

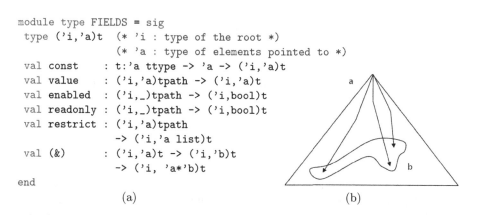

```
module type FIELDS = sig
  type ('i,'a)t   (* 'i : type of the root *)
                  (* 'a : type of elements pointed to *)
  val const    : t:'a ttype -> 'a -> ('i,'a)t
  val value    : ('i,'a)tpath -> ('i,'a)t
  val enabled  : ('i,_)tpath -> ('i,bool)t
  val readonly : ('i,_)tpath -> ('i,bool)t
  val restrict : ('i,'a)tpath
                   -> ('i,'a list)t
  val (&)      : ('i,'a)t -> ('i,'b)t
                   -> ('i, 'a*'b)t
end
```

(a)                                                     (b)

**Fig. 4.** The FIELDS module type (a) and an example of a `fields` value composed of three fields (b)

A value of type `(a,b)fields` for some a and b represents a set of located fields inside the type a. The diagram in Fig. 4(b) illustrates a case where the `fields` value is composed of three fields within a.

The `const` function provides functionality for expressing a constant field value whereas the `value` function gives access to the content of a field. The functions `enabled` and `readonly` give access to a field's enabled property and readonly property, respectively (as boolean values). The `restrict` function makes it possible to refer to the restricted set of valid values for a field; when used in the target of a rule, the set of valid values for a field may be restricted dynamically.

The `&` operator may be used to compose field values, as we have seen in the example. Most of the functions in the `Fields` module takes a `ttype` argument. In normal use of the module, the arguments are passed implicitly by the compiler and the programmer need not be explicit about these arguments, as can be seen in the example above.

```
module type RULE = sig
 type 'i t
 type ('i,'a) fields = ('i,'a) Fields.t
 val update   : ta:'a ttype -> tb:'b ttype
                -> ('i,'a)fields -> ('i,'b)fields -> ('a -> 'b) -> 'i t
 val validate : t:'a ttype -> ('i,'a)fields
                -> ('a -> string option) -> 'i t
 val button   : ta:'a ttype -> tb:'b ttype
                -> ('i,'a)fields -> ('i,'b)fields
                -> ('a -> 'b) -> ('i,unit)tpath -> 'i t
 val grid     : ('i,'a)fields -> ('i,'b list)tpath -> ('a * 'b)t -> 'i t
 val grid_add : t:'a ttype -> ('i,'a)fields -> ('i,'b list)tpath
                -> ('b,'c)fields -> ('a -> 'c) -> 'i t
 val default  : t:'a ttype -> ('i,'a)fields -> (unit -> 'a) -> 'i t
 val subpath  : ('i,'a)tpath -> 'a t -> 'i t
 val all      : 'i t list -> 'i t
 val iso      : ta:'a ttype -> tb:'b ttype
                -> ('i,'a)fields -> ('i,'b)fields
                -> ('a -> 'b) -> ('b -> 'a) -> 'i t
 val weak_upd : ta:'a ttype -> tb:'b ttype
                -> ('i,'a)fields -> ('i,'b)fields -> ('a -> 'b) -> 'i t
 ...
end
```

**Fig. 5.** The RULE module type

The module type for the `Rule` module is presented in Fig. 5. As we have seen earlier, the `update` function takes as arguments a source field specification, a target field specification, and an appropriate MLFi function that matches the source and target specifications. In addition, the function takes as argument two `ttype` arguments. As described in Sec. 4, these arguments are provided implicitly whenever the call site context provides the appropriate values.

Fig. 6(a) illustrates the semantics of the `update` rule. Intuitively, when a source field is modified, either by an end user or by another rule, the source values are extracted to form an argument for the MLFi rule function. Hereafter

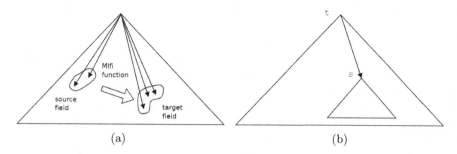

**Fig. 6.** Illustration of (a) the `update` rule and (b) the `subpath` rule

the function is applied and the result is stored into the target fields denoted by the target field specifier.

The implementation takes care that each rule is evaluated only once for each field modification performed by an end user. Rules are not allowed to form cycles, except through the `iso` and `weak_upd` rules (see below), thus rules may be topologically ordered. Instead of evaluating rules eagerly when triggered by a change in a source field, rules are dynamically added to a heap structure when a source field changes value. The heap structure is evaluated by repeatedly evaluating the topologically lowest ordered rule in the heap. Given that no cycles appears in the graph defined by the rules and given that each rule satisfies some validity constraints, the rule evaluation strategy guarantees that rules are evaluated on consistent data and that each rule is evaluated at most once in reaction to a field update.

The `validate` function takes only a source field specifier and a function that optionally returns an error message (besides from an appropriate `ttype` argument). The implementation guarantees that validate functions that have a specific field in its source field specifier are evaluated before other rules that have the same field in its source field specifier.

The `button` function takes four non-ttype arguments, (1) a source field specifier, (2) a target field specifier, (3) an evaluation function, to be evaluated when the button is pressed, and (4) a type path to a unit type, which serves to identify the button in the generated layout.

The `grid` function lifts a rule that works on a pair of auxiliary GUI data and data for a grid row to a rule that works on an entire grid, represented as a list of values (i.e., a list of rows). The `grid_add` function is used to specify field data for new rows added to the grid (by the user). The supplied type path points to the grid. The supplied function takes as argument data specified by the first fields specifier. The result of the supplied function matches a field specifier relative to the data for a row in the grid. Those fields in the added row that are not mentioned in the relative field specifier are filled with default values.

The `default` function provides functionality for specifying default values other than the built-in defaults or defaults specified using type properties.

The `subpath` function makes it possible to lift a rule for some type `s` to a rule for a type `t` that contains `s` in the sense that there exists a type path from `t` to s. The relation between t and s is illustrated in Fig. 6(b). The all function makes it possible to treat a list of rules as one rule. These two functions are important for building new rules from existing ones.

The last two rule functions shown, iso and weak_upd, allow for certain kinds of cycles in the fields dependency graph formed by a particular set of rules. The iso rule allow the programmer to set up an isomorphism between fields—it is the obligation of the programmer to guarantee that the supplied functions form an isomorphism. The weak_upd rule function works like the update function, except that the rule is triggered only when the change in a source field is due directly to a modification by an end user. This latter function has proven to be useful, for instance, for implementing a generic "fill out utility" that allows a user to select a value in a dropdown box and thereby get the effect that a series of fields are filled out with computed data, but in such a way that if some value in the set of filled out fields is edited, the wittness in the dropdown-box is erased. By using weak update rules for both the "fill out" functionality and the erase functionality, cycles in the rule evaluation is avoided.

## 6    Implementation

The implementation of typelets in the SimCorp Dimension asset-management system, targets the .NET platform via an extension to Microsoft's Windows Forms library. Whereas all rules are specified and analyzed in MLFi, the Windows Forms control tree is generated at the .NET side based on a serialized variant-representation of the type that specifies the layout of the typelet. Besides from the control-tree, a container tree is also constructed at the .NET side based on the (variant-representation of the) typelet type. Once both the container-tree and the control-tree are constructed, the containers are bound to the controls, which has the effect that changes in the containers will have a visible effect in the controls. Information about rules is also serialized and communicated to the .NET side. For each update rule, for instance, event handlers are attached to the source controls, by traversing the GUI control structure using type-indexed functions that iterate on the variantized version of the relevant type paths. At runtime, an attached event handler will, when triggered, collect the argument represented by a fields value, serialize the argument into MLFi representation, call the registered MLFi function, and store the result in the fields represented by the target fields value.

The typelet mechanism is by no means tied to the .NET platform. If desired, it should be straightforward to replace the .NET part of the framework with, for instance, a JavaScript/HTML backend using, for instance, SMLtoJs [8] or js_of_ocaml [23].

### 6.1    A Computation Monad

The MLFi runtime system is single-threaded and not reentrant, which make it impractical to let MLFi functions make queries to the database and call expensive functions (e.g., monte-carlo simulations for contract pricing [13]) on the

.NET side. For this reason, the actual interface provided to the rule programmer is a slight modification of the RULE module type given in Fig. 5. The actual RULE module type exposes a monadic interface to computations [18], through a monad of type 'a m. In effect, the type for the update rule function actually takes the following form:

```
val update : ta:'a ttype -> tb:'b ttype
             -> ('i,'a)fields -> ('i,'b)fields -> ('a -> 'b m) -> 'i t
```

Functionality on the .NET-side are exposed to the MLFi programmer as monadic computations, which may be composed with direct MLFi computations using the monad's return and bind functionality. Now, because the composed computations are driven from the .NET-side, the MLFi runtime system is blocking for entrance only when it is busy computing.

### 6.2   A Functional-Relational Mapping Scheme

The typelet implementation is also augmented with a typed functional-relational mapping scheme for mapping data in a typelet into a form acceptable for a relational database system and vice versa. The mapping forms an isomorphism between the data in the database and the data in the typelet and is used both for loading and saving typelet data. In this paper we have focused on the more dynamic behavior of typelets and we shall not discuss the functional-relational mapping scheme in more detail here, except by stating that the mapping scheme is applied for screens where the user may load particular stored data into the screen, either for presentation purposes or for the purpose of making changes to the data. Similarly, the mapping mechanism is used whenever data in a screen needs to be stored.

## 7   Separating Concerns Using Typelet Layouts

A front-end programmer may specify a complete redesign of a typelet using a set of combinators to form a so-called typelet layout. Besides from basic combinators for grouping controls in tab pages and group controls, two basic combinators are available, namely the pick combinator, which selects (using a type path) a component from the typelet (an entire group or a concrete control) and the apply combinator, which replaces a subcomponent in a layout with an alternative layout. As we shall see, the typelet layout combinators are guaranteed not to alter the rule semantics of the underlying typelets.

The front-end programmer may choose to redesign the entire standard layout (as induced by the type for the underlying typelet) or use parts of the standard layout in the defined layouts. Typelet layouts are first class entities and there is no limit to the number of layouts that can be associated with a typelet. Typelet layouts are typed in the sense that they are defined for particular typelets (or typelet library components). The typing ensures that we can give appropriate meaning to a typelet layout.

```
module type LAYOUT = sig
  type 'i t                            (* Layout for 'i-typelets *)
  type caption = string
  type halign = Left | Center | Right
  type valign = Top | Middle | Bottom

  val grp     : 'i t -> 'i t                    (* Grouping environment *)
  val (%%)    : 'i t -> 'i t -> 'i t            (* Horizontal sequencing *)
  val (@@@)   : 'i t -> 'i t -> 'i t            (* Vertical stacking *)
  val box     : caption -> 'i t -> 'i t         (* Wrap box around a layout *)
  val tab     : 'i t list -> 'i t               (* Show boxes as tabs *)
  val halign  : halign -> 'i t -> 'i t          (* Horizontal alignment *)
  val valign  : valign -> 'i t -> 'i t          (* Vertical alignment *)
  val hspace  : int -> 'i t                     (* Horizontal space *)
  val vspace  : int -> 'i t                     (* Vertical space *)
  val caption : caption -> 'i t -> 'i t         (* Use the provided caption *)
  val pick    : ('i,'a)tpath -> 'i t            (* Pick standard layout item *)
  val apply   : ('i,'a)tpath -> 'a t            (* Apply alternative layout *)
              -> 'i t -> 'i t

  (* Derived combinators *)
  val emp     : 'i t                            (* Empty layout *)
  val all     : 'i t                            (* Complete type layout *)
  val hide    : ('i,'a)tpath -> 'i t            (* Hide pointed-to item *)
              -> 'i t
  val lift    : ('i,'a)tpath -> 'a t            (* Lift pointed-to item *)
              -> 'i t
  val (%)     : 'i t -> 'i t -> 'i t            (* Padded sequencing *)
  val (@@)    : 'i t -> 'i t -> 'i t            (* Padded stacking *)
end
```

**Fig. 7.** The LAYOUT module type

Typelet programmers write typelet layouts in an embedded domain specific language for layouts. Fig. 7 lists the module type for the language.

The grouping environment introduced by grp allows the layout programmer to organize layouts in a grid style with proper alignment of columns and rows. In a group environment (e.g., in an argument to grp or box), the programmer may use the % and @@ combinators to separate items and rows (of items), respectively.

The alignment and space combinators give programmers control over the positioning of items without allowing programmers to work with absolute positioning. Notice that layouts should adapt properly to resizing of typelets and that layouts should position themselves properly, also on limited space.

The pick combinator allows the programmer to pick a layout from the type as pointed to by the type path argument. The apply combinator applies a given layout to a pointed-to item in a larger layout.

The tab combinator takes a list of boxes, which may either be constructed using the box combinator or picked from the typelet (by picking an existing tab element, a box, or an existing tab group).

It is possible, and often straightforward, to define derived combinators such as the `hide` and `lift` combinators. For instance, the `hide` combinator is implemented as follows:

```
let hide tp = apply tp emp
```

The interface imposes some restrictions. For instance, we have deliberately chosen not to allow the programmer to overwrite the default minimum size and width-flexibility of a control. Thus, picking a date control yields a date control with the same width, height, and caption as the picked control. Also, we do not attempt to capture, at the type level, which components are shown or whether an item is a box or another kind of object. This choice is deliberate; we want to keep the layout concept simple without cluttering the types with additional type parameters.

Fig. 8 demonstrates various features of the layout programming interface, including regrouping. Notice that the type `currency` is defined elsewhere as a sum datatype, which present themselves as a drop-down control.

```
type leg = {legno: int; underlying: string option;
            fixedrate: float option; currency: currency}
type tradedata = {tdata1: string; tdata2: string}
type tlet = {tradeid: string; nominal: float;
             receiveleg: leg; payleg: leg; tradedata: tradedata}
open Layout
let leg = pick(.underlying) @@
          pick(.fixedrate) @@
          pick(.currency)
let 12 : tlet t =
  pick(.tradeid) % pick(.nominal) @@
  grp(box "Receive"
        (lift(.receiveleg)leg) %
    box "Pay"
        (lift(.payleg)leg)) @@
  pick (.tradedata)
```

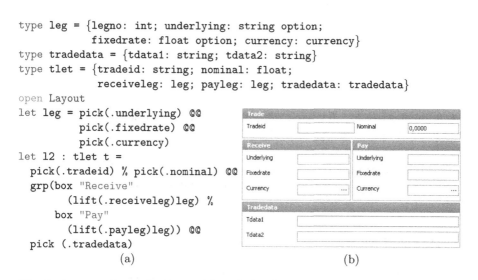

(a)                                   (b)

**Fig. 8.** An example typelet layout (a) and it's effect on the typelet presentation (b)

It is natural to ask for properties of the `pick` and `apply` combinators. In particular, we would expect the following property to hold:

*Property 1.* For all type paths $p$, it holds that `all = apply` $p$ `(pick` $p$`) all`.

Typelet layouts may be registered with the typelet at typelet definition time or loaded and linked dynamically using MLFi's dynamic linking features. Fig. 9 shows a layout for an input screen for an interest rate swap, a complex financial instrument used by most financial institutions for hedging interest rate risk.

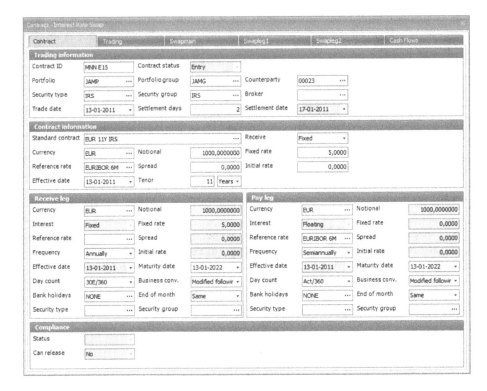

**Fig. 9.** Input screen for an interest rate swap, a complex financial instrument used by most financial institutions for hedging interest rate risk

Data can be entered by the user in any order and the rule machinery calculates a number of derived values whenever sufficient information is typed in by the user.

## 8   Related Work

There is a large body of related work. One strand of related work includes work on providing type-safe language bindings for constructing graphical user interfaces in functional languages [3, 14, 19] either using monads or by using the effectful features of a language for controlling the behavior of a GUI. A specific monadic combinator library for constructing GUI's is the Clean iTask library [17, 20], which primarily focuses on allowing the programmer to generate a workflow GUI from a declarative specification of the GUI and the workflow. Compared to the iTask framework, typelets do not address how windows are opened and closed, but rather on how fields, grids, and controls change upon changes in a field.

   Like the typelet library, many GUI libraries make use of phantom types [2, 9, 15] as a mechanism for providing increased type-safety, for instance through modeling single-inheritance [10]. Phantom types are used in the typelet implementation both for the `Fields`, `Rule`, and `Layout` modules to restrict the composability of values.

Another branch of related work is the large body of work on functional reactive programming [5–7, 16, 22], which has served as inspiration for the rule mechanism for typelets. In particular, using a topological ordering of rules and a heap data structure to guarantee that rules are triggered at most once upon a change of input is directly influenced by previous work on implementations of functional reactive programming [8]. The work on flowlets [1] combines work on functional reactive programming with formlets [4], which, as typelets, focuses much on composability of GUI components.

Other related work investigates the possibility of synthesizing user interfaces and event handling code for interdependent fields based on formal descriptions specified by the programmer in a domain specific language for specifying the logic dependencies. Both the work on property models [12] and the work on Plato [21], a compiler for interactive web forms, follows this direction. In the typelet approach, cyclic dependencies are only supported in a controlled way, through iso-rules and weak rules, and programmers need to be explicit about such cyclic dependencies, which makes it straightforward to express to programmers the requirements for composing user interface components.

## 9 Conclusion

We have presented the concept of typelets, which have been designed for constructing trade screens for the SimCorp Dimension asset management system. Each trade screen can have more than 400 individual fields located in nested tab-structures and group controls. Together with a functional-relational mapping (for storing and loading database content), the typelet implementation forms a dynamic GUI mechanism, which is declarative and statically typed, but also highly flexible.

**Acknowledgments.** The authors want to thank the Instrument Modelling Language team at SimCorp for many interesting discussions and the PADL'14 reviewers for their helpful and insightful feedback. This research has been partially supported by the Danish Strategic Research Council, Program Committee for Strategic Growth Technologies, for the research center HIPERFIT: Functional High Performance Computing for Financial Information Technology (`hiperfit.dk`) under contract number 10-092299.

## References

1. Bjornson, J., Tayanovskyy, A., Granicz, A.: Composing reactive GUIs in F# using WebSharper. In: Hage, J., Morazán, M.T. (eds.) IFL 2010. LNCS, vol. 6647, pp. 203–216. Springer, Heidelberg (2011)

2. Blume, M.: No-longer-foreign: Teaching an ML compiler to speak C "natively". In: Workshop on Multi-language Infrastructure and Interoperability (BABEL 2001) (September 2001)

3. Carlsson, M., Hallgren, T.: Fudgets–a graphical user interface in a lazy functional language. In: Proceedings of the ACM Conference on Functional Programming and Computer Architectures (FPCA 1993), pp. 321–330. ACM Press (1993)

4. Cooper, E., Lindley, S., Yallop, J.: The essence of form abstraction. In: Ramalingam, G. (ed.) APLAS 2008. LNCS, vol. 5356, pp. 205–220. Springer, Heidelberg (2008)

5. Courtney, A., Nilsson, H., Peterson, J.: The Yampa arcade. In: Proceedings of the 2002 ACM SIGPLAN Workshop on Haskell, pp. 7–18. ACM Press (2002)

6. Courtney, A., Elliott, C.: Genuinely functional user interfaces. In: Proceedings of the 2001 Haskell Workshop (September 2001)

7. Elliott, C., Hudak, P.: Functional reactive animation. In: ICFP 1997. ACM, New York (1997)

8. Elsman, M.: SMLtoJs: Hosting a Standard ML compiler in a web browser. In: Proceeding of ACM SIGPLAN 2011 International Workshop on Programming Language and Systems Technologies for Internet Clients (PLASTIC 2011). ACM Press (October 2011)

9. Elsman, M., Larsen, K.F.: Typing XHTML Web Applications in ML. In: Jayaraman, B. (ed.) PADL 2004. LNCS, vol. 3057, pp. 224–238. Springer, Heidelberg (2004)

10. Fluet, M., Pucella, R.: Phantom types and subtyping. In: International Conference on Theoretical Computer Science (TCS 2002) (August 2002)

11. Frisch, A.: Runtime types. In LexiFi blog (December 2011), http://www.lexifi.com/blog/runtime-types

12. Järvi, J., Marcus, M., Parent, S., Freeman, J., Smith, J.N.: Property models: from incidental algorithms to reusable components. In: 7th International Conference on Generative Programming and Component Engineering (GPCE 2008), pp. 89–98 (October 2008)

13. Jones, S.P., Eber, J.-M., Seward, J.: Composing contracts: an adventure in financial engineering. In: Fifth International Conference on Functional Programming (ICFP 2000) (September 2000)

14. Leijen, D.: wxHaskell: A portable and concise GUI library for Haskell. In: Proceeding of the 2004 ACM SIGPLAN Haskell Workshop. ACM Press (September 2004)

15. Leijen, D., Meijer, E.: Domain specific embedded compilers. In: ACM Conference on Domain-Specific Languages. ACM Press (2000)

16. Meyerovich, L.A., Guha, A., Baskin, J., Cooper, G.H., Greenberg, M., Bromfield, A., Krishnamurthi, S.: Flapjax: a programming language for ajax applications. In: OOPSLA 2009. ACM, New York (2009)

17. Michels, S., Plasmeijer, R., Achten, P.: iTask as a new paradigm for building GUI applications. In: Hage, J., Morazán, M.T. (eds.) IFL 2010. LNCS, vol. 6647, pp. 153–168. Springer, Heidelberg (2011)

18. Moggi, E.: Notions of computation and monads. Information and Computation 93, 55–92 (1989)

19. Noble, R., Runciman, C.: Gadgets: Lazy functional components for graphical user interfaces. In: Swierstra, S.D. (ed.) PLILP 1995. LNCS, vol. 982, pp. 321–340. Springer, Heidelberg (1995)

20. Plasmeijer, R., Achten, P., Koopman, P., Lijnse, B., van Noort, T., van Groningen, J.: iTasks for a change—type-safe run-time change in dynamically evolving workflows. In: Proceedings of the 20th International Workshop on Partial Evaluation and Program Manipulation (PEPM 2011), pp. 151–160. ACM Press (2011)
21. Hinrichs, T.L.: Plato: A compiler for interactive web forms. In: Rocha, R., Launchbury, J. (eds.) PADL 2011. LNCS, vol. 6539, pp. 54–68. Springer, Heidelberg (2011)
22. Sage, M.: FranTk - a declarative GUI language for Haskell. In: Proceedings of the Fifth ACM SIGPLAN International Conference on Functional Programming (ICFP 2000), pp. 106–117. ACM Press (2000)
23. Vouillon, J.: Js_of_ocaml. Documentation at
    http://ocsigen.org/js_of_ocaml/manual/

# Expand: Towards an Extensible Pandoc System

Jacco Krijnen[1], Doaitse Swierstra[1], and Marcos O. Viera[2]

[1] Department of Computer Science, Utrecht University, Utrecht, The Netherlands
[2] Instituto de Computación, Universidad de la República, Montevideo, Uruguay
`jaccokrijnen@gmail.com, doaitse@swierstra.net, mviera@fing.edu.uy`

**Abstract.** The *Pandoc* program is a versatile tool for converting between document formats. It comes with a great variety of readers, each converting a specific input format into the universal *Pandoc* format, and a great variety of writers, each mapping a document represented in this universal format onto a specific output format.

Unfortunately the intermediate *Pandoc* format is fixed, which implies that a new, unforeseen document element cannot be added. In this paper we propose a more flexible approach, using our collection of Haskell libraries for constructing extensible parsers and attribute grammars. Both the parsing and the unparsing of a specific document can be constructed out of a collection of precompiled descriptions of document elements written in Haskell. This collection can be extended by any user, without having to touch existing code.

The Haskell type system is used to enforce that each component is well defined, and to verify that the composition of a collection components is consistent, i.e. that features needed by a component have been defined by that component or any of the other components. In this way we can get back the flexibility e.g. offered by the packages in the LaTeX package eco-system.

**Keywords:** Document Formatting, Pandoc, Attribute Grammars, Parsing, Haskell, Type System.

> The nice thing about standards is that there are so many to choose from.
>
> — Andy Tanenbaum

# 1 Introduction

## 1.1 The Starting Point

The world is littered with document standards, from very simple ones such as *markdown* for easily expressing markup in wiki based systems up to very elaborate ones such as LaTeX, not to mention all the proprietary standards associated with programs like *Word* and its numerous brothers and sisters. It goes without

M. Flatt and H.-F. Guo (Eds.): PADL 2014, LNCS 8324, pp. 200–215, 2014.

saying that, besides all the differences, these standards have a lot in common, and so do the programs which are used to process and generate documents based on these standards. Unfortunately, once a document is created in one of these formats there is no easy way back; your formatting commands have effectively been stolen by the vendor of your document processing program.

*Pandoc* is a popular Haskell program which tries to alleviate such problems; its architecture is centered around a "universal document format", together with a collection of *readers* which map documents written using some other format onto this universal format, and a collection of *writers*, each mapping a document represented in this universal format onto the desired output format.

The design of this intermediate format is no sinecure, since on the one hand it is unrealistic to expect that it can represent all document elements which are introduced by any of the existing or future standards, and on the other hand it should not be so restricted that it cannot represents a substantial subset of these elements.

When we look back at the mother of all document formatters, TEX, we see no such limitations, since the language standard contains, besides a collection of primitives, a powerful macro mechanism which can be used to express the formatting of new document elements when the need arises. It is this extensibility which has kept TEX alive and the TEX ecosystem growing over the last 40 years.

A first shortcoming, albeit not such a serious one, is that all formatting commands are following the same lexical and syntactic structure. As a result of this some people prefer to use something like the *markdown* format when typing a document or to use a preprocessor like *lhs2TeX* which was used to add LATEX formatting commands to the input for the paper you are reading, making the Haskell code fragments look good. By using an adaptable syntax there are just fewer symbols to type and the structure of the final document is better visible in the input format of the document.

The second, but probably most serious shortcoming, is that the macro mechanism of TEX can hardly be seen as a modern programming environment. Building abstraction layer on top of abstraction layer by implementing what are effectively programming language interpreters using TEX's macro mechanism, makes resulting systems extremely slow and unforgiving in case the input contains any small mistake. Those who have used *TikZ* in combination with *lhs2TeX* in the *beamer* environment, which may cause a single slide to take seconds to format, can only agree with this observation. Abstraction is nice, but comes at a large cost if the abstraction mechanism itself is expensive. Furthermore the sequential nature of TEX processing makes it cumbersome to collect information and make it available at other places in the output. In those cases we have to recur to writing data into files and reading it back in the next run.

The question we seek to answer in this paper is whether we can deploy an extensible document structure with a way to collect and distribute information in the document, sharing common parts between the various readers and writers, and in which we can describe how an element is to be formatted in a modern, strongly typed programming language.

## 1.2   Our Approach

In this paper we present our solution to the problems mentioned in the previous subsection, demonstrating the use of the *CoCoCo*[1] libraries written in Haskell, which we developed over the years for constructing compilers in a compositional way [9]. From now on we will talk about *parsers* instead of *readers* and about *semantics* instead of *writers*, thus following conventional compiler construction terminology. The full code can be found in the Haskell package `expand`[2].

One of the libraries we base our solution on is the `murder`[11,10][3] library which can be used to explicitly represent mutually recursive values. In our case these will be grammar fragments which jointly describe the structure of the document to be formatted or converted. Notice that each grammar fragment is represented as a Haskell value, which can be combined, inspected, transformed, abstracted from, etc. Once we have all grammar fragments, which together describe our document, available we can construct the final grammar and map this grammar onto an error correcting parser, using e.g. the `uu-parsinglib`[4] library.

For describing the semantics of the document, i.e. the mapping of the recognised structure onto the desired output format, we use `AspectAG`[13][5]. This library provides a set of combinators for describing attribute grammar based fragments of evaluators. Also here such fragments (or aspects) of the final semantics are described by plain Haskell values, which are to be combined into the overall semantics of the final document structure. Instead of using the fixed *Pandoc* format our parsers and semantics are related to each other by an underlying abstract document format *for this specific class of documents*.

Hence each *Document Element Description* (DED) consists of the following elements:

1. some possibly new document kinds (non-terminals in the grammar) or new element alternatives, thus extending the structure relating the reading and writing phase of the document mapping
2. grammar fragments telling us how to recognise these new elements and how they are to be mapped onto the intermediate document structure
3. common semantics to all possible output formats, such as the construction of a table of contents
4. a description, in attribute grammar terms, describing how to map the newly defined elements onto specific output formats.

## 1.3   Outline of the Paper

In the paper we will describe how we reimplemented a subset of the intermediate *Pandoc* data type in such a way that it can be easily extended with new document

---

[1] http://www.cs.uu.nl/wiki/Center/CoCoCo

[2] http://hackage.haskell.org/package/expand

[3] http://hackage.haskell.org/package/murder

[4] http://hackage.haskell.org/package/uu-parsinglib

[5] http://hackage.haskell.org/package/AspectAG

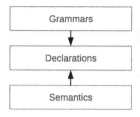

**Fig. 1.** Architecture

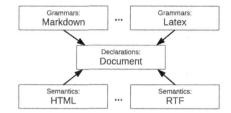

**Fig. 2.** Multiple Parsers and Semantics

elements. We assume that the reader is familiar with Haskell and its various extensions, since our libraries depend on them. Emphasis will however be on the underlying processes and techniques, and not so much on completeness.

In our example we start by showing how the usual top level structure of a document, including its sections, subsections and paragraphs, may be represented and mapped onto HTML. At the same time we show how some of the microformatting, such as bold and italic text are realised. Emphasis will be here on how we express the grammar for the input document, and how to generate some simple output. In no way we claim that something spectacular is going on here; it mainly serves as a basis from which we start to define our extensions in such a way that we can leave the initial code completely intact, and do not even have to recompile it. In the rest of the paper we describe two such extensions: the labeling of section headers with their index number, and the addition of a *table of contents* element, which displays information that is collected from various places in the input text.

## 2   Implementing expand

The architecture of **expand**, which stands for "Extensible Pandoc", is depicted in Figure 1; boxes represent (groups of Haskell) modules and arrows denote **import** relations.

The **expand** library is divided into three parts:

1. **Declarations** of abstract syntax for the general document format
2. **Grammars** that describe the parsers for concrete syntax of input languages.
3. **Semantics** that describe the unparsing for the concrete syntax of output languages.

each of which contain modules that serve as a collection of building blocks for the programmer.

As we show in Figure 2, multiple parsers (e.g. *markdown*, LaTeX) and semantics (e.g. generating HTML, RTF) can be defined following the same approach as *Pandoc* does. What makes the difference between our approach and *Pandoc* however, is that we can also extend, in a modular way, the parsers, semantics and intermediate representations of documents. For example, in Figure 3 we extend the generation of HTML by adding a numbering system to the headers.

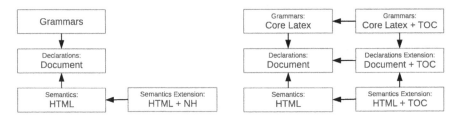

**Fig. 3.** Generating HTML and Numbered **Fig. 4.** Documents with Table of Contents Headers

Notice that the original modules are neither inspected nor modified; they are just imported. Thus there is no need to access to the source files of the former semantics, which could have been distributed as binary code. In our approach, extensions can be done to any of the three parts that compose to a complete definition. For example, in Figure 4 we show how extensions to the grammar and the intermediate document type and the semantics (may) depend on earlier modules. Here we start with a subset of LATEX which does not include the possibility to define a table of contents and to which we will refer to as the LATEX core; we extend the parser to recognise the \tableofcontents command, the document structure to represent its abstract syntax, and the semantics describing how to collect the information, distribute the information in the document, and the final formatting of this table. Note that the first two of these semantic aspects are likely to be defined separately, since they are not HTML specific and can be shared between different output formats.

In the following subsections we will show what such definitions look like. As an example we will show how to construct a program that translates core LATEX to HTML. We will also show how the extensions of figures 3 and 4 are expressed in Haskell.

## 2.1   Declarations

In our attribute grammar fragments we use names[6] to refer to children of nodes, names to refer to attributes and names to refer to the non-terminals of the abstract grammar. We use Template Haskell to generate such names from conventional Haskell data type definitions as in Figure 5.

A document (*Document*) consists of a list of blocks (*BlockL*), each being either a header or a paragraph. A header consists of an *Int* representing its level (*level_header*), and its text (*InlineL*). A paragraph contains text, some of which can be bold or italic. The function *deriveAG* generates the necessary labels and types to be used in the attribute grammars fragments describing computations over trees described by the above types. The function *deriveLang* generates a record data type containing a field for each non-terminal. Such a field holds the function which maps the inherited attributes of the corresponding non-terminal to its to synthesised attributes. Once such a record is constructed by combining

---

[6] We use the **HList** label model as defined in the module *Data.HList.Label4*.

**data** *Document = Document { blocks :: BlockL }* **deriving** *Show*
**type** *BlockL = [ Block ]*
**data** *Block   = Header     { level_header    :: Int*
                                *, inlines_header :: InlineL }*
                *| Paragraph { inlines_par     :: InlineL }*
        **deriving** (*Show*)
**type** *InlineL = [ Inline ]*
**data** *Inline  = Plain      { str_plainInl    :: String }*
                *| Bold       { inlines_boldInl :: InlineL }*
                *| Italics    { inlines_italInl :: InlineL }*
        **deriving** (*Show*)
$ (*deriveAG* "*Document*)
$ (*deriveLang* "Doc" [ "*Document*, "*BlockL*, "*Block*, "*InlineL*, "*Inline* ])

**Fig. 5.** The Haskell data types describing our document structure

*document* → *block**
*block*    → *paragraph* | *header*
*paragraph* → "\begin"  "{" "paragraph" "}" *inline**"\end" "{" "paragraph" "}"
*header*   → "\section"        "{" *inline**"}"
           | "\subsection"     "{" *inline**"}"
           | "\subsubsection" "{" *inline**"}"
*inline*   → "\plain"  "{" *text*   "}"
           | "\textbf" "{" *inline**"}"
           | "\textit" "{" *inline**"}"

**Fig. 6.** The EBNF for our input language

all attribute grammar fragments for all non-terminals we pass it to the parser, so
the parser can apply the appropriate function for each recognised non-terminal.
Notice that we use a deforestated approach: the intermediate tree never comes
into existence, but is instead directly represented by its semantics, i.e. a function
mapping the inherited attributes of the root to its synthesised ones. We use
plenty of **type** synonyms, so we have names for all types that play a role as
non-terminal in the actual parser.

## 2.2 Grammars

In this subsection we show how to construct a parser. For a deeper explanation
and more information on the types involved, see [9] section 3.3. For simplicity
reasons we assume here that plain text is explicitly marked using the commands
\plain{...} and \begin{paragraph}. Such commands can be inserted by a
preprocessor, or be omitted by writing a more elaborate parser. The EBNF
expressing the concrete input syntax is given in Figure 6, where *text* is a string,
excluding the special characters: \, &, %, $, #, _, {, }, ~ and ^.

$gLatex\ sem = \mathbf{proc}\ ()\ \rightarrow \mathbf{do}$
   $\mathbf{rec}$
      $document \leftarrow addNT \prec \|\ (pDocument\ sem)\ blockL\ \|$
      $blockL \quad \leftarrow addNT \prec pFoldr\ (pBlockL\_Cons\ sem, pBlockL\_Nil\ sem)$
                         $\|\ block\ \|$
      $block \quad\ \leftarrow addNT \prec \|\ header\ \| \texttt{<|>} \|\ paragraph\ \|$
      $paragraph \leftarrow addNT \prec \|\ (pParagraph\ sem)\ \texttt{"\textbackslash\textbackslash begin" "\{" "paragraph" "\}"}$
                                 $inlineL$
                               $\texttt{"\textbackslash\textbackslash end" "\{" "paragraph" "\}"}\ \|$
    $header \quad\ \leftarrow addNT \prec \mathbf{let}\ h\ (x, name) = \|\ (pHeader\ sem\ x)\ \texttt{"\textbackslash\textbackslash"}\ name$
                                          $\texttt{"\{"}\ inlineL\ \texttt{"\}"}\ \|$
                        $headers \quad = [(1, \texttt{"section"})$
                                     $, (2, \texttt{"subsection"})$
                                     $, (3, \texttt{"subsubsection"})]$
                    $\mathbf{in}\ foldr1\ (\texttt{<|>})\ (map\ h\ headers)$
    $inlineL \quad \leftarrow addNT \prec pFoldr\ (pInlineL\_Cons\ sem, pInlineL\_Nil\ sem)$
                              $\|\ inline\ \|$
    $inline \quad\ \leftarrow addNT \prec \|\ (pPlain\ sem)\ \texttt{"\textbackslash\textbackslash plain"}\quad \texttt{"\{"}$
                                  $(someExcept\ \texttt{"\textbackslash\textbackslash\&\%\$\#\_\{\}\textasciitilde\textasciitilde"})\ \texttt{"\}"}\ \|$
                  $\texttt{<|>} \|\ (pBold \quad sem)\ \texttt{"\textbackslash\textbackslash textbf"}\ \texttt{"\{"}\ inlineL\ \texttt{"\}"}\ \|$
                  $\texttt{<|>} \|\ (pItalics\ sem)\ \texttt{"\textbackslash\textbackslash textit"}\ \texttt{"\{"}\ inlineL\ \texttt{"\}"}\ \|$
  $exportNTs \prec exportList\ document\ (\ export\ cs\_document\ document$
                                   $\circ\ export\ cs\_blockL \quad\ blockL$
                                   $\circ\ export\ cs\_paragraph\ paragraph$
                                   $\circ\ export\ cs\_header \quad\ header$
                                   $\circ\ export\ cs\_inline \quad\ inline$
                                   $\circ\ export\ cs\_inlineL \quad inlineL)$

**Fig. 7.** Our EBNF encoded as a series of grammar transformations

With the abstract and concrete syntax in mind, we use combinators from the **murder** library to straightforwardly encode this grammar fragment in Haskell, as shown in Figure 7. Note that we can freely use Haskell abstractions where this comes in handy, as in the case where we deal with various levels of section headers; as a result our abstract grammar is more expressive than our input grammar.

## 2.3 Arrows and Their Syntax

A grammar fragment in the **murder** library is expressed using the arrow interface, which generalises the notion of a function, modelling effectful computations with input and output. In our case we maintain a state containing an environment holding the productions for each of the non-terminals introduced thus far.

Because arrow syntax [3] can be a bit daunting, we give some analogies to functions. When writing **proc** *inp* → ... (arrow abstraction), we define the arrow equivalent of writing λ*inp* → ... for functions. The *pat* ← *a* ≺ *alternatives* syntax is used in a recursive do block (**do rec**), indicating that we apply the arrow *a* to *alternatives* and match the output to the pattern *pat* (≺ is written as -< in Haskell code). Such a **do** block allows for recursive bindings, similar to a **let** block. Finally, we indicate the output of the grammar fragment with *a* ≺ *input* (which should be the last statement in the do block), meaning that the output of arrow *a* will be the final output of our grammar fragment arrow.

In the case of grammar fragments, the input of such an arrow provides information how to refer to earlier introduced elements of the grammar under construction (in this case we call the fragment a *grammar extension*). The empty structure () indicates that our fragment does not need to refer to any other fragment (we say the current fragment is an *initial grammar*).

In Figure 7 we introduce new non-terminals using the *addNT* arrow. A call to *addNT* extends the state with a new non-terminal, it takes the initial productions of this new non-terminal as input and returns a reference to the newly introduced non-terminal, which we can use as non-terminal in further fragments. Fragments as defined in Figure 7 are combined by means of arrow composition, as we will see later.

Each production is expressed using the so called *idiom brackets*[7] (iI and Ii in Haskell code). The brackets enable a notation which closely follows the common CFG notation, but reduce to normal applicative combinators. We have used class overloading to let the type of each element decide what kind of parser to construct. For example, when we write:

⟦ (*pBold sem*) "\\textbf" "{" *inlineL* "}" ⟧

we construct a parser that parses the strings "\\textbf" and "{", next applies the parser for the non-terminal *inlineL* and finally parses the string "}". The strings are not used and the result of the complete parse is constructed by selecting the appropriate semantic function (*pBold*) from the overall semantics *sem*, and applying it to the result of the parser *inlineL*.

Using the function *exportList* a list of non-terminals is constructed that can be used in later extensions. Its first argument expresses that the starting point of the grammar is *document* and that the extensible non-terminals are *document*, *blockL*, *paragraph*, *header*, *inline* and *inlineL*; they can be accessed using the labels *cs_document*, *cs_blockL*, *cs_paragraph*, *cs_header*, *cs_inline* and *cs_inlineL* which were generated by Template Haskell.

Note that the above grammar fragment is parameterised with a record *sem* containing for each production its associated semantic function. The type of this record is imported from the *Declarations* modules and was generated by *deriveLang*. In this way we have decoupled what to do with the recognised structure form the recognition process itself.

---

[7] http://www.haskell.org/haskellwiki/Idiom_brackets

## 2.4 Semantics

We can compute useful information from an abstract syntax tree by using an attribute grammar. In an attribute grammar, each node in a parse tree is decorated with a set of values, called attributes. There exist two kinds of attributes: synthesised and inherited. Synthesised attributes are used to pass information up to the parent node, while inherited attributes are used to pass information down to children nodes. Attribute value computations can refer to inherited attributes of the parent and synthesised attributes of the children. Attribute grammar based specifications differ from function definitions in the way that in case of the latter we have to specify both all arguments at the same time, and the various parts of a computed result together in the body at the same time, whereas in the former situation this specification can be given incrementally. For a proper understanding it suffices to see each introduction of an inherited attribute as adding an extra parameter to the semantics of a non-terminal and each introduction of a synthesised attribute as an extension of its result.

We will now show how, using the **AspectAG** library, we define a synthesised attribute containing the HMTL code for a piece of parsed input text. This library allows us to define attribute grammar fragments which can be type-checked, compiled, distributed and composed as any normal Haskell value. For naming the individual attributes of a node we follow the same approach as we did with naming the children and the non-terminals: we again use heterogenous lists [5] (**HList** package), in which values of different types can be stored and accessed by using a unique type as index.

Depending on whether we think of the abstract syntax as data type, a tree, or a grammar we use the following words as synonyms:

1. "data type", "parent node" and "left-hand-side (non-terminal)"
2. "data constructor", "current node" and "production"
3. "data constructor field", "child node" and "right-hand-side non-terminal"

Before introducing the definitions of the new attribute, we first create a unique label *html*, using the Template Haskell function *attLabels*:

$ (*attLabels* [ "html" ])

For every production of the abstract syntax with which we associate the synthesized *html* attribute, we provide a *rule* that states how to compute that attribute *html* (a *String*); we use the *syn* function to specify the rules:

$$
\begin{aligned}
document\_html &= syn\ html\ \$\ \textbf{do}\ blocks \leftarrow at\ ch\_blocks \\
&\qquad\qquad\qquad\quad return\ \$\ blocks\ \#\ html
\end{aligned}
$$

$$
blockLnil\_html = syn\ html\ \$\ return\ ""
$$

$$
\begin{aligned}
blockLcons\_html &= syn\ html\ \$\ \textbf{do}\ block\ \leftarrow at\ ch\_hd\_BlockL\_Cons \\
&\qquad\qquad\qquad\qquad blocks \leftarrow at\ ch\_tl\_BlockL\_Cons \\
&\qquad\qquad\qquad\qquad return\ \$\ block\ \#\ html \mathbin{+\!\!+} blocks\ \#\ html
\end{aligned}
$$

We define the rule for the only production (constructor) of the *Document* type and the two productions of the *BlockL* type (derived form the list type definitions). We use the *Reader* monad to get access to a small heterogenous record containing the attributes of the child nodes (constructor field). The (#) operator is used to access the fields of those records. Thus, to compute the *html* attribute for the production *Document*, we just return the value of the *html* attribute of its only child. Note that we are not working with the actual data types, but merely use the labels (i.e. *ch_blocks*, *ch_hd_BlockL_Cons* etc) that were *generated* from the data types (this method is key to achieve extensibility of the AST). We show two more rules, for the *Block* productions:

$$header\_html \quad = syn\ html\ \$\ \textbf{do}\ level \leftarrow at\ ch\_level\_header$$
$$inls \leftarrow at\ ch\_inlines\_header$$
$$return\ \$\ \texttt{"<h"} + show\ level + \texttt{">"}$$
$$+ inls\ \#\ html$$
$$+ \texttt{"</h"} + show\ level + \texttt{">"} + \texttt{"\textbackslash n"}$$
$$paragraph\_html = syn\ html\ \$\ \textbf{do}\ inls \leftarrow at\ ch\_inlines\_par$$
$$return\ \$\ \texttt{"<p>"} + inls\ \#\ html + \texttt{"</p>"} + \texttt{"\textbackslash n"}$$

In order to construct the semantic record using the defined attribute rules, we use the generated function *mkDoc* (which explains the role of the "Doc" parameter in the Template Haskell) which was also generated by *deriveLang* (see section 2.1), and which collects the semantic rules for all productions. The definitions of the other functions follows the same pattern as above.

$$semHtml = mkDoc\ blockLcons\_html$$
$$blockLnil\_html$$
$$bold\_html$$
$$document\_html$$
$$header\_html$$
$$inlineLcons\_html$$
$$inlineLnil\_html$$
$$italics\_html$$
$$paragraph\_html$$
$$plain\_html$$

The *mkDoc* function returns exactly the record structure with which we parameterised the grammar fragments.

## 2.5  Composing the Tool

Now that we have a definition for the semantics, we can finally put the tool together that maps LATEX onto HTML. We start by writing a small utility function to build the converter:

$$buildConverter\ gram\ att\ input = \textbf{let}\ parser = compile\ \$\ closeGram\ gram$$
$$res = result\ (parse\ parser\ input)$$
$$\textbf{in}\ res\ emptyRecord\ \#\ att$$

Thus, *buildConverter* takes an extensible grammar (e.g. a grammar fragment), an attribute with which we can index in the heterogenous record with the synthesized attributes of the root element, and an input string for the parser. We use the **murder** functions *compile* and *closeGram* to generate the parser, and *parse* to run it. With *result* we drop extra information from the parsing process and obtain the result: a function that takes a heterogenous record with inherited attributes (in our case none, thus *emptyRecord*) and returns a record containing the synthesized attributes, of which we select the one specified using (#).

We can now construct a converter tool for our language, by passing the defined semantic functions to the parser description, and using *buildConverter* to build and run the parser.

$$latex2html :: String \rightarrow String$$
$$latex2html = buildConverter\ (gLatex\ semHtml)\ html$$

## 3  Extending Our Definitions

In this section we show how our design can be extended in three different ways: extending the set of attributes, adding new non-terminals to the abstract syntax and extending the grammar describing the input language.

### 3.1  Extending the Semantics: Numbered Headers

As a first use case, we extend the HTML generation. In LATEX section headers are automatically numbered. In order to integrate this aspect into the HTML generation, we define some extra attributes.

We model a header number as a value of type $[Int]$, taking the level of headers into account, e.g. 3.1.4 is represented as [3,1,4]. We write a small function to format such an index

$$formatNH :: [Int] \rightarrow String$$
$$formatNH = intercalate\ "."\ \circ\ map\ show$$

We introduce an attribute *cHeaderNum*, a chained header number, which threads (or chains) the header indexes through the tree, updating it whenever a header is encountered. Such a chained attribute is by convention a pair of an inherited and a synthesised attribute having the same name, and has the same effect as using a *StateT* monad transformer. We also define a *local* attribute *headerNum*, which is only accessible from within the header node.

```
$ (attLabels ["cHeaderNum", "headerNum"])
  -- the non-terminals which have chained cHeaderNum attributes:
cHeaderNum_NTs = nt_BlockL .*. nt_Block .*. hNil
  -- by default the attribute is copied in a state monad like fashion:
default_cHeaderNum   = chain cHeaderNum cHeaderNum_NTs
  -- initialise the list of Integers at the root of the document:
document_cHeaderNum = inh cHeaderNum cHeaderNum_NTs $ do
                      return (ch_blocks .=. ([] :: [Int]) .*. emptyRecord)
  -- compute a local attribute containing the new list of numbers:
```

$header\_headerNum \qquad = loc \;\; headerNum \;\; \$ \; \textbf{do}$
$\qquad\qquad\qquad\qquad\qquad lhs \quad\;\; \leftarrow at \; lhs$
$\qquad\qquad\qquad\qquad\qquad level \;\; \leftarrow at \; ch\_level\_header$
$\qquad\qquad\qquad\qquad\qquad return \;\$\; updateHeaderNum \; level \,(lhs \,\#\, cHeaderNum)$

-- return the updated list of numbers:

$header\_cHeaderNum \qquad = syn \;\; cHeaderNum \;\; \$ \; \textbf{do}$
$\qquad\qquad\qquad\qquad\qquad loc \quad\;\; \leftarrow at \; loc$
$\qquad\qquad\qquad\qquad\qquad return \;\$\; loc \,\#\, headerNum$

-- auxiliary function which computes the next header number:

$updateHeaderNum :: Int \to [\,Int\,] \to [\,Int\,]$
$updateHeaderNum \; level \; par = zipWith \;(+)\; par' \,(zeros \,+\!\!+\, [\,1\,])$
$\qquad \textbf{where} \; par' \;\; = par \,+\!\!+\, repeat \; 0$
$\qquad\qquad\quad zeros = replicate \,(level - 1)\; 0$

Note that the computation of this new attribute is independent of the output language. Therefore, this attribute definition is defined in a separate module and can be shared across different output languages. It is now easy to access this attribute in our new definition of the *html* generation, where *synmodM* creates a rule that will overwrite the original rule when extending it.

$header\_html' = synmodM \; html \;\$\; \textbf{do} \; level \leftarrow at \; ch\_level\_header$
$\qquad\qquad\qquad\qquad\qquad\qquad\quad inls \;\; \leftarrow at \; ch\_inlines\_header$
$\qquad\qquad\qquad\qquad\qquad\qquad\quad loc \;\; \leftarrow at \; loc$
$\qquad\qquad\qquad\qquad\qquad\qquad\quad \textbf{let} \; num = loc \,\#\, headerNum$
$\qquad\qquad\qquad\qquad\qquad\qquad\quad return \;\$\; \texttt{"<h"} \,+\!\!+\, show \; level \,+\!\!+\, \texttt{">"}$
$\qquad\qquad\qquad\qquad\qquad\qquad\qquad\qquad +\!\!+\, formatNH \; num \,+\!\!+\, \texttt{" "}$
$\qquad\qquad\qquad\qquad\qquad\qquad\qquad\qquad +\!\!+\, inls \,\#\, html$
$\qquad\qquad\qquad\qquad\qquad\qquad\qquad\qquad +\!\!+\, \texttt{"</h"} \,+\!\!+\, show \; level \,+\!\!+\, \texttt{">"} \,+\!\!+\, \texttt{"\textbackslash n"}$

We can now construct a new semantic record for *html* generation by combining both the *html* and the *cHeaderNum* aspects:

$semHtml' = mkDoc \;(default\_cHeaderNum \; `ext` \; blockLcons\_html)$
$\qquad\qquad\qquad (default\_cHeaderNum \; `ext` \; blockLnil\_html)$
$\qquad\qquad\qquad bold\_html$
$\qquad\qquad\qquad (document\_cHeaderNum \; `ext` \; document\_html)$
$\qquad\qquad\qquad (header\_headerNum \; `ext` \; header\_cHeaderNum$
$\qquad\qquad\qquad\qquad\qquad\qquad\quad `ext` \; header\_html'$
$\qquad\qquad\qquad\qquad\qquad\qquad\quad `ext` \; header\_html)$
$\qquad\qquad\; inlineLcons\_html$
$\qquad\qquad\; inlineLnil\_html$
$\qquad\qquad\; italics\_html$
$\qquad\qquad\; (default\_cHeaderNum \; `ext` \; paragraph\_html)$
$\qquad\qquad\; plain\_html$

This is where the actual composition of semantics happens. The original *header_html* rule is extended from right to left, with rules for *cHeaderNum*, *headerNum* and a redefinition for the *html* attribute.

212    J. Krijnen, D. Swierstra, and M.O. Viera

## 3.2   A Table of Contents

As our second extension we show how to extend the grammar, abstract syntax and semantics by computing a table of contents of the document.

We start out by computing the table of contents as a synthesised attribute, since this computation requires no extension of the abstract syntax. Again, we would like this attribute to be reusable for different output languages, so we model the table as a value of type $[([Int], String)]$, i.e. a list of section headers tupled with the name of the section.

We start by defining two attribute labels: $sToc$ contains the synthesised table of contents, and $toc$ the complete table of contents, to be passed down the tree as an inherited attribute. In this way information collected from all over the document is made available at all places where we might insert the table of contents.

$(attLabels ["sToc", "toc"])$
$sToc\_NTs = nt\_Document\ .*.\ nt\_Block\ .*.\ nt\_BlockL\ .*.\ HNil$
$default\_sToc = use\ sToc\ sToc\_NTs\ (\!\!+\!\!)\ []$
$header\_sToc = syn\ sToc\ \$\ \mathbf{do}\ loc \leftarrow at\ loc$
$\qquad\qquad\qquad\qquad\qquad\qquad inls \leftarrow at\ ch\_inlines\_header$
$\qquad\qquad\qquad\qquad\qquad\qquad return\ [(loc\ \#\ headerNum, inls\ \#\ sInlStr)]$

For $sToc$ we provide a default rule that aggregates the synthesized table of contents. The $use$ function from the **AspectAG** library takes an operator to combine the synthesized tables from all the child nodes, and a default value if a child does not define the attribute. Next, we write a specific rule defining how to synthesize a table of contents at the header node. We ask for the local attributes, and reuse the $headerNum$ attribute, defined in the previous subsection. We also use the $sInlStr$ attribute which formats the $InlineL$ text as a simple string, while ignoring text formatting such as bold and italics (we omit its implementation).

We now add an extension to the abstract syntax to be able to indicate where the table of contents is to be inserted:

**data** $EXT\_Block = Toc$
$(extendAG\ ''\ EXT\_Block\ [])$
$(deriveLang\ "DocToc"\ [''\ EXT\_Block])$

The $EXT\_Block$ should be read as an extension of the $Block$ data type (defined in section 2.1), thus introducing a new production for the table of contents. The function $deriveLang$ will also produce a new record type containing the semantic function of the $Toc$ production. Now that we have this semantic record available, we can extend the LaTeX grammar

$gLatexToc\ sem = \mathbf{proc}\ imported \rightarrow \mathbf{do}$
$\qquad\qquad\qquad \mathbf{let}\ block = getNT\ cs\_block\ imported$
$\qquad\qquad\qquad toc \leftarrow addNT \prec\ \|\ (pToc\ sem)\ "\backslash\backslash tableofcontents"\ \|$
$\qquad\qquad\qquad addProds \prec (block, \|\ toc\ \|)$
$\qquad\qquad\qquad exportNTs \prec imported$

We retrieve the non-terminal *block* defined in the fragment from section 2.2 and introduce a new non-terminal *toc* that recognises the LaTeX command. We then add this new non-terminal as an extra alternative to the block non-terminal. Now we can also define the synthesis of the *html* attribute for the *Toc* production:

$$toc\_html = syn\ html\ \$\ \mathbf{do}\ lhs \leftarrow at\ lhs$$
$$return\ \$\ formatToc\ (lhs \# toc)$$
$$formatToc :: [([Int], String)] \rightarrow String$$
$$formatToc = foldr\ f\ ""$$
$$\mathbf{where}\ f\ (x, section)\ table = \texttt{"<a href=\#"} + show\ x + \texttt{">"}$$
$$+ (formatNH\ x) + \texttt{" "} + section$$
$$+ \texttt{"</a><br />\textbackslash n"} + table$$

We use the inherited attribute *toc* (the complete table) and format it using a small helper function. From this, we can derive the required semantic record.

$$semHtmlToc = mkDocToc\ (default\_toc\ `ext`\ toc\_html\ `ext`$$
$$default\_cHeaderNum\ `ext`\ default\_sToc)$$

We also redefine the synthesised *html* attribute for the header node, using its *headerNum* as a value for `id` in the HTML tag. This gives us a navigation mechanism within the HTML document. We omit the implementation since it closely resembles the *html* rule defined in section 3. We also do not show the construction of a new semantic record *semHtml''* with *mkDoc* since it is similar to *semHtml'* in section 3, except for the addition of the newly defined rules. We now have all the building blocks to create the new conversion tool:

$$latex2html'' :: String \rightarrow String$$
$$latex2html'' = buildConverter\ (gLatex\ semHtml''\ \texttt{+>>}\ gLatexToc\ semHtmlToc)\ html$$

The combinator **+>>** composes grammar fragments, such that its second argument extends the grammar in its first. It just composes two arrows, passing the output of the first one (exported non-terminals) as input to the second one.

# 4    Conclusions, Related and Future Work

We have shown how our libraries can be used to construct a more flexible and extensible *Pandoc* system. We have shown how to extend the underlying parsers for the input language, how to extend the intermediate representation, and how to extend and change computations over this intermediate data structure. The consistency of all definitions is done by the Haskell compiler. We foresee a system in which a document may come with references to the definitions of used document elements (like DTD's) *including* their semantics, i.e. how these elements are to be formatted in combination with other elements.

We heavily lean of the Typed Transformations of Typed Abstract Syntax [1] technique in realising this. One of the questions which arises is whether such flexibility might have been achieved otherwise. On his website[8] the designer of

---
[8] http://johnmacfarlane.net/pandoc/scripting.html

*Pandoc*, John Macfarlane, shows how some of the things we are doing using our attribute grammar system may be achieved by some form of scripting, which boils down to constructing the abstract syntax tree of the document, and subsequently applying functions to this tree, before writing the tree out in some specific format. We believe that, although this technique may work for simple transformations, this is not the way to go. Such approaches look simple at first, but become cumbersome to use once many (related) transformations are to be applied. They are inefficient since the tree is to be inspected over and over again, and worse, the programmer has to be aware of all the transformations, what they do to the tree, what information to leave in the tree for further transformations, and where to pick it up in further steps. Once one tries to use the Haskell type system to check for the consistency of this process the types of the intermediate trees change, defeating the whole underlying *Pandoc* philosophy. Of course this problem can be circumvented by storing attributes in the tree in the form of dictionaries, but then we move to the untyped world, where the type system does not guarantee that entries referred to are present. If one wants to resort to such untyped techniques one might look at systems which have been designed to support this approach such as Stratego [2] (see however [4] for an extension of transformation systems with attribute grammar facilities). The fact remains however that in all these approaches the life of the programmer becomes much more complicated because he loses strong typing and has to make the evaluation order and the storage and retrieval explicit, whereas this is implicitly done by the lazy evaluation underlying the attribute grammar approach. In a technical report we show the viability of our approach in implementing a compiler for the language Oberon0 in a stepwise fashion [9]. Other systems pursuing solutions along these lines are Kiama [6] which uses Scala as the (host) implementation language and Silver [8].

Once we have introduced a lot of attributes, the tree structures may grow, and accessing the individual attributes may start to add to the overall cost. In [12] we have described how the `AspectAG` code we have shown may be generated by the Utrecht University Attribute Grammar Compiler (*uuagc*) from a less verbose format. Another option which becomes available that way is to group attributes such that they can be accessed faster [12]. The *uuagc* compiler can also read a large collection of attribute grammar fragments, analyse the overall dependencies and generate the tree-walk evaluators which have to be constructed by hand in the more explicit approaches. In this way we can easily generate a very fast compiler for the document type at hand.

Although we have hardly used the full power of the attribute grammar formalism we want to mention that for many kinds of computations over trees they are the tool of choice: *attribute grammars form a domain specific language for describing computations over trees*, where we do not have to limit ourselves to non-circular grammars at all when we use an lazy evaluated underlying language. In the online computation of pretty printed documents we essentially use lazy evaluation to be able to evaluate a circular attribute grammar; something which is not easily transformed into an explicitly scheduled version [7].

# References

1. Baars, A.I., Swierstra, S.D., Viera, M.: Typed transformations of typed abstract syntax. In: TLDI 2009: Proceedings of the 4th International Workshop on Types in Language Design and Implementation, pp. 15–26. ACM, New York (2009)
2. Bravenboer, M.: Exercises in Free Syntax. Syntax Definition, Parsing, and Assimilation of Language Conglomerates. Ph.D. thesis, Utrecht University, Utrecht, The Netherlands (January 2008)
3. Hughes, J.: Generalising monads to arrows. Sci. Comput. Program. 37(1-3), 67–111 (2000)
4. Kats, L., Sloane, A., Visser, E.: Decorated attribute grammars: Attribute evaluation meets strategic programming. In: de Moor, O., Schwartzbach, M.I. (eds.) CC 2009. LNCS, vol. 5501, pp. 142–157. Springer, Heidelberg (2009), http://dx.doi.org/10.1007/978-3-642-00722-4_11
5. Kiselyov, O., Lämmel, R., Schupke, K.: Strongly typed heterogeneous collections. In: Proc. of the 2004 Workshop on Haskell, pp. 96–107. ACM Press (2004)
6. Sloane, A.M., Kats, L.C.L., Visser, E.: A pure object-oriented embedding of attribute grammars. In: Proc. of the Ninth Workshop on Language Descriptions, Tools, and Applications (March 2009)
7. Swierstra, S.D., Chitil, O.: Linear, bounded, functional pretty-printing. Journal of Functional Programming 19(01), 1–16 (2009)
8. Van Wyk, E., Bodin, D., Gao, J., Krishnan, L.: Silver: An extensible attribute grammar system. Sci. Comput. Program. 75(1-2), 39–54 (2010)
9. Viera, M.: First Class Syntax, Semantics and Their Composition. Ph.D. thesis, Utrecht University, Department of Information and Computing Sciences (2013)
10. Viera, M., Swierstra, S.D., Dijkstra, A.: Grammar Fragments Fly First-Class. In: Proc.of the 12th Workshop on Language Descriptions Tools and Applications, pp. 47–60 (2012)
11. Viera, M., Swierstra, S.D., Lempsink, E.: Haskell, Do You Read Me?: Constructing and composing efficient top-down parsers at runtime. In: Proc. of the First Symposium on Haskell, pp. 63–74. ACM, New York (2008)
12. Viera, M., Swierstra, S.D., Middelkoop, A.: UUAG Meets AspectAG. In: Proc. of the 12th Workshop on Language Descriptions Tools and Applications (2012)
13. Viera, M., Swierstra, S.D., Swierstra, W.: Attribute Grammars Fly First-Class: How to do aspect oriented programming in Haskell. In: Proc.of the 14th Int. Conf. on Functional Programming, pp. 245–256. ACM, New York (2009)

# Generic Generic Programming

José Pedro Magalhães[1] and Andres Löh[2]

[1] Department of Computer Science, University of Oxford, Oxford, UK
jpm@cs.ox.ac.uk
[2] Well-Typed LLP, Oxford, UK
andres@well-typed.com

**Abstract.** Generic programming (GP) is a form of abstraction in programming languages that serves to reduce code duplication by exploiting the regular structure of algebraic datatypes. Over the years, several different approaches to GP in Haskell have surfaced. These approaches are often similar, but certain differences make them particularly well-suited for one specific domain or application. As such, there is a lot of code duplication across GP libraries, which is rather unfortunate, given the original goals of GP.

To address this problem, we define conversions from one popular GP library representation to several others. Our work unifies many approaches to GP, and simplifies the life of both library writers and users. Library writers can define their approach as a conversion from our library, obviating the need for writing metaprogramming code for generation of conversions to and from the generic representation. Users of GP, who often struggle to find "the right approach" to use, can now mix and match functionality from different libraries with ease, and need not worry about having multiple (potentially inefficient and large) code blocks for generic representations in different approaches.

## 1 Introduction

GP can be used to reduce code duplication, increase the level of abstraction in a program, and derive useful functionality "for free" from the structure of datatypes. Over the past few years, many approaches to GP have surfaced. Including pre-processors, template-based approaches, language extensions, and libraries, there are well over 15 different approaches to GP in Haskell [7, Chapter 8]. This abundance is caused by the lack of a clearly superior approach; each approach has its strengths and weaknesses, uses different implementation mechanisms, a different generic view [4] (i.e. a different structural representation of datatypes), or focuses on solving a particular task. Their number and variety makes comparisons difficult, and can make prospective GP users struggle even before actually writing a generic program, since they first have to choose a library that is appropriate for their needs.

We have previously investigated how to model and formally relate some Haskell GP libraries using Agda [9], and concluded that some approaches clearly subsume others. The relevance of this fact extends above mere theoretical interest, since a comparison can also provide means for converting between approaches. Ironically, code duplication across generic programming libraries is evident: the same function can be nearly identical in different approaches, yet impossible to reuse, due to the underlying differences

M. Flatt and H.-F. Guo (Eds.): PADL 2014, LNCS 8324, pp. 216–231, 2014.

in representation. A conversion between approaches provides the means to remove duplication of generic code.

In this paper we show how to automatically derive representations for many popular GP libraries, all coming from one single compiler-supported approach. The base approach, generic-deriving [10], has been supported in the Glasgow Haskell Compiler (GHC), the main Haskell compiler, since version 7.2.1 (August 2011). From generic-deriving we define conversions to other popular generic libraries: regular [13], multirec [14], and syb [5, 6]. Some of these libraries are remarkably different from each other, yet advanced type-level features in GHC, such as GADTs [16], type functions [15], and kind polymorphism [18], allow us to perform these conversions.

Using the type class system, our conversions remain entirely under the hood for the end user, who need not worry anymore about which GP approach does what, and can simply use generic functions from any approach. As an example, the following combination of generic functionality is now possible:

```
import Generics.Deriving           as GD
import Generics.Regular.Rewriting as R
import Generics.SYB.Schemes        as S
import Conversions ()

data Logic α = Var α | Logic α :∨: Logic α | Not (Logic α) | T | F
                 deriving (GD.Generic)

rewriting :: Logic Char
rewriting = let elim2Not = R.rule $ λx → Not (Not x) :⤳: x
                in R.bottomUp (R.rewrite elim2Not) $ T :∨: Not (Not (Var 'p'))

size :: Int
size = S.everything (+) (const 1) $ Var 'p' :∨: Var 'q'

rename :: Logic String
rename = GD.gmap ('_':) $ T :∨: Var "p"
```

Here, the user defines a *Logic* datatype, and lets the compiler automatically derive a *Generic* representation for it (from generic-deriving). Three examples then show how functionality specific to three separate GP libraries can be used from this single representation:

- In *rewriting*, a rewrite rule is applied to a logical expression. The rewriting system requires a fixed-point view on data for encoding expressions extended with metavariables [13]. This fixed-point view is provided by the regular library. The term *rewriting* evaluates to $T :\vee: Var\ 'p'$.
- Expression *size* showcases the combinator approach to GP typical of syb, reducing all leaves to 1, and combining them with the $(+)$ operator. The term *size* evaluates to 5.
- Expression *rename* uses a map on the *String* parameter of *Logic* to rename all the variables. This makes uses of the support for parameters of generic-deriving. The term *rename* evaluates to $T :\vee: Var\ "\_p"$.

All this functionality can be achieved using only the *Generic* representation of generic-deriving, and by importing the conversion instances defined in some module

*Conversions* (provided by us); there is no need to derive any generic representations for regular or syb. Previously, combining the functionality of these libraries would also require generic representations for regular and syb. This would bring a dependency on Template Haskell [17] for deriving regular representations, and added code bloat.

Generic library writers also see an improvement in their quality of life, as they no longer need to write Template Haskell code to derive representations for their libraries, and can instead rely on our conversion functions. Furthermore, many generic functions can now be recognised as truly duplicated across approaches, and can be deprecated appropriately. Defining new approaches to GP has never been easier; GP libraries can be kept small and specific, focusing on one particular aspect, as users can easily find and use other generic functionality in other approaches.

We say this work is about *generic generic programming* because it is generic over generic programming approaches. Specifically, we define conversions to multiple GP libraries (Sections 3 to 5), covering a wide range of approaches, including libraries with a fixed-point view on data (regular and multirec), and a library based on traversal combinators (syb). In defining our conversions to other libraries, we also update their definitions to make use of the latest GHC extensions (namely data kinds and kind polymorphism [18]). This is not essential for our conversions (i.e. we are not changing the libraries to make our conversion easier), but it improves the libraries (while these libraries were always type safe, our changes make them more kind safe).

Moreover, our work brings forward a new way of looking at GP, where new, special-purpose GP libraries can be easily defined, without needing to repeat lots of common infrastructure. Users of GP can now simply cherry-pick generic functions from different libraries, without having to worry about the overhead introduced by each GP approach.

**Notation.** In order to avoid syntactic clutter and to help the reader, we adopt a liberal Haskell notation in this paper. We assume the existence of a **kind** keyword, which allows us to define kinds directly. These kinds behave as if they had arisen from datatype promotion [18], except that they do not define a datatype and constructors. We omit the keywords **type family** and **type instance** entirely, making type-level functions look like their value-level counterparts. When we use the same name for a constructor and a type, the "level" of the expression is clear from the context. Additionally, we use Greek letters for type variables, apart from $\kappa$, which is reserved for kind variables.

This syntactic sugar is only for presentation purposes. An executable version of the code, which compiles with GHC 7.6.2, is available at http://dreixel.net/research/code/ggp.zip. We rely on many GHC-specific extensions to Haskell, which are essential for our development. Due to space constraints we cannot explain them all in detail, but we try to point out relevant features as we use them.

**Structure of the Paper.** We first provide a brief introduction to the generic-deriving library for GP (Section 2). We then see how to obtain other libraries from generic-deriving: regular (Section 3), multirec (Section 4), and syb (Section 5). We then conclude with a discussion in Section 6. Along the way, we also show several examples of how our conversion enables seamless use of multiple approaches.

## 2    Introduction to `generic-deriving`

We begin our efforts of homogenising GP libraries by introducing `generic-deriving`, the library from which we derive the other representations.

**kind** $Un_D = V_D \mid U_D \mid K_D\ KType\ \star$
$\qquad \mid M_D\ Meta_D\ Un_D$
$\qquad \mid Un_D :+:_D Un_D$
$\qquad \mid Un_D :\times:_D Un_D$
**kind** $Meta_D = D_D\ MetaData$
$\qquad \mid C_D\ MetaCon$
$\qquad \mid F_D\ MetaField$
**kind** $KType = P \mid R\ RecType \mid U$
**kind** $RecType = S \mid O$

**data** $[\![\, \alpha :: Un_D \,]\!]_D :: \star$ **where**
$U_{ID} \quad :: [\![\, U_D \,]\!]_D$
$M_{ID} \quad :: [\![\, \alpha \,]\!]_D \to [\![\, M_D\ \iota\ \alpha \,]\!]_D$
$K_{ID} \quad :: \alpha \to [\![\, K_D\ \iota\ \alpha \,]\!]_D$
$L_{ID} \quad :: [\![\, \phi \,]\!]_D \to [\![\, \phi :+:_D \psi \,]\!]_D$
$R_{ID} \quad :: [\![\, \psi \,]\!]_D \to [\![\, \phi :+:_D \psi \,]\!]_D$
$:\times:_D :: [\![\, \phi \,]\!]_D \to [\![\, \psi \,]\!]_D \to [\![\, \phi :\times:_D \psi \,]\!]_D$

**Fig. 1.** Universe and interpretation of `generic-deriving`

**Universe.** The structure used to encode datatypes in a GP approach is called its *universe* [12]. The universe of `generic-deriving` can be seen on the left in Figure 1. It represents datatypes as a sum of products, additionally keeping track of meta-information. Since GP approaches often use the same names for similar representation types, we use the "D" subscript for `generic-deriving` names.

Datatypes are sums (choices between constructors, encoded with $:+:_D$) of products (constructors with several arguments, encoded with $:\times:_D$). The sum can be nullary ($V_D$), in case the datatype has no constructors, and so can each of the products ($U_D$), in case the constructor takes no arguments. Constructor arguments (encoded with $K_D$) can either be the (last) parameter of the datatype ($K_D\ P$), an occurrence of a datatype, which can be the same as the one we are defining ($K_D\ (R\ S)$) or some other datatype ($K_D\ (R\ O)$), or something else (such as an application of a type variable, encoded with $K_D\ U$). The annotations given by *KType* and *RecType* will prove essential when converting to approaches with a fixed-point view on data (Section 3 and Section 4), as there we need explicit knowledge about the recursive structure of data.

**Interpretation.** The interpretation of the universe defines the structure of the values that inhabit the datatype representation. Datatype representations are types of kind $Un_D$. We use a GADT [16] $[\![\, \_ \,]\!]_D$ to encode the interpretation of the universe of `generic-deriving`, which can be seen on the right in Figure 1. The top-level inhabitant of a datatype representation is always a constructor $M_{ID}$ (with type $[\![\, M_D\ (D_D\ \iota)\ \alpha \,]\!]_D$), which serves only as a proxy to store the datatype metadata on its type. An $M_{ID}$ appears also around each constructor (but then with type $[\![\, M_D\ (C_D\ \iota)\ \alpha \,]\!]_D$, and each constructor field (but then with type $[\![\, M_D\ (F_D\ \iota)\ \alpha \,]\!]_D$). Constructors can be on the left ($L_{ID}$) or right ($R_{ID}$) side of a sum. Constructor arguments are encoded in a product structure ($:\times:_D$), or can be empty ($U_{ID}$). Constructor fields are all encoded with $K_{ID}$, which is used with different types to encode the meta-information of the field in question (similarly to $M_{ID}$). We encode the last parameter of the datatype with $K_{ID} :: K_D\ P\ \alpha$, datatype occurrences with $K_{ID} :: K_D (R\ \iota)\ \alpha$, with $\iota$ being $S$ if the datatype is the same we are encoding and $O$ otherwise, and anything else with $K_{ID} :: K_D\ U\ \alpha$.

**Conversion to and from User Datatypes.** Having seen the generic universe and its interpretation, we need to provide a mechanism to mediate between user datatypes and our generic representation. We use a type class for this purpose:

> **class** $Generic_D\ (\alpha :: \star)$ **where**
> $\quad Rep_D\ \alpha :: Un_D$
> $\quad from_D :: \alpha \to [\![ Rep_D\ \alpha ]\!]_D$
> $\quad to_D \quad :: [\![ Rep_D\ \alpha ]\!]_D \to \alpha$

In the $Generic_D$ class, the type family $Rep_D$ encodes the generic representation associated with user datatype $\alpha$. The class methods *from* and *to* perform the conversion between the user datatype values and the interpretation of the generic representation. From here on, we shall omit the $to_D$ direction, as it is always entirely symmetrical to $from_D$.

**Example Encoding: Lists.** We now show an example of how a user datatype is encoded in `generic-deriving`. (Users never have to define the encodings manually; GHC can automatically derive $Generic_D$ instances.) We omit the encoding of metadata in the datatype, constructors, and selectors, as these are not relevant to our developments in the rest of the paper. The simplified instance looks as follows:

> **instance** $Generic\ [\alpha]$ **where**
> $\quad Rep\ [\alpha] = U_D :+:_D ((K_D\ P\ \alpha) :\times:_D (K_D\ (R\ S)\ [\alpha]))$
> $\quad from\ [] \quad\quad = L_{ID}\ U_{ID}$
> $\quad from\ (h : t) = R_{ID}\ (K_{ID}\ h :\times:_D\ (K_{ID}\ t))$

The first argument of the $(:)$ constructor is tagged as being the parameter (with $P$), and the second as being a recursive occurrence of the datatype being defined ($R\ S$).

## 3  From `generic-deriving` to `regular`

In this section we show how to obtain `regular` representations from `generic-deriving`. The `regular` library, first described in the context of generic rewriting [13], encodes datatypes using a "fixed-point view". As such, it abstracts over the recursive position of the datatype, allowing for the definition of recursive morphisms such as cata- and anamorphisms. It was previously thought that a fixed-point view was a requirement for defining recursive morphisms generally, or that it would be very hard or messy in other views. Here we show that this need not be the case, as our conversion to `regular` comes from a non-fixed point view, and is rather simple.

**Encoding `regular`.** We show a simplified encoding of the universe of `regular` (subscript "R"), omitting the constructor meta-information:

> **kind** $Un_R = U_R \mid I_R \mid K_R \star \mid Un_R :+:_R Un_R \mid Un_R :\times:_R Un_R$

As before, we have a type for encoding unitary constructors $(U_R)$ and a type for constants $(K_R)$. However, we also have a type $I_R$ to encode recursion. The regular library supports abstracting over single recursive datatypes only, so $I_R$ need not store the index of what type it encodes. Sums and products behave as in generic-deriving.

The interpretation of this universe is parametrised over the type of recursive positions $\tau$, which is used in the $I_R$ case:

**data** $[\![ \alpha :: Un_R ]\!]_R (\tau :: \star)$ **where**
$\qquad U_R \quad :: [\![ U_R ]\!]_R \tau$
$\qquad I_R \quad\;\; :: \tau \to [\![ I_R ]\!]_R \tau$
$\qquad K_R \quad :: \alpha \to [\![ K_R\, \alpha ]\!]_R \tau$
$\qquad L_R \quad\;\; :: [\![ \alpha ]\!]_R \tau \to [\![ \alpha :+:_R \beta ]\!]_R \tau$
$\qquad R_R \quad :: [\![ \beta ]\!]_R \tau \to [\![ \alpha :+:_R \beta ]\!]_R \tau$
$\qquad (:\times:_R) :: [\![ \alpha ]\!]_R \tau \to [\![ \beta ]\!]_R \tau \to [\![ \alpha :\times:_R \beta ]\!]_R \tau$

The *Regular* class witnesses the conversion between user-defined datatypes and their representation in regular. Note how the $\tau$ parameter of $[\![ \alpha ]\!]_R$ is set to $\alpha$ itself:

**class** *Regular* $(\alpha :: \star)$ **where**
$\qquad PF\, \alpha :: Un_R$
$\qquad from_R :: \alpha \to [\![ PF\, \alpha ]\!]_R\, \alpha$

This means that regular encodes a one-layer generic representation, where the recursive positions are values of the original user datatype, not generic representations.

**Type Conversion.** We now show the first conversion in this paper, which serves as an introduction to the structure of our conversions. We use a type family to adapt the representation, and a type-class to adapt the values. The first step is then to convert the representation types of generic-deriving into representation types of regular using a type family:

$\qquad D_{\to}R\, (\alpha :: Un_D) :: Un_R$

For units, meta-information, sums, and products, the conversion is straightforward:

$\qquad D_{\to}R\, U_D \qquad\qquad = U_R$
$\qquad D_{\to}R\, (M_D \imath\, \alpha) \quad\;\, = D_{\to}R\, \alpha$
$\qquad D_{\to}R\, (\alpha :+:_D \beta) = D_{\to}R\, \alpha :+:_R D_{\to}R\, \beta$
$\qquad D_{\to}R\, (\alpha :\times:_D \beta) = D_{\to}R\, \alpha :\times:_R D_{\to}R\, \beta$

The interesting case is that for constructor arguments, as we have to treat recursion into the same datatype differently:

$\qquad D_{\to}R\, (K_D\, (R\, S)\; \tau)\; = I_R$
$\qquad D_{\to}R\, (K_D\, (R\, O)\; \alpha) = K_R\, \alpha$
$\qquad D_{\to}R\, (K_D\, P \qquad \alpha) = K_R\, \alpha$
$\qquad D_{\to}R\, (K_D\, U \qquad \alpha) = K_R\, \alpha$

One might wonder what would happen if the generic-deriving representation had an inconsistent use of $K_D\, (R\, S)\, \tau$ where $\tau$ is not the type being represented. This would lead to a type error, as we explain in the next section.

**Value Conversion.** Having performed the type-level conversion, we have to convert the values in a type-directed fashion. The conversion of the values is witnessed by the $Convert_{D \to R}$ type class:

> **class** $Convert_{D \to R} (\alpha :: Un_D)\ \tau$ **where**
> $d_{\to}r :: [\![ \alpha ]\!]_D \to [\![ D_{\to}R\ \alpha ]\!]_R\ \tau$

(We omit the $r_{\to}d$ direction, as it is entirely symmetrical.) This is a multiparameter type class because we need to enforce the restriction that the recursive occurrence under $K_D (R\ S)\ \tau$ has to be of the expected type $\tau$:

> **instance** $Convert_{D \to R} (K_D (R\ S)\ \tau)\ \tau$ **where** $d_{\to}r (K_{ID}\ x) = I_R\ x$

The tag $R\ S$ expresses this restriction informally only; the formal guarantee is given by the type-checker, since this instance requires type equality, encoded in the repeated appearance of the variable $\tau$ in the instance head. We omit the remaining instances as they are unsurprising.

To finish the conversion, we provide a *Regular* instance for all $Generic_D$ types. It is here that we set the second parameter of $Convert_{D \to R}$ to the type being converted ($\alpha$):

> **instance** $(Generic_D\ \alpha, Convert_{D \to R} (Rep_D\ \alpha)\ \alpha) \Rightarrow Regular\ \alpha$ **where**
> $PF\ \alpha = D_{\to}R (Rep_D\ \alpha)$
> $from_R\ x = d_{\to}r (from_D\ x)$

With this instance, functions defined in the regular library are now available to all generic-deriving supported datatypes. This is remarkable; in particular, functions that require a fixed-point view on data, such as the generic catamorphism, can be used on generic-deriving types without having to provide an explicit *Regular* instance. From the generic library developer point of view there are other advantages. When defining a new generic function that fits the fixed-point view naturally, a developer could implement this function easily in regular, but would then require the users of this function to use regular, and manually write *Regular* instances for their datatypes, or use the provided Template Haskell code to derive these automatically. Alternatively, the developer could try to define the same function in generic-deriving, but this would probably require more effort; the advantage would be that users wouldn't need an external library to use this function, and could rely solely on GHC.

With the instance above, however, the developer can implement the function in regular, and the users can use it through the **deriving** $Generic_D$ extension of GHC. In fact, regular can be simplified by removing the Template Haskell code for generating *Regular* instances altogether. Given that this code often requires updating due to new releases of GHC changing Template Haskell, this is a clear improvement, and helps reduce clutter from the GP libraries themselves.

## 4    From generic-deriving to multirec

Having seen how to convert from generic-deriving to a fixed-point view for a single datatype, we are ready to tackle the challenge of converting to multirec, a library with a fixed-point view over *families* of datatypes [14].

**Encoding** multirec. The universe of multirec is similar to that of regular, only $I_M$ is parametrised over an index (since we now support recursion into several datatypes), and we have a new code $\triangleright:_M$ for tagging a part of the representation with a concrete index:

**data** $Un_M \ \kappa = U_M \mid I_M \ \kappa \mid K_M \star \mid Un_M \ \kappa \ \triangleright:_M \ \kappa$
$\qquad \mid \ Un_M \ \kappa :+:_M \ Un_M \ \kappa \mid Un_M \ \kappa :\times:_M \ Un_M \ \kappa$

Tagging is used to differentiate between different datatypes within a single representation. As an example, we show a family of two mutually-recursive datatypes together with the type-level representation in multirec:

**data** $Zig = Zig \ Zag \mid ZigEnd$
**data** $Zag = Zag \ Zig$
$ZigZagRep = \qquad ((I_M \ Zag :+:_M \ U) \ \triangleright:_M \ Zig)$
$\qquad\qquad :+:_M \ ((I_M \ Zig) \qquad\quad \triangleright:_M \ Zag)$

The multirec library encodes indices by using the datatype itself as an index. As such, in our example above, the index $\kappa$ is $\star$. This turns out to be convenient for our conversion, so we will always use $Un_M$ instantiated to kind $\star$.

The interpretation of the multirec universe is parametrised not only by the representation type $\alpha$, but also by a type constructor $\tau$ that converts indices into their concrete representation, and a particular index type $\iota$:

**data** $\llbracket \alpha :: Un_M \ \kappa \rrbracket_M \ (\tau :: \kappa \to \star) \ (\iota :: \kappa)$ **where**
$\quad U_M \quad :: \llbracket U \rrbracket_M \ \tau \ \iota$
$\quad I_M \quad :: \tau \ o \to \llbracket I_M \ o \rrbracket_M \ \tau \ \iota$
$\quad K_M \quad :: \alpha \quad \to \llbracket K_M \ \alpha \rrbracket_M \ \tau \ \iota$
$\quad Tag_M \ :: \llbracket \alpha \rrbracket_M \ \tau \ \iota \to \llbracket \alpha \ \triangleright:_M \ \iota \rrbracket_M \ \tau \ \iota$
$\quad L_M \quad :: \llbracket \alpha \rrbracket_M \ \tau \ \iota \to \llbracket \alpha :+:_M \ \beta \rrbracket_M \ \tau \ \iota$
$\quad R_M \quad :: \llbracket \beta \rrbracket_M \ \tau \ \iota \to \llbracket \alpha :+:_M \ \beta \rrbracket_M \ \tau \ \iota$
$\quad :\times:_M \ :: \llbracket \alpha \rrbracket_M \ \tau \ \iota \to \llbracket \beta \rrbracket_M \ \tau \ \iota \to \llbracket \alpha :\times:_M \ \beta \rrbracket \ \tau \ \iota$

In other words, the interpretation $\llbracket \alpha \rrbracket_M \ \tau \ \iota$ can be seen as a family of datatypes, one for each particular index $\iota$. The $Tag_M$ constructor introduces a type equality constraint on the tagged index; this is how the interpretation is restricted to a particular index.

Finally, user datatypes are converted to the multirec representation using two type classes, $Fam_M$ and $El_M$:

**newtype** $I_{0M} \ \alpha = I_{0M} \ \alpha$
**class** $Fam_M \ (\phi :: \star \to \star)$ **where**
$\quad PF_M \ \phi :: Un_M \ \star$
$\quad from_M :: \phi \ \iota \to \iota \to \llbracket PF_M \ \phi \rrbracket_M \ I_{0M} \ \iota$
**class** $El_M \ (\phi :: \kappa \to \star) \ (\iota :: \kappa)$ **where**
$\quad proof_M :: \phi \ \iota$

The class $Fam_M$ takes as argument a *family* type $\phi$. Here we instantiate the $\tau$ in $\llbracket \_ \rrbracket_M$ to an identity type $I_{0M}$; other applications in multirec, such as the generalised catamorphism, make use of the generality of $\tau$. The $El_M$ class associates each index type $\iota$ with its family $\phi$.

This is all best understood through an example, so we show the encoding for the family of datatypes $Zig$ and $Zag$ shown before. The first step is to define a GADT to represent the family. This datatype contains elements of either type $Zig$ or $Zag$:

> **data** $ZigZag\ \iota$ **where**
> $ZigZag_{Zig} :: ZigZag\ Zig$
> $ZigZag_{Zag} :: ZigZag\ Zag$

The type $ZigZag$ now describes our family, by providing two indices $ZigZag_{Zig}$ and $ZigZag_{Zag}$. This is made concrete by the following instances:

> **instance** $Fam_M\ ZigZag$ **where**
> $PF_M\ ZigZag = ZigZagRep$
> $from_M\ ZigZag_{Zig}\ (Zig\ z)\ = L_M\ (Tag_M\ (L_M\ (I_M\ (I_{0M}\ z))))$
> $from_M\ ZigZag_{Zig}\ ZigEnd = L_M\ (Tag_M\ (R_M\ U_M))$
> $from_M\ ZigZag_{Zag}\ (Zag\ z) = R_M\ (Tag_M\ (I_M\ (I_{0M}\ z)))$
>
> **instance** $El_M\ ZigZag\ Zig$ **where** $proof_M = ZigZag_{Zig}$
> **instance** $El_M\ ZigZag\ Zag$ **where** $proof_M = ZigZag_{Zag}$

**Type Conversion.** The first step in converting a family of datatypes representable in generic-deriving to multirec is to convert a single datatype. This is the task of the $D_{\rightarrow}M$ type family:

> $D_{\rightarrow}M\ (\alpha :: Un_D) :: Un_M \star$
>
> $D_{\rightarrow}M\ U_D\qquad\qquad = U_M$
> $D_{\rightarrow}M\ (M_D\ \iota\ \alpha)\quad\ = D_{\rightarrow}M\ \alpha$
> $D_{\rightarrow}M\ (\alpha\ :+:_D\ \beta) = D_{\rightarrow}M\ \alpha\ :+:_M\ D_{\rightarrow}M\ \beta$
> $D_{\rightarrow}M\ (\alpha\ :\times:_D\ \beta) = D_{\rightarrow}M\ \alpha\ :\times:_M\ D_{\rightarrow}M\ \beta$

The most interesting case is that for constants, which we now need either to turn into indices, or to keep as constants. We turn recursive occurrences into indices, and leave the rest as constants:

> $D_{\rightarrow}M\ (K_D\ (R\ \iota)\ \tau)\ = I_M\ \tau$
> $D_{\rightarrow}M\ (K_D\ U\quad \alpha) = K_M\ \alpha$
> $D_{\rightarrow}M\ (K_D\ P\quad \alpha) = K_M\ \alpha$

Having defined $D_{\rightarrow}M$ to convert one datatype, we are left with the task of converting a *family* of datatypes. We encode a family as a type-level list of datatypes, and define $D_{\rightarrow}M_{Fam}$ parametrised over such a list:

> **data** $\bot$
>
> $D_{\rightarrow}M_{Fam}\ (\alpha :: [\star]) :: Un_M \star$
>
> $D_{\rightarrow}M_{Fam}\ []\qquad = K_M\ \bot$
> $D_{\rightarrow}M_{Fam}\ (\alpha : \beta) = (D_{\rightarrow}M\ (Rep_D\ \alpha))\ :\triangleright:_M\ \alpha)\ :+:_M\ D_{\rightarrow}M_{Fam}\ \beta$

We convert a list of datatypes by taking each element, looking up its representation in generic-deriving using $Rep_D$, converting it to a multirec representation using $D_{\rightarrow}M$, and tagging that with the original datatype. The base case is the empty list, which we encode with an empty representation (since multirec has no empty representation type, we define an empty datatype $\bot$ and use it as a constant).

**Value Conversion.** Converting a value of a single type is done in exactly the same way as for the regular conversion:

**class** $Convert_{D_{\rightarrow}M}$ $(\alpha :: Un_D)$ **where**
$d_{\rightarrow}m :: [\![\alpha]\!]_D \rightarrow [\![D_{\rightarrow}M\ \alpha]\!]_M\ I_{0M}\ \iota$

As before, we omit the instances, as they are without surprises.

We're left with dealing with the encapsulation of values within a family. We represent families as lists of types, but a value of a family is still of a single, concrete type. We use a GADT to encode the notion of a value within a family:

**data** $(\alpha :: [\star])$ :@: $(\beta :: \star)$ **where**
$This ::\qquad\qquad (\alpha : \beta)$ :@: $\alpha$
$That :: \beta$ :@: $\alpha \rightarrow (\gamma : \beta)$ :@: $\alpha$

For example, the value *This ZigEnd* has the type $[Zig, Zag]$ :@: $Zig$, and the value *That (This (Zag ZigEnd))* has the type $[Zig, Zag]$ :@: $Zag$.

The application of :@: to a single argument is of kind $\star \rightarrow \star$, and it encodes precisely the notion of a multirec family. We make this explicit by providing $El_M$ instances stating that a type $\alpha$ is either at the head of the list, and can be accessed with *This*, or it might be deeper within the list, in which case we have to continue indexing with *That*:

**instance** $\qquad\qquad\qquad El_M$ $((\alpha : \beta)$ :@:$)$ $\alpha$ **where** $proof_M = This$
**instance** $(El_M$ $(\beta$ :@:$)$ $\alpha) \Rightarrow El_M$ $((\gamma : \beta)$ :@:$)$ $\alpha$ **where** $proof_M = That\ proof_M$

Converting a value within a family requires producing the appropriate injection into the right element of the family, plus the tag (with $Tag_M$). We use our :@: GADT for this (which results in a right-biased encoding of the family):

**instance** $(FamConstrs\ \alpha) \Rightarrow Fam_M$ $(\alpha$ :@:$)$ **where**
$PF_M$ $(\alpha$ :@:$) = D_{\rightarrow}M_{Fam}\ \alpha$

$from_M\ This\qquad x = L_M$ $(Tag_M$ $(d_{\rightarrow}m\ (from_D\ x)))$
$from_M\ (That\ k)\ x = R_M$ $(from_M\ k\ x)$

The constraints on this instance are not trivial, as each type in the family needs to have a $Generic_D$ instance and be convertible through $Convert_{D_{\rightarrow}M}$. The *FamConstrs* constraint family expresses these requirements:

$FamConstrs$ $(\alpha :: [\star])$ :: $Constraint$
$FamConstrs\ []\quad\ = ()$
$FamConstrs\ (\alpha : \beta) = (\ Generic_D\ \alpha, Convert_{D_{\rightarrow}M}\ (Rep_D\ \alpha)$
$\qquad\qquad\qquad\qquad\quad, Fam_M\ (\beta$ :@:$), FamConstrs\ \beta)$

**Example.** To test this conversion, assume we have some generic function $size_M$ defined in multirec which computes the size of a term. Assume we also have $Generic_D$ instances for the *Zig* and *Zag* types in generic-deriving (derived by the compiler). These give rise to a $Fam_M$ ($[Zig, Zag]$ :@:) instance (this section). As such, we can call $size_M$ directly on a value of type *Zig*:

$$size_M :: (Fam_M \; \phi, \ldots) \Rightarrow \phi \; \iota \to \iota \to Int$$
$$size_M = \ldots$$

$$zigZag :: Zig$$
$$zigZag = Zig \; (Zag \; (Zig \; (Zag \; ZigEnd)))$$

$$test_{d \to m} :: Int$$
$$test_{d \to m} = size_M \; (proof :: [Zag, Zig] \; :@: Zig) \; zigZag$$

Our test value $test_{d \to m}$ evaluates to 4 as expected. The use of :@: makes multirec easier to use than before; unlike in our example in Section 4, it is not necessary to define a family type; we can simply use :@:. The index (first argument to $size_M$) is automatically computed from the type signature of *proof*, so there is no need to explicitly use *This* and *That*. Finally, families can be easily extended: the code for $test_{d \to m}$ works equally well if we supply *proof* as having type $[Zag, Zig, Int]$ :@: *Zig*, for instance.

## 5    From generic-deriving to syb

The syb library, unlike the others we have seen so far, does not encode the structure of user datatypes at the type level. Instead, it views data as successive applications of terms; generic functions then operate on this applicative structure. The interface presented to the user hides this view, and is instead based on various traversal operators. In this section we show how to obtain syb representations of data from generic-deriving. We use the syb encoding of Hinze et al. [3] as the basis of our development instead of the "official" encoding shipped with GHC, but this does not make our conversion any less applicable or general.

**Encoding** syb. The basis of syb is the *Spine* datatype, which defines a view on data as a sequence of applications. A value of type *Spine* is either a constructor, or an application of a *Spine* with functional type to an argument:

**data** $Spine :: \star \to \star$ **where**
   $Con :: \alpha \to Spine \; \alpha$
   $(:\diamond:) :: (Data \; \alpha) \Rightarrow Spine \; (\alpha \to \beta) \to \alpha \to Spine \; \beta$

The *Data* constraint will be explained later.
   The *Spine* datatype is both *Functor*ial and *Applicative*, and we can also *fold* it:

**instance** *Functor Spine* **where**
   $fmap \; f \; (Con \; x) = Con \; (f \; x)$
   $fmap \; f \; (c :\diamond: x) = fmap \; (f \circ) \; c :\diamond: x$
**instance** *Applicative Spine* **where**
   $pure = Con$

$$Con\,f \quad <*>\,x \quad\quad = fmap\,f\,x$$
$$(c :\diamond: x) <*> Con\,y \;\;= fmap\,(\lambda f\,x \to f\,x\,y)\,c :\diamond: x$$
$$(c :\diamond: x) <*> (d :\diamond: y) = (fmap\,(\lambda f\,d\,y \to f\,(d\,y))\,(c :\diamond: x) <*> d) :\diamond: y$$
$$foldSpine \;::\; (\forall \alpha\,\beta.Data\,\alpha \Rightarrow \phi\,(\alpha \to \beta) \to \alpha \to \phi\,\beta)$$
$$\to (\forall \alpha.\alpha \to \phi\,\alpha) \to Spine\,\alpha \to \phi\,\alpha$$
$$foldSpine\,f\,z\,(Con\,c) = z\,c$$
$$foldSpine\,f\,z\,(c :\diamond: x) = foldSpine\,f\,z\,c\;`f`\,x$$

Although the type of *foldSpine* might look intimidating at first, its first argument is simply the replacement for the $:\diamond:$ constructor, and the second is the replacement for *Con*.

The *Data* class is used to embed conversions between user datatypes and the *Spine* generic view:

**class** $(Typeable\,\alpha) \Rightarrow Data\,\alpha$ **where**
$\quad spine \;::\; \alpha \to Spine\,\alpha$
$\quad gfoldl \;::\; (\forall \gamma\,\beta.Data\,\gamma \Rightarrow \phi\,(\gamma \to \beta) \to \gamma \to \phi\,\beta)$
$\quad\quad\quad \to (\forall \beta.\beta \to \phi\,\beta) \to \alpha \to \phi\,\alpha$
$\quad gfoldl\,f\,z = foldSpine\,f\,z \circ spine$

The *Data* class has *Typeable* as a superclass for convenience, because many generic functions in syb make use of type-safe runtime cast. The *gfoldl* method is the basis of all generic consumer functions in syb, and we see that it is just a variant of *foldSpine*.

The way syb is implemented in GHC, *gfoldl* is a primitive, and its definition is automatically generated by the compiler for user datatypes using the **deriving** mechanism. In our presentation, the *spine* method is the primitive, from which *gfoldl* follows.

The encoding of user datatypes in syb using *Spine* is very simple. As an example, here is the encoding of lists:

**instance** $(Data\,\alpha) \Rightarrow Data\,[\alpha]$ **where**
$\quad spine\,[] \quad\;\; = Con\,[]$
$\quad spine\,(h:t) = Con\,(:) :\diamond: h :\diamond: t$

Base types are encoded trivially:

**instance** $Data\,Int$ **where** $spine = Con$

We show a simplified version of syb, in particular omitting meta-information and the *gunfold* function. These are cosmetic simplifications only; Hinze et al. [3] describe how to support meta-information in the *Spine* view, and Hinze and Löh [2] describe how to define *gunfold*.

**Value Conversion.** To convert the generic representation of generic-deriving into that of syb we only need to convert values, as syb has no type-level representation. As such, we require only a type class:

**class** $Convert_{D \to S}\,(\alpha :: Un_D)$ **where**
$\quad d_{\to}s :: [\![\alpha]\!]_D \to Spine\,([\![\alpha]\!]_D)$

The idea is to first build a representation of type $Spine$ ($[\![\,\alpha\,]\!]_D$), and later transform this into $Spine\ \alpha$. The instances are unsurprising, and follow the functorial nature of $Spine$:

**instance** $Convert_{D\to S}\ U_D$ **where** $d_{\to}s\ U_{ID} = Con\ U_{ID}$

**instance** $(Convert_{D\to S}\ \alpha, Convert_{D\to S}\ \beta) \Rightarrow Convert_{D\to S}\ (\alpha\ :+:_D\ \beta)$ **where**
$\quad d_{\to}s\ (L_{ID}\ x) = fmap\ L_{ID}\ (d_{\to}s\ x)$
$\quad d_{\to}s\ (R_{ID}\ x) = fmap\ R_{ID}\ (d_{\to}s\ x)$

**instance** $(Convert_{D\to S}\ \alpha, Convert_{D\to S}\ \beta) \Rightarrow Convert_{D\to S}\ (\alpha\ :\times:_D\ \beta)$ **where**
$\quad d_{\to}s\ (x\ :\times:_D\ y) = pure\ (:\times:_D) <\!*\!> d_{\to}s\ x <\!*\!> d_{\to}s\ y$

**instance** $(Data\ \alpha) \Rightarrow Convert_{D\to S}\ (K_D\ \iota\ \alpha)$ **where**
$\quad d_{\to}s\ (K_{ID}\ x) = Con\ K_{ID}\ :\diamond:\ x$

**instance** $(Convert_{D\to S}\ \alpha) \Rightarrow Convert_{D\to S}\ (M_D\ \iota\ \alpha)$ **where**
$\quad d_{\to}s\ (M_{ID}\ x) = fmap\ M_{ID}\ (d_{\to}s\ x)$

With these instances in place, we can define a $Data$ instance for all $Generic_D$ types:

**instance** $(Generic_D\ \alpha, Convert_{D\to S}\ (Rep_D\ \alpha), Typeable\ \alpha) \Rightarrow Data\ \alpha$ **where**
$\quad spine = fmap\ to_D \circ d_{\to}s \circ from_D$

We first convert the user type to its generic-deriving representation with $from_D$, then build a $Spine$ representation using $d_{\to}s$, and finally adapt this representation with $fmap\ to_D$.

To test our conversion, assume that we had *not* given the $Data\ [\alpha]$ instance earlier in this section; the $Generic_D\ [\alpha]$ instance of Section 2 would then cascade down into a $Data\ [\alpha]$ instance using the conversion defined in this section. Assuming also generic functions *everywhere* (to apply a transformation to all subterms) and *mkT* (to transform a type-specific query into a generic query), as defined in syb, the expression $everywhere\ (mkT\ (\lambda n \to n + 1 :: Int))\ [1,2,3 :: Int]$ evaluates to $[2,3,4]$, as expected, *without* ever having to derive $Data$ instances directly.

The code defined in this section, albeit straightforward, allows GHC developers to scrap the current code for deriving $Data$ instances, as these can be obtained automatically from $Generic_D$ instances (which are currently derivable in GHC). Furthermore, it brings the combinator-style approach to GP of syb within immediate reach of the other approaches. It is also worth nothing that uniplate, another GP library, can derive its encodings from syb [11, Section 5.3]; therefore, by transitivity, we can also provide uniplate encodings from generic-deriving.

## 6 Discussion and Conclusion

We conclude this paper with a review of related work, and a discussion of concerns regarding the pratical implementation of the conversions as shown in the paper.

**Related Work.** We have defined conversions between GP approaches before, in Agda [9]. Those conversions were of a more theoretical nature, as the intention was to formally compare approaches. Furthermore, generic-deriving was not involved. Our work can be seen as providing conversions between views. In particular, while the

Generic Haskell compiler had generic views defined internally, whose adaptation required changing the compiler itself [4, Section 5], our work allows new views to be defined simply by writing a new universe and interpretation together with a conversion (as in Section 3).

Other approaches to providing functionality mixing different views have been attempted. Chakravarty et al. [1] mention support for multiple views, but do this through duplication of the universe, interpretation, and datatype representations. The Hackage pages instant-zipper and generic-deriving-extras provide functionality usually associated with a fixed-point view on a library without such a view, respectively, a zipper in instant-generics, and a fold in generic-deriving. This is achieved by extending the non fixed-point view libraries, rather than by converting between representations, as we do.

**Performance.** One aspect that we have not addressed in this paper is the potential performance penalty that the conversions might bring. We find it very likely that such an overhead exists, given that the conversions are not trivial. However, we also believe that this overhead should be fully removable by the compiler, using techniques similar to those described by Magalhães [8]. Performance concerns are relevant, as these are crucial for user adoption of our conversions. However, optimisation concerns often result in cumbersome code where the original idea is obscured. As such, we preferred to focus on presenting the conversions and their potential applications, and defer performance concerns to future work.

**Practical Implementation.** Performance concerns are just one of the aspects to consider when deciding how to best integrate our conversions with the existing GP libraries. While we have tried to remain faithful to the original libraries in our encoding, a few modifications to the way generic-deriving handles the tags in $K_D$ and $Rec_D$ were necessary to support the conversion to multirec. These changes, besides being minor, actually improve generic-deriving, as the current implementation is rather ill-defined with respect to which tag is used when. Furthermore, we know of no generic function currently relying on these tags; our conversion in Section 4 might be the first example.

We have used datatype promotion in all approaches, and encode meta-information at the type level, instead of using type classes. These changes are not backwards compatible because the current implementation of datatype promotion requires choosing different names for a representation type (e.g. $U_R$) and its interpretation (also named $U_R$), while these are often the same in the current implementations of the libraries. While the implementation of datatype promotion might change to allow avoiding name clashes, it might be preferable to have a new release for each library that breaks backwards compatibility, requires GHC $\geqslant 7.6$, but homogenises naming conventions and meta-data representation across libraries, for instance. Alternatively, we could introduce a new library, intended to sit at the top of the hierarchy, from which all other conversions could be derived. This library would not be intended for direct use, allowing it to be easily adapted to support new libraries. This would further enhance the new approach to GP in Haskell that we advocate: a particular library is just a particular way to *view* data, and all libraries interplay seamlessly because they all share a common root.

**Conclusion.** In the past, there was a lot of apparent competition between different approaches to GP. While it is reasonably easy to use Template Haskell to derive the encodings of the datatypes needed to use a particular library, most users seemed to prefer the libraries that had direct support within GHC, such as syb or generic-deriving. On the other hand, users had a difficult decision to make, operating under the assumption that they have to pick a single library among the many that are available, perhaps afraid to make the wrong choice and to then stumble upon a programming problem that cannot easily be solved using the chosen library.

Those times are over. GP library authors no longer have to feel embarrassed if they present a new library suitable only for a specific class of GP programming problems. All they need to do is to define a conversion, and their library will be integrated better than ever before, without any need for Template Haskell. Users should no longer worry that they have to make a particular choice. All GP libraries interact nicely, and they can simply pick the one that offers the functionality they need right now—we have arrived in the era of truly generic generic programming!

**Acknowledgements.** The first author is supported by the EP/J010995/1 EPSRC grant. We thank Nicolas Wu for suggesting the title of this paper, and Sean Leather for encouraging us to include multirec in our considerations. Jeremy Gibbons, Ralf Hinze, Johan Jeuring, Sean Leather, the members of the reading club at Utrecht University, and anonymous reviewers provided helpful feedback on an earlier draft of this paper.

# References

[1] Chakravarty, M.M.T., Ditu, G.C., Leshchinskiy, R.: Instant generics: Fast and easy (2009), http://www.cse.unsw.edu.au/~chak/papers/CDL09.html

[2] Hinze, R., Löh, A.: "Scrap Your Boilerplate" revolutions. In: Uustalu, T. (ed.) MPC 2006. LNCS, vol. 4014, pp. 180–208. Springer, Heidelberg (2006), doi:10.1007/11783596_13

[3] Hinze, R., Löh, A., Oliveira, B.C.d.S.: "Scrap Your Boilerplate" reloaded. In: Hagiya, M. (ed.) FLOPS 2006. LNCS, vol. 3945, pp. 13–29. Springer, Heidelberg (2006), doi:10.1007/11737414_3

[4] Holdermans, S., Jeuring, J., Löh, A., Rodriguez Yakushev, A.: Generic views on data types. In: Uustalu, T. (ed.) MPC 2006. LNCS, vol. 4014, pp. 209–234. Springer, Heidelberg (2006), doi:10.1007/11783596_14

[5] Lämmel, R., Peyton Jones, S.: Scrap your boilerplate: a practical design pattern for generic programming. In: Proceedings of the 2003 ACM SIGPLAN International Workshop on Types in Languages Design and Implementation, pp. 26–37. ACM (2003), doi:10.1145/604174.604179

[6] Lämmel, R., Peyton Jones, S.: Scrap more boilerplate: reflection, zips, and generalised casts. In: Proceedings of the 9th ACM SIGPLAN International Conference on Functional Programming, pp. 244–255. ACM (2004), doi:10.1145/1016850.1016883

[7] Magalhães, J.P.: Less Is More: Generic Programming Theory and Practice. PhD thesis, Universiteit Utrecht (2012)

[8] Magalhães, J.P.: Optimisation of generic programs through inlining. Accepted for publication at the 24th Symposium on Implementation and Application of Functional Languages, IFL 2012 (2013)

[9] Magalhães, J.P., Löh, A.: A formal comparison of approaches to datatype-generic programming. In: Chapman, J., Levy, P.B. (eds.) Proceedings Fourth Workshop on Mathematically Structured Functional Programming. Electronic Proceedings in Theoretical Computer Science, vol. 76, pp. 50–67. Open Publishing Association (2012), doi:10.4204/EPTCS.76.6

[10] Magalhães, J.P., Dijkstra, A., Jeuring, J., Löh, A.: A generic deriving mechanism for Haskell. In: Proceedings of the 3rd ACM Haskell Symposium on Haskell, pp. 37–48. ACM (2010), doi:10.1145/1863523.1863529

[11] Mitchell, N., Runciman, C.: Uniform boilerplate and list processing. In: Proceedings of the ACM SIGPLAN Workshop on Haskell, pp. 49–60. ACM (2007), doi:10.1145/1291201.1291208

[12] Morris, P.: Constructing Universes for Generic Programming. PhD thesis, The University of Nottingham (November 2007)

[13] Van Noort, T., Rodriguez Yakushev, A., Holdermans, S., Jeuring, J., Heeren, B.: A lightweight approach to datatype-generic rewriting. In: Proceedings of the ACM SIGPLAN Workshop on Generic Programming, pp. 13–24. ACM (2008), doi:10.1145/1411318.1411321

[14] Rodriguez Yakushev, A., Holdermans, S., Löh, A., Jeuring, J.: Generic programming with fixed points for mutually recursive datatypes. In: Proceedings of the 14th ACM SIGPLAN International Conference on Functional Programming, pp. 233–244. ACM (2009), doi:10.1145/1596550.1596585

[15] Schrijvers, T., Peyton Jones, S., Chakravarty, M., Sulzmann, M.: Type checking with open type functions. In: Proceedings of the 13th ACM SIGPLAN International Conference on Functional Programming, pp. 51–62. ACM (2008), doi:10.1145/1411204.1411215

[16] Schrijvers, T., Peyton Jones, S., Sulzmann, M., Vytiniotis, D.: Complete and decidable type inference for GADTs. In: Proceedings of the 14th ACM SIGPLAN International Conference on Functional Programming, pp. 341–352. ACM (2009), doi:10.1145/1596550.1596599

[17] Sheard, T., Peyton Jones, S.: Template meta-programming for Haskell. In: Proceedings of the 2002 ACM SIGPLAN Workshop on Haskell, Haskell 2002, vol. 37, pp. 1–16. ACM (December 2002), doi:10.1145/581690.581691

[18] Yorgey, B.A., Weirich, S., Cretin, J., Peyton Jones, S., Vytiniotis, D., Magalhães, J.P.: Giving Haskell a promotion. In: Proceedings of the 8th ACM SIGPLAN Workshop on Types in Language Design and Implementation, pp. 53–66. ACM (2012), doi:10.1145/2103786.2103795

# Author Index

Areias, Miguel    168

Bracker, Jan    65

Campeotto, Federico    152
Chakravarty, Manuel M.T.    136
Clifton-Everest, Robert    136

Dal Palù, Alessandro    152
Devriese, Dominique    17
Dovier, Agostino    152

Elsman, Martin    184

Fioretto, Ferdinando    152

Gill, Andy    65

Jagannathan, Suresh    1

Keller, Gabriele    136
Krijnen, Jacco    200

Lakin, Matthew R.    81
Le, Tiep    87
Lierler, Yuliya    49
Löh, Andres    216

Magalhães, José Pedro    216
McDonell, Trevor L.    136

Pereira, Luís Moniz    104
Petricek, Tomas    33
Phillips, Andrew    81
Piessens, Frank    17
Pontelli, Enrico    87, 152

Rocha, Ricardo    168

Saptawijaya, Ari    104
Schack-Nielsen, Anders    184
Schrijvers, Tom    17
Sivaramakrishnan, K.C.    1
Son, Tran Cao    87
Swierstra, Doaitse    200
Syme, Don    33

Tarau, Paul    120
Truszczynski, Miroslaw    49

Viera, Marcos O.    200

Winant, Thomas    17

Ziarek, Lukasz    1